A Nietzschean Bestiary

A Nietzschean Bestiary

Becoming Animal Beyond Docile and Brutal

Edited by
Christa Davis Acampora
and Ralph R. Acampora

ROWMAN & LITTLEFIELD PUBLISHERS, INC.
Lanham • Boulder • New York • Toronto • Oxford

ROWMAN & LITTLEFIELD PUBLISHERS, INC.

Published in the United States of America
by Rowman & Littlefield Publishers, Inc.
A wholly owned subsidiary of The Rowman & Littlefield Publishing Group, Inc.
4501 Forbes Boulevard, Suite 200, Lanham, Maryland 20706
www.rowmanlittlefield.com

PO Box 317
Oxford
OX2 9RU, UK

British Library Cataloguing in Publication Information Available

Library of Congress Cataloging-in-Publication Data

A Nietzschean bestiary : becoming animal beyond docile and brutal / edited by
Christa Davis Acampora and Ralph R. Acampora.
p.   cm.
Includes bibliographical references and index.
ISBN 0-7425-1426-9 (alk. paper)—ISBN 0-7425-1427-7 (pbk : alk.
paper)
1. Nietzsche, Friedrich Wilhelm, 1844–1900.   2. Animals (Philosophy)
3. Metaphor.   I. Acampora, Christa Davis, 1967–   II. Acampora, Ralph R.,
1965–
B3318.A54N54   2004
193—dc22   2003015203

Printed in the United States of America

♾ ™ The paper used in this publication meets the minimum requirements of American
National Standard for Information Sciences—Permanence of Paper for Printed Library
Materials, ANSI/NISO Z39.48-1992.

For Sam

*Cursed I call all who have only one choice:
to become evil beasts or evil tamers of beasts;
among such men I would not build my home.*
       —Thus Spoke Zarathustra

Contents

Abbreviations   xiii–xiv

Translations   xv–xvii

Acknowledgments   xix–xx

Introduction   xxi–xxxii
   Christa Davis Acampora and Ralph R. Acampora

Nietzsche's Feral Philosophy: Thinking through an
Animal Imaginary   1
   Ralph R. Acampora

Part I: On "Lowly" Origins

Ape   Who Is Zarathustra's Ape?
       Peter S. Groff   17

Camel   A Sketch (*Riß*) of the Camel in *Zarathustra*
       Charles S. Taylor   32

Polyp   Polyp Man
       Brian Domino   42

Part II: Zarathustra's Animals

Dog   Dogs, Domestication, and the Ego
       Gary Shapiro   53

Spider	Arachnophobe or Arachnophile? Nietzsche and His Spiders *Alan D. Schrift*	61
Snake	The Eternal-Serpentine *Nickolas Pappas*	71
Bird	The Halcyon Tone as Birdsong *Gary Shapiro*	83
Cow	"Even Better than a Cow, O Zarathustra!" *Tracey Stark*	89
Ass	Nietzsche and the Mystery of the Ass *Kathleen Marie Higgins*	100

Part III: Beasts of Prey

Lion	Zarathustra's Laughing Lions *Paul S. Loeb*	121
Blond Beast	Nietzsche's "Blond Beast": On the Recuperation of a Nietzschean Metaphor *Gerd Schank*	140
Beasts of Prey	How We Became What We Are: Tracking the "Beasts of Prey" *Daniel W. Conway*	156

Part IV: Human Animals (*Unter, Halb,* and *Über*)

Woman	Women as Predatory Animals, or Why Nietzsche Philosophized with a Whip *Thomas H. Brobjer*	181
Woman	Circe's Truth: On the Way to Animals and Women *Jennifer Ham*	193
Satyr	Human-Animality in Nietzsche *Lawrence J. Hatab*	211
Overhuman	The Overhuman Animal *Vanessa Lemm*	220

Part V: Animal Nietzsche

Mole   On Nietzsche's Moles
Debra B. Bergoffen   243

Cat   The Cat at Play: Nietzsche's Feline Styles
Martha Kendal Woodruff   251

Lizard   Nietzsche's *göttliche Eidechsen*: "Divine Lizards," "Greene Lyons," and Music
Babette E. Babich   264

Afterword   Paws, Claws, Jaws, and Such: Interpretation and Metaphoric Modalities
Christa Davis Acampora   285

Bibliographic Essay   Traces of the Beast: Becoming Nietzsche, Becoming Animal, and the Figure of the Transhuman
Jami Weinstein   301

Sources for the Metamorphoses: The Ages of Man and the Three Metamorphoses of the Spirit
Richard Perkins   319

Index to Animals in Nietzsche's Corpus
Brian Crowley   329

General Index   361

About the Contributors   367

Abbreviations

Abbreviations of Nietzsche's texts have been standardized throughout the volume, conforming to the style preferred by the North American Nietzsche Society. References are given in the body of the book. In cases in which Nietzsche's prefaces are cited, the letter "P" is used followed by the relevant section number, where applicable. When a section is too long for the section number alone to be useful, the page number of the relevant translation is also provided. In the cases in which the *KGW* and *KSA* are cited, references provide the volume number (and part for *KGW*) followed by the relevant fragment number and any relevant aphorism (e.g., *KSA* 10: 12[1].37 refers to volume 10, fragment 12[1], aphorism 37).

A   *The Antichrist*
AOM   *Assorted Opinions and Maxims*
BGE   *Beyond Good and Evil*
BT   *The Birth of Tragedy*
CW   *The Case of Wagner*
D   *Daybreak*
DS   *David Strauss, the Writer and Confessor*
EH   *Ecce Homo* [sections abbreviated "Wise," "Clever," "Books," "Destiny"]
FEI   "On the Future of our Educational Institutions"
GM   *On the Genealogy of Morals*
GS   *The Gay Science*
HC   "Homer's Contest"
HCP   "Homer and Classical Philology"
HH   *Human, All Too Human*

HL   *On the Use and Disadvantage of History for Life*

KGB   *Briefwechsel: Kritische Gesamtausgabe*

KGW   *Kritische Gesamtausgabe*

KSA   *Kritische Studienausgabe*

LR   "Lectures on Rhetoric"

NCW   *Nietzsche Contra Wagner*

PTA   *Philosophy in the Tragic Age of the Greeks*

RWB   *Richard Wagner in Bayreuth*

SE   *Schopenhauer as Educator*

TI   *Twilight of the Idols* [sections abbreviated "Maxims," "Socrates," "Reason," "World," "Morality," "Errors," "Improvers," "Germans," "Skirmishes," "Ancients," "Hammer"]

TL   "On Truth and Lies in an Extra-moral Sense"

UM   *Untimely Meditations*

WDB   *Werke in drei Bänden*

WP   *The Will to Power*

WPh   "We Philologists"

WS   *The Wanderer and His Shadow*

Z   *Thus Spoke Zarathustra* [References to Z list the part number and chapter title followed by the relevant section number when applicable. Chapter titles are abbreviated in the index.]

Translations

The following translations of Nietzsche's works are utilized in this volume. Authors indicate the relevant translator as the occasion requires. In cases in which no translation is indicated, the author has supplied his or her own translation.

The Antichrist (written in 1888). In *The Portable Nietzsche*. Ed. and trans. Walter Kaufmann. New York: Viking Press, 1968. Also translated as *The Anti-Christ*. In *Twilight of the Idols/The Anti-Christ*. Trans. R. J. Hollingdale. New York: Viking Penguin, 1968.

Assorted Opinions and Maxims (1879). Vol. 2, part 1 of *Human, All Too Human*. Trans. R. J. Hollingdale. Cambridge: Cambridge University Press, 1986.

Beyond Good and Evil: Prelude to a Philosophy of the Future (1886). Trans. Walter Kaufmann. New York: Vintage Books, 1966. Also *Beyond Good and Evil: Prelude to a Philosophy of the Future*. Trans. R. J. Hollingdale. London: Penguin Books, 1990.

The Birth of Tragedy, Or: Hellenism and Pessimism (1872). In *The Birth of Tragedy and The Case of Wagner*. Trans. Walter Kaufmann. New York: Vintage Books, 1967. Also *The Birth of Tragedy*. Trans. Francis Golffing. New York: Anchor Books, 1956; and *The Birth of Tragedy*. Trans. Shaun Whiteside. London: Penguin Books, 1993.

Daybreak: Thoughts on the Prejudices of Morality (1881). Trans. R. J. Hollingdale. Cambridge: Cambridge University Press, 1982.

Ecce Homo: How One Becomes What One Is (written in 1888). In *On the Genealogy of Morals and Ecce Homo*. Trans. Walter Kaufmann. New York: Vintage Books, 1969.

The Gay Science (1882 and 1887 [Book V added]). Trans. Walter Kaufmann. New York: Vintage Books, 1974.

"Homer's Contest" (written in 1871). Trans. Christa Davis Acampora. *Nietzscheana* 5/6, 1996. Also "Homer on Competition." Trans. Carole Diethe. In *"On the Geneaology of Morals" and Other Writings*. Ed. Keith Ansell-Pearson. Cambridge: Cambridge University Press, 1994. Excerpts also translated as "Homer's Contest." In *The Portable Nietzsche*. Ed. and trans. Walter Kaufmann. New York: Viking Press, 1968.

Human, All Too Human: A Book for Free Spirits, Vol. 1 (1878). Trans. R. J. Hollingdale. Cambridge: Cambridge University Press, 1986. Also *Human All Too Human: A Book for Free Spirits*. Trans. Marion Faber with Stephen Lehmann. Lincoln: University of Nebraska Press, 1986.

On the Genealogy of Morals (1887). In *On the Genealogy of Morals and Ecce Homo*. Trans. Walter Kaufmann and R. J. Hollingdale. New York: Vintage Books, 1969. Also *"On the Geneaology of Morals" and Other Writings*. Ed. Keith Ansell-Pearson. Trans. Carol Diethe. Cambridge: Cambridge University Press, 1994.

"On Truth and Lies in a Nonmoral Sense" (written in 1873). In *Philosophy and Truth: Selections from the Notebooks of the 1870s*. Trans. Daniel Breazeale. Atlantic Highlands, New Jersey: Humanities Press, 1979.

"On the Use and Disadvantage of History for Life" (1874). In *Untimely Meditations*. Trans. R. J. Hollingdale. Cambridge: Cambridge University Press, 1983. Also translated as "History in the Service and Disservice of Life." In *Unmodern Observations*. Trans. Gary Brown. New Haven: Yale University Press, 1990.

Richard Wagner in Bayreuth (1876). Trans. Richard T. Gray. In *The Complete Works of Friedrich Nietzsche Volume 2: Unfashionable Observations*. Stanford: Stanford University Press, 1995.

"Schopenhauer as Educator" (1874). In *Untimely Meditations*. Trans. R. J. Hollingdale. Cambridge: Cambridge University Press, 1983.

Thus Spoke Zarathustra (1883 [Parts 1–2]; 1884 [Part 3]; 1885 [Part 4]). In *The Portable Nietzsche*. Ed. and trans. Walter Kaufmann. New York: Viking Press, 1968.

Twilight of the Idols (written in 1888). In *The Portable Nietzsche*. Ed. and trans. Walter Kaufmann. New York: Viking Press, 1968.

The Wanderer and His Shadow (1880). Vol. 2, part 2 of *Human, All Too Human*. Trans. R. J. Hollingdale. Cambridge: Cambridge University Press, 1986.

The Will to Power (selected notes from 1883–1888). Ed. Walter Kaufmann. Trans. Walter Kaufmann and R. J. Hollingdale. New York: Vintage Books, 1967.

Nietzsche's Works in German

Kritische Studienausgabe. Ed. Giorgio Colli and Mazzino Montinari. Berlin and New York: Walter de Gruyter, 1967–1988.

Kritische Studienausgabe Sämtliche Briefe. Ed. Giorgio Colli and Mazzino Montinari. Berlin and New York: Walter de Gruyter, 1986.

Kritische Gesamtausgabe. Ed. Giorgio Colli and Mazzino Montinari. Berlin and New York: Walter de Gruyter, 1967-.

Werke in drei Bänden. Ed. Karl Schlechta. 3 vols. Munich: Carl Hanser, 1954–1956.

Acknowledgments

This project had a number of estimable forefathers, not the least of whom is Graham Parkes. In his *Composing the Soul: Reaches of Nietzsche's Psychology* (Chicago, 1994), Parkes writes, "We can now inquire into the 'ecology' of the soul understood as the *logos* of its *oikos*, the way it speaks of its household and the denizens thereof, of its inner ménage and menagerie. Specifically, what kinds of relations obtain between animal forces contained within the household and those that are in the wild, undomesticable? And under what organization of the passions of the soul, imagined as potentially domesticable energies, would we flourish best? The richest field for this inquiry is *Thus Spoke Zarathustra*, which contains an abundance of faunae unmatched in any other work of Western philosophy. Not since Aristotle's magnificent treatises on animals has such a vast and varied bestiary crawled, soared, swum, trotted, and slithered through the pages of a philosophical text. Over seventy different species are mentioned by name, ranging from domestic animals to wild beasts, from fishes to birds, insects to reptiles" (p. 215). Although this project was already underway prior to the publication of Parkes' book, it nevertheless is greatly indebted to the work and its author. We are specifically grateful to Parkes for advice and support, for his taking time to read and comment upon papers even though his schedule did not permit him to contribute an essay.

The work on the index of animal references in Nietzsche's works would not have proceeded as smoothly as it did were it not for the helpful suggestions and advice supplied by the group of editors for the *Nietzsche Dictionary* project, particularly Paul van Tongeren, Herman Siemens, Gerd Schank, and Alexander-Maria Zibis. Brian Crowley deserves special recognition for the assistance he provided numerous contributors as he shared with them drafts of his entries for the index. He has a fine and promising philosophy career ahead of him. For his assistance with the general index, we thank Robert Spinelli.

Earl Nitschke selected the images incorporated in the cover design and created several of the illustrations in the body. We are most thankful for his contributions to what we think is a rather handsome book.

Audiences at the meetings of the International Association for Philosophy and Literature (Stony Brook, 2000) and the Society for Phenomenology and Existential Philosophy (Penn State, 2000) heard several of the papers presented in early drafts. We are grateful for their stimulating discussion and supportive enthusiasm, both of which buoyed the project. We are also grateful for comments we received from anonymous reviewers. One reviewer in particular offered especially helpful encouragement that we reconsider the organization of the volume. We think our efforts to take up that suggestion resulted in a book that is better than it might have been otherwise.

Hunter College provided financial assistance in the form of two grants, including a Hunter Grant for Teaching and Excellence in Research and the Eugene Lang Student-Faculty Award, which supported the acquisition of research materials and travel to Nijmegen. Christa also benefited from release time made possible by a grant awarded by the Research Foundation of the Professional Staff Congress of the City University of New York.

Finally, a word of gratitude to acquisitions editor Eve DeVaro, editorial assistants John Wehmueller and Tessa Fallon, and editor-in-chief Jon Sisk for acquiring the project. As university presses are slashing lists and discontinuing acquisitions in many areas, there has never been a more urgent need for quality independent academic publishers. We are most grateful for the association.

Introduction

Christa Davis Acampora and Ralph R. Acampora

In the first chapter to her *Philosophical Imaginary*, Michèle Le Doeuff asks, "If someone set out to write a history of philosophical imagery, would such a study ever be as much an accepted part of the historiography of philosophy as histories of philosophical concepts, procedures or systems?"[1] She continues, "If one further argued that existing histories of philosophy are at the very least incomplete, not to say mutilating, in that they never present us with any individual philosopher's image-album, would such a reproach be deemed worthy of serious consideration?" Jacques Derrida, at least, has taken such questions seriously enough to direct their force upon himself and answer in the voice of animal autobiography: "It [his imaginary] would have amounted at the same time to something more and less than a bestiary."[2] Perhaps an accounting of philosophic imagery along the animal axis can also be mounted with respect to other philosophers, living and historical. To accomplish this, of course, a great deal of disciplinary inertia would have to be overcome. Images, Le Doeuff correctly observes, are considered by most professional philosophers to be *extrinsic* to the real theoretical labor of a philosopher's writings. To dwell upon them is much like focusing on the wrapping of the gift of truth that the philosopher is supposed to give. Nietzsche's image-album is so extensive and so vivid that it has hardly gone unnoticed. Indeed, it might be said that it is precisely *because* Nietzsche's works are laden with images that there was, and perhaps continues to be, such reluctance to recognize his work *as* philosophy rather than literature. Le Doeuff's work endeavors to show that images are not only rhetorically interesting but that, despite various philosophers' protests to the contrary, such images play

xxi

an essential role in the properly philosophic development of ideas (i.e., aside from questionable persuasive functions, such as slipping in unjustified claims and asserting dogmatic positions). Risking what Derrida calls "the troubling stakes of a philosophical bestiary, of a bestiary at the origin of philosophy," our intention in this volume is to display object lessons in support of Le Doeuff's gambit as it applies to Nietzsche.[3] One of the project's motivations, then, is to enable an appreciation for the philosophic purposes of Nietzsche's metaphorical expression by focusing on this particular and prominent set of terms, perhaps illuminating paths for others to follow.

Another motivation for this project was our desire to intervene in contemporary discussions on the traditional concept of "human nature" and in the emerging field of "animal studies." Research in the life sciences by figures as diverse as Frans de Waal, Steven Pinker, and Donna Haraway have given new currency to old debates regarding the definition of humanity as such.[4] Controversies of an earlier generation over the political ramifications of sociobiology have morphed into philosophic disputes about the ontological import of primate ethology, evolutionary psychology, and cyborg biotechnology.[5] In addition, as walls of anthropocentrism are deconstructed, a multidisciplinary movement across the domains of science and "the humanities" is busily forming to reconsider the nature of nonhuman lives and cross-species encounters.[6] In the context of these explorations, we believe, an investigation of Nietzsche's "animal imaginary" can serve to illuminate historical developments of zoological constructs of other animals as well as self-conceptions of human animality.[7]

Following the keynote chapter that provides a thematic entryway into the topos of Nietzschean animality, the main body of the book is divided into five parts. The first one, "On 'Lowly' Origins," is populated by animals that are given a low priority both in cultural currency at large and, at least superficially, in Nietzsche's own philosophic imaginary. The characteristics of these animals are typically associated with what is base and brutish in animality generally, with what humans pride themselves on having overcome. Each of the chapters in this division addresses Nietzsche's ambivalence toward these creatures and shows how they offer resources for what Nietzsche envisions as necessary to the future development of humanity as such. The second part, "Zarathustra's Animals," continues to develop the issues explicitly raised in the preceding part and ties them to prominent concerns in *Thus Spoke Zarathustra*, including the ideas of eternal recurrence and the overcoming of morality and humanity. The third part focuses on the most infamous creature in Nietzsche's bestiary, namely, the beast of prey, who is also associated with the blond beast, black beast, and lion. The three contributions to this division work together to trace Nietzsche's sources for this animal, its relation to creativity and violence, and the role it plays in his conception of the human animal. Various forms of human animality, including deficient and enigmatic forms, hybrids, and possible future forms are the subjects of the fourth division, "Human Animals." In these chapters, the authors consider the ways in which their subjects are figured as animals in order to devise a diagnostic tool or measure of the fitness of the human in relation to other animals. Nietzsche's goal in these cases is to develop therapies that would enable a more vibrant possibility for the human animal's future. The fifth and final part focuses upon Nietzsche's conception of himself as animal. These chapters reveal how Nietzsche thinks of his own "inner animal" and how he conceives the enterprise of philosophizing as drawing upon and cultivating various animal energies to appropriate different animal "styles." Finally, we conclude the volume with a set of reflections on Nietzsche's philosophic use of metaphor, focusing on the metamorphoses effected in his accounts of animal parts—paws, claws, and jaws—for the purposes of both imagining and instigating the transformation of human *physis*. This afterword is followed by materials that we expect to be especially useful to those who wish to pursue the themes of the volume, including a brief discussion of source materials for Nietzsche's famous account of the metamorphosis in *Thus Spoke Zarathustra,* a bibliographic essay that explores how Nietzsche's conception of animality is developed in the work of philosophers following Nietzsche, and an index of animal references in Nietzsche's works. The index is by no means exhaustive, but it does constitute the most substantial survey available in English, noting exemplary passages for the multiple purposes to which Nietzsche's references are put.

The chapters in the volume were generally written to stand on their own, and many supply entrées to Nietzsche's works for specialists and non-specialists alike. The reader might well read them out of order, dipping in and out of the book as one might do with the bestiaries of popular and classical literature, which supply brief moral lessons based on the trials and tribulations of various animal characters.[8] Nevertheless, the assembly of the chapters is not haphazard, and the reader might welcome further direction about what one can expect to find between these covers. The following overview introduces the topics of each of the chapters and highlights their points of intersection, diversion, and dialogue.

The first creature to appear is the ape, who is at once closest to the human and an object of ridicule even in Nietzsche's bestiary. Peter S. Groff skillfully explores how Nietzsche's figure of the ape emerges in the context of Nietzsche's naturalism, his reception of Darwin, and his self-proclaimed efforts to overcome the inflated sense of human value that is derived from the kind of anthropomorphism he strives to surpass. Nietzsche's reclamation of the animal in the human appears to reiterate a hierarchy that places the ape in a decidedly low position, one in which the beast is base relative to what Nietzsche takes to be *properly* human potentialities. Groff focuses on the connection between the ape and *mimesis*, in which case the apishness of imitation appears to be the chief target of Nietzsche's derision. The essay concludes with a brief discussion of Zarathustra's speech on the three metamorphoses of the spirit at the beginning of *Thus Spoke Zarathustra*. Groff thereby relates the transformation of imitation—which is how "the human being is more ape than any ape"—to the playfulness of the child in the final stage.

Charles Senn Taylor focuses on the apparent distinction between the camel and the lion in the same speech in *Zarathustra* and challenges the standard reading, which denigrates the camel for its reverence and valorizes the lion for its boldness. Recalling Nietzsche's instruction in *Human, All Too Human*, "Of First and Last Things," he explores the crucial role the camel plays as the "first thing" in the process of development that leads to the "last thing" that human beings are or can become. By calling attention to the essential function being-camel plays in exemplifying the nature of becoming, Taylor helps us see how the camel represents not merely a stage through which one hopes to pass on the way to child: the teaching of the camel affords opportunities for rumination about the process of sublimation through which our concepts, including those highest and most cherished by metaphysical philosophy, develop and obscure their origins.

It is the possible instruction for overcoming the metaphysical conception of the self as something singular, fixed, and determined that gives shape to Brian Domino's chapter on the smallest and seemingly simplest creature in the book, the polyp. Specifically, Domino focuses on the psychological effect of thinking of ourselves as a polyp-like collection of drives in which the various motives that organize our lives are thought of as so many arms of a polyp. These "arms" are nearly autonomous and autogenetic, and each seeks nourishment at the expense of the others. Domino does not so much as consider how the polyp *represents* something else that Nietzsche is endeavoring to describe as he explores the therapeutic value of the polyp as metaphor for life. Ultimately, Domino claims, Nietzsche's polyp psychology supplies new forms for conceiving the self, the intellect, and the soul—with the upshot that the intellect acts less as the chief manager or tamer of the soul and more as a barometer of the degree to which the drives that constitute the self are harmonious.

The first among Zarathustra's animals to be discussed, the dog, similarly offers instruction about the conception of the ego as one of the metaphysical errors that Nietzsche claims we need to overcome. Gary Shapiro opens his chapter with discussion of *Zarathustra*'s "On the Vision and the Riddle," in which the dog is joined by the spider and the snake in a passage devoted to Zarathustra's thought of eternal recurrence. Although the spider and the snake are most frequently discussed in relation to Zarathustra's idea, as elaborated below, Shapiro claims it is the dog who has the most active role in that section of the book insofar as the dog figures into our attachment to the ego and the idea of the self that the eternal recurrence appears to threaten. Focusing on how the training of dogs also involves disciplining those who would train them, Shapiro suggests that our prideful sense of individuality might very well be a result of the process through which we have pursued the domestication of other animals, including the so-called bestial elements of ourselves. In our exercise of power as domesticators, we have simultaneously disciplined ourselves into becoming the animals we are. If we truly respond to the howl of the dog, we shall understand that eternal recurrence requires us to give up the "dog we call 'ego.'"

The figure of the spider is similarly woven into Nietzsche's concerns about metaphysical ideas that are debilitating or limiting and about the promise that the idea of eternal recurrence might somehow afford us a prospect of freeing ourselves from their webs. Alan D. Schrift develops these themes as he explores Nietzsche's ambivalent relation to arachnid potencies. Nietzsche's spider exhibits creativity (as self-creating genius) and deadly violence (as life-sucking), which Nietzsche likens to both an artist (as using materials at once delicate and strong) and metaphysician (as sick and a sickening spinner of concepts). Ultimately, Schrift concludes, Nietzsche appears to be more fearful than admiring of the spider, who acts more as "cunning trapper than a true predator" and threatens to catch poor Nietzsche in webs of philosophical concepts and to potentially infect him with the poison of life-denying morality.

Fear of poisonous infection is also at issue in Nietzsche's treatment of the snake, as Nickolas Pappas describes. But this is not all. As Pappas helpfully elaborates, the snake has multiple senses in Nietzsche's works and "does not slither straight to an index card to be filed under 'enemy' or 'knowledge' or 'temptation.'" Nietzsche's snake both retains and transforms the registers of meaning it acquires in Judeo-Christian theology as well as in the polytheistic and other literary traditions with which Nietzsche was familiar. It is the snake's role in the transmission of the knowledge of eternal recurrence that Pappas finds particularly interesting. Nietzsche's animal imaginary appears to trade ophiophobia (the fear of snakes) for gynophobia in figuring the snake as the symbol of eternity, for it seems that even as Nietzsche favorably transforms the meaning of the knowledge that the snake conveys, he retains the gender of the snake as masculine. Nietzsche's masculine symbol of eternity figures it in terms of a future that has no maternity. For all his rhetorical prowess and cunning in the revaluation of values, Nietzsche might, in the end, feel a bite on the tail: by drawing upon such varied symbolic registers, Nietzsche's creatures cannot possibly all reside together in the same philosophical menagerie.

The connection between the feminine and the process of becoming other that informs the idea of eternal recurrence is also explored by Gary Shapiro in his chapter on the bird. Shapiro notices that Nietzsche associates the significance of his "gift to humanity," his work *Thus Spoke Zarathustra*, with sounding a halcyon tone. As a figure of self-sufficiency, dislocation, transformation, and fecundity, the female bird who builds her nest on the sea embodies what Nietzsche describes as his bird wisdom. Recalling illuminating features of the story of Alcyone, whose metamorphosis to the halcyon Ovid describes, Shapiro reveals how Nietzsche's bird wisdom is conveyed as "Alcyone and Zarathustra become-bird by entering into an alliance with winged creatures." The effect of this alliance is a new economy of desire, one figured not in terms of lack but rather as being drawn into a process of becoming other than what one is, and this new conception of desire and love recasts the significance of the feminine.

Shapiro frames Nietzsche's sense of becoming-animal as an Orphean trope, and it is precisely the music that Zarathustra plays on a new lyre and the new songs of eternal recurrence he sings that are the subjects of Tracey Stark's chapter on the cow. Stark considers how Zarathustra's teaching relates to rumination, making him "even better than a cow," as the voluntary beggar describes him in the fourth book of *Thus Spoke Zarathustra*. By illuminating the parallels between Zarathustra's quest and the mythical journey of the heroic Cadmus, who was led by a cow to the site where his city should be established, Stark endeavors to show how Zarathustra takes on the role of a cow leading his readers to a place in which new values and new forms of life can be founded.

Kathleen Marie Higgins rounds off the section devoted to Zarathustra's animals by picking up the theme of Zarathustra as a value-giver. Focusing on the humor of Nietzsche's use of the ass metaphor in "The Awakening" and "The Ass Festival" in the fourth and final part of *Thus Spoke Zarathustra*, Higgins establishes the context of the medieval Ass Festival, which often included church clergy who disported themselves in presence of their flocks. The ass festival in *Zarathustra*, much like its historical model, Higgins argues, effectively undermines the power of ecclesiastical authority *gaily*; that is, humorously, creatively. In affronting those in whom such authority was invested, it models self-overcoming. Higgins emphasizes the comedic nature of this revaluation process, which stands in stark contrast to the grave character of the moralizing it overturns. By highlighting the ass as symbol of spiritual transformation, Higgins offers a highly suggestive reading of *Thus Spoke Zarathustra* that extends the metamorphic process initially described in terms of camel-lion-child in the prologue to include a fourth stage, that of the ass. This is not to say that Nietzsche sees asinine characteristics as the markers of the highest form of spirit, but rather that the innocence of the child is also informed by lessons learned and perspectives acquired through folly, which give Zarathustra's revaluating laughter a gnostic quality.

The character of laughter in *Zarathustra* is at issue in Paul Loeb's chapter on the lion, which provides the segue to the section devoted to the animal image that is most recognized in Nietzsche's corpus—the beasts of prey. We note that these are plural, since, as it will become clear from reading Gerd Schank's survey of Nietzsche's use of the terms "beast," "bestial," and "blond beast," Nietzsche drew upon various models and applied the terms in a variety of contexts. Daniel Conway further illuminates the *bestiality* of the beast as he provides a fascinating account of the place of the beast of prey in Nietzsche's philosophical anthropology. The part devoted to *Beasts of Prey* begins with Paul S. Loeb's careful exploration of the connection between the lion of *Thus Spoke Zarathustra* and the blond beast of *On the Genealogy of Morals*. Loeb rightly points out that many commentators seek to mollify the ferocity and brutality of the beast of prey in GM by gesturing back to Nietzsche's *Zarathustra*. The blond beast, it is claimed, is identical to, or is at least a close cousin of, the leonine stage of spiritual development. Thus linked, the predacious activities associated with the beast of prey are described as merely figurative descriptions of the development of spirit and do not refer to any anticipated *actual* violence against other living beings, particularly human beings. While Loeb agrees that these lion images are connected, he offers an original account of the character of the lion in Nietzsche's *Zarathustra*. Stemming from a novel interpretation of the narrative structure of the conclusion of the book, Loeb establishes the basis for the claim that the laughter of Zarathustra's lions signals not a spiritual gaiety associated with transcendence but rather the sinister delight in wanton destruction and physical violence.

Gerd Schank's chapter, skillfully translated by Jennifer Ham, is an edited version of materials written for the massive project that will eventually be published as *The Nietzsche Dictionary*. Schank's extensive research on the contexts of Nietzsche's uses of the terms "blond," "beast," "bestial," and other related words reveals that Nietzsche's use of "blond beast" is not intended to lionize the German peoples. Schank emphasizes that Nietzsche's admiration of the blond beast is tied to his concern to effect an agonized relation between Nature and culture. Nietzsche's beasts of prey are more intimately tied to that project, Schank claims, than to any racist vision of the future of humanity.

Steering a course somewhat between the two preceding chapters, Daniel Conway considers the blond beast as "a *biomorphism*, i.e., a human/hominid type"; creatures who "act like wild animals toward other human beings." Emphasizing the *brutality* of the blond beast, Conway recovers the more terrifying characteristics that have been minimized in the course of the effort to distance Nietzsche from his Nazi appropriations, but at the same time Conway indicates how these very same characteristics are conceived by Nietzsche as life-giving. As Conway traces the development of Nietzsche's philosophical anthropology, he suggests that the beast of prey, rather than simply referring to the "wild" state of prehuman history, provides a kind of missing link between our animal past and the sickly domesticated species we have become. In a discussion that is akin to Gary Shapiro's chapter on the dog, which notices that the enforcement of a kind of forming or shaping of others has the effect, a kind of backlash, of domesticating or training the trainer, Conway claims that the disappearance of the beast of prey is explained as the result of the beasts' particular ways in which they seized their captives. By domesticating their captives, the beasts of prey were transformed, virtually to the point of their own extinction. Conway masterfully situates Nietzsche's discussion of the ascetic priest in this context and anticipates a renascence of the beast of prey that would give it wings.

The chapters relating to human animals and hybrids continue to pursue Nietzsche's accounting for the development of the human animal, its deformations, and its prospective reformations. Three human animal forms illuminate these possibilities: that which is under (woman), that which is liminal (the satyr), and that which is overcoming (the overhuman).[9] It is to the double nature of humanity (as both herd animal and predator) that Thomas

Brobjer looks in his provocative chapter on Nietzsche's conception of the animality of women. Brobjer reveals that although Nietzsche appears to share some fairly commonplace misogynistic ideas about the nature and place of women, the way he characterizes their animality reveals how Nietzsche thinks about human animality more generally. It is not that Nietzsche discredits women for their herd mentality, as one might expect; he is, rather, cautious of their *predatory* nature, which has not been *sufficiently* tamed. Brobjer casts new light on the sources of Nietzsche's ideas and his vision of the specific disciplining of wildness Nietzsche imagines for at least some human beings. This bears on the relation between nature and culture, cultivation and destruction, and domestication and wildness that are prominent themes in other chapters.

Jennifer Ham emphasizes how Nietzsche's discussion of women reveals certain aspects of how Nietzsche thinks about freedom and the relation between the sexes (and species). Referring to practices of animal training contemporaneous with Nietzsche, she shows that he was actually quite concerned with the cruelty of taming projects as they might apply to both zoological and gender relations. This insight leads her to the thesis that "in grouping women with animals, Nietzsche was arguing vociferously for their liberation within the context of a new, posthuman order." The latter transvaluation is marshaled by and in Nietzsche's sexually charged imagery of animal/female "ensphinxment" and seduction by the figure of Circe as woman/ truth. In treating these images, Ham's stimulating study raises interest in questions of the liminal and hybridity—issues that are key to the next two chapters (on satyrs and on the *Übermensch*).

The satyr is a hybrid figure who occupies a liminal niche in the ecology of Nietzsche's bestiary. Lawrence Hatab brings into the spotlight this creature's exuberance of eroticism, dance, and playfulness and finds in these traits a Nietzschean emblem of the intermixture of nature and culture. The satyr, Hatab demonstrates, also played a role in the articulation and development of Greek theater by serving as an intermediary between tragedy and comedy. Its comic leanings and behaviors associated it with the boisterous banter and anti-authoritarian borderline obscenity prevalent in the Dionysian gatherings, or *komos*. Yet, as Hatab argues, the satyr is not reducible to a piece of vulgar humor; rather, it is "an experiment with inversions and crossovers on the fringe, meant not so much to destroy as to renew human culture."

That renewal, of course, is famously centered for Nietzsche on the ideal of the *Übermensch*. The Nietzschean narrative of transhumanity is the focus of Vanessa Lemm's contribution. Her interpretation reaffirms Nietzsche's take on (natural) history as a revolutionary endeavor in which "overcoming takes the form of a return to the beginning, to the animal." Lemm shows that and how Nietzsche's conceptions of humanity, animality, the human animal, and the overhuman animal are determined by the antagonism of memory and forgetfulness, of promise and subversion. The figure of the over-human animal pioneers the future of what Nietzsche calls the *Umgekehrten*, those free animal spirits capable of transvaluatory endeavors that overcome the cultural, political and moral meaning of civilization towards freer forms of human animal life and culture.

The last part of the bestiary proper, "Animal Nietzsche," groups together three chapters that treat Nietzsche's self-identifications with a variety of animal forms. Debra Bergoffen sheds light on, or rather tries to get to the bottom of, the anti-metaphysical work of the mole, discovering in her endeavor that this creature will not admit illumination in any transparent sense. The mole, that is, serves sometimes as a *doppelgänger* for and sometimes as a double agent against Nietzsche as author and philosopher, alternately contesting and affirming his own duplicities, such as trying to remain faithful to the earth even as he champions heights and (sun)light. These aspects of the mole metaphor are craftily interpreted by Bergoffen as signs of Nietzsche's ambivalent ideals of genealogy/under-going and *Übermensch*/over-coming.

Ambivalence, likewise, is the watchword for Martha Kendal Woodruff's reading of the cat image in and for Nietzsche. According to Woodruff, while he has some nasty things to say about feline deceit and the sensual (reminiscent of his notorious remarks about women), "the traits Nietzsche attributes to cats he also seeks for his own life-affirming laughter, embodiment, and artistry." This last point is best seen and appreciated by consideration of the cat as a writerly mascot for Nietzschean stylism, and it is just such a consideration that anchors Woodruff's interpretation. Ultimately, she reveals how— like a cat—Nietzsche "approaches his goals crookedly and indirectly, curving around meanings, arching his back in the 'archness' of irony, purring with secret pleasure."

Our review of Nietzsche's bestiary closes with a meditation on a seemingly inconsequential creature, the lizard. But as Babette E. Babich ingeniously shows, Nietzsche's lizard is anything but insignificant as it elicits reflection on the very heart of his philosophical aspirations. Skimming a path from Nietzsche's interest in alchemic transfigurations—that is, his abiding concern for revaluation and the transformation of what is base into something exceptional and rare—Babich considers how Nietzsche endeavored to bring about not merely a renewed concern for matters of style but, more important, a transformation of language itself. By tying Nietzsche's investigations of rhetoric to his interest in music and his conception of tragedy, Babich illuminates how Nietzsche sought to bring a new sense of time to his philosophical thinking and writing, one that would make it possible for us to finally "hear with our eyes" and become aware of the *soundings* of the Dionysian. As a figure of the fleeting character of thought, the lizard "is a metaphor . . . for lapidary, illuminated insights." In its capacity for regeneration, the lizard symbolizes alchemical transformation, and in its ectothermic regulatory functions, the lizard is a marker of convalescence and renewed health. Thus, our book of Nietzsche's animals concludes by uniting many of the threads sown throughout the volume and by sounding some of the most significant themes in Nietzsche's philosophy.

The final materials in the volume provide touchstones and tools for future development of these and related ideas. Christa Davis Acampora's chapter takes its starting point from consideration of what might be called Nietzsche's "Parts of Animals" and considers the ontological import of Nietzsche's use of metaphor. Bibliographic and source materials provide readers with ample resources for their own explorations. Jami Weinstein provides an extremely helpful bibliographic essay that sheds light on how Nietzsche's conception of animality gives shape to the works of those who follow him, particularly those of Deleuze and Guattari, Heidegger, Foucault, and Irigaray. Richard Perkins discusses fables and other literary texts that supply the key images for Nietzsche's Zarathustra's metamorphosis of camel-lion-child. And, finally, Brian Crowley collects and organizes an index of Nietzsche's references to most of the animals treated in the book, in which he notes not only their prevalent senses but also deviations, sources, and their development over time. We greatly look forward to seeing the fruit this research will bear.

Notes

1. Michèle Le Doeuff, *The Philosophical Imaginary*, trans. Colin Gordon (London: Athlone Press, 1988), 2.

2. Jacques Derrida, "The Animal That Therefore I Am (More to Follow)," trans. David Wills, *Critical Inquiry* 28 (Winter 2002): 405.

3. Derrida, "The Animal That Therefore I Am," 407.

4. Frans B. M. de Waal, *The Ape and the Sushi Master: Cultural Reflections by a Primatologist* (New York: Basic Books, 2001); Steven Pinker, *The Blank Slate: The Modern Denial of Human Nature* (New York: Viking, 2002); Donna Haraway, *The Haraway Reader* (New York: Routledge, 2003).

5. See Mary E. Clark, *In Search of Human Nature* (New York: Routledge, 2002); and Maxine Sheets-Johnstone, *The Roots of Power* (Chicago: Open Court, 1994) and *The Roots of Thinking* (Philadelphia: Temple University Press, 1990). See also Barbara Noske, *Beyond Boundaries: Humans and Other Animals* (Buffalo, N.Y.: Black Rose, 1997); and N. Katherine Hayles, *How We Became Posthuman* (Chicago: University of Chicago Press, 1999).

6. Lynda Birke and Ruth Hubbard, eds., *Reinventing Biology* (Bloomington: Indiana University Press, 1995); Jennifer Wolch and Jody Emel, eds., *Animal Geographies: Place, Politics, and Identity in the Nature-Culture Borderlands* (New York: Verso, 1998); H. P. Steeves, ed., *Animal Others: Ethics, Ontology, and Animal Life* (Albany: State University of New York Press, 1999); Jennifer Ham and Matthew Senior, eds., *Animal Acts: Configuring the Human in Western History* (New York: Routledge, 1997); Erica Fudge, *Animal* (London: Reaktion Books, 2002); and Cary Wolfe, ed., *Zoontologies: The Question of the Animal* (Minneapolis: University of Minnesota Press, 2003).

7. See Adrian Franklin, *Animals and Modern Cultures: A Sociology of Human-Animal Relations in Modernity* (London: Sage, 1999).

8. Books of beasts, or bestiaries, are common in a variety of cultures. The Greek *Physiologus* dates to the second century. The medieval version is not only a collection of various animal forms but also a survey of a variety of poetic forms. So, for example, the entry for the lion is written in leonine hexameters. A survey of the bestiary background can be found in Boria Sax, *The Mythical Zoo: An Encyclopedia of Animals in World Myth, Legend, and Literature* (Santa Barbara: ABC-CLIO, 2001). See also Arnold Clayton Henderson, "Medieval Beasts and Modern Cages: The Making of Meaning in Fables and Bestiaries," *Proceedings of the Modern Language Association* 97 (1982): 40–49. A source available during Nietzsche's lifetime is Friedrich von Lauchert, *Geschichte des Physiologus* (1877; reprint, Strassburg: K. J. Trübner, 1889). It includes chapters on "Der griechische Physiologus" (229–279) and "Der jüngere deutsche Physiologus" (280–299).

9. Of course, Nietzsche regards "man" as an animal, too, but his references specifically to males in relation to other animal types are few and far between; thus, there is not an essay that treats "man" in the way that there are entries for "woman" in this section. Certainly an essay treating the figure of the child, particularly as it plays a role in the "three metamorphoses of the spirit" in *Thus Spoke Zarathustra* would be appropriate for this section. It is one of our regrets that we were unable to secure an appropriate entry for this human animal. Interested readers are directed to the existing literature on this figure and its connection to Nietzsche's conception of creativity. See, for example, Robert Gooding-Williams' extended discussion of "The Three Metamorphoses" and frequent references to the child in his *Zarathustra's Dionysian Modernism* (Stanford: Stanford University Press, 2001); and consult the index for relevant discussions of the child in numerous chapters herein.

~

Nietzsche's Feral Philosophy: Thinking through an Animal Imaginary

Ralph R. Acampora

This chapter sounds some of the main themes for the volume as a whole and furnishes readers with an interpretive key for tuning into its subject matter. It seeks to locate and familiarize a promising (though certainly not the only) overarching topos in which the bestiary may be appreciated. A collection of this kind need not be read straight through, completely, or in sequential order—any more than the traditional tomes it recalls must be. Although it does not aim at a slavish reproduction of them, the present book shares an aspect of *bricolage* with some of the medieval bestiaries: there are lessons to be learned here and there that do not require acquaintance with all the reflections lying between. In this respect, to use a more modern analogue, the experience of engaging the various entries within might resemble listening to a compilation of recorded music rather than reading a monograph.[1] Yet, as in a "concept-album," organization is indeed discernible if desired—and this chapter supplements the systematic roadmap of the introduction by explicating themes that underlie many of the essays on particular beasts.

It cannot be taken for granted that Nietzsche was a thinker of animality, let alone an avant-garde one. In fact, a recent commentator has it that he "perpetuated the old stereotypes of animals . . . unfortunately supporting [their] long-standing devaluation."[2] On this view, references to animals in his corpus are little more than rhetorical tactics, writerly embellishments, or metaphors pointing toward other (broadly humanistic) themes and issues of greater import for Nietzsche.[3] Hence, it is even held that to him "animals are not of interest purely in themselves."[4] This gesture occurs on physical as well as psychic planes, according to Nietzsche—for whom, it has been said, "Health of the body and health of the mind are not only physiologically related, but operate according to parallel principles of resistance, struggle, and creative overcoming."[5]

Such claims should not be dismissed; clearly Nietzsche was not exclusively a zoologist, nor was he an advocate for animal rights. Nonetheless, the present compendium gathers significant evidence that he deserves to be counted a visionary philosopher of what it means to live as an animal being. Indeed, it can be argued that, even if his concern remains largely with humankind, Nietzsche perceives and presents the cultural enterprise of humanity as an agonistic confrontation between animalistic forces of devolutionary domestication and magnanimous atavism (representing degradation and enlargement of spirit, respectively). For the Nietzsche therapeutically interested in the "psychophysics" of culture, the European herd-history of common civilization has produced animals spiritually sickened by becoming all-too-humanly *tame*; their illness can, however, be overcome by transhuman (*übermenschlich*) individuals who have the courage and control to instinctually and artistically reappropriate—redeem and transvalue—ancestral animality from the prehistoric wild. One finds such ideas introduced in T. J. Reed's "Nietzsche's Animals: Idea, Image and Influence" in *Nietzsche: Imagery and Thought*,[6] and Margot Norris characterizes Nietzsche's enterprise as a "recuperation" of zootic principles.[7] In calling for and cultivating an experimental education of the human animal from civilized domesticity to atavistic wilderness, Nietzsche can be seen to develop a feral philosophy of cultural zoology. In other words, he advances his philosophical anthropology within a broader, zoologically natural history of culture. The point of this experiment is to recharge humanity's wild animal energy, which has waned while suffering centuries of overcivilizing ideologies and institutions. T. J. Reed pioneered the sustained study of Nietzschean animality, and his delineation of Nietzsche's program still appears valid: first, there is a diagnostic project aimed at the "revelation" of animality beneath the overlays of theological and humanistic constructions (this unfolds in a scientifico-logical fashion); second, there is a therapeutic project, the goal of which is the "restoration" of wildness in the human animal (this proceeds in an aesthetico-literary mode).

Throughout the corpus of his works, one discovers Nietzsche arguing against the idealized homo-exclusive anthropology embedded in Euro-Christian culture, and for the zoological recontextualization of humanity as an organic life form set in the natural (versus a metaphysical or supersensory) environment. In this broad sense of naturalizing humankind, Nietzsche participates in a Darwinian thoughtscape, and yet he is notoriously critical of Darwin(ism). A number of scholars have looked into this paradox, and the results are mixed. Some have seen a Nietzsche who badly mistakes Darwinian thought as a teleological justification of humanity—"one might almost say," it is suggested, "that Nietzsche was a Darwinist without knowing it";[8] or again, "at the points at which Nietzsche thinks he is differing from Darwin, he is in fact endorsing a subtler Darwin he never cultivated an appreciation of."[9] Others claim that it is hermeneutically idle to bring Nietzsche before a tribunal of biological correctness, that larger conceptions of nature are at stake, and thus the profile between Nietzschean and Darwinian ontologies of life has purchase in that the former emphasizes superfluity of power whereas the latter stresses selectivity of survival.[10] However one reads his relation to Darwin, it is clear that Nietzsche is humored by the irony of modern European self-consciousness, which—infected by the hubris of Hegelian history—construes its tame, sick, lowly constitution as the pinnacle of world order: "the pretension of the tiny human worm is surely the most comical, the funniest scene on the face of the earth" (HL 9).[11] After this joke has spent its energy, laughter subsides into recognition and identification of falsehood: Nietzsche eventually lists four basic errors according to which humans have heretofore miseducated themselves; the third one is that "he [man] placed himself in a false order of rank in relation to [other] animals and nature" (GS 3:115).[12]

What is the meaning of Nietzsche's evaluation? How can the error be corrected? Proposing an answer to the latter question may help shed light on the former. In Beyond Good and Evil, Nietzsche issues a command that provides a strong clue for the correction of humankind's erroneous zoological/ecological self-image: "the basic text of homo natura must again be recognized," he asserts (230). Given Nietzsche's radically hermeneutic epistemology, to call homo natura a "text" (rather than an interpretation) is to cognitively valorize this image of humanity with an astonishingly honorific title. Of course, some of the astonishment vanishes when Nietzsche sets it as the preeminent task of anthropological knowledge-seekers "to translate man back into nature" (BGE 230, emphasis added). As Sarah Kofman has argued, text is not non-perspectival for Nietzsche—because translation (and hence interpretive appropriation) is still required because of the already metaphorical nature of figuring humanity in terms of discourse and because the will-to-power revealed in the image of homo natura reinstalls the applicability of perspectivism.[13] Methodologically, the proposed translation is to be conducted with "Odysseus ears, deaf to the siren songs of old metaphysical bird catchers who have been piping at him [man] all too long, 'you are more, you are higher, you are of a different origin!'" (*BGE* 230). Substantively, humanity's animal genesis is at stake here for Nietzsche.

"We have learned better," Nietzsche reports in *The Anti-Christ(ian)*, "We no longer trace the origin of man in the 'spirit', in the 'divinity', *we have placed him back among the animals*" (A 14, emphasis added). Homo-exclusive ontotheology of human origination swept aside, any residual traces found in similar teleologies of biological development become suspect: "we guard ourselves against . . . the vanity *that man is the great secret objective of animal evolution*. Man is absolutely not the crown of creation: *every creature stands beside him at the same stage of perfection*" (A 14, emphasis added). Here, in this position that Nietzsche shares with standard evolutionary theory, we can come to understand the meaning of *The Gay Science*'s attack on false zoological hierarchy. That attack is central to Nietzsche's "negative" or diagnostic project of stripping away animal-concealing ideology; it represents an overcoming of the ontological anthropocentrism that runs through religiously domesticated civilization's supernaturality.

Yet if it is the supernatural that is (to be) overcome, Nietzsche's own naturalism is ambiguous. Consider the following pair of passages:

> When one speaks of *humanity*, underlying this idea is the belief that it is humanity that *separates* and distinguishes human beings from nature. But, there is, in reality, no such distinction: the "natural" qualities and those properly called "human" grow inseparably. Human beings in their highest and noblest capacities are wholly nature and bear within themselves its uncanny dual character. Those abilities that are thought to be terrifying and inhuman are perhaps even the fruitful soil from which alone all humanity can grow in emotions, deeds, and works. (*HC*)

This view and the next could hardly stand in greater contrast. The first presents humankind and nature as entirely intertwined, whereas the second separates and even opposes them (indirectly, by implication).

> According to nature you want to *live*? O you noble Stoics, what deceptive words these are! Imagine a being like nature, wasteful beyond measure, indifferent beyond measure, without purposes and consideration, without mercy and justice, fertile and desolate and uncertain at the same time; imagine indifference itself as a power—how *could* you live according to this indifference? Living—is that not precisely wanting to be other than this nature? (*BGE* 9)

We must thus ask how it is that Nietzsche "naturalizes" humanity: given that the human being is not *above* nature, does that being operate *with* or *against* it? Perhaps the answer is twofold: humankind lives as (or "with") organically natural animacy, while still struggling to assert itself in (or "against") the natural environment's comparatively inorganic indifference.[14] The distinction at work here—even if ultimately only heuristic—might enable us at least partially to express the intuition or impulse driving Nietzsche's attempt to forge a pivotal role for animality as a cultural force and value.

When Nietzsche proclaims that "apart from the ascetic ideal, man, the human *animal*, [has] had no meaning so far" (GM III:28), the announcement effectively exhorts his audience toward a trans-signification of human being's animal nature that avoids the hatred of animality ascetic ideals seem to take as their originary gesture. In the process of zoologically retranslating humankind into nature, Nietzsche continually stresses the importance of feeling humanity's kinship to notoriously "evil" or predaceous species—beasts and birds of prey, snakes, etc.[15] The infamy of such species is understandable, "for the fear of wild animals, that was bred in man longest of all, including the animals he harbors inside himself and fears: *Zarathustra calls it the 'inner beast'*" (Z:4, "On Science," emphasis added). Nietzsche's point, however, is that "this hidden core needs to erupt from time to time, *the animal has to get out again and go back to the wilderness*" (GM I:11, emphasis added). Thus *homo natura* is felt to have a distinctly wild side that is keenly needful of expression.

Parenthetically, notice here that a figure of much bad press comes to the fore, namely, "the blond beast."[16] Walter Kaufmann endeavored to peel away the Teutonic mythology and dubious ideology surrounding what is probably an imagistic term for one of Nietzsche's poetic companion animals, the lion.[17] Further, although bestial wildness is lionized for its primordial energies, it is not a terminal point for the development of the human animal that Nietzsche champions.[18] In Zarathustran terms, the childlike creator is to be the noble successor to both the camel (qua beast-of-burden) and the lion (qua predator) in human being; in other words, playful creation is to succeed both the docile existence of the human herd and the raw energy of the barbarian wilderness.

Yet, lest we cast a too-gentle glow upon Nietzsche's portrayal (something that the child image risks), it is worth emphasizing that Nietzschean creativity never entirely sheds, but rather spiritually incorporates, its animal roots (including the wild strains). In *Human, All Too Human*, for instance, the cultural weight of such incorporation is made manifest. There Nietzsche praises the embodiment of great, opposing forces of culture in an individual life's architecture—and he dreams of this cultural genius in zoomorphic terms: "he is a centaur, half human, half animal" (241, see also 276). Later in the unfolding of Nietzsche's thought, the heroic *Übermensch* figure takes on the task of cultivating and transforming animality through a spiritual overture of sublimation. It is important to remember that a necessary condition of noble overcoming is atavistic going-under (*Untergang*).[19] For Nietzsche, in R. J. Hollingdale's words, "where there is 'the sublime' there must have been that which was *made sublime*—sublimated—after having been for a long time not sublime."[20] As Richard Schacht puts it, the spiritual task of high culture—noble education transcending herd civilization—is at bottom a zoological affair "possible only by drawing on one's human animality, which is fundamentally but a piece of nature."[21] For Nietzsche *übermenschlich* cultivation sublimates naturally primitive zoological drives in a way that does not annihilate or eviscerate wildness—in other words, it spiritually (intellectually or artistically) transforms the brutality of Zarathustra's "inner beast" while yet preserving its wild animality.[22] With this claim I part company from interpreters such as Kaufmann and Schacht who stress transcendence of animality to the point of denying, or leaving dubious, the preservation part of the *Aufhebung* at issue. Seeded early on in his work, Nietzsche's humanizing transformation of animality blossoms into the full-fledged *redemption*—not *rejection*—of animal *physis*. In the later image of a Zarathustran metaphor, humanity appears as a rope tied between animalism and the superhuman (Z:P3). That rope is never cut by Nietzsche—rather, the braiding of its strands is only tightened and celebrated: "*esprit* and happy exuberance in favor of the animal in man is in [cultivated] ages the most triumphant form of spirituality" (WP 1019).

When discussing the Nietzschean transfiguration of (animal) nature, Kaufmann shies away from the concept of redemption, the salvific overtones of which he takes to be misleadingly supernaturalistic.[23] However, it is clear that Nietzsche himself did not conceive of the matter along the lines of a Christian model. There can be little doubt that his naturalism has a strongly redemptive aspect, as in *The Gay Science*'s rhetorical question, "When may we begin to '*naturalize*' humanity in terms of a pure, newly discovered, newly *redeemed* nature?" (109, only latter emphasis added). Yet such anti-anthropocentrist redemption is actually quite *anti*-Christian: it buys back animal nature at a higher human value than had been European civilization's theological custom. Using a Kantian formula to phrase Nietzsche's view, one can say that while animality without humanity may be relatively blind, still humanity without animality is decidedly empty.[24]

One reason why Kaufmann and others do not draw this conclusion is that they are caught in a false dilemma of interpretation. For them, animality comes in only two states: tame or wild. And, reasoning on Kaufmann's terms, Nietzsche wants to avoid both stagnation in "animal conformity" and development of "super-brutes."[25] So, this interpretation implicitly argues, the human transmutation of animal nature cannot (or shall not) maintain the integrity of its *transmutandum*. Such an argument is interpretively unsound from the start, however, for its major premise places before us only the false animal alternatives of herd-like docility or bestial brutality. As another commentator once put it, "Nietzsche's *scalae naturae* consists of two basic groups: the weaker '*Sklaventiere*,' or domesticated animals in the service of man, and the '*Raubtiere*,' the less slavish animals of prey."[26] Zoologically speaking, however, it is possible for an animal to be neither fully tame nor entirely wild but rather liminally feral.[27] Ferity, then, is the hermeneutic middle excluded from standard readings of Nietzschean animality; ironically, it is central to Nietzsche's own retranslation of the text he calls *homo natura*.[28] That Nietzsche does not subscribe to any supposed law of the excluded ferine middle, that in fact his affirmative vision of human animality is positioned between the extremes of pure domesticity and raw wilderness, can be appreciated by considering his conception of the philosopher.

The philosopher, as a central figure in Nietzsche's cultural zoology, subliminally fuels intellectual activity with a deep draft of wild animality. Philosophy, that is, draws on a whole complex of animal instincts; far from the stereotype of cool contemplation, the Nietzschean thinker is *la bête philosophe*—at once bestial and noble.[29] This kind of philosopher is a paradoxical avatar of culture, for his flight from civilization is charged with a prized mission of cultivation and education (see *SE*, e.g.). Neither a completely docile "herdsman" or "shepherd," nor a thoroughly savage "exception," he is rather a *feral* "deserter" or "fugitive" (*TI* "Maxims" 37 and *WP* 1009). *Tame-gone-wild*, the philosopher qua cultural critic/constructor looks back at, while running ahead of, his society and epoch: he cultivates (implants ideals) by educating (literally, "leading out"). Thus, philosophy for Nietzsche has the task of riding and remapping the liminal frontier between domesticity and wilderness, culture and nature, human and animal. With its feet in two worlds, "domestico-wild" philosophy demands that its practitioners have a double persona. Janus-faced, though far from hypocritical, feral philosophy must scale and plumb the extremities of surplus and defect in human animality.

Its cultural work is agonistic—to think and live, that is, on the creatively tense threshold between principles of outlandish transcendence and civilized historicity.

Before concluding this foray into ferine philosophizing, we would do well to notice that because it is not wholly wild, feral philosophy's "cultivated transcendence" can court confusion with the domesticative disease infecting civilization (as seen by Nietzsche). There is, however, a distinction that may be drawn between the residential and the carceral. Perhaps it is Nietzsche's hope that the house of culture to be built by his free spirits of the future will not be like the jail cell of European Christendom. Construction of a cultural home, in other words, does not have to be *oppressively* domestic—rather than repressing wild animality, it might be flexible enough to let the animal in us emerge and return occasionally to the wilderness (recall GM I:11). Beyond this point, furthermore, there is an aspect of Nietzsche that positively affirms what could be called "training without taming."[30] Indeed, the (new) philosopher's cultural advent and pedagogical practice is described in terms of discipline and cultivation (*BGE* 203, *WP* 980). More broadly, Nietzsche is clear that an important part of any spiritual growth is a "going-under" that requires taking on burdens of pain and involves deep distress. In *Beyond Good and Evil*, he asks rhetorically:

> That tension in the soul in unhappiness which cultivates its strength, its shudders face to face with great ruin, its inventiveness and courage in enduring, persevering, interpreting, and exploiting suffering, and whatever has been granted to it of profundity, secret, mask, spirit, cunning, greatness—was it not granted to it through suffering, through the discipline of great suffering? (225)

This kind of phenomenon echoes the disciplinary virtues described in *Zarathustra*'s "Three Metamorphoses."[31] It is also tied to what Nietzsche calls breeding, something that he explicitly discriminates from taming and extols for its vivifying potency:

> There is no worse confusion than the confusion of breeding with taming: . . . Breeding as I understand it, is a means of storing up the tremendous forces of mankind so that the generations can build upon the work of their forefathers—not only outwardly, but inwardly, organically growing out of them and becoming something stronger.(*WP* 398)

How, then, can this sort of training be distinguished from the domestication process Nietzsche so often excoriates? One way would be to lean on the distinction drawn between a dispositional mode of being and a directional application thereof (*WP* 281). For Nietzsche, the Christian/democratic form of domestication uproots our biological makeup and infects us with a life-denigrating orientation (disposition or being-mode), whereas the cultivation he promotes would train (harbor and apply) certain organic drives in a life-enhancing direction or vector.[32] In terms of a Nietzschean bestiary, the beast of burden outranks the herd animal—because working as the former can serve a genuinely culture-building function (as in the camelesque self-discipline of learning, en route to overcoming, a tradition) and thus breeds a vital nobility or dignity that the latter lacks and even counteracts through its debilitating regime of civilization (as in the acceptance of conformity and complacency seen in the devolved figure of the flea-like "last man" [*Z:P* 5]).[33]

Let us now recapitulate. Nietzsche holds that in the past "the *meaning of all culture* is the reduction of the beast of prey 'man' to a tame and civilized animal, a *domestic animal*" (GM I:11). Because he evaluates herd-society negatively as the moribund decay of primordially wild animal energies, Nietzsche envisions a need for atavistically reinfusing humanity with its more bestial nature. Positing a Euro-historic duality between life-denying civilization and life-affirming culture (where *life* is biologically reducible to "will-to-power"), Nietzsche's thought challenges free-spirited philosophers of the future to undertake the naturalistically redemptive task of cultivating human animality in its full richness. Thus, the broad project of philosophical education spins out of the creatively fertile agonism between (healthy) culture and (sick) civilization (BGE 61 and *WP* 121; cf. *WP* 966). This program requires an understanding of domesticity, a retranslation of *homo natura* as animal, and an experimental willingness to psychosomatically transfigure oneself into a sublim(at)e(d) embodiment of wilderness—it calls, in other words, for *Übermenschen* of cultural zoology to act as feral philosophers. Ferity then is a liminal mode of human animality tapped by Nietzsche's project of biological naturalization in order to redeem humanity's animal *physis* while avoiding the tame and wild extremes of civilized captivity and uncultivated barbarity. Thus, transvaluatory maintenance of carnate animality throughout the spiritual overtures of cultural sublimation serves as a corrective for, and a continuing check on, the false evolutionary consciousness manifested in what Nietzsche identifies as the error of homo-hubristic hierarchy over other organisms.

Finally, intrinsic to this portrait of human animality is a certain compensatory predilection on Nietzsche's part for representing images of nonhuman animals that display the wilder possibilities of living existence. (At times, admittedly, what might appear a fetish for beasts and birds of prey can take on the aspect of *over*compensation—but even this tactic may be read as a recognition that wildness is not all fun and games, not simply childlike.) In many instances, it seems that Nietzsche is using another animal type as an analogy to, or role model for, the human species. Does he thereby overlook the real differences between humans and other animals? Not necessarily, at least not if his analogies and models are read as images of becoming (rather than comparisons between beings)—for, as one contributor has already shown, "becoming is an experience of difference which unites instead of divides, an experience of the line or boundary as a drawing together, a configuring, not a drawing apart."[34] It may be tempting to wring out of such affiliation an "animal lover" or humane protectionist in Nietzsche—yet his appreciation of animality is not readily serviceable for anti-cruelty causes of animal welfare.[35] The Nietzschean outlook is indeed based on a "biosophy," as it were, but it is not necessarily kind in nature. As a precursor of the present project concluded, "only a radical variant of these [benign] philosophies, one that essentially advocated returning the earth to a feral state, would approximate a genuine biocentric vision."[36] It is this sort of vision that fascinates Nietzsche and that the "zoographers" herein explore, further, and/or contest. *Ecce animot!* [37]

Notes

1. Cf. Brian Massumi's advice on similarly approaching G. Deleuze and F. Guattari's *A Thousand Plateaus* (Minneapolis: University of Minnesota Press, 1987), xiii ff.

2. Monika Langer, "The Role and Status of Animals in Nietzsche's Philosophy," in *Animal Others: On Ethics, Ontology, and Animal Life*, ed. H. Peter Steeves (Albany: State University of New York Press, 1999), 90.

3. On the complexity of metaphor in Nietzsche's animal imaginary, see C. D. Acampora's afterword in the present volume.

4. Langer, "Role and Status of Animals," 90.

5. Alfred I. Tauber, *Confessions of a Medicine Man* (Cambridge: MIT Press, 1999), 44.

6. T. J. Reed, "Nietzsche's Animals: Idea, Image and Influence," in *Nietzsche: Imagery and Thought*, ed. M. Pasley (Berkeley: University of California Press, 1978), section 1, esp. 160f.

7. Margot Norris, *Beasts of the Modern Imagination: Darwin, Nietzsche, Kafka, Ernst, and Lawrence* (Baltimore: Johns Hopkins University Press), 22.

8. C. U. M. Smith, "'Clever Beasts Who Invented Knowing': Nietzsche's Evolutionary Biology of Knowledge," *Biology and Philosophy* 2 (1987): 73. (N.B.: Nietzsche was dependent on German translations of or commentaries on Darwin's writing.) See Martin

Heidegger's argument that Nietzsche's bio-epistemology is ultimately metaphysical—*Nietzsche, Volume III: The Will to Power as Knowledge and Metaphysics*, trans. and ed. D. F. Krell et al. (San Francisco: HarperCollins, 1987/1991), Part 1, chapter 16.

9. Keith Ansell-Pearson, "Nietzsche contra Darwin," in *Nietzsche: Critical Assessments*, ed. D. Conway and P. Groff (London: Routledge, 1998), 4:8.

10. Pieter Mostert, "Nietzsche's Reception of Darwinism," *Bijdragen tot de Dierkunde* 49, no. 2 (1979): 235–246 (esp. 236, 242). This perspective is in basic agreement with Heidegger's position that Nietzsche's thought is not in the final analysis biologistic—see *Nietzsche: Volume III*, Part 1, chapter 6. See Paul J. M. van Tongeren's anti-essentialist reading that highlights the human being's status as the "as-yet-undetermined animal," "Nietzsche's Naturalism" (presented to the Nietzsche Society in 1997 at St. Andrew's University-U.K., typescript 5ff.; to be published in *Nietzsche and the German Tradition*, ed. Nicholas Martin [Berne: Peter Lang, 2003]).

11. For translations of Nietzsche's works, I rely mostly upon the standard series of texts by Kaufmann and/or Hollingdale. Other renderings referred to include William Arrowsmith's edition of *Unmodern Observations* (New Haven, Conn.: Yale University Press, 1990); *Human, All Too Human*, trans. Marion Faber (Lincoln: University of Nebraska Press, 1984); "Homer's Contest," trans. Christa D. Acampora, in *Nietzscheana* 5/6 (1997).

12. See also *WP* 684: "man as a species does not represent any progress compared with any other animal."

13. Sarah Kofman, *Nietzsche and Metaphor*, trans. Duncan Large (London: Athlone Press, 1993), 92–100, especially her insight that "arriving at the text of *homo natura* means risking the truth which the weak cannot admit, that there is no truth" (93). In agreeing that Nietzsche "does not express a romantic desire to return, in literal fashion, to a natural state or condition of humanity," Wayne Klein explicates that because translation requires at least two languages and a translator, it "can be no more certain and make no more claims to correctness and decidability than interpretation can." *Nietzsche and the Promise of Philosophy* (Albany: State University of New York Press, 1997), 178/6.

14. According to C. D. Acampora (personal communication), the latter moment harbors the significance of art for Nietzsche: appealing to the "veil of individuation" from *BT*, we can appreciate how art saves us from the recognition of ourselves as purposeless, amoral, uncertain, and indifferent. Yet see Alistair Moles, *Nietzsche's Philosophy of Nature and Cosmology* (New York: Peter Lang, 1990), whose work arguably undermines the sort of differentiation I invoke. See also Christoph Cox, *Nietzsche: Naturalism and Interpretation* (Berkeley: University of California Press, 1999), who claims that "Nietzsche comes to construe the natural world . . . as a continuum with many differentiations but no radical breaks" (79). In this context, I would stress that the relevant distinction between organic and inorganic may be one of relative degree rather than absolute kind.

15. For examples, see *BGE* 44 and *GM* I:13.

16. Other (wild) animals significant to Nietzsche's Zarathustran persona are the serpent and the eagle, symbols of ("evil") wisdom and pride, respectively. See Z:P10 and Z:4 "The Song of Melancholy" 1. For commentary, see Heidegger's *Nietzsche, Volume II: The*

Eternal Recurrence of the Same, trans. D. F. Krell (San Francisco: HarperCollins, 1984/ 1991), Part 1, chapter 7.

17. See also Daniel Conway's contribution to the present volume (wherein he contests this view).

18. See Kaufmann's comments in his translation of GM (12) and in *The Portable Nietz-sche* (116).

19. Recall, e.g., Zarathustra's dictum, "I must go under" (Z:P1).

20. *Twilight/Anti-Christ,* appendix F, 196. Hollingdale goes on to formulate a criterion of Nietzschean value thus: "everything good proceeds from sublimated 'will-to-power,' everything bad from the absence of this 'will' or the absence of sublimation" (196). This formula would devalue any pure humanization (lacking all primal animal urges), yet it also rules out the sociopathic or psychopathic personage from *Übermensch* status. For text that supports Hollingdale on this point, see *WP,* where Nietzsche goes so far as to describe will and power as "the antithesis of the vicious and unbridled" (871).

21. "Unmodern Observations," intro. to *SE,* 155.

22. Indeed, "the 'wild animal' has not been exterminated at all; it lives, it thrives, it has only become—deified" (cited and translated from *BGE* by Norris, 10).

23. *Nietzsche,* 4th ed. (Princeton, N.J.: Princeton University Press, 1974), 172f.

24. See *WP* 1045: "the splendid 'animal' must be given first—what could any 'human-ization' matter otherwise!" Again, compare this transvaluatory rescue with Kaufmann's tendency to treat animality as a condition of cultural bankruptcy (of merely marginal worth at most).

25. Kaufmann, *Nietzsche,* 176.

26. Jennifer Ham, "Taming the Beast: Animality in Wedekind and Nietzsche," in *Animal Acts: Configuring the Human in Western History,* ed. J. Ham and M. Senior (New York: Routledge, 1997), 159. Compare Gilles Deleuze and Felix Guattari's post-Nietzschean, tripartite typology of Oedipal animals, State animals, and demonic animals in *A Thousand Plateaus,* 240f.

27. Think, for examples, of trickster figures such as the edge-dwelling coyote or of escape artists such as stray dogs and alley cats. These sorts of animals can make their way in (i.e., have behavioral repertoires capable of negotiating) a variety of environments, natural and built, across territories diversified in degrees of cultural modification. Com-pare also rats, roaches, and other "weedy species" in David Quammen's "Planet of Weeds," *Harper's* 297, no.1781 (October 1998): 57–69 (esp. 66ff.). Nietzsche's own illus-tration is a human sub-species, so to speak—the philosopher.

28. There is an inkling of this in the mid-century secondary literature: Phyllis Morris sees Nietzsche as moving midway within the traditional dichotomy between the "pallid" and "sour" views of the human as either a "creature of sweetness and light" or else a "creature of sinful bestiality" in her "The Laughing Lion: Nietzsche's Vision of the Over-man," *The Western Humanities Review* 15 (Autumn 1961): 356.

29. See GM III:7 and *TI* "Maxims" 3. Compare *WP* 1027.

30. This term is Graham Parkes's, to whom I am indebted for provoking me into con-sideration of the present theme (personal correspondence).

31. In the present volume, see Charles Taylor's essay on the camel and compare Paul Loeb's essay on the lion.

32. See Parkes's *Composing the Soul: Reaches of Nietzsche's Psychology* (Chicago: University of Chicago Press, 1994), esp. Part 2.

33. Think, for instance, of the twentieth-century artist Francis Bacon. He taught and trained himself in the traditional skills of painting and yet transfigured his work and life into projects that rarely strike anyone as tame. See the critical biography by Christophe Domino, *Francis Bacon: Painter of a Dark Vision*, trans. R. Sharman (New York: Abrams, 1997 [1996]).

34. Ham, "Taming the Beast," 158. Norris also, speaking of a similar phenomenon, refers to "this suture over the great cleft produced in our human being by the repression of the animal and the living body," and she dubs it "this Nietzschean *Anknüpfung.*" *Beasts of the Modern Imagination*, 3.

35. No, the spirit moving Nietzsche's zoomorphology is too ferine; it is more like Deleuze and Guattari's notion of transformation: "Becomings-animal are basically of another power, since their reality resides not in an animal one imitates or to which one corresponds but in themselves, in that which suddenly sweeps us up and makes us become—a *proximity, an indiscernibility* that extracts a shared element from the animal far more effectively than any domestication, utilization, or imitation could: 'the Beast'"; *A Thousand Plateaus*, 279. Yet for a possible avenue of rapprochement between Nietzsche's stance on animality and latter-day animal advocacy, see Brian Luke's "Taming Ourselves or Going Feral?" in *Animals and Women*, ed. Carol J. Adams and Josephine Donovan (Durham, N.C.: Duke University Press, 1995).

36. Norris, *Beasts of the Modern Imagination*, 24.

37. As Jacques Derrida has declared in a related context, "The Animal That Therefore I Am (More to Follow)," trans. David Wills, *Critical Inquiry* 28 (Winter 2002): 369–418 (see esp. 405 n.27).

PART ONE

ON "LOWLY" ORIGINS

A P E

Who Is Zarathustra's Ape?

Peter S. Groff

The ideal "ape" could one day stand before humanity—as a goal.

KSA 10:1[38] (July-August 1882)[1]

Do you merely want to be the ape of your god?

KSA 13:20[28] (Summer 1888)

In *The Gay Science*, a book originally published only one year before the first part of *Thus Spoke Zarathustra*, Nietzsche presents an experimental naturalistic program that can be read as adumbrating the entirety of his philosophical activity. There, having proclaimed the death of God (GS 108, 125) he calls for the "de-deification" of nature, along with the "naturalization" of the human being (GS 109). The first part of this ambitious program requires us to expunge the residual "shadows of God" from our conceptions of nature, rooting out any vestiges of stability, immutability, and purpose—characteristics that Nietzsche sees as wishful "aesthetic anthropomorphisms" and resentful falsifications of the sovereignty of becoming (GS 109). The second part requires that humankind itself be "translate[d] . . . back into nature" (*BGE* 230), in both anthropological and axiological terms.[2] This involves, among other things, a more modest reconceptualization of the human being's place within the aleatory flux of nature—particularly with regard to the "false order of rank" that we have mendaciously read into our relation to other animals (GS 115).

Toward this end, Nietzsche generally seizes every opportunity to valorize non-human nature while deflating the self-serving myths of that sick, not-yet-fully-determined ascetic animal, the human being (BGE 62, GM III:13 and 28). The following passage from the Antichrist(ian) summarizes this aspect of his naturalism most economically:

> We have learned differently. We have become more modest in every way. We no longer derive the human being from "the spirit" or "the deity"; we have placed him back among the animals. We consider him the strongest animal because he is the most cunning: his spirituality is a consequence of this. On the other hand, we oppose the vanity that would raise its head again here too—as if the human being had been the great hidden purpose of the evolution of animals. The human being is by no means the crown of creation: every living being stands beside him on the same level of perfection. And even this is saying too much: relatively speaking, the human being is the most bungled of all the animals, the sickliest, and not one has strayed more dangerously from its instincts. But for all that, he is of course the most interesting. (A 14; cf. GM III:25)

However, if we take Nietzsche's ostensibly non-hierarchical naturalism at face value, there is at least one respect in which his own writings fall short of this radical vision of nature. For Nietzsche himself consistently and almost systematically disparages what might be seen as the most significant and symbol-laden animal in late nineteenth-century Europe's psychological bestiary: the ape (Affe). This is particularly evident in Thus Spoke Zarathustra, a work dedicated to the affirmation and redemption of the earth, and appropriately, one in which animals are most plentiful and most celebrated. There, unlike the rest of Zarathustra's myriad beasts (whom Nietzsche for the most part valorizes), the ape is presented alternately as an object of shame, loathing, and derision.[3] Perhaps this is because, of all the beasts that appear in this book, the ape is most closely affiliated with the human being in both pre- and post-Darwinian taxonomy. Indeed, in the third part of Zarathustra, the figure dubbed "Zarathustra's ape" turns out to be human.[4] But in order to understand the anomalous status of the ape in this book, it is necessary first to trace out the various characteristics and traits that Nietzsche associates with this "all-too-human" beast.

The Ape as Representative of the
Pudenda Origo of the Human

Nietzsche's most well-known reference to the ape occurs in the prologue to *Zarathustra*, where his neophyte prophet first attempts to present the doctrine of the *Übermensch* to a less-than-appreciative audience in the town marketplace:

> What is the ape to the human being? A laughingstock or a painful embarrassment. And the human being shall be that for the *Übermensch*: a laughingstock or a painful embarrassment. You have made your way from worm to human being, and much in you is still worm. Once you were apes, and even now, too, the human being is more ape than any ape. (Z:1, "Prologue," 3; cf. KSA 10:4[181] and 10:5[1] 255)

First let us note an obvious fact that misled many of *Zarathustra*'s earliest readers: Nietzsche is in this passage exploiting Darwin's popularly caricatured, but still scandalous, insight into the human being's evolutionary descent from primates. Partly as a result of this, Nietzsche has been often been cast as a Darwinian thinker, a misunderstanding that has since for the most part been dispelled.[5] If anything, contemporary readers emphasize his *opposition* to Darwinian conceptions of life. But although Nietzsche attempted to distance himself from the famed English naturalist on a number of philosophical points—and indeed, could not countenance Darwinian interpretations of the *Übermensch* (EH "Books" 1)—he nonetheless gladly appropriated Darwin's overall evolutionary model, along with its more radical implications. These are: (1) that biological nature has a history; (2) that the human being can no longer be understood as essentially other than nature (but rather as a product of chance and necessity, like any other natural organism); and (3) that the deeply entrenched prejudice of human superiority with regard to other species no longer has any legitimate purchase, at least as traditionally conceived.

Given Nietzsche's "Darwinism" with respect to these matters, it is worth noting in the above-quoted passage the vestigial anthropocentric conceit of human beings as *higher* animals than apes. A similar residual speciesism[6] can be found in other works, even where Nietzsche is obviously trying to naturalize the human being. A few examples will suffice. First, a note from the *Nachlass*, written between the spring and fall of 1881:

> The age of the experiment! The assumptions of Darwin have to be tested—through the experiment! Likewise the genesis of higher organisms out of the lowest ones.

Experiments must be performed for thousands of years! Apes must be brought up [*erziehen*] to be human beings! (*KSA* 9:11[177])

Note the "false order of rank" that Nietzsche seems to presuppose here: human beings are "higher" organisms, and apes, if not necessarily the "lowest," are undoubtedly *lower* on the natural hierarchy. Now admittedly, Nietzsche's naturalism by no means undermines the very possibility of rank-ordering altogether; indeed, if it were thoroughly non-hierarchical, even with regard to different human types, it would leave his own proclamations and evaluations bereft of any normative leverage whatsoever. However, it *would* appear to leave him without the conceptual resources necessary to draw a distinction between "higher" and "lower" animals—especially when that distinction is drawn in such a traditional, anthropocentric manner, i.e., between the human being and the ape.

When Nietzsche attempts to establish a general rank-ordering between higher and lower types, he uses as his evaluative criteria power, health, and sometimes complexity.[7] Assuming that human beings would in most respects be at a disadvantage with regard to the first two criteria,[8] might the last one be used to salvage Platonic and Christian presumptions of human superiority? Even this seems dubious on Nietzschean grounds:

> [T]he human being as a species does not represent any progress compared with any other animal. The whole animal and vegetable kingdom does not evolve from the lower to the higher—but all at the same time, in utter disorder, over and against each other. The richest and most complex forms—for the expression "higher types" means no more than this—perish more easily: only the lowest preserve an apparent indestructibility. The former are achieved only rarely and maintain their superiority with difficulty; the latter are favored by a compromising fruitfulness. (*KSA* 13:14[133]; *WP* 684)[9]

Note the ambiguity in this passage: even as Nietzsche rejects the notion of evolutionary progress and the possibility of establishing an interspecies hierarchy, he recasts the notion of the "higher type" in terms of complexity. Setting aside Nietzsche's marked ambivalence about the advantages and disadvantages of complexity, this move appears to be something of a non sequitur. For why would it follow that a more complex organism is necessarily "higher"? Again, we are faced with the question of why Nietzsche reinscribes the false order of rank that he elsewhere so forcefully challenges.

This apparent inconsistency crops up with some frequency in Nietzsche's published writings as well. Take for instance the following aphorism from the first volume of *Human, All Too Human* (1878):

> *Circular orbit of humanity.*—Perhaps the whole of humanity is no more than a stage in the evolution of a certain species of animal of limited duration: so that the human being has emerged from the ape and will return to the ape, while there will be no one present to take any sort of interest in this strange comic conclusion. Just as, with the decline of Roman culture and its principle cause, the spread of Christianity, a general uglification of the human being prevailed within the Roman Empire, so an eventual decline of the general culture of the earth could also introduce a much greater uglification and in the end animalization of the human being to the point of apelikeness [*Affenhafte*].—Precisely because we are able to visualize this prospect we are perhaps in a position to prevent it from occurring. (*HH* 247)

This aphorism exhibits a dynamic similar to the previous two passages we have examined. Nietzsche begins by experimentally proffering a quasi-cyclical, anti-teleological model of evolution (one that anticipates his later doctrine of the eternal return), thus undermining the notion of evolution as a kind of goal-driven, linear progression. However, having gestured toward a more modest vision of the human's place within nature, he quickly compromises the radicality of his own suggestion. For the "circular orbit of humanity" is framed in terms of the human being's possible "return" to the ape, a development that is associated with the "decline," "uglification," and "animalization" of the human being. The reversion to "apelikeness" represents a base and ignoble possible future that Nietzsche's language suggests ought to be prevented if at all possible.

Two years later, in the second volume of *Human, All Too Human* (1880), Nietzsche returns to the theme of humanity's place in nature relative to other creatures, again rather traditionally choosing the ape as his foil: "*The human being, the comedian of the world.* . . . If a god created the world then he created human beings as the *apes of god*, so as always to have on hand something to cheer him up in his all-too-protracted eternities. The music of the spheres encompassing the earth would then no doubt be the mocking laughter of all other creatures encompassing humanity" (*WS* 14). Once again, this aphorism picks up on the standard motifs of Nietzsche's naturalism, attacking the ideas that the human being stands over against nature (or even that we stand in a unique or particularly high order of rank within nature) and that evolution is a progressively linear and teleological process with the human being as its goal. If the God-hypothesis is experimentally retained (purely for comedic purposes, one assumes), humankind is nonetheless taken down a notch and subjected to the "mocking laughter" of other creatures. But once again, the demotion of the human being, and the demolition of its false order of rank, is predicated upon a residual speciesism. In short, if human beings are now to be reconceived as the "apes of god," then the beasts' mocking laughter is at least in one case self-directed: the joke is still on the ape.

But the question remains whether Nietzsche's own position is as myopic and inadequately thoroughgoing as these passages seem to suggest. In order to address this, I want to draw attention to one more passage. In an aphorism from *Daybreak* (1881), whose title underlines one of the crucial themes of Nietzsche's naturalism—"*The new fundamental feeling: our conclusive transitoriness*"—he writes:

> Formerly one sought the feeling of grandeur of the human being by pointing to its divine *origin*: this has now become a forbidden way, for at its portal stands the ape, together with other gruesome beasts, grinning knowingly as if to say: no further in this direction! One therefore now tries the opposite direction: the way humankind is *going* shall serve as proof of our grandeur and kinship with god. Alas this, too, is vain! At the end of this way stands the funeral urn of the last human being and gravedigger (with the inscription '*nihil humani a me alienum puto*'). However high humankind may have evolved—and perhaps at the end it will stand even lower than at the beginning!—it cannot pass over into a higher order, as little as the ant and the earwig can at the end of its 'earthly course' rise up to kinship with God and eternal life. The becoming drags the has-been along with it: why should an exception to this eternal spectacle be made on behalf of some little star or for any little species on it! Away with such sentimentalities! (D 49)

Here, as in the Prologue from *Zarathustra*, Nietzsche is more than happy to draw upon the striking Darwinian imagery still fresh in his readers' consciousness. Such a picture, with its unsentimental recognition of the human being's "*pudenda origo*" (D 42, 102) on the one hand, and our "conclusive transitoriness" on the other, is inimical to human pride and vanity. It forces us to abandon the false order of rank in relation to animals and nature that has for so long bestowed upon us a cheap, unearned dignity. No longer can humanity be seduced by the metaphysician's flattering conceit that "you are more, you are higher, you are of different origin!" (BGE 230). But once again, it would seem that this edifying insight is achieved only at the expense of the much-abused ape (now flanked by other beasts) who is relegated to the role of exemplifying our "shameful origins."

Now, having cited these various passages, one must ask whether Nietzsche really thinks that our animal origins are "shameful," and whether humans are really "higher" than the primates. For when we compare the probity and rigor (as well as the surprising cohesiveness) of Nietzsche's naturalism with his more traditional and anthropocentric remarks about apes, the latter seem conceptually insubstantial and incoherent. As we have seen, Nietzsche's naturalism questions the very speciesism that he himself occasionally falls back upon. But precisely because the tension between these two elements is so obvious and explicit, we should be careful not to draw hasty conclusions about the consistency of Nietzsche's thought. It seems unlikely that a thinker as nuanced—and as sensitive to the art of writing—as Nietzsche would have so quickly forgotten his own insights. Rather, when Nietzsche exhumes the traditional anthropocentric assumptions about primates, he is more probably exploiting his readers' popular prejudices for rhetorical effect, while at the same time retaining an ironic distance from such conceits.

However, as we shall see, Nietzsche has other reasons for strategically belittling the ape, the most obvious of which is its behavioral proximity to the human being. In particular, Nietzsche is concerned with the phenomenon of *mimêsis*, which, interestingly, he sees as one of the chief characteristics of both the human and the simian. But in order to examine this dimension of the function of the ape in Nietzsche's texts, we will have to turn our attention to a speech from the third book of *Zarathustra*, which revolves around the figure called "Zarathustra's ape."

The Ape as Representative of Superficial Mimicry and Imitation

We began our inquiry into the status of the ape in Nietzsche's naturalism by looking at Zarathustra's first speech on the *Übermensch*. So far, we have focused only on his characterization of the ape as a "laughingstock or painful embarrassment," something indicative of the "shameful origins" of the human being. But Zarathustra's oration continues with the following observation, which we have not yet examined: "Once you were apes, and even now, too, the human being is more ape than any ape" (Z:1 "Prologue" 3; cf. *KSA* 10:3[1]403). Yes, in a manner of speaking, once we were apes, but in what respect is the human being "more ape than any ape"? In order to answer this question, we will need to look at a later speech of Zarathustra's in book 3 entitled "On Passing By."

In the third part of the book, as Zarathustra begins winding his way home to his mountain cave, he comes to the gate of an unnamed metropolis known only as "the *great city*."[10] Here he is confronted by an overzealous disciple who has modeled his activities on Zarathustra, albeit in a course and unflattering way: "[A] foaming fool jumped toward him with outspread hands and barred his way. This, however, was the same fool whom the people called "Zarathustra's ape": for he had gathered something of his phrasing and cadences and also liked to borrow from the treasures of his wisdom" (Z: 3, "On Passing By"). Now, if there is one constant in the four books of *Zarathustra*, it is the incapacity of those audiences to whom Zarathustra addresses himself to apprehend fully the radical import of his gradually developing doctrines. Zarathustra's (presumably human) "ape," however, represents perhaps the most striking example of the ways in which these doctrines can be misinterpreted and misrepresented. The lengthy and repetitive speech in which he warns Zarathustra to "spit on the city and turn back" is a simplistic caricature of Zarathustra's political teaching, borrowing decontextualized fragments from some of his earlier speeches, but with a mode of expression that is vulgar and embarrassingly heavy-handed. Without attempting to reconstruct it in its entirety here, we can note that the ape's speech is marked by two vices: (1) it exemplifies superficial imitation without understanding; and (2) it is motivated by base and ignoble resentment rather than a great love and longing.[11] Zarathustra finally interrupts the ape's tedious harangue by putting a hand over his mouth. His counter-speech, in which he expresses his own disgust at the ape's disgust with the city ("I despise your despising," he retorts), is similarly coarse but nonetheless contains two important insights. First, having identified the desire for revenge at work in his ape's disparagement of the great city, he ruminates: "But your fool's words injure me, even where you are right. And even if Zarathustra's words *were* a thousand times right, still *you* would always *do* wrong with my words" (Z:3 "On Passing By"). Zarathustra's point here seems quite similar to Kierkegaard's identification of truth with subjectivity. There are "true" propositions that in the mouths of certain people become untrue, inasmuch as truth is something that must be *lived*. The ape's words are indeed "right" in two respects: (1) they are in many cases cribbed from Zarathustra's previous speeches; and (2) the great city *is* as terrible as Zarathustra's ape claims: Zarathustra himself admits to being nauseated by it. Nonetheless, in existential terms, the ape *does* wrong with Zarathustra's words. Although superficially similar, the ape's speech is an expression of resentment rather than great love and longing. Thus, because of the sort of person Zarathustra is, because of his history, because of his inner experience, because of his actions and their motives, his evaluation of the great city is true. Because of the sort of person Zarathustra's *ape* is, because of *his* history, because of *his* inner experience, because of *his* actions and their motives, the same evaluation is false. This realization—that the existential truth value of a doctrine is contingent upon who expresses it—leads to the second key insight of Zarathustra's speech, which he offers to his ape as a "parting gift": "where one can no longer love, there one should *pass by*" (Z:3 "On Passing By").

What does all this have to do with Zarathustra's prior claim that "the human being is more ape than any ape"? In this speech, we have an example of an individual human being characterized as an ape—presumably because he "apes," or crudely mimics, Zarathustra's teaching instead of creating his own truth, and even worse, imitates it without understanding it either intellectually or emotionally.[12] Elsewhere, Nietzsche similarly characterizes general *types* of people as apes. Actors, for instance, are in Nietzsche's estimation "ideal apes":

> *Psychology of actors.*—Great actors have the happy delusion that the historical personages they play really felt as they do when they play them—but they are strongly in error: their power of imitation and divination, which they would dearly love to pretend is a capacity for clairvoyance, penetrates only sufficiently far to understand gestures, tones of voice, facial expressions and the superficial in general; that is to say, they catch the shadow of the soul of a great hero, statesman, warrior, man of ambition, jealousy or despair, they press close to the soul but not into the spirit of their object. . . . [L]et us never forget that the actor is no more than an ideal ape, and so much of an ape that he is incapable of believing in 'essence' or the 'essential': with him everything becomes play, word, gesture, stage, scenery and public. (D 324)

This is an odd passage that plays with residual metaphysical distinctions of appearance and reality, interiority and exteriority, the essential and the accidental. The main point of interest to us, however, is that the actor—like the ape—can only imitate superficial expressions, at most capturing the "shadow" of another's soul [Seele], but never the spirit [Geist].[13] Nietzsche similarly characterizes various other groups of human beings as apes. Children, for example, are "born apes" who imitate adults' inclinations and aversions and later try to justify their acquired affects (D 34). The French are "apes and mimes" of the English (BGE 253) and the Germans want to be apes like the French, although their "wonderful talent" (i.e., their "peculiar natural inclination for seriousness and profundity [Schwer- und Tiefsinn]") all too often gets in the way (*KSA* 7:35[12]).[14] Thus, certain types of human beings, inasmuch as they have a penchant for superficial mimicry, are "ape-like." But this is a quality that Nietzsche will at times find in *all* human beings. In a *Nachlass* note from 1880, for instance, he observes, "Imitation, the 'apish' [*das Affische*], is the actual and oldest human quality—to the extent that we eat only the food that tastes good to others. No animal is as much ape as the human being. Perhaps human pity belongs here also, insofar as it is an instinctive, inner imitation" (*KSA* 9:3[34]).[15] Following the thread of remarks associating apes and imitation, we thus encounter a variant of Zarathustra's earlier observation that the human being is more ape than any ape: "No animal is as much ape as the human being." This *Nachlass* note can, I think, be taken as a kind of missing link between Zarathustra's remark in Z:1 "Prologue" 3 and the significance of Zarathustra's ape in Z:3 "On Passing By": the human being is more ape than any ape because so much of what it is and does is rooted in superficial imitation. But as we shall see, this may not be an altogether bad thing.

On Nietzschean Ideals: Apes, Camels, Lions, and Children

An examination of the earliest ape references in Nietzsche's writings suggests that his use of this figure was initially drawn from classical Greek sources.[16] For instance, in one of Nietzsche's unpublished notebooks from 1873, we find the following entry: "'The wisest human being is an ape in the face of god' Heraclitus" (*KSA* 7:26[2]).[17] Nietzsche seems to have been quite fond of this fragment. Several entries later, it appears again, this time reformulated in a slightly more Nietzschean spirit: "According to Heraclitus: the cleverest philistine (human being) is an ape in the face of genius (God)" (*KSA* 7:27[67]; cf. Z:2 "On the Pitying"). Apart from the Heraclitus fragment, Nietzsche occasionally gestures in his early philological writings toward a figure he calls "Heracles' ape." Presumably, Nietzsche was thinking of the *cercôpes*, dwarflike mythical trickster figures famous for their cunning deceit and thievery. In earlier Greek myths, the *cercôpes* are twin brothers (sons of Oceanus and Theia) who attempt to steal Heracles' arms while he sleeps. Heracles awakes and captures them, with the intent of doing them harm, but ultimately lets them go because they amuse him with their clever jokes. In subsequent myths, however, the *cercôpes* (now cast as an entire race rather than two brothers) do not fare so well: they anger Zeus with their trickery and deceit, and he accordingly transforms them into monkeys (see Ovid, *Metamorphoses* XIV.88–100; cf. Z:3 "On Passing By"). Most probably, the tale of this metamorphosis, and the figures' popular depiction as monkeys, grows out of their original name—*cercôpes* means "tailed ones"—which according to most accounts is a function of their cunning and thievery. There is some reason to believe that Zarathustra's ape is at least in part modeled on these mythic figures. However, in Nietzsche's writings, Heracles' "ape"—he uses the singular, for some reason—is associated not so much with cunning and deceit as with thievery and superficial mimicry. He becomes a symbol of those who, instead of creating new works and values, merely imitate the great achievements of the past (or plunder them) without ever really understanding them. Heracles' ape, as Nietzsche describes him, "merely knew how to deck himself out in the ancient pomp" (*BT* 10; cf. *KSA* 1:549).

Let us for the moment set aside the ape figure itself, with all its troublesome connotations, and examine the phenomenon that Nietzsche is descrying here. For surely there is nothing wrong with appreciating the insights and great cultural achievements of the past, or even appropriating them—indeed, Nietzsche himself (qua philologist) was something of a connoisseur in this respect. Nor can one become a creator in the robust Nietzschean sense without first subordinating oneself to the discipline of tradition, i.e., the greatest works of previous creators. Zarathustra himself makes this point quite powerfully in a speech, discussed in numerous other contributions to this volume, entitled "On the Three Metamorphoses," which describes the processes through which "the spirit becomes a camel; and the camel a lion; and the lion, finally a child" (Z:1). Typically, the last two transformations in this allegory—those of the destructive lion and the creative child—are valorized, often at the expense of the rather prosaic camel stage. But seemingly mundane as it may be, this first metamorphosis of the spirit is indispensable to the realization of Zarathustra's ideal: for neither the destruction nor the creation of values is possible without the camel's reverent spirit and initial subordination to the discipline of tradition. The notion, for instance, that a creative genius simply picks up a musical instrument, bypasses all received conventions, and effortlessly creates the possibility of an entirely novel aesthetic experience is empirically dubious at best. It is only through the tedious and sometimes painful acquisition of pre-existing bodies of knowledge (both intellectual and somatic) that one can ever move beyond them to genuine innovation. And much of this initial ascetic drudgery—what might be characterized as the "prehistory" of aesthetic creativity—is necessarily mechanical and imitative. Our entry into any discipline always involves a good deal of habituation, repetition, and superficial mimicry—not to mention theft— which can perhaps be understood as a sublimated version of the cruelty and stupidity at the bottom of all good things (cf. *BGE* 229 and *GM* II:3). Nietzsche never tired of emphasizing the productive, creative capacities of such subordination; it is only through subjecting oneself for a long time to artificial, "unnatural," and frustrating constraints that one achieves genuine spontaneity and creative freedom.[18] Such are the "shameful origins" of our highest achievements. Mimicry—understood now as the lowly but necessary origin of all great cultural creativity—is thus not as base and ignoble as Nietzsche/Zarathustra's rhetoric might lead us to expect.

The problem is not imitation per se, but the inability to move beyond mere imitation. In a *Nachlass* note from the end of 1880, Nietzsche quotes an anonymous Spaniard: "At 40 years man is a camel; at 70 an ape" (*KSA* 9:7[4]). What might Nietzsche have found have illuminating about this obscure remark? To make any sense of it we must bear in mind what it is to be a camel in the Nietzschean sense. To be a camel is to be a beast of burden: strong, reverent, willing to take on difficult tasks, willing to subordinate oneself to values and bodies of knowledge created by others, indeed, to incorporate and internalize them, to allow these heteronomous elements to shape and mold oneself. As I have suggested here, this is good—or at least necessary—but it is only the first stage in the productive transfiguration of the human spirit. Unless one pushes beyond this stage, unless one becomes a lion, and then a child, one eventually "devolves" into an ape, thoughtlessly imitating (or stealing from) the great creations of the past, "decking oneself out in the ancient pomp," incapable of any new creation or even of genuine understanding. As suggested by the figure of Heracles' ape, there is something frivolous, and perhaps even base, about this. The heritage of great aesthetic and cultural innovations is reduced to a fund of "arts and manners through which life is made pretty," rather than something "through which life is transfigured and illuminated" (*KSA* 7:35[12]).[19] The trick, then, is to subordinate oneself provisionally to past cultural achievements without remaining forever at the level of slavish imitation or parasitic appropriation. Indeed, Nietzsche seems to suggest that only through further creative innovation (which necessarily involves a destructive overcoming) can we understand and appreciate those achievements in the first place. "To have joy in originality without becoming the ape of it," he observes, "will be perhaps one day be the sign of a new culture" (*KSA* 9:3[151]).

As we have seen in the course of this chapter, Nietzsche primarily associates the figure of the ape with shameful origins and superficial mimicry. However, as I have argued, the ape, understood as an ineliminable moment in our natural history (our collective "becoming"), and imitation, understood as a necessary formative stage in our individual becoming, turn out to be considerably more important to Nietzsche's own thought than his rhetoric might initially suggest. A truly thoroughgoing naturalism of the kind Nietzsche envisioned would need to affirm these things just as much as what might arise out of them. Of course, within the allegory of the "Three Metamorphoses," the telos of Zarathustra's nomothetic legislation is the child, a figure typically identified with the *Übermensch*: "The child is innocence and forgetting, a new beginning, a game, a wheel rolling out of itself, a first movement, a sacred 'Yes'" (Z:1 "On the Three Metamorphoses"). One could argue that this passage constitutes a kind of thumbnail sketch, not only of the Zarathustrian ideal of the *Übermensch* (in relation to which the human being stands as the ape stands to the human being) but also the more modest and realistic "ideals" one finds scattered throughout Nietzsche's other writings: e.g., the genius, the sovereign individual, the great human being.[20] Such creatures, on Nietzsche's quasi-Heraclitean account, seem as far from the ordinary human being as a god is from an ape.[21] They are, in a manner of speaking, this-worldly "gods" in Nietzsche's new de-deified nature: like Heraclitus's image of *aiôn* as a "playing child," they represent a "sacred 'Yes'" in the "game of creation."[22] But although Nietzsche's later works retain vestiges of such a nomothetic telos (e.g., TI "Skirmishes" 44, 48 and 49; and A 3–4), he seems to grow increasingly suspicious of the abuse and misrepresentation to which such ideals are invariably subject. Will the human being ever overcome its own "apishness"?[23] Or does "the becoming drag the has-been along with it" (D 49), as Nietzsche once suggested? As his productive career drew to a close, amid all the cheerful and immodest hyperbole of the 1888 works, one can nonetheless detect a note of resignation: "The disappointed one speaks. I searched for great human beings; I always found only the apes of their ideals" (TI "Maxims" 39).[24]

Notes

1. With the exception of occasional emendations in favor of greater literalness, I rely chiefly on Walter Kaufmann's translations for Viking Press/Random House and R.J. Hollingdale's translations for Cambridge University Press. Translations from *KSA* are my own.

2. To get a sense of what this entails, see *BGE* 9, 188, and 230, and the introduction to this volume.

3. One other exception is noteworthy here: the tarantula (Z:2 "On the Tarantulas").

4. The only other exception is the leech [*Blutegel*], from the satirical and deliberately unpublished fourth part of *Zarathustra* (Z:4 "The Leech").

5. For an excellent discussion of Nietzsche's proximity and opposition to Darwin, see Keith Ansell-Pearson, "Nietzsche contra Darwin," in *Nietzsche: Critical Assessments*, ed. Daniel W. Conway with Peter S. Groff (London: Routledge, 1998), 4:7–31.

6. I rely here upon Richard Ryder's awkward, but nonetheless useful, coinage. See his seminal essay "Experiments on Animals," in *Animals, Men and Morals,* ed. Stanley and Roslind Godlovitch and John Harris (New York: Taplinger Pub. Co., 1972), 81, as well as his book *Victims of Science* (London: Davis-Poynter, 1975), 16.

7. See e.g., *KSA* 12:7[9]/*WP* 644, *KSA* 12:2[76]/*WP* 660, and *KSA* 13:14[133]/*WP* 684. Compare *SE* 6 and *TI* "Skirmishes" 14.

8. But compare *A* 14 for another perspective.

9. The passage continues, with a focus on the human: "Among human beings, too, the higher types, the lucky strokes of evolution, perish most easily as fortunes change. They are exposed to every kind of decadence: they are extreme, and that almost means decadent. . . . This is not due to any special fatality or malevolence of nature, but simply to the concept 'higher type': the higher type represents an incomparably greater complexity—a greater sum of coordinated elements: so its disintegration is also incomparably more likely. The 'genius' is the sublimest machine there is—consequently the most fragile."

10. The "great city" is *not* Zarathustra's beloved town, "The Motley Cow," a detail that is made clear in the subsequent section (Z:3 "On Apostates").

11. Various commentators have drawn attention to the fact that the ape's vulgarization is a bit too close for comfort. See, for example, Laurence Lampert, *Nietzsche's Teaching: An Interpretation of* Thus Spoke Zarathustra (New Haven, Conn.: Yale University Press, 1986), 165. Stanley Rosen takes a more critical stance in his *The Mask of Enlightenment: Nietzsche's* Zarathustra (New York: Cambridge University Press, 1995), 191–192.

12. Michel Foucault links Zarathustra's ape to the "shameful origins" motif examined earlier in his "Nietzsche, Genealogy, History," in *Language, Counter-Memory, Practice,* ed. Donald F. Bouchard, trans. Donald F. Bouchard and Sherry Simon (Ithaca, N.Y.: Cornell University Press, 1977), 143.

13. Although Nietzsche sometimes characterizes consciousness [*Bewusstsein*] as a "surface," he generally associates spirit [*Geist*] with depth [*Tiefe*] and interiority.

14. Not surprisingly, Richard Wagner (that most Germanic of composers) has his own "clever apes" (*CW,* Second Afterword). Numerous peripheral remarks reinforce this connection between imitation and apelikeness in Nietzsche's writings, e.g., *KSA* 11:26[460].

15. For the sake of economy, I eschew discussion of Nietzsche's suggestive hypothesis, casually introduced at the end of this *Nachlass* note, that the ostensibly deep, interior experience of pity or compassion [*Mitleiden*, literally "suffering with"] is itself a kind of "instinctive, inner imitation." Those wishing to pursue the topic might consult *BGE* 222, *HH* 247, and Z:3 "On Passing By." Considering the link between pity and imitation, it is

no surprise that Nietzsche disparagingly characterizes the ape as a *herd* animal (*KSA* 9:11[130]). Ironically, he even suggests that apes "anticipate the human being" in their penchant for cruel and pleasurable penal practices in GM II:6.

16. The first four references to the ape in Nietzsche's corpus are to be found in the unpublished lecture from 1870 entitled "Socrates and Tragedy," *The Birth of Tragedy* 10, and two entries in the *Nachlass*, circa 1873, *KSA* 7:26[2] and 27[67]. All draw upon classical sources, i.e., a Heraclitus fragment and a myth of Heracles.

17. Cf. H. Diels and W. Kranz, *Die Fragmente der Vorsokratiker* (Berlin, 1952), 22B fragments 82–83 and Charles Kahn, *The Art and Thought of Heraclitus* (New York: Cambridge University Press, 1979), 173–174. It should be noted, however, that *kallistos* can also be translated as "noble," and *aischros* as "base," a resonance that Nietzsche certainly would have been attuned to. It is unclear whether this gnomic pronouncement is attributable to Heraclitus: the fragment is questionable, in part because it is culled from Plato, *Hippias Major* 289a, a dialogue the authenticity of which is disputed.

18. For some passages where Nietzsche emphasizes the importance of subjecting oneself to constraint as a means of achieving a higher naturalness, spontaneity, or freedom, see *KSA* 7:29[118 and 119], *KSA* 8:23[7], *HH* 221 and 278, Z:1 "On the Thousand and One Goals," *GS* 341 and 377, and *BGE* 188 and 225.

19. Compare *HL* 10, where Nietzsche claims that "culture can be something other than the decoration of life." As opposed to the Roman notion of culture as ornamentation and concealment ("mere dissimulation and disguise"), he appropriates the classical Greek conception of culture as "transfigured *physis*" (*SE* 3) and even a "new and improved *physis*" (*HL* 10).

20. For a good treatment of the difference between Zarathustra's "ideal" and ideals articulated in Nietzsche's other books, see Daniel W. Conway, "The Genius as Squanderer: Some Remarks on the *Übermensch* and Higher Humanity," *International Studies in Philosophy* 30, no. 3 (1998): 81–96.

21. Some human beings are awkwardly situated between god and ape, for example, Paganini, Liszt, and Wagner, whom Nietzsche characterizes as "dubiously placed in the middle between 'god' and 'ape' . . . determined equally for 'imitation' as for invention, for creation in the art of imitation" (*KSA* 11:41[2]).

22. Compare *PTA* 6; *KSA* 12:2[130]/*WP* 797; and Z:3 "Before Sunrise." Also see Diels and Krantz, *Die Fragmente der Vorsokratiker*, 22B, fragment 52.

23. The answer to this question depends in part upon how we understand "overcoming" and "self-overcoming" in Nietzsche's texts. Nietzsche himself uses two different terms to express this idea: *Selbstüberwindung* and *Selbstaufhebung*, the second of which has more pronounced Hegelian connotations. I take this as suggesting that the self-overcoming of the human entails not only destruction but also at the same time a preservation and lifting up of what is most important.

24. I would like to thank my colleagues Jeff Turner and Mark Padilla, as well as my research assistant, Kelly Rhoads, whose helpful input during the writing of this chapter is greatly appreciated.

A Sketch (*Riß*) of the
Camel in *Zarathustra*

Charles S. Taylor

We shall be thinking here about the camel in *Thus Spoke Zarathustra* 1.[1] As
this volume makes manifestly clear, Nietzsche wrote frequently about many
kinds of animals, and much of what he had to say falls into the distinction
between the beast of burden and the beast of prey. As a representation of
this distinguishing, we could hardly have a more obvious starting place than
his references to the camel and the lion in Z:1, "On the Three Metamorphoses." Reading this passage straightforwardly gives us the same basic evaluation
one sees throughout Nietzsche's writings: the domesticated beast of burden
receives little if any esteem, while the beast of prey is presented as a higher
level of development of *Geist*. The camel is merely "reverent," while the lion
is courageous enough to steal the freedom to create new values. If, however,
we pay heed to Heidegger's suggestion that covering and uncovering are fundamental modes of Being, then we might well ask what remains covered, or
has been covered up, by the standard reading of Nietzsche's beast of burden/
beast of prey distinction. In this distinction there is generally an explicit
dualistic value judgment; and yet, in his initial description of the metamorphoses of spirit in Z:1, there is no simple dualism separating the camel and

the lion or the lion and the next evolutionary level, the child. The creative child is Spirit that was *necessarily* first camel and then lion. If we start by paying heed to the apparent necessity of the camel, we may ask more carefully just what it is that gives this beast of burden importance in Nietzsche's thought.

In "On the Three Metamorphoses" Nietzsche begins by recalling many difficult things a strong weight-bearing Spirit might undertake. We start, it must be noted, with our focus precisely on the *strong* Spirit rather than on a weak form of Spirit generally attributed to obedient, passive domesticated animals. The strong Spirit does not, as the many think, have an easy life because of its strength. Neither does it want the easy life. Rather, Nietzsche says, it wants to be well laden. Indeed, the strong Spirit wants the *heaviest* load so that in taking upon itself what *for it* is the most difficult, its own strength becomes therein a joyful thing (*meiner Stärke froh werde*). Strength, of course, is not always joyous. It can easily be connected to fear or self-control or hatred or practical activities or revenge—none of which are in essence joyous. We must ask, then, precisely about this *joy* that accompanies strength in Nietzsche's thinking here. The weight-bearing Spirit asks those who are heroes (and not the many assembled in the marketplace) what for them is the heaviest so that similarly difficult burdens may be undertaken. There is in such thinking about the camel a divergence from the standard view of the beast of burden. The camel, as understood by Nietzsche, does not simply meet the incessant, tedious daily demands of life (through *Arbeit, travailler*); nor does it pragmatically, unimaginatively merely carry out the demands of daily tasks efficiently. Safely driving to and from work is a desirable achievement, but it is not likely a way in which one's strength becomes a joyous thing. As everywhere in his thinking, there is Heracleitean complexity in Nietzsche's view of the camel.

Perhaps the richest word Nietzsche uses in relation to the camel comes when he says that *Ehrfurcht* dwells in this strong Spirit. Thomas Common (and later Walter Kaufmann) chose "reverence" to translate this word, while R. J. Hollingdale used "respect and awe." If we think of *Ehrfurcht* literally as "honor + fear," we might begin to see more clearly traces of the initially hidden, deep ambiguity in what Nietzsche thinks about the camel. A simple way to understand fear in the strong Spirit attempting difficult things is to consider the normal fear that one is not strong enough for a task. "Who tied my son to this plow?"—asks an old Scottish saying. One might at the same time, conscious of various difficult obstacles, feel respect specifically for tasks that demand unusual strength (the strength of *Helden*). The higher values of reverence and honor seem to be explored later in Z:1 in "On the Thousand and One Goals." Ranking above a difficult task is one that is also indispensable. Indispensable tasks seem worthy of honor. And above these is a task that liberates and therein evokes awe. The collection of ideas Nietzsche presents to us here does not fit together comfortably. But all of them—fear, heroism, awe, strength, respect, honor, reverence, difficulty, joy—are unmistakable parts of any sketch of the camel.

Nietzsche lists in "On the Three Metamorphoses" diverse examples of heroes taking upon themselves the heaviest burdens—suggesting that this passage is not the first time he had reflected on these things. It is at this point quite helpful to return to earlier versions of Nietzsche's ideas, as is often the case. Returning to his earlier writings with this questioning of *Ehrfurcht* as our guide we actually discover many passages worthy of renewed consideration. "The Greatest Weight" in *Gay Science* 341 is surely one example. One finds more complete exploration of this theme in *Human, All Too Human* in the collection of aphorisms titled "The Souls of Artists and Writers" (*HH* 145–223). In these early aphorisms one begins to see the core elements that eventually were distilled into the comments on the camel in *Zarathustra* 1.

To follow Nietzsche's discussion of artists and writers in *HH* one must first recall the fundamental theme set in that book's opening section, "Of First and Last Things." In "Chemistry of Concepts and Feelings" (*HH* 1), Nietzsche immediately makes clear that the opposition to dualistic metaphysics, which appears implicitly in *The Birth of Tragedy*, has now become an explicit theme. In the beginning of *HH*, Nietzsche develops this opposition through a contrast between metaphysical and historical philosophy. Metaphysical philosophy has for the past 2,000 years, he suggests, solved the basic problems of philosophy by a dualistic separation between fundamental concepts, such as rationality vs. irrationality, sentience vs. the dead, contemplation devoid of interest vs. covetous desire, and altruism vs. egoism. *Last*, ultimate things such as rationality cannot, according to metaphysical philosophy, have originated in opposite *first* things such as irrationality. Ultimate things have instead a miraculous origin (*Wunderursprung*) directly from the so-called in-itself (*An-sich*). Historical philosophy, on the other hand, rejects the dualism of metaphysical philosophy as a mistake of reason (*Vernunft*). If one apprehends things correctly, there is never *pure* contemplation devoid of interest as proposed by Kant and Schopenhauer. What actually happens is that the *first* thing, covetous desire (or, irrationality, egoism), becomes sublimated.

Sublimation (*Sublimierung*) is here used in its scientific sense as the process by which a solid passes directly into a gaseous state without passing through the liquid state. On the surface of an ice cube, for example, most solid ice molecules will melt into water, and then the liquid water molecules (when heated more) will become steam. However, from the surface of the ice cube some rigid ice molecules do directly enter into the gaseous state without passing through the liquid phase. Because the last thing (water vapor) is sublimated from the first thing, one has not seen the transition one sees in normal change; the first and last things no longer appear connected. Steam and ice appear as different things. In *pure* contemplation, fully sublimated selfish desire is so dispersed that it can be observed only if intentionally sought out by the most careful observation. Immersion in the play of one's understanding and imagination while following a theme and its astonishing variations through Schubert's String Quartet no. 15 conceals all traces of personal desire. Such contemplation appears to be a totally different experience from the sensuous pleasure one feels in touching a piece of cashmere or velvet cloth—the sublimation conceals all connection.

There are two basic points here. One is that our highest concepts have gone through a process of development. The second is that our highest concepts developed out of "lesser" forms of human activity—very human, all-*too*-human activities. These two themes of development and of the lowly origins of the highest on which we so pride ourselves permeate Nietzsche's thinking in *HH*. Based on this lesson about careful observation from the natural sciences (which had long failed to apprehend sublimation), Nietzsche calls for a chemistry of moral, religious, and aesthetic concepts and sensations that inspects just this kind of hidden growth. He proceeds to work on developing this "chemistry" in his three books immediately preceding *Zarathustra*. Nietzsche's project of disclosure here is a precursor of Heidegger's thinking about the uncovering and covering of Being. One finds this discussion of covering and revealing throughout Heidegger's writings as, for example, in *The Question Concerning Technology*, where the standard definition of technology as tools made by humans for practical purposes is shown in its great clarity to conceal the essence of technology.

In "The Souls of Artists and Writers," Nietzsche is working on a "chemistry" of aesthetic concepts and sensations. *Human, All Too Human* 145 starts with the usual understanding that a perfect thing cannot have gone through the process of *becoming*, thus incorporating the assumption of Parmenidean-Platonic metaphysics that ideals are eternally perfect and unchanging and wholly separated from their opposites (e.g., Diotima's description of the idea of beauty, *Symposium* 211a). The effective work of art produces a belief in the magical suddenness of its origination (instantaneous perfection) and does not give any sense of development. Artists, believing in this pure, complete origination, add to their works elements of inspired unrest or blindly groping disorder as the only possible kind of horizon for perfect art. The idea of a sudden emergence of perfection must, Nietzsche insists in opposition, be observed in a scientific (*wissenschaftlich*) way in order to see the process of gradual development hidden from sight by the dazzling presence of the completed artistic product.

Nietzsche's approach to disclosing the mistake that lies in not perceiving development in art is to explore a set of related questions. *Human, All Too Human* 149, titled "The Slow Arrow of Beauty," suggests that the noblest kind of beauty does not attack us stormily and intoxicatingly (*welche nicht stürmische und berauschende Angriffe macht*). The noblest beauty does not transport us *suddenly*. Such art often disgusts. Rather, the noblest art infiltrates slowly; we carry it with us unnoticed and only eventually does it take possession of us after having lain a long time modestly in our hearts. One may carefully, single-mindedly study Cézanne's still-life paintings at every opportunity and only at a much later time be captivated by his paintings of Mont St. Victoire—even though one had seen many of them (in passing) while moving through a museum to look at his glorious fruit and pottery arranged on that table. Here, then, we have the question of instantaneity presented for consideration. One misses the direction of Nietzsche's thinking if one sees this as a comparison of two differing (subjective) descriptions of aesthetic experience—stormy attack vs. slow infiltration. Speed is not the issue. The emphasis upon slowness for Nietzsche is tied primarily to the correlation between duration and the process of *becoming*. This is clarified if we consider another passage in the same section.

Instantaneous, complete perfection is typically considered the product of genius. The habit of adapting the methods of natural science to his own uses in *HH* was strong enough that even in the discussion of *HH* in *Ecce Homo*, Nietzsche still writes, "One error after another is coolly placed on ice; the ideal is not refuted—it *freezes* to death. Here, for example, "the genius" freezes to death . . ." (*EH* "Books" HH:1). The cooling down of instantaneous perfection produced by genius occurs in several stages. Although artists have a vested interest in fostering the belief in sudden inspiration, notes Nietzsche again in *HH* 155, the truth is that the *imagination* of the *good* artist (or thinker, or poet) regularly produces not only the good but also the mediocre and the bad. The real achievement of the *imagination* is prolificacy. What distinguishes the *good* artist is not sudden inspiration. The driving force behind the good artist is rather a most highly sharpened and constantly used judgment (*Urteilskraft*). It is the *judgment* of the great artist that rejects, selects, and then ties together the worthy products of the imagination. Beethoven's *Notebooks*, Nietzsche points out, show that his greatest music was *gradually* put together out of many different attempts. The passage on the slowness of the affect of the beautiful points at growth, at development in the spectator. Here it is the work of art that also is seen to undergo a process of development. Genius is not "refuted" but rather cooled down by the observation that selection plays an essential role in art.

Well-dispersed within genius there is, we have just seen, the regular, hard work of *judgment*. With this acknowledgement of hard work we seem to have found a place for Nietzsche's later praise of the camel. Hard work, understood as passing judgment on one's own creations, does seem open to the issues of fear that we noted to be included in the *Ehrfurcht* of the camel. One's ego may well be afraid to admit that one has made the merely mediocre and surely will not acknowledge readily that one has made something bad or ugly. Much strength is needed to discard one's own creations—or to be self-critical enough to labor at making them better. Respect for one's own creations is far more authentic when one has demanded much of oneself. Those who do not know this experience of hard work in judging one's own creations will think of creativity as a sublime gift of genius quickly, effortlessly achieved and not as sublimated hard work.

Prior to *HH*, Nietzsche had devoted much time to reflection on the Greeks. Traces of that thinking persist throughout his writings. *Human, All Too Human* 170 thinks about Greek artists writing in order to triumph. Their work cannot be thought of without competition. Hesiod's good *Eris*, ambition (*Ehrgeiz*), gave wings to their genius. This *Ehrgeiz* (honor + greed) demands that their work achieve the highest excellence—in their *own* eyes, as *they* understand excellence, without reference to reigning taste or common opinion. Sophocles' self-criticism, then, was based on his own critical judgment of his work. His unwillingness to accept his own work unless it was (in his own uncompromising eyes) actually the best was his most difficult burden. Likewise, one might ask, following Nietzsche here, whether it is not the *Ehrgeiz* of Aristophanes that underlies his presentations of Socrates in *The Clouds* and Euripides in *The Frogs*. Nietzsche points out in *HH* 170 that a writer such as Æschylus wanted *to be* authentically excellent (*wollen wirklich vortrefflicher sein*). There is joy in triumph only over the worthy opponent. So there must, as noted, be a true contest, and in *this* contest one's strength becomes joyous for having reached its highest achievement. Only outsiders think that great accomplishments happen effortlessly. The overwhelming impact of a completed work blinds the spectator to the extreme effort that lies behind the completed last thing. The camel for Nietzsche symbolizes, among other things, this inescapable element of immense struggle.

To this point we have been considering the significance of the camel/artist in one of the two modes mentioned—the essential role of becoming in the production of perfection. The gradual development of beauty, through the hard work of distinguishing the good from the bad and the mediocre, points primarily to the final product. We have not yet considered how *first* things are sublimated into last things. To this we must now turn.

Hard work in passing judgment on one's creations is not the only feature of genius that plays a role in "freezing" this metaphysical ideal. More reflection on genius in HH 162 proposes no fundamental difference between the activity of the artist and that of the inventor of machines or the scholar of astronomy or history or the master of tactics. All of these reveal themselves as the activities of those:

1) whose thinking is active in one direction;
2) who put everything to use as material;
3) who observe with zeal their own inner life and that of others;
4) who see everywhere models and stimulation;
5) who never become tired of combining material.

This is an instructive explication of hard work. In each of these activities, one can observe a connection between things that often appear wholly separate. The *thinking in one direction*, what many call "being focused" today, is presented as a quality of the actions of the scholar, the inventor, and the artist. The most immediate reading of this could be to extend the term "creative" (and probably "genius") to all of them and not restrict it to the artist. In doing only this, however, one simply fills out the meaning of *last* things. Last things result from tireless work, using all possible materials, finding inspiration wherever one turns, and having an authentic sense of one's inner life. Nietzsche allows us to go further and see a connection between first and last things.

One can tirelessly work hard in a single direction and not produce anything of lasting value. Or, one might perform the same tasks with the same material again and again or with no sense of others involved—give the same lecture on Descartes' dream argument for twenty years without change. Can one use a story from the morning news to elucidate Cartesian doubt, or does one use the same examples one heard as an undergraduate? Every human activity can be marvelously complicated, Nietzsche notes, but none is a "miracle." In the previously considered criticism of the instantaneous production of genius, there was no clear sense of first things being sublimated into last things. But now we must note that tirelessness, single-mindedness, and adaptability are by themselves normal human traits. The question might be asked: What, if anything, separates the single-mindedness of Hölderlin from that of a student pursuing a university degree consciously expending the absolute minimal amount of energy? First and last things seem not so separate in this context.

Human, All Too Human 163, "The Seriousness of Craft" suggests that one can easily point to many great artists who were very little "gifted." There is no problem speaking of the genius of a Beethoven, because then the concept (traditionally understood) is accepted to be a rarely appearing gift—the vanity of the normal person is not offended by the "miraculous" presence of "gifts" in the very few. But now Nietzsche is looking at the great artist who developed greatness through the earnestness of craftsmanship. Such a "worker" learns first to form all the individual parts properly and completely before attempting the great whole. Such workers make sure that they have all the time needed to make each of the parts correctly because they get more pleasure in the actual making of the parts than they get in the effect of the completed whole. Recalling Cézanne's oft-quoted, "I will astound Paris with an apple" helps us grasp Nietzsche's thought here. This detailed working on parts sounds merely tedious to usual (metaphysical) thinking, so one does not ever speak positively of the need for this kind of work. But here too one sees something of Nietzsche's praise of the camel and the associated joy in one's strength. This strength is different from the strength of judging one's own creations noted earlier. Here we have the professor who after twenty-five years can still (for perhaps the fifty-seventh time) bring to life in class Socrates' questioning of the slave boy in the *Meno*—the great teacher. This joy and strength of the camel becomes still clearer in a passage in *The Wanderer and His Shadow*.

"Dancing in Chains" (WS 140) draws together the points just considered about the great Greek artists seeking to triumph over their peers and the notion that one becomes a genius out of earnest craftsmanship. Greek artists, Nietzsche proposes, through self-imposed *new constraints*, so charmed their contemporaries that they stimulated imitation. Any invention in meter, for example, was a self-imposed fetter. "Dancing in chains" is a distinct artistic achievement disclosed to us by the Greeks—making things difficult for themselves and then casting over everything the illusion of easiness. As early as Homer, Nietzsche notes, one can perceive an abundance of artistic formulas and rules of epic narrative within which he had to dance. Starting out by following established artistic rules and then gracefully conquering those very rules brings before us for our admiration both triumph and constraint. This kind of artistic achievement is difficult to grasp in our postmodern world, where rejection of all established rules is the only starting point.

There is, to be sure, a fundamental ambiguity in this notion of dancing in chains. And it would seem that this same ambiguity also lies in the essence of the camel in *Zarathustra*. For Nietzsche, the beginning is Spirit allowing itself to be laden with the greatest burden. Said more carefully, the beginning is Spirit taking upon itself the most difficult. One starts not knowing if one will get the field plowed with *that* plow. Fear might well lead to choosing a smaller plow—and doing less. But for Nietzsche, the goal in either case is not simply completing the task. And yet, neither is the goal giving up the job at hand. As we have seen, meticulously making all the needed pieces of a machine or an artwork (or getting the field plowed even into the corners) is an indispensable part of astonishing Paris with an apple. The task undertaken is not done gratuitously. Completion, nonetheless, is not the goal. One does not follow a poetic constraint so that one can then announce, "See how well I wrote my dactylic hexameter!" Obedience is not sufficient. Again, one can point to much obedience (most obedience?) that seems clearly far removed from dancing and much closer to fear of punishment or to hope for reward or to desire for comfort and calm. We seem to be at the point of trying to see the solid ice molecule sublimate into water vapor.

It would be easy to resolve these questions about the interplay of constraint and joy by attributing joyousness only to the playing child in *Zarathustra*. In the same way, one can readily think about dancing after chains have been removed, or without their ever having existed. But Nietzsche gives us no such dualistic clarity. It has already been noted that one form of the joy of the camel does come from the achievement of great tasks. This would be dancing after the chins were removed. The Greek poets danced *in* chains. The camel's strength grasped now in this way becomes joyous while taking on the greatest burden, not afterward. In *HH* 164, Nietzsche suggests that it is very useful for great spirits to gain insight into their own power and its origin. This means grasping what purely human (*rein menschlichen*) qualities have flowed together in them and what fortunate circumstances exist for them—never-ending energy, first of all; resolute working toward single goals;

great personal courage; and then the luck of an upbringing that offered from the earliest years the best teachers, models, and methods. We see here that "*menschlich*" does not always have a pejorative meaning for Nietzsche. Perhaps this is the ground upon which to think about dancing in chains. Struggling with chains and lifting heavy burdens are clearly *rein menschlichen* activities. The camel, we are told in "On the Three Metamorphoses," willingly takes on the heaviest burdens. This is not a matter of passivity or domination but rather a choosing to struggle with the difficult. If these activities grow in time out of their initial negative natures into dancing and joy then the connection is observable between first and last things. Such observations help overcome the mistake of metaphysical philosophy.

Notes

1. The source for quotations is *WDB*. Translations are my own.

P O L Y P

Polyp Man[1]

Brian Domino

This is an essay about Nietzsche's one-time use of the polyp in his published writings.[2] Specifically, it is about the role of the polyp in the project of Book II of *Daybreak*. The polyp is not a well-known animal. Indeed, it wasn't until 1740 that polyps were known to be animals at all. Most people today upon hearing the word "polyp" don't think of plants or animals. I discovered this bit of sociological trivia while working on this chapter. Colleagues would ask what I was working on. "Nietzsche's polyp" I would cheerily reply, only later realizing that I had given the impression that I was aiming for a publication in the *Annals of Proctology*.[3]

From Machine Man to Polyp Man

Polyps were not always so philosophically obscure. Abraham Trembley's discovery that polyps were not plants but animals spawned an intense period of polyp research. A key discovery was that a polyp cut into pieces became as many polyps. Some creatures can regenerate particular organs (think of a lizard and its tail); the polyp is truly autogenetic. While polyps piously require eight days for their acts of (re)creation, the materialists were less religious. As Lange puts it in his *History of Materialism*: "The polyp cut up by

Trembley had in itself the causes of its reproduction. Only ignorance of natural forces has made us take refuge in a God."[4] The polyp killed more than God. According to some materialists' not unproblematic reasoning, the polyp's self-regenerative ability demonstrated that the soul could not be "in" the head or heart as previously believed and that it was divisible and hence material. Although several philosophers discuss the lowly polyp and its role in such divine metaphysical thinking, none relied on it more than La Mettrie, who used polyps repeatedly in his *Machine Man*.[5] While Nietzsche may not have read La Mettrie's works directly, Lange mentions him over two dozen times and in all three volumes of his *History of Materialism* and even devotes an entire chapter to him. Given Nietzsche's praise and multiple readings of Lange's study, it is almost certain that he was familiar with La Mettrie's thought.[6]

Mindful, then, of the little creature's philosophical might, Nietzsche uses the polyp as an analogy for the psyche in his revolutionary project to achieve "the autosuppression [*Selbstaufhebung*] of morals" (D Preface 4). I will argue that the appropriate question is not whether the psyche is "really" analogous to a polyp but whether believing it is helps us flourish. One feature of turning to *Daybreak* is that Nietzsche has yet to discover decadence, which throws an epistemic wrench into the philosophic project of self-improvement. Specifically, by 1888 Nietzsche realizes that we are likely to be infected with decadence and hence will believe that thinking or acting in particular ways adds to our flourishing when the opposite is true. Fortunately, in *Daybreak*, Nietzsche is still several years from discovering decadence, so we can learn from a clearer picture of the psyche. I can, therefore, ask rather straightforwardly whether thinking of myself—that is, my drives and intellect—as a collection of polyp arms, some wielding my intellect in their fight for domination, helps me flourish. First let me develop Nietzsche's account of the psyche in terms of the polyp.

Nietzsche states his polyp psychology in a few sentences: "Every moment of our lives sees some of the polyp-arms of our being grow and others wither, all according to the nutriment that the moment does or does not bear with it. [. . .] And as a consequence of this chance nourishment of the parts, the whole, fully grown polyp will be something just as accidental as its growth as been" (D 119). On this account, the psyche is polyp-like, with each polyp arm representing a drive. Experience washes over the tentacles, accidentally nourishing some while others "will be neglected and starved to death" (D 119). Nietzsche gives a homey example of how this plays out in everyday life. He lists six different responses to hearing someone laugh at us as we pass by, ranging from "think[ing] about what is ridiculous *per se*" to being "pleased at having involuntarily contributed to add a ray of sunshine and mirth to the world" (*D* 119). That people respond differently to being laughed at is due to different polyp arms being nourished. For example, the person who responds by trying "to pick a quarrel on account of it" is so doing because his combativeness tentacle happened upon the event. The Pollyannaish response is explained similarly: it was the polyp arm of benevolence that was nourished. Since Nietzsche neither presents an exhaustive list of the drives nor a strategy for limiting their number, this account seems vulnerable to the objection of explanatory circularity that he lodges against Kant in *Beyond Good and Evil* 11. Just as Kant and his followers invented faculties any time they needed to explain a human ability, so it seems that Nietzsche multiplies drives as needed. I think this objection misses Nietzsche's point, but that won't be clear until we develop his point. For the moment, let's think along Nietzsche's lines and return to this issue later.

Another consequence of one polyp arm being nourished by a particular event is that none of the other tentacles are. This in turn means that the nourished tentacle will grow while the others will wither. If one polyp arm repeatedly seized all the nourishment, it would come to dominate while the others would become feeble and eventually die. A similar fate awaits the tentacle denied an opportunity to discharge its strength. After "a few days or a few months of non-gratification, it will wither away like a plant that has not been watered" (*D* 119). If either circumstance occurred, people would soon become the psychological equivalents of the inverse cripples of *Zarathustra* 2 ("On Redemption"), always becoming combative, benevolent, and so on. Elsewhere in *Daybreak*, Nietzsche uses the example of the drive for pity. "Supposing that it [pity] prevailed, even if only for one day, it would bring humanity to utter ruin" (*D* 134). Fortunately, only the hunger drive requires something real. Our other polyp arms are content with "imaginary dishes." While the interpretive freedom afforded by dreams are the polyp arms' smorgasbords, waking life offers only slightly lighter fare. Either way, events are interpreted so as to nourish the other polyp arms.

Having completed our account of the polyp psychology of *Daybreak*, we must return to the objection of circularity. The obvious way out involves an appeal to the natural sciences, but this route is epistemologically impossible: "However far a man may go in self-knowledge, nothing can be more incomplete than his image of the totality of *drives* that constitute his being. He can scarcely name even the cruder ones: their number and strength, their ebb and flood, their play and counterplay among one another, and above all the laws of their *nutriment* remain wholly unknown to him" (*D* 119). The unknowability of the drives means, as Nietzsche learned from Lange, that philosophers can present, not scientific truths—for none are to be had—but rather what Kant called regulative ideals.[7] That is, philosophers can present claims whose truth status cannot be known, but that help us to flourish if we believe in them.[8] Thus the charge of explanatory circularity is misguided for Nietzsche is not offering a scientific explanation but rather is offering us a reasonable belief whose acceptance ought to improve our lives. In other words, the question is not "Are we really polyps, psychologically speaking?" but "Does adopting Nietzsche's polyp perspective improve our lives?"[9]

From Polyp Science to Polyp Politics and Psychology

So now the question is: How would accepting Nietzsche's polyp psychology help us flourish? The answer is to be found in the history of morals. For most of human history, actions were grouped into altruistic and free, on the one hand, and egoistic and unfree, on the other. On the basis of this "supposed and profound intrinsic difference" (*D* 148) we valued the first kind of actions more, so they were performed more frequently. If we accept Nietzsche's polyp psychology, we must abandon this distinction. As this error and its related mistakes gradually lose their habitual hold, we will come to prefer to act as we have wanted to all along, namely egoistically. This in turn means that life itself will no longer be viewed as evil. The polyp will undo the original sin that the serpent brought us. This auto-suppression of morals is the broader and distant political goal of *Daybreak* Book II. Since this will take a long time to happen, there must be some egoistic reason for the individual to begin to act this way. This is what I want to explore now.

In addition to its ethicopolitical value, this polyp psychology seems immanently practical in the quest for self-improvement. Indeed, earlier in *Daybreak*, Nietzsche gives an exhaustive list of six strategies for "combating the vehemence of a drive" (*D* 109). The list includes avoidance—what we would now call aversion therapy—and negative association, among others. This list gives no clear indication that beliefs are involved at all. All the techniques, perhaps save aversion therapy, work in training non-human animals, animals bereft of beliefs. It is as if the rational self needs to train the non-rational body. Nietzsche ends this section, however, by radically distancing himself from this Platonic-Cartesian assertion:

[T]hat one *desires* to combat the vehemence of a drive at all, however, does not stand within our own power; nor does the choice of any particular method; nor does the success or failure of this method. What is clearly the case is that in this entire procedure our intellect is only the blind instrument of *another drive* which is a *rival* of the drive whose vehemence is tormenting us. [. . .] While 'we' believe we are complaining about the vehemence of a drive, at bottom it is one drive *that is complaining about another*; that is to say: for us to become aware that we are suffering from the *vehemence* of a drive presupposes the existence of another equally vehement or even more vehement drive, and that a *struggle* is impending in which our intellect is going to have to take sides. (D 109)

This leaves Nietzsche in much the same place as Hume was in, given that they broadly agree that reason is the slave of the passions. On Nietzsche's account, reason is only the tool of some drive trying to quell another. This reduces reasoning to rationalizing. One way to think about what this means for philosophy is to say that it shifts the topos of philosophy from truth to health (in the broadest sense). Following Nietzsche's many autobiographical examples in his works, I will examine a trivial aspect of my life.

Of Polyps and Other Little Things

As often as I can, I walk from my house to the library where, free of distractions, I can think and write. About every other week, I am nearly hit by a vehicle. From my perspective, these brushes with fatality are always due to driver error. Before thinking deeply about Nietzsche's polyp psychology, my reaction to these pseudo-accidents could best be described as indignation. I would be angry at the drivers for nearly hitting me because they were preoccupied fiddling with their stereos or chatting on cell phones. More accurately, I was angry at them for choosing to engage in such activities, which further divided their already meager intellectual resources, with the smaller part apparently going toward watching for pedestrians in general and me in particular. My indignation would spread a miasma over the next few hours, which, needless to say, thwarted my work.

Thinking of myself as having a large polyp arm (representing my "combativeness" drive) scouring my experiences for people and situations about which to get angry (more accurately: to interpret as situations about which I should be angry and so thereby to find nutriment) certainly conformed to the "data" I had. Upon reflection, it did seem that I was on the prowl for anger-producing situations and people. Strangely, just adopting this perspective calmed me. I then looked at Nietzsche's six methods for self-control.

Since I was trying to tame that polyp arm precisely so that I could engage in "a particularly difficult and fatiguing task" (D 109), Nietzsche's fifth technique of engaging in such a task seemed a poor choice. He also warned against the third technique of giving yourself over to "unrestrained and unbounded gratification of the drive," lest one follow "the rider who rides his horse to death and breaks his own neck in doing so" (D 109). I had to agree that becoming "the indignant professor" would probably be a poor career move. Without detailing my selection process, I decided that the fourth technique, namely, that of associating the gratification of the drive with some painful thought, would work best. After all, Nietzsche reports that it has been successfully used by such diverse people as Napoleon, Christians in general, and Lord Byron.

Now comes the stumbling block. I easily slipped back into my dogmatic slumbers in which I believed that this monolithic 'I' is choosing to attack one of its polyp arms by associating its pleasure with some greater displeasure and that this choice is rational. What really is happening is that some other drive—let's call it my tenure drive—is engaged in a battle with my anger drive and has enlisted the help of my intellect. As Graham Parkes points out in his *Composing the Soul*, what Nietzsche means by intellect is not particularly clear in *Daybreak*.[10] Fortunately, Nietzsche soon clarifies his meaning in both the *Gay Science* (GS 333) and in *Beyond Good and Evil* (BGE 36). The intellect is a disposition or configuration of the drives toward each other. This view has two things to recommend it. First, it explains why humans have identified the self with the intellect for so long. Second, it explains why Hume could never find his self, only various passions or drives. Just as the polyp has no definite parts (in the sense that a trunk severed from its arms will regenerate new arms and the "old" arms a new trunk), the intellect is not different from the drives; it is not their overlord.

My self, then, is a collection of drives, each having a disposition toward the others and each vying for domination over the others. The project of self-improvement can be thought of as continuously shifting allegiances among the drives. Some combinations allow for the greater exercise of various drives and so for the flourishing of the whole, while other combinations are lethal, as shown previously. There is some combination (or combinations) of drives that allows for the individual's maximal flourishing. Finding this disposition is the project of becoming who you are. The value of Nietzsche's polyp psychology is that it recasts the role of the self, intellect, or soul in the project of self-improvement, the quintessential philosophical project. The intellect is not the conductor of the drives but rather an indicator of the extent to which they are acting harmoniously. How to read our intellectual mood, and how to overcome the decadence that corrupts our readings, is the task of Nietzsche's later works, especially *Ecce Homo*. The value of this now is that it allows for moods to be philosophically important. Before Nietzsche, morality was considered apart from or despite moods. At best, being ill-disposed toward a particular action only added to its pedigree. Nonetheless, the pessimism ("skepticism" seems more accurate, but Nietzsche writes "pessimism" in his preface) that *Daybreak* engenders, especially in Book 2, can help us take a first step toward flourishing; namely, to achieve "the autosuppression [*Selbstaufhebung*] of morals" (*D* Preface 4). Reshaping the task of philosophy is certainly a remarkable achievement, and it probably explains why Nietzsche, when looking back on *Daybreak* in *Ecce Homo*, sees not his former polyp self but a sea monster (*Seegethier*) (*EH* "Books" D 1). But what is a hydra but a mythologized polyp?

Notes

1. Unless otherwise noted, citations are drawn from Walter Kaufmann's and R. J. Hollingdale's translations with minor emendations. I would like to thank Christa Davis Acampora, Ralph Acampora, and Graham Parkes for their insightful comments on earlier drafts of this essay.

2. Nietzsche does mention the animal polyp at least twice in his notebooks. The first (*KGW* 2:12[5]) is nearly unintelligible, but it seems to draw a parallel between humans and polyps, likening science to the mountains that polyps build. Since polyps don't build mountains, it is difficult to understand what Nietzsche is up to here (I thank James Hanges and Justin Erik Halldór Smith for their help in trying to understand this notebook entry.) In the second entry (KGW VII3:36[43]), Nietzsche uses "Polypen" to mean octopi, as he cites Theognis's observation that they take on the colors of the rock to which they adhere.

3. Even Nietzsche's use of the term is usually in a medical sense. See, for example, GM 2:21 and *The Case of Wagner* 1.

4. Frederick Albert Lange, *History of Materialism*, trans. Ernest Chester Thomas (London: Kegan Paul, Trench, Trübner, and Co., 1890), 2:72.

5. For an excellent overview, see Aram Vartanian, "Trembley's Polyp, La Mettrie, and Eighteenth-Century French Materialism," *Journal of the History of Philosophy* 11, no. 3 (June 1950): 259–286.

6. On this issue, see George Stack, *Lange and Nietzsche* (New York: de Gruyter, 1983), 139–141.

7. See Nietzsche's letter to Gersdorff in August 1866. Also see *WP* 477.

8. The details of this account can be found in George J. Stack's "Kant, Lange, and

Nietzsche: Critique of Knowledge," in *Nietzsche and Modern German Thought*, ed. Keith Ansell-Pearson (New York: Routledge, 1991), 30–58. Also see his *Lange and Nietzsche*, 10f.

9. A similar shift occurs in the passage from *Beyond Good and Evil* cited earlier: "[F]or the Kantian question 'How are synthetic a priori judgments possible?' it is high time to substitute another question: 'why is the belief in such judgments *necessary*?'—it is time to understand that for the purpose of preserving creatures of our kind, we must *believe* that such judgments are true; which means, of course, that they could still be *false* judgments" (*BGE* 13).

10. Graham Parkes, *Composing the Soul: Reaches of Nietzsche's Psychology* (Chicago: University of Chicago Press, 1994), 353.

PART TWO

ZARATHUSTRA'S ANIMALS

DOG

Dogs, Domestication, and the Ego

Gary Shapiro

Fondly, for three bitches: Blacky, Amber, and Annie

In *Zarathustra*'s "On the Vision and the Riddle," three animals—a spider, a snake, and a dog—make significant appearances, as do three human or quasi-human figures—Zarathustra himself, the dwarf known as the Spirit of Gravity, and the shepherd who must bite off the head of the snake. Of these animals, it is the dog who receives the most extended attention. Here, in the passage that along with "The Convalescent" (with its eagle and serpent) is usually and rightly taken to be Nietzsche's most articulate and yet highly veiled approach to explaining the teaching of eternal recurrence, the riddling vision involves animals. This is scarcely the only passage in Nietzsche to deal with the figure of the dog, although it is the one in which the dog has the most active role; frequently the name of the animal appears only in figurative speech. Here, even if the entire passage is a figure for the meaning of recurrence, the dog is as lively and noisy within the text as any of the other protagonists. Unfolding the vision and the riddle, or perhaps at least discovering what questions it asks, requires a confrontation with the figures of the animals and that howling dog. The parallel passage in *The Gay Science* (341) includes a demon rather than a dwarf and a spider spinning in the moonlight but no dog and no shepherd choked by a snake. Let us note, before proceeding further, that of all these animals, it is only the dog who is domesticated in the "real world." Eagles and serpents may speak in fairy tales (or at the beginning of Genesis), but they are fundamentally without language, although we suspect that the style of a dog's whining and whimpering and perhaps its howling may have something to do with its domestication. The need for a more subtle exploration of the role of the animal in the presentation of the thought of recurrence emerges when we realize that nowhere in Nietzsche's published writings is the teaching ever articulately affirmed by a human voice; yet in the two chapters of *Zarathustra* just mentioned, its dramatic presentation is staged with diverse animals.[1] The discussion of recurrence in "On the Vision and the Riddle" reaches a turning point when the *Märchen*-like dwarf has just "murmured contemptuously 'All truth is crooked; time itself is a circle.'" Zarathustra's reply to this reductionistic oversimplification is to pose a series of questions with very little in the way of affirmation, his last question being "must we not eternally return?" But he tells his audience—the searchers, researchers, and guessers of riddles—that with such questions his voice became increasingly soft, for he was afraid of his own thoughts and the thoughts behind them.

It is with this cessation of the voice that

> suddenly I heard a dog howl nearby. Had I ever heard a dog howl like this? My thoughts raced back. Yes, when I was a child, in the most distant moment of childhood: then I heard a dog howl like this. And I saw him too, bristling, his head up, trembling, in the stillest moonlight, when even dogs believe in ghosts—and I took pity: for just then the full moon, silent as death, passed over the house; just then it stood still, a round glow—still on the flat roof, as if on another's property—that was why the dog was terrified, for dogs believe in thieves and ghosts. And when I heard such howling again I took pity again.

On one level this records an experience of déjà vu. Zarathustra sees and hears a dog howling just as he did when he was a small child. It does not seem to be an identical repetition of the same experience, for the dog of childhood memory howled as the moon rose over a house; here there is no house and the moon had already risen, for the spider was spinning its web in the moonshine (although since we are dealing with the comparison of a vision and an early childhood memory recollected within that vision, we must be cautious when speaking of identity and comparison). So far the dog is just a marker of such an experience, an experience that might indicate the possibility of a stricter form of recurrence, one that might require great courage and resolution to comprehend and internalize. But what is a dog, this domesticated animal, that whimpers, whines, and howls, believes in ghosts and thieves, bristles and trembles?[2] Does the dog tell us something about the human ego, its breeding and training? In a note for *Zarathustra*, Nietzsche writes: "And wherever I climb, my dog follows me everywhere; he is called 'ego'" (*KSA* 10:4[188]). We imagine ourselves as sovereign individuals who train the lesser animals. In fact when we "train" dogs, we ourselves are being trained to be dog trainers and owners (as anybody who has been to obedience school with their pet can testify). The ego too is something that has been bred, appearing first in the herd. Zarathustra is quite clear, by the way, about seeing early humans as herd animals rather than pack animals such as dogs:

> The delight in the herd is more ancient than the delight in the ego [*Ich*]; and as long as the good conscience is identified with the herd, only the bad conscience says: I [*Ich*]. . . . Verily, the clever ego, the loveless ego that desires its own profit in the profit of the many—that is not the origin of the herd but its going under. (Z:1 "On the Thousand and One Goals")

Dogs were once wolves, beasts of prey; now they are domesticated, like too many human beings. Indeed, our experience of domesticating and training dogs has served as an implicit model for training humans. There is no doubt about the baneful aspects of the process: "Virtue is what makes modest and tame: with it they make the wolf into a dog and man himself into man's best domestic animal" (Z:3 "Of the Virtue That Makes Small"). However, it is just the domestication of humans that leads to such astonishing results as an animal that is capable of making promises and that is therefore pregnant with a future beyond the alternatives of domestication, the herd, or the pack (GM II:1).

Part of life's difficulty for most people most of the time is that they fail to see the ego as a dog. Aphorism 312 of *Gay Science* reads: "My *dog*.—I have given a name to my pain and call it 'dog.' It is just as faithful, just as obtrusive and shameless, just as entertaining, just as clever as any other dog—and I can scold it and vent my bad mood on it, as others do with their dogs, servants, and wives." How liberating it would be if we could see our "pain"—the sum of our resentments and frustrations, for example—as a dog that frequently amuses us but needs to be kept in its place and can serve as an outlet for our bad temper. This would be far superior to seeing ourselves as identical with the pain, and the same holds true for our relation to the ego, which follows us about like a dog.[3]

The dog is rather consistently a figure of slavish obedience, as contrasted with other animals. A note from the first half of 1883 praises the superior strength and fitness of beasts of prey (*Raubtiere*) and explains that cats and dogs are both degenerate (*entartete*) versions of such beasts (KSA 10:7[42]). Yet Nietzsche admires the playfulness and cunning of the cat, while having some reservations about its dishonesty.[4] One might say that the dog does not have enough imagination for the feline style of dishonesty. In the epilogue to *The Wanderer and His Shadow*, as the light is failing the Wanderer takes leave of the Shadow, who has been dogging his steps and thoughts for a whole long day. Rejecting the Shadow's tentative offer to be his slave, the Wanderer replies:

> [T]he sight of one unfree would embitter me for all my joy; I would find even the best things repulsive if someone *had* to share them with me—I want no slaves around me. That is why I will not have even a dog, that lazy tail-wagging parasite who has become "doglike" only through being the slave of man and who is even commended for loyalty to his master and willingness to follow him like his—

"Like his shadow," his fading companion completes the sentence and goes on to compare himself with a dog lying at his master's feet and then with the "philosophical 'dog'" Diogenes, the Cynic, or canine, who asked Alexander the Great to step out of his light. The Cynics can be taken to be doglike not only in their espousal of a "back to nature" lifestyle and their contempt for culture but also in their retention and exaggeration of the "I," that individuality that they seek to preserve by doing without, living in tubs, and expressing their disdain for a society that has taught them to be the dogs that they are.[5]

From the beginning of *Zarathustra*, the shepherd, always associated with his dog, has been an object of suspicion. After Zarathustra has carried away and buried the tightrope walker—who is mockingly called a "dead dog" by one of the townsfolk—he codifies his new insight: "[L]et Zarathustra speak not to the people but to companions [*Gefährten*]. Zarathustra shall not become the shepherd and dog of a herd [*einer Heerde Hirt und Hund*]" (Z:P 9). In the notes for *Zarathustra*, Nietzsche writes, "If you want to take life easy, always stay with the herd. Forget yourself in the herd! Love the shepherd and respect his dog's bite!" (KSA 10:4[38]). Yet if the trained dog is not the ideal companion, the way of liberation does not involve setting the wild dogs loose from their imprisonment in their cellars. This is what Zarathustra teaches the pale youth in "On the Tree on the Mountainside," whose imagination of freeing his imprisoned instincts still reflects a prison mentality. From the post-human perspective of the *Übermensch*, the human ego will appear as a result of training and breeding not dissimilar to that of the training and breeding of dogs. We may imagine that our discipline is directed toward others, but it is directed just as much toward ourselves. Michel Foucault helps to show this, following Nietzsche, in *Discipline and Punish*; in *The History of Sexuality*, he argues that what we conventionally take to be liberatory, the discourse of sexuality in modern therapeutic theory and practice, is in fact a disciplining of individuals and part of a biopower directed toward certain populations.[6]

There is nothing wrong with the herd as such. It is simply the condition of the animal. The problem arises when the individual claims to be an independent "I" or ego but continues to think, feel, and live, unbeknownst to herself, as a member of the herd. So it becomes possible to speak of "the herd of independent minds." In their domesticated state, dogs frequently live as solitary pets. Their owners find them charmingly individual and human, thus confirming their sense of their own individuality. But what if that vaunted individuality were something into which they had been domesticated and trained, as obedience school teaches them to be good dog owners? In a liberal, democratic, consumer society one expresses one's individuality in one's style of consumption, one's vote at the polls, one's choice of entertainment—the content may vary from person to person, but not the general matrix within which choices, conscious or unconscious, are made. Another note of Nietzsche's puts the point succinctly: "Once the ego [*das Ich*] was hidden in the herd: and now the herd is still hidden in the ego" (*KSA* 10:5[1] 273). Dogs over the years have been bred to be amenable to certain forms of training; this is the herd that lies hidden in the family pet. Humans over the years have also been bred to be amenable to certain kinds of training, and this is the herd that lies hidden in what we call education and freedom. So when Nietzsche notoriously speaks of the desirability of "breeding" human beings of a certain sort, he does so at a certain point in a long history in which breeding has proceeded in a happenstance and unreflective fashion.

"Dogs believe in thieves and ghosts." Both are intruders who do not belong, even if one is "real" and the other not. It is a philosophical joke of Plato's, in the *Republic* (376a), that the dog is the most philosophical animal because it distinguishes friend and foe on the basis of knowledge. These are the friends and enemies of the house, the *domus*, and this knowledge of the watchdog is a domesticated knowledge. In the episode of "The Leech" in Z, we hear that it is a matter of accident whether a particular man and a particular dog become friends or enemies. Nietzsche never tires of pointing out how we (and all animals) require simplified schemas of recognition in order to get on with the business of life. These schemas are both necessary and problematic; they provide quick and easy means of sorting things out, while they channel attention in predetermined ways and so hinder fresher, more spontaneous responses. The ghost is the intruder par excellence, the reification and fetishization of whatever is other and incomprehensible.

Having focused on the howling dog and the childhood memory it evokes, Zarathustra realizes that the dwarf, the spider, and the gateway have all disappeared—but not the dog, whose howling indicates the plight of the shepherd choking on a snake: "*But there lay a man*. And there—the dog, jumping, bristling, whining—now he saw me coming; then he howled again, he *cried*. Had I ever heard a dog cry like this for help? And verily, what I saw—I had never seen the like." The watchdog, probably the shepherd's dog, his loyal and faithful ego, knows that something is terribly wrong. He seems to recognize Zarathustra as a possible friend or helper. Many commentators on this passage assert without argument that the shepherd *is* Zarathustra's double, who dramatizes the difficulty of acknowledging and confronting the thought of recurrence. If this is so, then we could think of the dog as his own ego, appalled and confused by those thoughts that had led to his falling silent in the colloquy with the dwarf. Why should the thought of recurrence make the ego cry desperately for help? In a note from August 1881, just a few days after the first jottings in Nietzsche's notebooks on the thought of recurrence, he writes of a series of errors, schemas of recognition and conceptualization, including that of individuality:

> The species is the cruder error, the individual the more refined error, it comes *later*. The individual struggles for its existence, for its new taste, for its relatively *unique* position among all things—it considers these as better than the universal taste and despises the latter. It wants to *rule*. But then it discovers that it itself is something changing and has a taste that changes, with its subtlety it sees into the secret that there is no individual, that in the smallest twinkling of the eye [*im kleinsten Augenblick*] it is something other than it is in the next and that its conditions of existence are those of no end of individuals: *der* **unendlich kleine Augenblick** is the higher reality and truth, a lightning image [*Blitzbild*] out of the eternal flow [*Fluss*]. So the individual learns: how all *satisfying* knowledge rests on the crude error of the species, the subtler error of the individual and the subtlest error of the creative *Augenblick*. (KSA 9:11[156])

We are constrained to think in terms of species: humans, dogs, elephants, leeches, and so on. But as both Darwinian biology and the Nietzschean

ontology of differential will to power imply, the species is simply a convenient fiction. In the light of such a realization, we may come to give pride of
ontological and ethical place to the individual, the "I." But to think recurrence, as the shepherd and Zarathustra struggle to do, takes us beyond the
individual, beyond the dog we call "ego." To affirm recurrence is to give equal
weight to all my experiences, both before and after thinking the thought. It
leads to no coherent narrative of my own life but suggests that I am immersed
in the stream of becoming. If "the innocence of becoming" frees me from
guilt, it also radically transforms the very terms of "I" and "me" with which
I began to pose such questions—the thoughts and hinter-thoughts that were
interrupted by the howling dog. In the conversation with the dwarf, it was
suggested that the passing moment or twinkling of the eye (*Augenblick*) is
that which eternally recurs. Perhaps that too was a necessary oversimplification; the closest approximation to the real that escapes conceptualization.
Once the shepherd bites off and spews out the head of the snake we hear no
more of the noisy dog. If this biting and spewing involves acknowledging
the anti-individualistic thrust of the teaching of recurrence, the role of the
domesticated ego necessarily falls away. And the shepherd, in his superhuman laughter, becomes something other than a shepherd. He will no longer
be either domesticated or domesticator, for reflection on the canine condition reveals that these are two sides of the same coin.

Notes

1. I have made this point in *Alcyone: Nietzsche on Gifts, Noise, and Women* (Albany:
State University of New York Press, 1991), 94–96.

2. Compare "the dog howls, the wind: is not the wind a dog? It whines, it yelps, it
howls" (Z:4 "The Drunken Song" 8).

3. For some perceptive thoughts on *Gay Science* 312, see Kathleen Marie Higgins,
Comic Relief: Nietzsche's Gay Science (New York: Oxford University Press, 2000), 167–
172. Consider two additional passages from the earliest and latest of Nietzsche's books
dealing with canines as dogged followers. (1) In his reflections on Albrecht Dürer's
Knight, Death, and the Devil he notes that the knight, who he identifies with Schopenhauer, is "alone with his horse and his dog" (*Birth of Tragedy* 20). As is quite clear in the
woodcut, the knight rides the horse and is accompanied by his dog, which has an air of
attention and devotion. Might this faithful companion be Schopenhauer's ego? (2) In
Ecce Homo ("Why I Am So Clever" 1), Nietzsche describes his nutrition, an issue that
he says is more important than all of theology for the salvation of humanity; indeed, he
refers to his eating and drinking practices as "my morality." There he writes of his rejection of alcohol but notes "I prefer towns in which opportunities abound for dipping from

running wells (Nizza, Turin, Sils); a small glass accompanies me like a dog" (*ein kleines Glas läuft mir nach wie ein Hund*—literally "a small glass runs after me like a dog"). Nietzsche embraces his animal self, scouting out his territory in terms of fresh running water; he enjoys the habit of the glass but keeps it in the subordinate position of the helpful and amusing animal companion.

4. See Martha Kendal Woodruff's chapter in this volume.

5. The "Epilogue" should also be read in relation to the last aphorism of the book, which immediately precedes it (*WS* 350), in which Nietzsche writes of the need to free human beings from the chains of morality, religion, and metaphysics: "Only when this *sickness from one's chains* has also been overcome will the first great goal have been attained: the peeling off [*Abtrennung*] of man from the animals." This suggests not that humans will be freed from all aspects of their animal nature but that once they are no longer chained, they will no longer have the melancholy and resentment of chained animals; they will be able to pursue distinctive possibilities of the species that are not open to the other animals.

6. Michel Foucault, *Discipline and Punish*, trans. Alan Sheridan (New York: Vintage Books, 1979), especially Part 3, "Discipline"; Foucault, *The History of Sexuality*, trans. Robert Hurley (New York: Vintage Books, 1980), especially Part 5, "Right of Death and Power Over Life." In the early 1970s, when Foucault was intensely involved both with the study of prisons and with the politics of the prison system, he wrote an essay on a series of paintings of dogs by the contemporary French artist Paul Rebeyrolle. Foucault reads the series "*Chiens*," each of which shows a dog in a different state of being caged, suffering, and attempting escape, as an allegory of the contemporary prison system. See Foucault, "*La force de fuir*," in *Dits et écrits* (Paris: Gallimard, 1994), II:401–405. I discuss the essay and translate some excerpts in *Archaeologies of Vision: Foucault and Nietzsche on Seeing and Saying* (Chicago: University of Chicago Press, 2003), section 67, "The Prison of the Gallery and the Force of Flight." For a further exploration of the question of biopower that is indebted to Foucault, see Giorgio Agamben, *Homo Sacer: Sovereign Power and Bare Life*, trans. Daniel Heller-Roazen (Stanford, Calif.: Stanford University Press, 1998). Agamben argues, in effect, that contemporary society is rapidly adopting the principle that all life, human and animal, is a subject of political power. His perspective might be enlarged if he were to consider the intertwined history of the human domestication of animals and the normalization of human behavior.

Arachnophobe or Arachnophile?
Nietzsche and His Spiders

Alan D. Schrift

When he happen'd to be tired by having applyed himself too much to his Philosophical Meditations, he went down Stairs to refresh himself, and discoursed with the people of the House about any thing, that might afford Matter for an ordinary Conversation, and even about trifles. He also took Pleasure in smoaking a Pipe of Tobacco; or, when he had a mind to divert himself somewhat longer, he look'd for some Spiders, and made 'em fight together, or he threw some Flies into the Cobweb, and was so well pleased with that Battel, that he wou'd sometimes break into Laughter.

Colerus, *The Life of Benedict de Spinosa* (1706)[1]

References to the spider, *die Spinne*, and its spinning of webs are common throughout Nietzsche's works. Kant is a fatal spider (*A* 11) and Spinoza is a cunning one (*TI* "Skirmishes" 23).[2] God himself spun out the world as a spider spins its web. An apparently insignificant spider in the moonlight makes an appearance in the first formulation of the eternal recurrence in *The Gay Science* 341, and a spider reappears when eternal recurrence makes its initial appearance in *Thus Spoke Zarathustra*'s "On the Vision and the Riddle." In what follows, I want to briefly review Nietzsche's references to spiders in his published works and some of the more significant mentions in the unpublished works, and I will conclude by offering some observations on whether Nietzsche is an arachnophobe or, like his "precursor" Spinoza, an arachnophile.[3]

The first reference chronologically to a spider in the *Kritische Studienausgabe* is found in *Philosophy in the Tragic Age of the Greeks* 10, where Parmenides's hostility to the natural world leads him to turn away from natural philosophy, producing instead "bloodless truths" that sit like empty husks in a maze of spider's webs (*Spinnefäden*). While Parmenidean philosophy and the spider both produce victims, according to Nietzsche, the spider "undoubtedly wants the blood of his victims" and thereby stands as a natural counterpoint to the Parmenidean philosopher, who can only produce denatured abstract generalities that pass as "truths."

The spider figures twice in "On Truth and Lies in an Extramoral Sense." First is the spider's web as the culminating structure in Nietzsche's series of architectural metaphors for the construction of science: Nietzsche's story begins with the beehive of bustling, instinctual labor, then moves through ideas fortified like the towers of a medieval fortress to concepts mummified in the hierarchical pyramid and then to the charred remains of those concepts in a Roman columbarium before ending up with a spider's web, at once fragile yet resilient. What appeals here to Nietzsche about the image of the spider's web is, in fact, three things: first, that the web of a spider is delicate; second, that for all its delicate fragility, it is remarkably strong; and third, and most important, that the spider constructs its web not with material that it finds outside itself but rather that the spider manufactures its web from itself.[4] Where the bee or the ant are *bricoleurs,* working with what they find, the spider is a creative artist who serves as an image for man as the "genius of construction [*Baugenie*]" insofar as "man builds with the far more delicate conceptual material which he first has to manufacture from himself" (*TL*, p. 85). This is related directly to the second reference to the spider in "On Truth and Lies," which expands upon this genius of conceptual construction: the builders of these webs, "the practitioners of science," spin out their representations with the same necessity with which a spider spins its web, by which Nietzsche means that "all that we actually know about these laws of nature is what we ourselves bring to them—time and space, and therefore relationships of succession and number" (*TL*, p. 87).[5] Here we see Nietzsche at his most Kantian, and, although he does not yet link the spider to Kant (he will later, as we shall see), he does present the spider here in the context

of a fairly straightforward Kantian phenomenalism: scientists will have organized their experiences in terms of the Kantian forms of intuition and categories of the understanding as naturally and necessarily as will a spider spin
its web.

While Socrates spins a net impenetrably tight around existence in *Birth
of Tragedy* 15, the spider itself does not appear in the published works until
the second of the *Untimely Meditations* (*HL* 9, pp. 108–109). And here it is
not just any spider but a *grosse Kreuzspinne*, which Hollingdale translates literally as a "great cross-spider" and which Gray translates simply as a "great
spider."[6] A "Kreuz," of course, is a cross or crucifix, and so, on the one hand,
there is an allusion to Christianity that Nietzsche will make much more of
in his three later references to the *Kreuzspinne*.[7] But a *Kreuzspinne* is also,
quite simply, a "garden spider" and so may involve no reference to the
Church at all. We shall have to leave this question of the cross unresolved in
this passage, however, for although one could argue that Nietzsche *always*
alludes to Christianity, whether consciously or not, when he invokes the
Kreuz, he does not explicitly invoke Christianity in this case. Instead, it is
simply "the modern human being" who is the "great cross-spider at the center of the cosmic web [*die grosse Kreuzspinne im Knoten des Weltall-Netzes*]"[8]
and whose tireless unraveling and historicizing of all foundations has given
rise, on the one hand, to a certain sort of gloominess (a gloominess that will
later be called "nihilism") and, on the other hand, to what Nietzsche regards
as a humorous, albeit unconscious, parody of world history, namely, Eduard
von Hartmann's *Philosophy of the Unconscious* (1869).

The spider's next appearance is *Human, All Too Human* 427, where the
free spirit is warned against marriage because habits are like a net of spider's
webs (*Spinneweben*), and we must be vigilant against sitting in the middle of
our habits like "the spider who has caught himself and has to live on his own
blood." In the second volume of *Human, All Too Human, Assorted Opinions
and Maxims*, the spider makes several appearances. In *AOM* 32, we find the
first link between God and the spider as Nietzsche echoes Plato's critique of
the poets for weaving a web of beautiful deceptions around the world and
having those deceptions taken by the masses to be the "real reality." When
this poet comes to believe, like his audience, that he really *knows* what he
describes, Nietzsche concludes that he has deluded himself into thinking he
knows as much as "the great world-spider itself." In *AOM* 153, Nietzsche
tells us that one must spend time with a good book, "many hours must pass
over it, many a spider have spun its web on it." In *AOM* 171, we're told that
webs of forgetfulness are spun around works of art—and in particular musical
works—that are tied to a historical moment that has passed, while in *AOM*

172 we find that modern poets—incapable of the great creative ventures of the master poets of earlier times—are haunted by spiders and other unpleasant creatures. The spider's final appearance, in AOM 194, is representative of many of the spider references from this period in invoking self-generation, artifice, and predation and is short enough to cite in full. It is titled "Three thinkers equal a spider." The passage reads: "In every philosophical sect three thinkers follow one after the other in the following way: one produces out of himself the seed and sap, the second draws it out into threads and spins an artificial web, the third lurks in this web for victims who get caught in it—and tries to live off philosophy."

The spider—once again a great spider (*grosse Spinne*)—makes its next appearance in *Daybreak* 71 as the image of the Roman conqueror whose eternal constructions were established to "consume all blood wherever it might well forth." This is followed in D 117 by one of Nietzsche's significant statements of perspectivism: we are prisoners of our senses and all our knowledge is incapable of bringing us to the "real world"; rather, our knowledge only reflects back to us the limits of our sensory organs, and, as a result, "we sit within our net, we spiders, and whatever we may catch in it, we can catch nothing at all except that which allows itself to be caught precisely in *our* net."[9] In D 130, the belief in an ordered world of purposes and willed actions is described as a spider's web that is broken by the interventions of chance and accident, and later in this section we find a veiled allusion to God as a spider insofar as the belief in a loving God who in fact orchestrates precisely those chance interventions is described in terms of the spinning out of purposes and nets too refined for humans to understand.

In *The Gay Science*, the spider makes his first appearance in the famous section 341 as an image of insignificance to emphasize that the demon's challenge really does mean that *every* thing—even this insignificant spider—will recur. Whether this is the only reason for the spider is perhaps worth questioning and, as an aside, I'll offer what I hope is not a completely idle speculation; namely, that insofar as GS 341 follows the section titled "The dying Socrates," it seems plausible that the demon who steals after "you" in 341 is intended to recall Socrates' *daimon*. And if so, perhaps we are also supposed to think, subliminally, that this insignificant spider who would also recur is none other than Socrates himself, the first of the life-sucking spiders that populate the philosophical pantheon. I don't think this speculation can be proved conclusively by the text, but given all that is going on in the closing sections of the fourth book of *The Gay Science*, it might be worth some further speculation. In any case, the spider's final appearance, in the fifth book of *The Gay Science* (358), finds the God, or perhaps a generalized pope, of the Catholic Church alluded to as the "old spider" whose centuries of work were unraveled by that precocious peasant Martin Luther.

We next come to *Thus Spoke Zarathustra*, where the spider is a frequent character. His first appearance, a tarantula's appearance really, is in the chapter of that name, where the tarantulas, those preachers of equality who are in fact teachers of revenge, are described as poisonous spiders (*Gift-Spinnen*) whose teachings, ultimately the teachings of the priests—Zarathustra's old enemies—are the very opposite of what Zarathustra teaches. In Z:2 "On Scholars," Nietzsche has his revenge on the philological moles who ridiculed his earlier work, describing them as spiders who lie in wait carefully preparing their poisons for those whose work is alive. In book three, spiders appear in six of the sixteen sections. First is in Z:3 "On the Vision and the Riddle," recalling the image of insignificance first presented in GS 341, as we are here told by Zarathustra that recurrence will include this slow spider and this moonlight. In Z:3 "Before Sunrise," we find praise of chance as the alternative to a no longer believable "eternal spider and spider's web of Reason [*ewige Vernunft-Spinne und -Spinnennetze*]." In Z:3 "On Virtue that Makes Small" 3, the nothingness of those whose virtues lead them away from life is itself "a spider's web and a spider which lives on the blood of the future." In Z:3 "Of Apostates" 2, the *Kreuzspinne*—the cross-spider—that we first saw in the second *Untimely Meditation* appears again, this time explicitly as an image of the priest, whose piety and deadly cleverness attract the other apostate spiders who are losing their loss of faith, luring them with the teaching that "under crosses one can spin well." This cross-spider appears twice more in book three of *Thus Spoke Zarathustra*. At the end of Z:3 "On the Three Evils," those who cannot appreciate the value of selfishness because they have no self—the world-weary and the priests—are called "world-weary cowards and cross-spiders." In Z:3 "On the Great Longing," Zarathustra sings to his soul of having brushed the dust, twilight, and spiders off of it. Here it is just plain spiders, not cross-spiders this time, though the cross might be implied given the other passages in book three. But the cross-spider makes one last appearance in the second of "The Seven Seals," where Zarathustra's wrath comes like a broom to cross-spiders (Z:3).

The spider's appearances in book four of *Thus Spoke Zarathustra* are much less numerous and significant than what we find in book three. In Z:4 "At Noon," we find Zarathustra's soul so content (or is it just fatigue?) that it leans against the earth like a ship nestled in a still cove that is moored there with nothing stronger than the threads spun by a spider. And the spider's final appearance in *Thus Spoke Zarathustra* comes in section 4 of Z:4 "The Drunken Song," a passage that recalls "On the Vision and the Riddle" in linking the howling of a dog with the shining of the moon, only this time the spider is not quite so devoid of thematic association, for here again it is the desire for blood that Zarathustra suggests animates the spider's spinning of its web.

After *Thus Spoke Zarathustra*, the spider reappears early in *Beyond Good and Evil*, this time in the guise of the philosopher and friend of knowledge who is described as, among other things, a "web-spinner of the spirit [*Spinneweber des Geistes*]" (BGE 25). What is noteworthy about this passage, though, is that it is the first time Nietzsche links the spider with Spinoza. This verbal linkage—Spinoza *als Spinne*—will reappear again, but in this first connection, it is made in the context of philosophers as lovers of truths whose truths are of no interest to the masses. The people's utter indifference to the wisdom of the philosophers turns these poor, ignored souls into "vengeance-seekers and poison-brewers."[10] The spider appears again much later, in BGE 209, once more as an image of blood-sucking, this time in the context of a parable of the fears of the father of Frederick the Great, who is concerned that young Frederick might fall victim to the blood-sucking "spider of skepticism" that his father Friedrich Wilhelm I associated with those clever Frenchmen—Montaigne, La Rochefoucauld, Voltaire—that Nietzsche so preferred to the British or the Germans.

In *On the Genealogy of Morals* III:9, in the context of a comment on the general hubris of contemporary philosophers and scientists, Nietzsche refers to the current "attitude toward God as some alleged spider of purpose and morality behind the great captious web of causality." Webs of the most malicious conspiracies, whose authors are unidentified (are they spiders or silkworms?), are woven by the sick and weak in GM III:14, while philosophers are ridiculed as "web-spinners and idlers" in GM III:17 insofar as they believe that feelings of displeasure will vanish as soon as the error in them is recognized.

In *Twilight of the Idols* ("'Reason' in Philosophy" 4), the philosophical mistake of valuing that which comes last as most valuable is disparaged as "the brainsick fantasies of sick web-spinners [*die Gehirnleiden kranker Spinneweber*]." In *TI* "Skirmishes" 23, in a passage uncharacteristic for its praise of Plato as a great erotic, Spinoza is again linked to the spider when he is put forward as the ultimate contrast to the Greek tradition of philosophizing in public: "Nothing is less Greek than the conceptual web-spinning [*Begriffs-Spinneweberei*] of a hermit, *amor intellectualis dei* in the manner of Spinoza."

In *The Antichrist(ian)*, the spider makes four significant appearances, and

I think it would be fair to hold these appearances as in many respects representative of many of the passages we have already surveyed in the later works. The first three come in the context of Nietzsche's condemning philosophy, especially German philosophy, for having been corrupted by theology (see A 10). The first, A 11, labels Kant a "fatal spider [*Verhängniss von Spinne*]" insofar as he provided a philosophical justification for the theological tendency to mistake its own notion of duty for the concept of duty in general. The other two, A 17 and 18, address the Christian concept of God as an impoverished god, which reflects the decadence of the people who created it. Having been transformed from the all-powerful god of a chosen people to the good god of the weak and the sick, this Christian God is so impotent that he has been mastered by the "the palest of the pale, [. . .] *messieurs* the metaphysicians, the conceptual albinos [who] have spun their web around him so long that, hypnotized by their movements, he himself became a spider, a metaphysician."[11] This metaphysician-god is then linked to the two modern philosophers who we have already seen conjoined with the spider, Spinoza and Kant, as Nietzsche concludes in A 17: "Thenceforward he span the world again out of himself—*sub specie Spinozae*—thenceforward he transformed himself into something ever paler and less substantial, became an 'ideal,' became 'pure spirit,' became '*absolutum*,' became 'thing in itself.' . . . *Decay of a God*: God became 'thing in itself.'" And this comment is immediately picked up in the following section, in which Nietzsche elaborates on the degeneration of God to a contradiction of life: "The Christian conception of God—God as God of the sick, God as spider, God as spirit—is one of the most corrupt conceptions of God arrived at on earth" (A 18). The *Nachlass* also has a passage that reflects this conjunction of God, metaphysics, and spiders, KSA 13:16[58]: "For the spider, the spider is the consummate being; for the metaphysician, God is a metaphysician, which is to say, he spins. . . ." In the final spider passage in A, it is not God but the priest who earns this label, as Nietzsche confesses to having recognized the priest for what he is: "the most dangerous kind of parasite, the actual poison-spider of life [*Giftspinne des Lebens*]" (A 38).

These are all the references to spiders in Nietzsche's published works and the more significant references in the *Nachlass*.[12] Before I conclude this survey, though, I suppose a final comment is in order concerning a reference to a particular species of spider—the tarantula. In addition to the section "On the Tarantulas" in *Thus Spoke Zarathustra*, about which I've already spoken, there is only one other reference to tarantulas in Nietzsche's works, but it is an interesting reference. The tarantula is, for Nietzsche, a particularly nasty spider known more for its bite than its web-spinning, and this one reference is to Rousseau, who in section three of the preface to *Daybreak* is referred to as a *moral* tarantula whose bite we are told infected poor old Kant with a moral fanaticism that was, among other things, what led Kant to his sympathies for the French Revolution.

I will close with two brief observations. First, there appears to be a progression in Nietzsche's references to spiders from the positive to the negative.[13] Where the spider begins, in "On Truth and Lies" and *Philosophy in the Tragic Age of the Greeks*, as a positive image of self-generating creation and predation, it ends as a much more negative image of cunning and capture. This progression, I would suggest, roughly parallels the progression of Nietzsche's thinking about one of the two philosophers he associates most closely with the spider, namely, Kant. When Nietzsche thinks about Kantian phenomenalism and the epistemological perspectives articulated in Kant's *Critique of Pure Reason*, he cannot help but notice the strong affinities between the Kantian position and his own. This Kantian spider spins out the webs of its knowledge necessarily and naturally, and Nietzsche cannot but affirm its activities. But as Nietzsche's attention turns to the universalization of duty in the *Critique of Practice Reason* and the disinterested observation of the *Critique of Judgment*, his sympathy disappears as he sees in Kant's ethics, religion, and aesthetics the deceptive web-spinning of a deadly spider that is resurrecting the metaphysical and supernatural illusions of the Platonic and Christian traditions.[14] And, as a consequence, this Kantian spider emerges as one of the prime examples of life-negation whose actions must be refused and revalued.

Finally, returning to my title, we must ask: Is Nietzsche an arachnophile or an arachnophobe? I think we have to answer: both. On the one hand, Nietzsche surely loves his spiders as a metaphor—they are one of the most commonly appearing members of his menagerie, appearing in no less than ten of his seventeen published works. They are master-builders who, moreover, can create out of themselves with a kind of necessity that Nietzsche can only admire. And they are invoked in the two main passages in the published works, GS 341 ("The Greatest Weight") and Z:3 "On the Vision and the Riddle," in which Nietzsche presents eternal recurrence. But, that said, Nietzsche seems more than a little afraid of them: they are blood-suckers, parasites. While Nietzsche admires the beasts of prey in *On the Genealogy of Morals*, he does not express much admiration for the predatory characteristics of the spider. Lacking the natural grace of the beasts of prey, the spider may be even more dangerous because as it seems so relatively benign and unthreatening. For this reason, Nietzsche is more attentive to the spider as a cunning trapper than a true predator. Perhaps he fears getting caught more than getting killed: caught in webs of philosophical concepts with which he has no sympathies, caught in the webs of the priests that will diminish if not negate his active strength, caught in the web of the great spider God whose values stand as that which must be overcome. It would seem, then, that the spider is more a slave than a master, and, while Nietzsche may not technically be an arachnophobe—spiders, at least as far as we can tell, did not lead to any "clinically significant impairment" of his behavior—he may share more with Little Miss Muffet than with Spinoza, who found the feeding of flies to spiders a source of entertainment if not hilarity.

Notes

1. I thank Michael Rosenthal for bringing this biography of Spinoza to my attention.

2. In general, I use the Hollingdale translations of A, AOM, D, HL, and TI; the Kaufmann translations of BGE, BT, GM, GS, and Z; and the Kaufmann-Hollingdale translation of WP.

3. Nietzsche refers to Spinoza as a "precursor," a *Vorgänger*, in a postcard from Sils Maria to Franz Overbeck, July 30, 1881.

4. Sarah Kofman makes a similar observation concerning the spider's web in *Nietzsche and Metaphor*, trans. Duncan Large (London: Athlone Press, 1993), 69.

5. Conceptual web-spinning actually makes its first appearance in the fourth of the "Prefaces to Unwritten Books," titled "On the Relationship of Schopenhauerian Philosophy to a German Culture"; see KSA 1, p. 780.

6. Friedrich Nietzsche, *Unfashionable Observations*, trans. Richard T. Gray, vol. 2 of *The Complete Works of Friedrich Nietzsche* (Stanford, Calif.: Stanford University Press, 1995).

7. It is worth noting here that nature and the German language have been kind to Nietzsche insofar as the common German "garden spider" has, in fact, a white marking on its back in the shape of a cross, a marking that gave rise to the name *Kreuzspinne*.

8. One might wonder here again whether or not there is an allusion to Christianity insofar as Nietzsche might conjoin the *Kreuzspinne* with "the modern human being" in order to indicate that modern humanity is itself marked by the cross, that Christianity is itself the cross that modern humanity must bear. Were this conjunction made in the latter works (BGE, GM, GS Book V), I would feel confident in arguing that the allusion to Christianity was intended, but at this point in his career (1874), I think the question must remain open. I thank Brian Domino for helping me to clarify this point.

9. This image is repeated in KSA 9:6[439]: "Wir thun *nicht* mehr mit der *Erkenntniß* als die Spinne mit Netz und Jagd und Aussaugen: wir stellen unsere Bedürfnisse und deren Befriedigung fest, dazu gehören Sonne Sterne und Atome, es sind umwege zu uns, ebenso

die Ablehnung eines Gottes. Auf die Dauer leiden wir *Schaden* an jeder fehlerhaften Relation (Annahme einer Relation) Deshalb hat an sich unsere Erkenntniß keinen Werth: es sind lauter optische Gesetze (gleichnißweise) Der Mensch selber, in seinem Raum von 5 Fuß Länge, ist eine willkürliche Annahme, auf Schwäche der Sinnesorgane hin *construirt*." See also *KSA* 9:9[15] and 15[9].

10. Might this be a case of the pot calling the kettle black? More than a few commentators have suggested that the increasing hysteria and vitriol in Nietzsche's works of his last years should be read in the context of his increasing frustration at not having found his audience.

11. *KSA* 11:38[7] also links German metaphysics (in this relatively long passage, Kant, Hegel, Schelling, Fichte, and Schopenhauer are named) with the spinning of conceptual webs: "Man meinte, der Weg zur Erkenntniß sei nunmehr *abgekürzt*, man könne unmittelbar den 'Dingen' zu Leibe gehen, man hoffte 'Arbeit zu sparen': und alles Glück, welches edle Müßiggänger, Tugendhafte, Träumerische, Mystiker, Künstler, Dreiviertels-Christen, politische Dunkelmänner und metaphysische Begriffs-Spinnen zu empfinden fähig sind, wurde den Deutschen zur Ehre angerechnet." See also *KSA* 12:2[6]. And in *KSA* 13:11[55]/*WP* 252, Christianity is criticized for, among other things, its absurd conceptual web-spinning.

12. There are other spinners—both animal spinners such as the silkworm and human spinners such as scholars (*GS* 366) or thinkers in general—but I have chosen to restrict my comments here more exclusively to spiders.

13. I thank Drew Hyland for first drawing this progression to my attention.

14. The locus classicus for this articulation is the chapter "How the True World at Last Became a Fable" in *Twilight of the Idols*.

SNAKE

The Eternal-Serpentine

Nickolas Pappas

"On the Adder's Bite"

The story begins with Zarathustra asleep under a fig tree (Z:1 "On the Adder's Bite"). An adder (*Natter*) slithers toward him, presumably out of that tree, and bites Zarathustra on the neck. The snake laments having inflicted this mortal wound on Zarathustra, but he boasts of carrying a greater poison than any snake's, and the adder gratefully licks the innocuous wound.

When Zarathustra tells his disciples this story they ask him for its moral; he says he is an annihilator of morals and that goes for morals of stories too. So he gives what you might call the unmoral of the story, roughly speaking an anti-sermon of amoral advice about responding to an enemy's injuries. The anti-sermon negates Christian injunctions: Don't bless those who curse you; don't repay evil with good.

Genesis 3 comes to mind as a source for this story's images, thanks to the snake and to the fig tree that appears the moment Adam loses his innocence (Genesis 3:7). But the tree also recalls John 1:48, in which Nathanael is said to have been sitting under a fig tree when Jesus sees him—supernaturally, from a distance—and chooses him as a disciple.

So although as the occasion for Zarathustra's commentary the adder only needs to be an enemy or a danger, it arrives in the book imbedded in images that make it function more specifically as a temptation to moralistic thinking. The Genesis serpent brings Adam and the woman to interpret themselves morally; Nathanael is drawn into discipleship. Whatever power lets Zarathustra escape the viper's poison also lets him escape a moralistic interpretation of the viper's bite—as evil for instance, as a thing that calls for redemption or forgiveness.

The third biblical story behind Zarathustra's and the most elaborately alluded to comes from Acts 28. There again the snake is an adder or viper [*ochidna*]. Paul is shipwrecked on Malta and has just sat down by a fire when the adder crawls out of one of the logs and bites his hand. His Maltese hosts read the snake's attack as a sign of divine justice. Paul must be a murderer. But Paul shakes the viper off his hand; it hasn't hurt him, and now the Maltese conclude that he must be a god.

Paul himself is not said to comment on the meaning of the viper. Acts leaves both moralizing interpretations to the Maltese: Paul is either atrociously guilty or a god. Barbarians though they are said to be, Paul's hosts uphold the terms of moral interpretation of Genesis, whose serpent promised divinity but delivered only great guilt.

Paul *has* become godlike though and impervious to snakes' effects thanks to the grace of Christ. The moralistic interpretation of his immunity to snakebite is right as far as it can go in its ignorance of Christian grace; only Paul's immunity does not follow from good deeds he's done or from divine birth but from his liberation from morality as morality has thus far been known.

Nietzsche amplifies one side of the story about Paul. Things have indeed changed, and snakes no longer represent either crime or the punishment for it, and the one who is not felled by their bites does stand above the concerns of petty justice: all this as in Acts. But whereas the witnesses in Acts decide that Paul is no murderer, Zarathustra forestalls the Christian interpretation by accepting the title of annihilator. Paul's miraculous preservation shows that he is not a murderer; Zarathustra's shows that he is one.

The fig tree's biblical associations moreover turn the snake into a representative of all morality and demonstrate Zarathustra's independence, greater than Paul's, from morality's bite.

These passages from *Zarathustra* suggest two lessons for the reader of Nietzsche who wants to discover what snakes can mean in his writings.

First, if a string of associations leads this adder to represent enmity in general but also moral interpretations of enmity (and then even the interpretation of Christianity as a moral enemy), Nietzsche's readers should take care not to decide in advance what any one reference to snakes has to mean. This story's adder does not slither straight to an index card to be filed under "enemy" or "knowledge" or "temptation." If anything, the desire to categorize it as uniquely symbolic betrays a habit of interpretive simplification, which is to say moralization.

Even the snake's venom should not be read as possessing an obvious significance. Kathleen Marie Higgins has pointed out how insistently *On the Genealogy of Morals* uses poison as a metaphor for morality's effects.[1] But she also points out Nietzsche's role in history as one who bites more of the same poison into his readers—like Zarathustra, he boasts of his own venom—to heighten its effect.[2]

Second, the adder's meanings emerge against the backdrop of the biblical narratives that Nietzsche inverts or parodies or otherwise tries to supersede. Nietzsche's symbol-construction cannot be understood without reference to the symbolic uses of snakes already in play.

Varieties of Snakes

The snake in Nietzsche's writings manages to represent numerous and disparate qualities. Partly taking over the animal's established meanings or stereotypes and partly inverting them, Nietzsche savors the polyvalent result in which knowledge and danger and concealment coexist with health and life and eternity.

Often enough when *die Schlange* (alone or in compounds) comes into Nietzsche's writing as no more than a tag, a quip, a turn of phrase, Nietzsche is talking about something else; at times, however, it is the snake in particular that he wants to talk about, usually in a transformed way; in *Thus Spoke Zarathustra*, snakes are even characters in the narrative. Among all these appearances of the word are some that let its significance be read right off the page. Thus, when the "Prelude of Rhymes" to *Gay Science* has a proverb describe itself as "dove and snake and pig all at once" (GS "Joke, Cunning, Revenge" 11), it is easy to chalk up that serpentine appearance as an invocation of the animal's proverbial cunning and dangerousness, just as the dove bespeaks a proverb's apparent peaceability.

The snake even retains its obvious and traditional sense in *Zarathustra* when it turns up in fleeting figures of speech: "Snakes' filth and bad odors" (Z:2 "On Immaculate Perception"); "lower than snake and swine" (Z:3 "On the Three Evils"). Deadly in a sneaky way, a thing that hides to plot its treachery, this version of the Nietzschean snake is the easiest to read. You might say these lines make the serpent's concealment a metaphor for the unconscious, but still that is a clearly decipherable metaphor.

Other uses of *die Schlange,* while classifiable as those just cited, reject the word's usual derogatory overtones. Nietzsche directly invokes the tempter of Genesis 3 to make something new out of it, as in GS 259 and *Ecce Homo* ("Books" BGE 2). As God's great opponent and morality's most concrete image of transgression, that snake serves Nietzsche when he wants to complicate the idea of opposition to morality, in other words, when he wants to show the opposition as something other than pure perverse evil. Transforming the wicked snake into a supramoral one thus repeats allegorically the reinterpretation of morals that Nietzsche more often carries out analytically.

In this spirit GS 259 pictures the serpent calling God's prejudices good and evil. A prejudice for Nietzsche is something like the limiting horizon of thought. Morality pictures the tempter or any other devil seeing good and evil as realities and deliberately choosing evil. But the cunning serpent as Nietzsche imagines it refuses to remain inside the prejudiced vocabulary of morality as that picture of deliberate choice would require it to. It has found a perspective from which it can examine the psychology of morals.

The blasphemy in GS 259 painstakingly rejects the old Satanic reading of the snake but keeps and adumbrates the animal's equally longstanding reputation for cleverness and knowledge. Nietzsche regularly appeals to that reputation. In many instances, he associates the snake with knowledge either directly or by way of more allusions to Genesis 3. Thus the two mentions of snakes in *Beyond Good and Evil* (BGE 152 and 202).

Such references to serpents, though reformations of their meaning, are still categorizable enough: the wise snake, the snake-philosopher, the snake beyond good and evil whose cunning exposes morality's errors. But other snakes in Nietzsche hint at more than they say clearly. Does "On the Adder's Bite" make its snake principally an emblem of danger or principally an emblem of morality?

Or take the Prelude to *The Gay Science* again. In a cryptic rhyme about shedding skin (GS "Joke, Cunning, Revenge" 8) Nietzsche describes his skin as cracking, speaks of "the snake in me [*in mir die Schlange*]"; the rhyme is about snakes eating earth and Nietzsche's own urge to keep consuming that snake food. Does Nietzsche's equation of himself with a snake mainly draw on a folk belief that snakes live off dirt, in which case he is announcing that his book's investigations will dig lower than philosophers before him dared to? Or does this snake stand for any submerged impulse in the way that the "bunch of wild snakes [*Knäuel wilder Schlangen*]," to which Zarathustra refers, represents the unworthy criminal's disarray of character (Z:1 "On the Pale Criminal")? In that case the rhyme points to a new authenticity that Nietzsche is claiming for himself—his willingness to embrace his own hidden drives—more than to the philosophical inquiry that feeds that authenticity.[3]

But a skin that cracks to release something new and larger-grown also seems to promise rebirth and rejuvenation. Snakes live on soil (or so Nietzsche pretends to believe); the earth keeps them strong and healthy; his need to keep renewing himself by digging into life's unsavory elements lies at the heart of Nietzsche's deepest inclinations. The sixty syllables that constitute the eighth verse of GS "Joke, Cunning, Revenge" twine together all three implications of the snake. Meanwhile of course this snake continues to function as a sign of knowledge, because the dirt that Nietzsche craves is the dirt on human morals. Snake as body, snake as the hidden, snake as the self-rejuvenating, the snake who knows: Nietzsche is the tempter snake in all these senses.

Nietzsche's appeals to the familiar meanings of snakes in his briefest references to them do not gainsay the spirit of GS "Joke, Cunning, Revenge" 8 and the other passages that bring new significance to the serpent. A passing illustrative figure of speech can only function by making immediate sense—it needs to clarify, not complicate. Similes presuppose some fixed meaning in the term of comparison. When Nietzsche positively addresses himself to the snake, he has a freedom to multiply and deepen its connotations that mere mentions do not allow.

And yet if Nietzsche's use of the serpent here and there does not betray his covert acceptance of its interpretation under Christian morality, still it does remind you that he is writing from within Christian language and culture. The general categories for understanding the serpent remain the categories of knowledge, concealment, fertility, and danger. Nietzsche may accept a derogatory stereotype of serpentine cunning in one place, metaphorize or parody it somewhere else, and invert the stereotype completely in a third passage, but each time he presupposes the moralizing tradition.

The Serpent in *Thus Spoke Zarathustra*

Given *Zarathustra*'s fondness for mythic language and narrative, it is not surprising that the book should contain Nietzsche's most frequent and most self-conscious mentions of the serpent. Aside from a few reversions to moralistic stereotypes about serpents (noted above: Z:2 "On Immaculate Perception" and Z:3 "On the Three Evils"), these mentions invest the animal with nearly divine properties.

The most visible snake is the one that along with an eagle lives in Zarathustra's cave with him. Even quick references to that particular snake (Z:1 "Prologue" 1; Z:2 "The Child with the Mirror"; Z:4 "The Voluntary Beggar"; Z:4 "The Song of Melancholy" 1; Z:4 "The Drunken Song" 2) establish Zarathustra's place outside the Christian-moralistic interpretation of nature and specifically antagonistic toward that interpretation. Imagine how the serpent himself might have written Genesis 3, Nietzsche is saying. Zarathustra calls his snake "the wisest animal" (Z:1 "Prologue" 10; Z:4 "The Magician" 2; Z:4 "The Ugliest Man"; see also Z:4 "On Science"), and the snake and eagle reteach him his own doctrine of the eternal return in "The Convalescent" (Z:3).

The serpent and eagle also hark back to *The Birth of Tragedy*, in which Nietzsche contrasts the masculine Aryan myth of sacrilege with the feminine original sin of Semitic myth (*BT* 9). A serpent instigated the Semitic sacrilege and came to enact part of the punishment for it, biting the woman's heel and her descendants' heels forever (Genesis 3:15). Prometheus steals fire on his own, but an eagle gnaws away his liver every day to punish him.

These animals that until now have reinforced morality's bonds on behavior appear in Zarathustra's story to give him heart and egg him on. No fear of sacrilege here. Precisely because he does not read these natural beings moralistically, Zarathustra remains free of the sanctions against blasphemy. The animals mean what they had meant but without the superaddition of those judgments that amount to prejudices.

The serpent's wisdom shows itself when the animals teach the eternal return back to Zarathustra: it is a wisdom about eternity. Other snake-references in *Zarathustra* likewise connote eternity and knowledge, whether they be the dangerous snake in the young shepherd's mouth symbolizing eternal return as an unwelcome teaching (Z:3 "The Vision and the Riddle") or the metaphorical description of life as a serpent (Z:3 "Other Dancing Song"). Maybe the present that Zarathustra's disciples give him—a staff topped with a golden snake wrapped around a sun (Z:1 "On the Gift-Giving Virtue")—also represents eternity.

The first of these examples makes a specially vexed case. Why should it be such a noxious serpent that stands for the eternal return? With what aspect of the doctrine does Nietzsche associate it? And why does Zarathustra bite off its head?

Paul Loeb's recent juxtaposition of "The Vision and the Riddle" with *Siegfried* II—Siegfried killing Fafner the dragon or snake—prods new meanings out of the serpent in Zarathustra's vision.

The consensus among commentators has been that Zarathustra's confrontation with this snake represents his struggle with the thought that even small humans will recur eternally.[4] But Zarathustra does not merely overcome his own nausea, he kills the snake itself. The snake therefore denotes "the eternally recurring human," whether great or small;[5] if the snake is more generally an image of time's loop, its head represents the present "while the 'tail' symbolizes the past that has transpired up to the present moment."[6] Beheading the snake therefore means destroying humanity as it exists at present.

If Loeb's interpretation holds, then the envisioned serpent combines direct appropriations of Eden's serpent with inversions of it. For Loeb, as for the consensus he rebuts, this snake is a tempter; but unlike Adam, Zarathustra defeats the temptation. As in Genesis this serpent forces the issue of humanity's survival, except that Zarathustra ends humanity when he vanquishes the serpent instead of in succumbing. And eternity is still the gift a serpent has to offer.

Nietzsche and Non-Christian Snake Imagery

Before Christianity and outside Judaism, snakes were linked to knowledge or wisdom and also to fertility. Taking eternity as the most extreme extension of fertility (or as a fertility separated from reproduction), it is tempting to conclude that Nietzsche restores the serpent to positive meanings it enjoyed before the Edenic serpent (later identified with Satan: Revelation 12:9) imposed a moral interpretation on a natural beast that left it shifty, malevolent, loathsome, and foul.

This temptation ought to be resisted. The fact is that biblical serpents already come trailing splendid enough associations, while polytheisms contain plenty of examples of a snake so inimical to civilization that it needs to be not only respected and resisted but supernaturally battled too—into subjugation, in fact.

Egypt provides one of several exceptions to the generalization that serpents in antiquity were not thought of pejoratively. Apophis the snake was perhaps the greatest demon and needed to be expelled by the sun god. Among the Hittites, the giant serpent Illuyanka threatened the divine order and similarly fell through the combined efforts of several gods; and the New

Hittite goddess Ishtar faced and vanquished a giant reptile. The story of Apollo and Python fits the same pattern. These serpents have to lose and not only lose but disappear; whatever *they* have to teach will not be learned.

The second inconvenience for a reading that has Nietzsche rehabilitating the serpent from Christianity's moralistic use of it is the animal's already multifarious appearance in the Bible. The Genesis snake does tempt the woman to eat the forbidden fruit, and insults such as the gospels' "generation of vipers" (Matthew 3:7, 12:34, 23:33; Luke 3:7) do express the loathing you would expect that event to have inspired. But if the Asclepian caduceus typifies the high regard in which Greek polytheism held snakes, it ought to matter that the Bible contains almost identical images. When Moses and Aaron turn their rods into serpents and back again (Exodus 4:3–4, 7:9–12), the act conjures up the caduceus's ties between snakes and wood. The lifesaving is biblical, too. Moses sets up a brass serpent in the desert that protects the Israelites from snakebite (Numbers 21:6–9). John 3:14–15 even reads this story as a foreshadowing of Christian soteriology in which the son of man will be lifted up like the snake in the desert and bring eternal life to all believers. Where is the negative stereotype in that comparison?

Meanwhile the Israelites need saving in the first place because God sent venomous serpents after them (see also I Corinthians 10:9). God frequently uses serpents to punish the wicked (Job 20:16; Isaiah 59:5; Jeremiah 8:17; and see Deuteronomy 32:24 and Job 26:13), which makes the animals as powerful as they are in Greek mythology—e.g., the snakes with which Hera intends to kill the infant Heracles—and no more intrinsically evil than the Greeks made them out to be, if they are doing a good God's work. (For more references to serpentine power see Isaiah 14:29 and 27:1; for fearsomely strong sea serpents see Isaiah 51:9, Psalm 74:14 and 104:26, and Job 26:12.)

The snake's agreeable scriptural meanings join together in the biblical serpent to which Nietzsche most often alludes. In King James English this beast is "subtil" (Genesis 3:1), has the power of speech, promises life if the woman eats the fruit (3:4), and promises knowledge of good and evil (3:5). Its evil nature aside, it is much the same serpent as in ancient polytheism.

Given Nietzsche's own allegiance to knowledge—a strange new kind of allegiance, but it is still an allegiance—he most frequently emphasizes the mental acumen of Eden's serpent when he alludes to that animal. It is not exactly that Nietzsche denies the evil of this serpent that knows about morality and immortal life, but rather that he denies the evil of that "evil." The meanings he would like to invest in the serpent are here already, only needing to be cut loose from moral judgment. The serpent is still an animal of concealment, but concealment does not have to mean a sinfulness that requires hiding; it is still a cunning animal, but Nietzsche prizes cunning treatments of morality. It is still a promise of long life—longer than ever, as a matter of fact; *eternal* life—but this serpent keeps its promise.

The Masculine Snake

Nietzsche's Dionysus might make a good symbolic counter to "the Crucified" but does not originate with that contrast, rather in a rich context outside Christian thought. Nietzsche does not have to make up the Dionysian by inverting aspects of the Christian.

Nietzsche's serpent, however, begins as a Judeo-Christian construction even if passages that pay special attention to the serpent transfigure that construction. The serpent in Nietzsche negates elements of the serpent in Christianity rather than affirming elements of the polytheistic one.

Does the point need to be harped on? Does it matter in the end if the anti-Christian serpent preponderates over the non-Christian one? Anti-Christian *everything* in Nietzsche preponderates over the non- or pre-Christian.

Still one difference is notable in the present case. The Bible's snakes are masculine figures. When they turn malevolent, they are malevolent toward women. Biblical figures of speech identify Dan, the son of Jacob, with a serpent (Genesis 49:17) but no women. Proverbs 30:18f. compares the serpent's crawl over a rock to "the way of a man with a maid." And John 3:14–15, as noted, takes the brazen serpent in the desert as an anticipatory figure for Christ.

Non-Christian serpents had masculine associations, but not exclusively. Athena appears holding a serpent nearly as often as with her primary mascot, the owl—and that freestanding serpent doesn't even count the Gorgon head on her breastplate wreathed with snakes. Minoan paintings show women holding serpents. Outside Greece there are the Egyptian snake goddesses Kebechet and Renenutet, the Hindu Manasa, and the Mahayana Buddhist Janguli. The Canaanite goddess Hepat is depicted holding serpents.

The Nietzschean serpent denies the biblical interpretation of it as perverse and foul, but along with knowledge and eternity it also preserves its biblical masculinity. The terrifying snake that brings news of the eternal return (Z:3 "On the Vision and the Riddle") thrusts phallically into the young shepherd's mouth in a scene tense with ambiguous language.[7] There is an intimacy between the shepherd and Zarathustra that they seem to need the snake to help them accomplish.

Zarathustra's own serpent, homier and unaggressive, represents in spite of *die Schlange*'s grammatical femininity a desexualized male comradeship. In the prologue, Zarathustra sees his eagle flying with his serpent coiled around its neck—"like a friend," the book says (Z:1 "Zarathustra's Prologue" 10)—no threat of either death or copulation in this embrace.

In Part 4 of *Zarathustra*, camaraderie goes as far as it can, considering that almost no one listens to Zarathustra and that those who do listen garble his teaching. Zarathustra dispatches the magician and beggar and other characters to his cave. He tells these would-be followers, all of them men, that they must learn from his animals. To someone who has read this far in the book, that specifically means that they need to learn of the eternal return from his serpent.

Both the deadly animal and the tame one therefore unite men in learning about eternity. As a phallic image the serpent homosexualizes relations among men; as an emblem of wisdom it desexualizes them. However, in general, the Christian serpent, though otherwise transformed, continues to block the news of eternity from passing between men and women.

Eternity Without Fertility

A word of context. Aristotle calls reproduction the means by which most living things share in eternity (*De Anima* II.4 415a29). Nietzschean eternity not only supersedes but even seems to require denying it. The serpentine masculinity is not an oddity, in other words, but true to Nietzsche's usual way of thinking.

Look at *Beyond Good and Evil*: it contains striking examples of Nietzsche's silence about procreation in the midst of his volubility about the life to come. The philosophy he looks forward to in that book will be practiced by the future's philosophers. But where do they come from? "Who would have time to wait for such servants?" Nietzsche asks (*BGE* 45), and well he might. "They obviously grow so rarely; they are so improbable in any age"—evidently so improbable that *Beyond Good and Evil* cannot say who might give birth to these future philosophers.

It isn't simply that Nietzsche overlooks the chance to speak about procreation. He keeps giving himself chances and then refusing to take them. Nietzsche's scandalizing comments about women (*BGE* 232–239) rule out any part for them to play in the new philosophers' births. But even supposing they would be qualified to mother a philosopher, women as Nietzsche describes them would hardly be able to. Putatively treating the subject of "women as such" and their sexuality, he says close to nothing about reproduction. The closest that *Beyond Good and Evil* does come to accounting for extraordinary new individuals are comments about large populations, somehow conducive to variety, that together with their usual product—the enfeebled modern European—occasionally throw up the exception, too (*BGE* 200, 29, and 242). Somehow, it just happens; put a lot of humans together and new ones emerge.

You might not want to speak with Klossowski of Nietzsche's "need to give birth to himself through himself."[8] Still, Nietzsche's obsession with eternity and his simultaneous prohibition of reproduction invite some kind of comment. And it is the same comment the Nietzschean serpent brings to mind.

Nietzsche might be the Bible's reigning parodist. He takes the evasiveness of the biblical snake and turns it into a psychological unconscious—he twists the essentially evil plotting/cunning of that snake into philosophical insight. But he remains faithful to the association between serpents and health, fertility, and longevity that the Bible shares with many polytheisms and even aggrandizes that characteristic into immortality.

Then, with still greater fidelity, Nietzsche retains the biblical serpent's masculinity. No ambiguities *here* all of a sudden.

The misfit between eternity and a masculine, infertile serpent is not the inadvertent effect of taking over a biblical image and negating some, but not all, of its aspects until a contradiction appears. The serpent's concatenation of attributes rather reflects a positive effort to keep procreation out of the picture even when it is the picture of a fertility symbol.

The snake's shifting meanings in Nietzsche's books—in "On the Adder's Bite," for instance, or the *Gay Science* poem—might even owe something to the impossibility of the symbolizing work Nietzsche puts it to. His symbol of eternity cannot be all the things he would like it to be: Is that why he sometimes (anxiously) keeps changing its job description?[9]

Notes

1. Kathleen Marie Higgins, "*On the Genealogy of Morals*—Nietzsche's *Gift*," in *Nietzsche, Genealogy, Morality: Essays on Nietzsche's "On the Genealogy of Morals*," ed. Richard Schacht (Berkeley: University of California Press, 1994), 450–451.

2. Higgins, "*On the Genealogy of Morals*—Nietzsche's *Gift*," 454–458.

3. This interpretation is further supported later in GS 307 in which Nietzsche likens truths to skins that cover what we are not yet able to see and that we shed, albeit "like a worm [*Gewürm*]" once our lives become other than what they were when we needed such

"truths." What induces the shedding—that is, the abandonment of ideas as "untruths"—is the growth of "living, driving powers [*lebendige treibende Kräfte*]" rather than the exercise of "reason."

4. Paul S. Loeb, "The Dwarf, the Dragon, and the Ring of Eternal Recurrence: A Wagnerian Key to the Riddle of Nietzsche's *Zarathustra*," *Nietzsche-Studien* 31 (2002): 94–96 summarizes the scholarship.

5. Loeb, "The Dwarf, the Dragon, and the Ring of Eternal Recurrence," 99.

6. Loeb, "The Dwarf, the Dragon, and the Ring of Eternal Recurrence," 104.

7. On this serpent, the teaching of eternity, and semen, see David Allison, *Reading the New Nietzsche* (Lanham, Md.: Rowman & Littlefield Publishers, 2001), 162–167.

8. Pierre Klossowski, *Nietzsche and the Vicious Circle*, trans. Daniel W. Smith (Chicago: University of Chicago Press, 1997), 188.

9. For both practical and inspiring comments on this piece I am grateful to my wife Barbara Friedman and to Christina Garidis, Hope Igleheart, and Joseph McElroy.

The Halcyon Tone as Birdsong

Gary Shapiro

Contained in one of Nietzsche's favorite words is the name of a seabird that flits back and forth across the landscapes and seascapes of Mediterranean reality, classical myth, and Nietzsche's imagination. Lexical authorities credit Nietzsche with reintroducing the word "halcyon [*halkyonisch*]" into the German language.[1] That word will recall the "halcyon days," part of the metamorphic complex in the story of Alcyone, who lost her husband Ceyx at sea but was transformed along with him into a pair of seabirds, the female having the extraordinary characteristic of building a floating nest, in which she hatched her eggs during the weeks following the winter solstice, the halcyon days of calm winds and waters arranged by the gods.[2] The story of the nest is generally accepted in the classical world, for example, by such sober authorities as Aristotle and Plutarch. At least three times, Nietzsche emphasizes that the book he regards as the "greatest gift to mankind"—to modern humans, who, in his view, are in need of deeper contact with the wild animal world—will fall on deaf ears unless one hears a certain tone for which this bird is famed. As he says about *Zarathustra* in *Ecce Homo*:

> Here no "prophet" is speaking, none of those gruesome hybrids of sickness and will to power whom people call founders of religions. Above all, one must *hear* aright

the tone that comes from this mouth, the halcyon tone, lest one should do wretched injustice to the meaning of its wisdom. (*EH* P 4)[3]

Nietzsche the musician, the lover of song and opera, with their deployment of the female (human) voice, imagines himself becoming a bird, one renowned for its song throughout the ancient world. The cry of the halcyon (or kingfisher) was said to be remarkably haunting, plaintive, and melancholy, while the halcyon days are bright, calm, and peaceful; Nietzsche writes of "that which is really noble in a work or human being, the moment when their sea is smooth and they have found halcyon self-sufficiency" (*BGE* 224). His frequent evocations of the halcyon are most obviously associated with the latter, but we may assume that both senses are relevant and that the very interplay of the two, as in the myth, is typically at work. The songs of Zarathustra include laments and are often tinged with melancholy. The halcyon has both a spatial/visual aspect and an auditory one. The play between these is evident in several texts where Nietzsche writes of the halcyon element in the music of Mendelssohn and its absence in Wagner.[4]

The refrain, Deleuze and Guattari point out, whether animal or human, is a primordial way of marking territory and making art.[5] One of Nietzsche's ways of becoming-animal is to sing the world, something that he attempts both in his own musical compositions (in the narrow sense), in his poetry, and, most to the point here, in the songs of Zarathustra. Might Nietzsche, with his talk of a new lyre, be thinking of Zarathustra (or himself) as a new Orpheus, whose song could charm the beasts and the birds? After the revelation of "The Convalescent," it is Zarathustra's chattering (not singing) animals that urge him to speak no more but to fashion new songs with a new lyre. He proceeds to do so in a series of three songs. These songs are sung in response to the terrible thought of recurrence, the thought whose consequence is that I am always becoming another. If Nietzsche expressed this eventually in the "mad" form "I am all the names of history," he might, as we shall see, have also said "I am all the names of natural history." The last of the three songs is called "The Seven Seals" in parodic reference to the otherworldly and decidedly anti-animal Christian Revelation. This song celebrates "bird-wisdom" and can be read as alluding to many features of the Alcyone story: freedom from geographical constraints, a magnificently endless world of sea and sky, marriage and maternity, and the supremacy of song. This final strophe in the last song of the cycle culminates in a lyric that aspires to birdsong:

If ever I spread tranquil skies over myself and soared on my own wings into my own skies; if I swam playfully in the deep light-distances, and the bird-wisdom of my freedom came—but bird-wisdom speaks thus: "Behold, there is no above, no below! Throw yourself around, out back, you who are light! Sing! Speak no more! Are not all words made for the grave and heavy? Are not all words lies to those who are light? Sing! Speak no more!" Oh, how should I not lust after eternity and after the nuptial ring of rings, the ring of recurrence?

Never yet have I found the woman from whom I wanted children, unless it be this woman whom I love: for I love you, O eternity. (Z:3 "The Seven Seals" 1)

For this Zarathustra-Nietzsche-becoming-bird, sea and sky are no longer the formless opposites of the land with its definite contours, but the dimensions open to a flying creature, which finds its home everywhere and nowhere ("no above, no below!"). If the latter was the (non)location of Cusanus's god, who was still all too spiritual, now it is envisioned in embodied terms as the playground of a bird-sage who moves and sings effortlessly, nomadically, to territorialize, deterritorialize, and reterritorialize itself with its surroundings. Bird-wisdom, insofar as it speaks, does so in order to renounce mere speech for song. The bird's flight and its song are forms of pure excess. It is not filling a lack or struggling simply to exist; it is overflowing with energy. In the story of Alcyone, the bird's life is geared to the cycle of the sun, itself the excessive energy source for all animal life and so the object of Zarathustra's veneration. It is at the sun's lowest point, the winter solstice, that the halcyon bird helps to celebrate nature's fecundity and rebirth with its miraculous nesting and hatching of young. Nietzsche was doubtless annoyed that Christianity, with its rejection of animal energy, appropriated this season for its own story of birth. In the sixth of the seven seals, Zarathustra sings "this is my alpha and omega, that all that is heavy and grave should become light; all that is body, dancer; all that is spirit, bird."

Hearing Nietzsche's halcyon tone and understanding Zarathustra's becoming-bird can help to clarify the vexed topic of Nietzsche's relation to the feminine. Since Jacques Derrida's *Spurs* and Luce Irigaray's *Marine Lover of Friedrich Nietzsche*, the question has been posed with new subtlety to what extent Nietzsche must be thought of as a misogynist. Derrida pointed out that Heidegger managed to overlook the emphasis that Nietzsche gave to "*it becomes woman*" in his capsule history of philosophy "How the True World Finally Became a Fable." He suggested that we must read the texts more carefully, attending to the confessions of personal bias ("these are my truths") as well as to the affirmative dimension of "suppose that truth is a woman" and the praise of those, including women, whose profundity lies in their realization that we are always dealing with surfaces. Irigaray's love letter takes Nietzsche to task for his narcissism, which expresses itself in his fantastic image of himself as a self-sufficient aerial creature and his avoidance of watery, feminine depths. She sees his or Zarathustra's image of having a child as a masculine attempt to appropriate female powers, asking whether his idea of will and eternal recurrence "are anything more than the dream of one who neither wants to have been born, nor to continue being born, at every instant, of a female other?"[6] Illuminating as both of these readings are, they remain anthropocentric, failing to recognize the full spectrum of life, which is the context for Nietzsche's discussion of sexuality and gender. He does not simply reduce human beings to the lowest common denominators of the reproductive roles that they share with other animals. Although Nietzsche does sometimes write of procreation as involving the eternal war of the sexes, he tends to portray the female as the stronger antagonist. However, what is omitted in both the anthropocentric and the reductively biologistic accounts of Nietzsche on sex and gender is the dimension of the animal and of metamorphosis. When we are overtaken by desire, Ovid, Nietzsche, and Deleuze and Guattari combine to claim, we are in a process of becoming-other, typically a becoming-animal. If we read Ovid—one of Nietzsche's favorite writers, who gives him the motto "we seek the forbidden"—in a flatly literal way, we get a series of incredible stories about humans transformed into trees, birds, dogs, and so on. Reading these stories of metamorphosis in a more generous spirit, stories that so frequently focus on the erotic, we can decipher them as narratives of what Deleuze and Guattari call molecular becoming; they are not about the imitation of external form, but internal transformation. As they write, "Unnatural participations or nuptials are the true Nature spanning the kingdoms of nature. . . . Sexuality is the production of a thousand sexes, which are so many uncontrollable becomings. *Sexuality proceeds by way of the becoming-woman of the man and the becoming animal of the human.*"[7] Desire is not about filling a lack (as a tradition from Plato to Freud would have it) but about becoming something other. Alcyone and Zarathustra become-bird by entering into an alliance with winged creatures.

An authoritative German encyclopedia of classical antiquity informs us that "the name Alcyone was bound up with the idea of faithful married love."[8] In "The Seven Seals," bird-wisdom presides over Zarathustra's proposed marriage with the "woman" eternity. Might we *hear* the halcyon tone of this text as the song of one who is becoming-woman and becoming-bird, singing of transformation, dislocation, and giving birth? On such a reading, or hearing, the sexual relation for Nietzsche would not be understood as a deconstructed binary issuing in a perpetual and complex play of "man" and "woman," the upshot of Derrida's *Spurs*. Nor would it be resolved into a narcissistic projection that must avoid the watery element, as in Irigaray's analysis. Rather, taking seriously the animal dimension of Nietzsche's philosophical rhetoric and poetics would offer a way of hearing his laments and love songs (often one and the same, like ours) as enacting becomings that are both very strange and surprisingly familiar. To hear the halcyon tone of Zarathustra's songs would be to hear one who is becoming-woman-becoming-bird, a double transformation. Yet we all know the sweet songs of loss, on the radio and in our hearts, the blues, which are the ineluctable flip side of the joyous affirmation of love just discovered. Nietzsche's attentive reader and Orphic disciple Rilke knows this in the *Duino Elegies*, which places the human between the animal and the angel. In *Zarathustra*, the hymeneal rejoicing of "The Seven Seals" does not eclipse the *Klage* of "The Night Song." The two deepen one another, because "pain too is a joy; curses too are a blessing." When Zarathustra chants this in the penultimate chapter of his book, "The Drunken Song," he is singing a metasong, a song of songs that explains the mutual imbrication of love and loss, "for all joy wants itself, hence it also wants agony." It is at this point that Zarathustra, after the song competition at his feast and ass festival, becomes the singing teacher, leading the higher men in a round of the "Midnight Song." It is part of Zarathustra's becoming-bird, marking his territory with a refrain. The higher men cannot follow him in this becoming, for they are only students of animals (like the scientist who studies the brain of the leech), their masters (the kings with their beasts of burden), or their imitators and pretended equals (like the voluntary beggar). The story of the new Orpheus ends as this singer welcomes the sign—lion and doves—that tells him that a new singing class ("my children") is on the way.

Notes

1. Hans Schulz, ed., *Deutsches Fremdwörterbuch* (Strassburg, 1913; reprinted Berlin, 1974), 261–262.

2. The story is told in Ovid's *Metamorphoses*, Book XI. For more detailed references to the Greek and Roman literature, see Gary Shapiro, *Alcyone: Nietzsche on Gifts, Noise, and Women* (Albany: State University of New York Press, 1991), 109–154.

3. See also *EH* "Books" Z:6; *GM* P 8.

4. *BGE* 245; *NCW* 10.

5. Gilles Deleuze and Félix Guattari, *A Thousand Plateaus*, trans. Brian Massumi (Minneapolis: University of Minnesota Press, 1987), 310–350; cf. 312: "the bird sings to mark its territory"; 316: "from this standpoint art is not the privilege of human beings."

6. Luce Irigaray, *Marine Lover of Friedrich Nietzsche*, trans. Gillian C. Gill (New York: Columbia University Press, 1991), 26.

7. Deleuze and Guattari, *A Thousand Plateaus*, 241 and 278–279.

8. *Pauly-Wissowa Realenzyklopädie der classischen Altertumswissenschaft*, vol. 1, col. 1581.

C O W

"Even Better than a Cow, O Zarathustra!"

Tracey Stark

> To be sure, one thing is necessary above all if one is to practice reading as
> an *art* in this way, something that has been unlearned most thoroughly now-
> adays—and therefore it will be some time before my writings are "read-
> able"—something for which one has almost to be a cow and in any case *not*
> a "modern man": rumination.
>
> (GM P 8)[1]

We find that the cow serves many roles in Nietzsche's works: from comforting
familiar (providing a sense of warmth to one suffering from chills and mistrust) to carrier of the bankrupt morality of the herd ("Except we turn back
and become as cows, we shall not enter the kingdom of heaven" [Z:4 "The
Voluntary Beggar"]), and, as cited above, as an example of how to read.
Nietzsche insists that when we read him we ruminate; that is, approach the
text as if one were a cow. Zarathustra himself demonstrates his proclivity for
such a contemplative awareness when he reflects on the words of others:
"What strange people have I found to talk with! Now I shall long chew their
words like good grains; my teeth shall grind them and crush them small till

they flow like milk into my soul" (Z:4 "The Ugliest Man"). What if Nietzsche were one of these "strange persons" whose words we have to crush until
they yield sweet milk? What if one was to ruminate on the role of this ruminating creature itself in Nietzsche's bestiary?

When Nietzsche reflects on his *Zarathustra* in *Ecce Homo*, he writes of the
"rancor of greatness," the awful price one pays for creating great art, of the
distance he feels between himself and others, and of the empty gazes he
encountered. He also writes about suffering from a variety of physical ail-
ments and his susceptibility to "feeling chills as well as mistrust—mistrust
that is in many instances merely an etiological blunder." Then comes this
surprising sentence: "In such a state I once sensed the proximity of a herd of
cows even before I saw it, merely because milder and more philanthropic
thoughts came back to me: *they* had warmth" (*EH* "Books" Z:5). Hypersensi-
tive to his natural surroundings—to landscape, climate, and time of day—
Nietzsche finds solace in nature for his terrible loneliness and inability to
communicate with human beings. It is thus that he is captivated by the
peaceful, composed strength of the cows. Suffering from silence and solitude
and inclined to cold and suspicion, Nietzsche is calmed and softened by the
mere thought of cows, who communicated warmth to him. This experience
underlies "The Voluntary Beggar," in Part 4 of *Zarathustra*, which begins:
"When Zarathustra had left the ugliest man, he felt frozen and lonely: for
much that was cold and lonely passed through his mind and made his limbs
too feel colder." But as he rambles on, he becomes warmer and heartier:
"something warm and alive refreshes me, something that must be near me."
As he looks around for the "comforters of his lonesomeness" Zarathustra sees
cows, those "brothers . . . whose warm breath touches my soul." In the midst
of these kindred souls, he sees a man sitting on the ground trying to persuade
the cows not to fear him. This man is the "voluntary beggar" (Preacher-on-
the-Mount), who proclaims that he seeks happiness on earth and believes
that the cows can teach it to him. He is angry because the cows were about
to speak when Zarathustra intruded. "Except we turn back and become as
cows," the beggar preaches, "we shall not enter the kingdom of heaven. For
we ought to learn one thing from them: chewing the cud. And verily, what
would it profit a man if he gained the whole world and did not learn this one
thing: chewing the cud!"

When he recognizes that the intruder is no stranger, but Zarathustra himself, the beggar jumps up in reverence. This "voluntary beggar" had given his
wealth and heart to the poor only to be spurned by them and had turned
instead to the animals and "to these cows." Humans, poor or rich, are not

blessed, he declares, "but the kingdom of heaven is among the cows." After Zarathustra chides him for his severity and anger, the beggar acknowledges his softer nature and says he seeks "gentle idlers and loafers." Hence the cows: "[T]hey invented for themselves chewing the cud and lying in the sun. And they abstain from all grave thoughts, which bloat the heart." At this, Zarathustra invites the beggar to his cave to talk of the "happiness of animals" with his own animals, the serpent and eagle, and he urges the "strange" one to leave his cows. This will be difficult: "For they are your warmest friends and teachers." "Excepting one whom I love still more," answers the beggar: "You yourself are good, and even better than a cow, O Zarathustra."

What is it that makes Zarathustra better than a cow? Perhaps all his ruminating has brought him not only the quiet warmth of the cows but also transcendence beyond mute/brute nature into the realm of eternal return. In preaching this greatest truth, the truth of the eternal return, and by conceiving "the totality of natural existence as an enormous interplay of dynamic and differential forces," Zarathustra "can advance an account of material reality as an ever-changing aggregation and reaggregation of force or energy."[2] For the beggar, Zarathustra's teaching of the eternal return gives even more comfort than the peaceful cows. Yet Zarathustra finds no consolation in this teaching, because it would also require the eternal return of the small human, the Last Man, who, even though God is dead, lives by principles of good and evil. Zarathustra himself is partly to blame for the existence of these small humans, because he had thus far taught a dualistic theology.[3] His mistake comes back to haunt him now as he contemplates endless generations of dualistically inclined human beings. His animals (oh those familiars, perhaps the hidden gods?) recognize his terror and tell him to think in a new way, *beyond* metaphysical dualities. "Do not speak on!" they cry, "rather even, O convalescent, fashion yourself a lyre first, a new lyre! For behold, Zarathustra, new lyres are needed for your new songs. Sing and overflow, O Zarathustra; cure your soul with new songs that you may bear your great destiny." It is a dangerous destiny, perhaps the great destiny Zarathustra prayed for. The teaching of the eternal return is Zarathustra's destiny, yet the very *thought* of it makes him queasy: "[H]ow could this great destiny not be your greatest danger and sickness too?" (Z:3 "The Convalescent").

Zarathustra's sickness is caused by the metaphysical dualism of the small human, the dualism of good and evil, and he must overcome it to fulfill his destiny. It is because he needs to overcome this way of thinking that he went to the mountain of the god Dionysus, the god of disintegration. Zarathustra is nauseated by his civilization and the thought of its eternal recurrence. Insofar as he himself preaches dualism, Zarathustra is also a sick man. There is a division in his soul and a division in the body social, and it cannot be healed in any of the ways Zarathustra has attempted to heal it; the gods are dead and utopian fantasies for the future are the fantasies of the Last Men. The only thing that can heal the sickness of the age (the illness that results from a sense of fragmentation and alienation from the cycle of life) is an overcoming of dualism and a transcending of the small human. This requires that we go beyond the ossified trappings of a used-up religion and blind devotion to science and that we sing "new songs." Until he sings these new songs, Zarathustra and his civilization will be ill, but ill in the sense that pregnancy is an illness. Zarathustra hasn't yet overcome dualism, but he prepares the way for the one who will: the overman. It is the birth of the overman that will renew an affirmation of life for a whole civilization.

In the Prologue to *Zarathustra*, the ancient wise one is descending from his mountain retreat to bring his "gift of honey" to the world. He enters the town of The Motley Cow, hoping to find someone there to accept his offering. What is this honey? What town is this? Perhaps the gift is semen, and Zarathustra is bringing inseminating words to the mother of the overman. Could it also be the gift of milk, nourishing our souls? In *Human, All Too Human*, Nietzsche argues that if you become a wanderer (like Zarathustra, perhaps), your life will obtain new meaning, and "the clouds of affliction hovering over you will yet have to serve you as udders from which you will milk the milk for your refreshment" (*HH* 292). Here and in other places, Nietzsche uses many images of cups overflowing, udders being full to the point of pouring out, even into the galaxy. Could the honey be wine, the gift of the god Dionysus, intoxicating us now not with alcohol, but with the *vision* of joy? "I say unto you: one must still have chaos in oneself to be able to give birth to a dancing star" (*Z:P* 5).

Zarathustra's first gift is the story of the great metamorphoses, from camel to lion to child. He bestows this gift upon "the town that is called The Motley Cow." What is this town, and why does Zarathustra descend here of all places? Is it the city of Thebes, founded by the hero Cadmus?[4] This interpretation makes sense for a variety of reasons: as Apollodorus, Hesiod, and others tell us, Cadmus founded Thebes and started a new civilization there after following a black and white cow to its destined place.[5] Also, it would follow that Nietzsche would want to return to the territory highlighted in the tragic plays he champions in *The Birth of Tragedy*, the city of Laius and Joscasta, of Oedipus and Antigone. It is significant that the mountain where Zarathustra resides, Mount Cithaeron, is also the home of the god Dionysus in Greek mythology. It is Dionysus on whom Nietzsche calls at the end of BT: "Thus the Dionysiac element, as against the Apollonian, proves itself to be the eternal and original power of art, since it calls into being the entire world of phenomena." This is not to say that the Apollonian isn't also needed to "catch and hold in life the stream of individual forms," but these two forms have developed out of proportion, with the Apollonian overwhelming the Dionysian (BT 25).

The Birth of Tragedy ended with a hope for a revival of tragedy, which had been destroyed by Socratic reason. Nietzsche endeavors to reawaken the Dionysian spirit in the modern world, the world in which "the inartistic and parasitical nature of Socratic optimism has shown itself both in our art, reduced to mere amusement, and in our lives, governed by empty concepts" (BT 24). This is the world Nietzsche wants to challenge. He addresses his "friends," those who "believe in Dionysiac music," and claims that this music "inspires the most extravagant hopes and promises oblivion of the bitterest pain." In BT, Nietzsche anticipates that this music will be reborn in his generation, brought about by those who will destroy the "evil dwarfs" who have kept the "German genius" enslaved (BT 24).

There is little doubt that Nietzsche believed Wagner to be such a savior; however, Wagner disappointed him, so Thus Spoke Zarathustra is Nietzsche's own attempt to bring tragedy back to us. Just as Wagner's Siegfried killed the dwarf, Mime, in The Ring of the Nibelung, so must Nietzsche's Zarathustra kill the "evil dwarf," the spirit of gravity, only now not out of a nationalist interest, but out of a hope for the overcoming of all dwarfish people with the coming of the overman.[6] What better place to do this than Thebes? It is the city of wisdom and has a history of being visited by questing heroes and those looking for lost wholeness. The very journey of the first hero, Cadmus, is founded on a loss, that of his sister, Europa (his feminine side), who has been carried off by the god Zeus. This is the first fragmentation Cadmus experiences, as the theft splits him into the dualities of "male" and "female." To reunite these two sides, Cadmus (like all heroes, including Zarathustra himself) must become a dragon-slayer and fight the ossified ways of the "being" in favor of the challenge of becoming.

Cadmus is a mythical hero, vanquishing those who trap the divine wisdom and bringing it down from the mountain. Zarathustra wants to become yet another mask of this same hero, retracing the steps of Cadmus and progenerating a new race. Yet Zarathustra cannot fulfill his mission because he is made impotent by that monster, dualism, which freezes him in the sickness of alienation. This is why his animals told him to make a "new lyre"; just as Cadmus killed the monster Typhus with the lyrical music of Zeus's thunder, so now Zarathustra has to reclaim the shattering thunder of the god.

We see that Zarathustra's journey mirrors Cadmus's again with the story of Cadmus's defeat of the snake of Ares. With Athena's inspiration, Cadmus stabbed it with the sacrificial knife and cut off its head. This killing signifies the cut that Cadmus must make from the past in order to be reborn in his marriage with Harmony, the daughter of Aphrodite and Ares. It is echoed in Zarathustra's biting off the head of the snake lodged in his throat. Like Cadmus, Zarathustra must also make a cut from the past, destroying the spirit of gravity and nausea that suffocates him. He must kill the idea of the eternal return of the small humans in favor of a world that recognizes the unity behind all dualisms. Hence, the eternal return signifies not the return of our frozen ways of thinking but the endless dance of creation and destruction. It is only once Zarathustra reconceptualizes the eternal return that he can he engage in the divine marriage with life itself. As Paul S. Loeb finds, rather than affirming the eternal return of that which nauseates him, Zarathustra "learns how to overcome that very thing which he rightly loathes and which rightly induces nausea in him, namely, the eternal recurrence of the small human."[7] I would add here that what nauseates Nietzsche about the small human is precisely that he or she does not see that dualisms are illusions and that what eternally returns is life itself. Once Zarathustra realizes this, he becomes the hero; he too can slay dragons and move humanity beyond the dualisms of good and evil, thus the laughter: "With this new laughter, Zara-thustra mocks and ridicules the small and dwarfish standards by which the spirit of gravity has so far assessed what is good and evil for all."[8] And what of the snake he killed, cutting off its head while leaving the coils writhing? Is this not the snake that lodged in the mouth of the shepherd? The snake he bit? The dismembered snake that sent the shepherd laughing? Is this not the very snake that Zarathustra counsels us to destroy if we want to be reborn?

Just as Cadmus had done long ago, Zarathustra wants to usher in a new spiritual awareness and an age of new gods. What better place to go than the city Cadmus founded, the city of The Motley Cow? It is at once the abode of a herd-like population, following the teachers of virtue and their herd val-ues, and the place from which higher humanity will arise out of the writings of the hero. We see that by alluding to the myth of the marriage of Cadmus and Harmony, Nietzsche is calling us back to the wisdom of tragedy, that art by which the Greeks were "superficial out of depth" (the lowly spotted heifer can point us to the divine) (cf. *BT*). We see that Cadmus brought the written alphabet to the Greeks that allowed them to write not only theogonies but also tragedies. It is the written tragedy and myths that save us from the oblivion of forgetfulness. Individuals die, the mythic hero is reborn. Further, with the written alphabet, we no longer require the full presence of the gods; they become a ladder that can be left behind once we have climbed to the heights of spiritual truth.

Hence we see Nietzsche's call to metamorphosis. We have abandoned the gods, but we have access to their wisdom in the words of the poet, words that can *change* us by killing the monsters of a frozen language of the common. Zarathustra does not teach the virtue of the Sage, but he does not discount its usefulness, for he knows that virtue can act as the "pedagogical prelude to the culminating insight, which goes beyond all pairs of opposites."[9] The Sage teaches that the youth became camels; but now they need to "go under." Here, we become god-like, for what were the Greek gods if not constantly changing shape?—Zeus a swan in this story, a bull in the next. Nietzsche is calling on us to be like Zeus, to undergo a metamorphosis, to live mythically, and to regain that superficiality that signifies depth. What better place to do it than in the land of the spotted cow?[10] What will cause the birth of such people if not the written word, the gift of Cadmus? Cadmus, who was not only adept at writing but was nursed on the milk of books; Cadmus, who knew the song of justice and played it on Apollo's harp; Cadmus, who married his words with Harmony, thus bringing poetry to life.

Zarathustra wants to enact a similar marriage. Not only are the people in his "cow country" (Boetia) sleeping but their virtue is the virtue of the herd. They *name* their virtues, thereby robbing them of their singularity: "[N]ow you have her name in common with the people and have become one of the people and the herd with your virtue." Once this virtue was new and jarring; now it has become commonplace. We must abandon this worn-out virtue and find a new living truth, one that hasn't yet passed into the common currency of language. It is better not to name it, to only speak of it in a stammering voice, saying, "This is *my* good; this I love; it pleases me wholly; thus alone do *I* want the good," (Z:1 "On Enjoying and Suffering the Passions").

This personal virtue is not the virtue of divine commands or human statutes; it is the virtue that cannot be spoken, for fear that it be misrepresented. It is a bird that "built its nest with me" and sits on my "golden eggs." It cannot be spoken because it is a truth beyond words, the truth of the oneness of good and evil. This is why Zarathustra preaches that we turn our passions into virtue and enjoy them, transforming poisons into balsams, wild dogs into songbirds, and the sour milk of the cow, melancholy, into something sweet. Is this not exactly what Cadmus did when he transformed loss into mythic return with his alphabet? Cadmus, who is the descendent of Io, that great mother cow? Perhaps this is why Zarathustra brings his word to the town of The Motley Cow: in this town they have the written word and can ruminate over Zarathustra's verse—filled with aphorisms, metaphors, and analogies—the stammered words of personal virtue. These are words that seem to display the simple-mindedness of a child, but they contain truths that are too great to be communicated directly: "The trance-susceptible shaman and the initiated antelope-priest are not unsophisticated in the wisdom of the world, nor unskilled in the principles of communication by analogy. The metaphors by which they live, and through which they operate, have been brooded upon, searched, and discussed for centuries—even millenniums."[11] Ruminating on these metaphors (and aphorisms) can facilitate the apprehension of the universality beyond "the colorful, fluid, infinitely various and bewildering phenomenal spectacle" to the truth or openness beyond. This can never be communicated in a straightforward fashion because our "forms of sensibility and the categories of human thought . . . are themselves manifestations of this power."[12] Our ordinary language confines the mind so that it is impossible to communicate such truth, yet analogy can overcome this, for with it, "forms and conceptions that the mind and its senses can comprehend are presented and arranged in such a way as to suggest a truth or openness beyond. And then, the conditions for meditation having been provided, the individual is left alone"[13] (to "ruminate," as it were). Zarathustra doesn't want to be read; he wants to be "learned by heart." It is through his use of metaphors that he can "lure many away from the herd."

"Of all that is written I love only what a man has written with his blood." Zarathustra can love only that which is sacred and life giving. Only a ritual sacrifice, the killing of a sacred cow, as it were, brings to light the experience that blood is spirit. Only once we have made such a sacrifice can we climb to divine elevations and experience the joy of the dance of the universe: "Who among you can laugh and be elevated at the same time? Whoever climbs the highest mountains laughs at all tragic plays and tragic seriousness." We can laugh at tragic plays and tragic seriousness because we know that life and death are united, that they are different perspectives on the same life force. Once one realizes this, one becomes "well disposed toward life, butterflies and soap bubbles and whatever among men is of their kind seem to know most about happiness" (Z:1 "On Reading and Writing"). When one goes beyond dualisms, such as those of good and evil, he or she becomes light, flies to the heights, dances. Rather than being filled with moral indignation or tragic pity and fear, Zarathustra calls on us to laugh the "Olympian laugh," where we see that our sorrows and tears are "suffused with the joy of a transcendent anonymity regarding [ourselves] in all of the self-centered, battling egos that are born and die in time."[14]

This call to transcend dualisms explains Nietzsche's claim that "Woman's love involves injustice and blindness against everything that she does not love. And even in the knowing love of a woman there are still assault and lightening and night alongside light." The "woman" here is divine truth, represented by a Queen Goddess or Holy Spirit. She is also life and the feminine side of Zarathustra himself, he who is trapped in the dualisms of gender. She is that side of him who is nauseated by the thought of the return of the small human and cracks this lie open with her moonlit arrows. She is the almighty bringer of life and harbinger of death, which she loves equally.

"Woman is not yet capable of friendship: women are still cats and birds. Or at best, cows" (Z:1 "On the Friend"). She is the cat who deceives by hiding the truth behind appearance, the bird who sits on my golden eggs, the cow who nourishes me with the milk of wisdom, but she is not my friend. As long as we need crutches, personifying this truth as a goddess or biblical character, it is distant from us as Harmony was from Cadmus. For Nietzsche, the friend (the feminine principle in each of us) should challenge us, but who is challenged anymore by the worn-out clichés of our culture?[15]

"Woman is not yet capable of friendship. But tell me, you men, who among you is capable of friendship?" (Z:1 "On the Friend") For Nietzsche, "joy" is that which we share in friendship. Our friend is an "overflowing" spirit who gives out of excess and challenges out of love (HH 189). The truth no longer challenges us (not yet, at least), but do we challenge each other? Who is willing to play the father, robbing us of our infantile cathexes and making us ready to take the reins for the future? Zarathustra hopes to become that person: "That I may one day be ready and ripe in the great noon: as ready and ripe as glowing bronze, clouds pregnant with lightning, and swelling milk udders—ready for myself and my most hidden will: a bow lusting for its arrow, an arrow lusting for its star—a star ready and ripe in its noon, glowing, pierced, enraptured by annihilating sun arrows—a sun itself and an inexorable solar will, ready to annihilate in victory!" (Z:3 "On Old and New Tablets").

Here we have images of insemination, pregnancy, and lactation. Each birth is entwined with death—with the birth of sun, we have the death of the star, yet life continues on; soon the moon will annihilate the sun as surely as Artemis's arrows hit their mark, and always, the cows. Zarathustra reaches for the height and he seeks the excess of the overflowing cup, the Cornucopia, Horn of Plenty: a cow's horn pouring forth all the fruits of the earth. Hence, when Zarathustra leaves the town of The Motley Cow, he preaches:

> Remain faithful to the earth, my brothers, with the power of your virtue. Let your gift-giving love and your knowledge serve the meaning of the earth. Thus I beg and beseech you. Do not let them fly away from earthly things and beat with their wings against eternal walls. Alas, there has always been so much virtue that has flown away. Lead back to the earth the virtue that flew away, as I do—back to the body, back to life, that it may give the earth a meaning, a human meaning. (Z:1 "On the Gift-Giving Virtue")

What is Zarathustra asking except that we turn away from the eternal return of the small human and its symbols of a frozen past and reaffirm *life* in all its ambiguity? (Zarathustra himself does this after overcoming his nausea and dancing and conversing with life—personified as a woman.) He is asking that we turn from the now-impotent myth of an eternal God and the Enlightenment myth that we can live without myth. We need new myths, for without the mythic structure to guide us, our lives are lonely and we are fractured. Inventing new myths will not be easy. Once the hero has slain the beast and made the sacred marriage, he must still return to the world, "where men who are fractions imagine themselves to be complete." He has yet to confront society with his "ego-shattering, life-redeeming elixir," and in turn face its questions, resentment and indifference.[16] This hero will be lonely, yet he or she is the bearer of the future:

> Wake and listen, you that are lonely! From the future come winds with secret wing-beats; and good tidings are proclaimed to delicate ears. You that are lonely today, you that are withdrawing, you shall one day be the people: out of you, who have chosen yourselves, there shall grow a chosen people—and out of them, the over-man. Verily, the earth shall yet become a site of recovery. And even now a new fragrance surrounds it, bringing salvation—and a new hope. (Z:1 "On the Gift-Giving Virtue" 2)

Notes

1. I use Golffing's translation of BT; Kaufmann's translations of BGE, EH, Z; Kaufmann and Hollingdale's translation of GM; and Hollingdale's translation of HH in my citations of Nietzsche's works.

2. David B. Allison, *Reading the New Nietzsche* (Lanham, Md.: Rowman & Littlefield, 2001), 121.

3. Zoroaster was of course a teacher of the Manichean theology, which posited the existence of both a good and an evil god.

4. Allison, *Reading the New Nietzsche*, 128–129.

5. As the Pythis in Delphi say to Cadmus when he asks where to find his sister:

> In vain, Cadmus, do you plant your wandering footsteps far and wide; you seek a bull never born to any cow; you seek a bull no mortal can find. Forget Assyria; take an earthly heifer as your guide and follow it; do not seek the Olympian bull. . . . Settle in a foreign land and found a city that will bear the name of your homeland, Thebes of Egypt. Found it in the place where the heifer, by divine inspiration, falls to the ground, stretching out her weary hooves.

Roberto Calasso, *The Marriage of Cadmus and Harmony*, trans. Tim Parts (New York: Knopf, 1993), 384.

6. See Paul S. Loeb, "The Dwarf, the Dragon, and the Ring of Eternal Recurrence: A Wagnerian Key to the Riddle of Nietzsche's *Zarathustra*," *Nietzsche-Studien* 31 (2002): 92–113.

7. Loeb, "The Dwarf, the Dragon, and the Ring of Eternal Recurrence," 96.

8. Loeb, "The Dwarf, the Dragon, and the Ring of Eternal Recurrence," 108.

9. J. Campbell, *The Hero with a Thousand Faces* (Princeton, N.J.: Princeton University Press, 1949), 44.

10. See Campbell, *The Hero with a Thousand Faces*, 121.

11. Campbell, *The Hero with a Thousand Faces*, 256.

12. Campbell, *The Hero with a Thousand Faces*, 258.

13. Campbell, *The Hero with a Thousand Faces*, 258.

14. Campbell, *The Hero with a Thousand Faces*, 46.

15. See Campbell, *The Hero with a Thousand Faces*, 249.

16. Campbell, *The Hero with a Thousand Faces*, 216.

A S S

Nietzsche and the Mystery of the Ass

Kathleen Marie Higgins

The time I first read *Thus Spoke Zarathustra*'s "The Awakening" may well be the first time I laughed aloud over Nietzsche. I was in the next room from my grandmother's bridge party, and I heard one of her guests ask what I was doing. "She's reading some of that dry old philosophy," my grandmother replied. I was reading *Zarathustra,* and I was just at the point of beginning "The Awakening," in which Zarathustra returns to his cave to discover that his dinner guests, the higher men, are worshipping an ass. The section was hilarious, and with my grandmother's comment in mind, I had tears in my eyes as I read.

Only later did I seriously question what the ass was doing in *Zarathustra.* My first thought, while reading at my grandmother's, was that Zarathustra's return to the higher men was a parody of Moses with his tablets returning to his followers, who were worshipping a golden calf. This allusion makes sense in the context. Zarathustra, like Moses, is the bestower of new values, values that his followers have not consistently internalized. But the excessive character of "The Awakening" suggests that the Moses allusion does not exhaust Nietzsche's purpose. Why, if the point were simply to reference Moses, does Nietzsche make an ass the center of attention?

In connection with the ass, Nietzsche observes the principle later formulated into Chekhov's dictum that if one brings a pistol onstage, one should fire it before the end of the act. An ass carrying a load for the kings in Part 4 might have passed as simply a kingly accompaniment, but Nietzsche goes out of his way to make the ass as obtrusive as a gun onstage would be. Zarathustra remarks when he first spies the ass and its owners, "Strange! Strange! How does this fit together? Two kings I see—and only one ass!" On encountering Zarathustra, the kings explain their purpose, making the ass the focus. "As with one voice," the kings declare, "We are on our way to find the higher man—the man who is higher than we, though we are kings. To him we are leading this ass" (Z:4 "Conversation of the Kings"). Nietzsche continues to emphasize the ass when Zarathustra responds to the kings' further complaint that higher men are not currently in positions of power.

> "What did I just hear?" replied Zarathustra. "What wisdom in kings! I am delighted and, verily, even feel the desire to make a rhyme on this—even if it should be a rhyme which is not fit for everybody's ears. I have long become unaccustomed to any consideration for long ears. Well then!" (But at this point it happened that the ass too got in a word; but he said clearly and with evil intent, Yea-Yuh.)" (Z:4 "Conversation of the Kings")[1]

The ass is given a conspicuous role again in "The Last Supper," the section describing Zarathustra's dinner party for the various higher men he has encountered during the day.

> On this occasion, as the soothsayer asked for wine, it happened that the king at the left, the taciturn one, got a word in too, for once. "For wine," he said, "we have taken care—I together with my brother, the king at the right; we have wine enough—a whole ass-load. So nothing is lacking but bread." (Z:4 "The Last Supper")[2]

Zarathustra announces the fare he will be serving.

> "The best belongs to my kind and to me; and when one does not give it to us, we take it: the best food, the purest sky, the strongest thoughts, the most beautiful women."
>
> Thus spoke Zarathustra; but the king at the right retorted: "Strange! Has one ever heard such clever things out of the mouth of a sage? And verily, he is the strangest sage who is also clever and no ass."
>
> Thus spoke the king at the right, and he was amazed; but the ass commented on his speech with evil intent: Yeah-Yuh. (Z:4 "The Last Supper")

Zarathustra mentions asses again in the subsequent section, "On the Higher Man," which recounts Zarathustra's long speech during the meal. In the psychologically salient final section, he proclaims, "What gives asses wings, what milks lionesses—praised be this good intractable spirit that comes like a cyclone to all today and to all the mob" (Z:4 "On the Higher Man"). The ass is again featured at the beginning of "The Awakening," when Zarathustra is first prompted to step outside his cave, leaving the higher men on their own.

> [S]ince all of the assembled guests talked at the same time and even the ass, thus encouraged, would no longer remain silent, Zarathustra was overcome by a slight aversion and by scorn for his company, although he enjoyed their gaiety. For this seemed to him a sign of convalescence. So he slipped out into the open and talked to his animals. (Z:4 "The Awakening")

While chatting to his animals outside the cave, Zarathustra is disturbed again by the sound of the ass: "And Zarathustra covered up his ears, for just then the Yeah-Yuh of the ass was strangely blended with the jubilating noise of these higher men" (Z:4 "The Awakening").

The recurrent emphasis on the ass in Part 4 is something of a mystery that is not fully unraveled when the reference to Moses is noted. One might point out that Nietzsche mentions asses elsewhere in *Zarathustra*, too, and in other works. But this is only to further motivate the question. What are asses to Nietzsche?

The German word *Esel*, which can be translated "ass" or "jackass," shares with those words the connotations of foolishness, stubbornness, and stupidity. Given Nietzsche's low opinion of many of his fellow human beings, perhaps it is not surprising that the term *Esel* recurs in his writing. And certainly the connotation of foolishness and stupidity is evoked by some of Nietzsche's ass-laden comments.[3] For example, when he considers the possibility of a teacher of his era encouraging students to be natural, he begins his comment with "even such a virtuous and guileless ass" (*BGE* 264). Despite the mention of virtue, this is no compliment. In *Ecce Homo*, Nietzsche makes another negative reference to the ass.

> All of us know, some even know from experience, which animal has long ears. Well then, I dare assert that I have the smallest ears. This is of no small interest to women—it seems to me that they may feel I understand them better.—I am the *anti-ass par excellence* and thus a world-historical monster—I am, in Greek, and not only in Greek, the *Antichrist*. (*EH* "Books" 2)[4]

In the context of a megalomaniacal passage, Nietzsche's calling himself an anti-ass appears to disparage the ass. In *Zarathustra*, too, we find uses of the word *Esel* in which it appears to have the connotation of "stupid fool." For example, consider Zarathustra's comment when he first sees the Kings, mentioned earlier, and the passage that immediately follows.

> "Strange! Strange! How does this fit together? Two kings I see—and only one ass!"
> The two kings stopped, smiled, looked in the direction from which the voice had come, and then looked at each other. "Something of the sort may have occurred to one of us too," said the king at the right; "but one does not say it." (Z:4 "Conversation of the Kings")

The comment of the King at the right underscores Nietzsche's pun here. The ass is the traditional "mount of kings,"[5] but the term is also applied to a foolish person, which presumably the King at the right takes his fellow to be.

However, some of Nietzsche's remarks on asses are not obviously negative. For example, in a letter to his sister in July 1883, Nietzsche describes himself and any man with a real goal as putting "a veritable asshide around his essence, so that one can beat him nearly to death." This person "prevails and goes his old way as the old ass, with his old Ya-Yuh."[6] One of his aphorisms in *Twilight of the Idols* also presents the ass rather sympathetically. "Can an *ass* be tragic?—To be crushed by a burden one can neither bear nor throw off? . . . The case of the philosopher" (*TI* "Maxims and Arrows" 3). The equation of asses and stupid people is inadequate for interpreting such passages.

Jörg Salaquarda was perhaps the first to notice that the ass, particularly the ass in *Zarathustra*, has a more complex role than the received view acknowledged. Gustav Naumann and others had earlier taken the ass to be a symbol of the mob, an interpretation that relies heavily on the association of the ass with stupidity and baseness. Salaquarda convincingly argues that this interpretation is inadequate.[7]

Salaquarda notes that the references to the ass in the first three parts of *Thus Spoke Zarathustra* do tend to associate the ass with the undistinguished crowd. He cites, for example, the following passage from "On Reading and Writing."

> You say to me, "Life is hard to bear." But why would you have your pride in the morning and your resignation in the evening? Life, is hard to bear; but do not act

so tenderly! We are all of us fair beasts of burden, male and female asses. What do
we have in common with the rosebud, which trembles because a drop of dew lies
on it?" (Z:1)

Again, in "On the Famous Wise Men," Nietzsche addresses the famous
ones, "As the people's advocates you have always been stiff-necked and clever
like asses" (Z:2 "On the Famous Wise Men"). Here the asses are not "the
people" themselves, but clever individuals who attract the people's attention.[8] Nevertheless, they are associated with the people through being
described as their advocates. In "On Apostates" common people of little
intelligence are again associated with asses. Zarathustra overhears night watchmen speculate that God doesn't prove anything because he considers faith
so important. He comments, "Verily, this will yet be my death, that I shall
suffocate with laughter when I see asses drunk and hear night watchmen thus
doubting God. Is not the time long past for all such doubts too?" (Z:3 "On
Apostates"). Similarly in "On the Spirit of Gravity," Zarathustra announces,
"Verily, I also do not like those who consider everything good and this world
the best. Such men I call the omni-satisfied. . . . [T]o chew and digest everything—that is truly the swine's manner. Always to bray Yea-Yuh—that only
the ass has learned and whoever is of his spirit" (Z:3 "On the Spirit of
Gravity").

Despite such passages in which asses are associated with common fools,
Salaquarda argues persuasively that Nietzsche often uses the term *Esel* in reference to more distinguished individuals and their mindlessly held convictions, particularly moral prejudices. Philosophers with their prejudices are
paradigmatic asses, for Nietzsche, as are those who have faith in "modern
ideas." Although Nietzsche does show scorn for the mob of humanity, he
heaps particular contempt on learned asses and the asses of politics.[9]

A particularly fascinating passage to which Salaquarda alludes occurs in
Beyond Good and Evil: "There is a point in every philosophy when the philosopher's 'conviction' appears on the stage—or to use the language of an
ancient Mystery: *Adventavit asinus, Pulcher et fortissimus* [Kaufmann's translation: The ass arrived, beautiful and most brave]" (*BGE* 8). The words of the
"ancient Mystery" are lines from "The Song of the Ass," sometimes attributed to Pierre de Corbeil, Archbishop of Sens, who died in 1222.[10] This song
played a role in a celebration of medieval times called Feast of Fools, the Ass
Festival, or Feast of Asses (*asinaria festa*), a connection that Salaquarda and
others have recognized.[11] Salaquarda credits Naumann with the recognition
that Nietzsche had referred to the Ass Festival procession in a letter to Carl

von Gersdorff,[12] as well as in the *Beyond Good and Evil* passage, but he regis-ters surprise that Naumann had not drawn consequences from these refer-ences for an interpretation of Nietzsche's ass metaphor.[13] Salaquarda himself sees Nietzsche's reference to the procession as providing support for his view that Nietzsche employs the image of the ass to criticize those who join the parade of true believers, burdened by their convictions.

Salaquarda does not, however, make much of the humor of Nietzsche's references to the medieval Ass Festival, except insofar as it is contemptuous. I will argue that the humorous character of "The Awakening" and the subse-quent section, "The Ass Festival," is likely to have been an important part of Nietzsche's agenda. The details of the historical feast reveal why Nietzsche may have found it both humorous and worthy of attention.

The Historical Ass Festival

From the late eleventh to the sixteenth centuries, the Ass Festival was cele-brated annually in various European cathedrals and churches at some point during the weeks after Christmas. It was most popular in France, although reports place it at various locations in Germany, Spain, England, Bohemia, and Poland.[14] The festival typically involved the sub-deacons, the lowest rank of the clergy, clownishly pretending to be their clerical superiors (often bishops) and engaging in carnivalesque activities such as "the using of masks, talking gibberish, making animal noises instead of articulated speech, men dressing in female clothes, etc."[15] Often the excesses went considerably fur-ther, to include clergy members playing dice and eating blood pudding at the altar, braying at Mass, singing wanton songs both inside and outside the church, dancing lewdly, burning old shoes and censing the altar with them, "baptizing" members of the clergy with buckets of water, and driving around town in carts while singing and making obscene gestures.

During the course of this festival, "The Song of the Ass," or "The Prose of the Ass," was commonly sung one or more times. This hymn, the one cited in *Beyond Good and Evil*, is preserved in various forms. The hymn praises the ass, making frequent reference to its strength; for the ass, it pro-claims, "no burden was too heavy." The ass bites the straw he eats "with strongest teeth" and thus becomes sated. Of particular interest for our pur-poses is the line "None can dance as thou."[16] In the last stanza, the ass is urged to say "Amen."

Nietzsche's song in "The Awakening" follows its model closely. When Zarathustra returns to his cave, he discovers the higher men "all kneeling like children and devout old women and adoring the ass. And just then the ugliest man began to gurgle and snort as if something inexpressible wanted to get out of him; but when he really found words, behold, it was a pious strange litany to glorify the adored and censed ass." The litany begins

> Amen! And praise and honor and wisdom and thanks and glory and strength be to our god, from everlasting to everlasting!
> But the ass brayed: Yea-Yuh.
> He carries our burden, he took upon himself the form of a servant, he is patient of heart and never says No; and whoever loves his God, chastises him.
> But the ass brayed: Yea-Yuh.
> He does not speak, except he always says Yea to the world he created: thus he praises his world. It is his cleverness that does not speak: thus he is rarely found to be wrong.
> But the ass brayed: Yea-Yuh. (Z:4 "The Awakening")

The Ugliest Man's litany follows the medieval model by including braying, censing, and the song praising the ass's strength and its satisfaction in food (it does not "despise food" [Z:4 "The Awakening"]). Later in the text, reports of the ass dancing are mentioned. The ass's hee-haw, rendered "I-A" in Nietzsche's German, sounds like "ja," the affirmative interjection. In effect, Nietzsche's ass says "Amen," as the medieval "Song of the Ass" urges, for "Amen" is the affirmative expletive "so be it."

The Ass Festival got its name not only from the hymn and the foolish behavior associated with it but also from the role played by an ass of the more literal sort. The feast involved a procession to the church that hosted it, often a feast including an ass. Chambers describes the "amazing account of the Beauvais ceremony" of the twelfth century described in the glossary of Ducange as revised by later editors.

> A pretty girl, with a child in her arms, was set upon an ass, to represent the Flight into Egypt. There was a procession from the cathedral to the church of St. Stephen. The ass and its riders were stationed on the gospel side of the altar. A solemn mass was sung, in which the *Introit*, *Kyrie*, *Gloria* and *Credo* ended with a bray. To crown all, the rubrics direct that the celebrant, instead of saying *Ite*, *missa est*, shall bray three times [*ter hinhannabit*] and that the people shall respond in similar fashion. At this ceremony also the "Prose of the Ass" was used, and the version preserved in the *Glossary* is longer and more ludicrous than that of either the Sens or the Beauvais *Officium*.[17]

Although the details of the celebrations varied, the ass was a common partic-
ipant. Chambers summarizes the account of the feast's celebration at Châ-
lons-sur-Marne in 1570:

> [T]he chapter provided a banquet on a theatre in front of the great porch. To this
> the 'bishop of Fools' was conducted in procession from the *maîtrise des fous*, with
> bells and music upon a gaily trapped ass. He was then vested in cope, mitre, pecto-
> ral cross, gloves, and crozier, and enjoyed a banquet with the canons who formed
> his "household." Meanwhile some of the inferior clergy entered the cathedral, sang
> gibberish, grimaced and made contortions. After the banquet, Vespers were precip-
> itately sung, followed by a *motet*. Then came a musical cavalcade round the cathe-
> dral and through the streets. A game of *la paume* took place in the market; then
> dancing and further cavalcades. Finally a band gathered before the cathedral,
> howled and clanged kettles and saucepans, while the bells were rung and the clergy
> appeared in grotesque costumes.[18]

The ass involved in such processions was not inevitably admitted into the
church. However, Chambers cites a number of reports that place the ass
inside, and he observes that the braying typical of these festivals already
brought the ass into church by making its cry a part of the service itself.[19]
Again, Nietzsche's version of the Ass Festival, with the ass processing to Zarathustra's inner sanctum and braying in response to the ugliest man's litany,
resembles its historical antecedents.

Not surprisingly, Church authorities were dubious of the Ass Festival.
Complaints by the papal legate in France to the bishop of Paris resulted in
an order for the reform of the ceremony as practiced at the Paris Cathedral
of Notre-Dame. Chambers and Gilhus both cite at length a letter addressed
in 1445 from the Theological Faculty of Paris to the French bishops and
chapters. It itemizes the offenses of participants in the Ass Festival and
reproves participants for their abominable behavior, which, the letter claims,
preserve the pagan traditions of Janus. These practices, it argues, are not
harmless relaxation but the consequence of original sin.[20]

Perhaps the most startling feature of these festivals in retrospect is the
significant participation of the clergy themselves. Those clergy who defended
the feast had argued prior to the Theological Faculty letter that "foolishness,
which is our second nature and seems to be inherent in man, might freely
spend itself at least once a year. Wine barrels burst if from time to time we
do not open them and let in some air."[21] In many parts of France, the history
of the feast involves the authorities making intermittent efforts to reform or

eliminate the festival, surrounded by periods in which the feast was celebrated with enthusiasm and spontaneity.

Several features of the historical Ass Festival might have recommended
themselves to Nietzsche. First, the "burlesque of the sacred and tedious ceremonies" that Chambers describes might well have struck a chord with Nietzsche who, as the son and grandson of Lutheran ministers, was also quite
painfully familiar with such services. He seems to enjoy lampooning these
ceremonies in the Ugliest Man's litany. At the same time, he is able to mock
the Catholic ecclesia, large portions of which engaged in a festival on the
order of what Nietzsche presents in "The Awakening."

Second, Nietzsche would likely have been pleased by the Ass Festival's
impact of undercutting the authority of the Church hierarchy. The medieval
festival deliberately reversed the status of the clergy, raising the sub-deacons
above the bishops. As some of the Church hierarchy seemed to recognize,
this pretended undermining of clerical authority *actually* undermined it. In
many of his works, Nietzsche analyzes Christian doctrine as formulated to
establish and reinforce the power of priests. The Ass Festival is a celebration
that reverses clerical power, and Nietzsche, who rejected the Christian
Church in both Catholic and Protestant forms, would have applauded this.
The fact that the participating clergy themselves were instrumental in
destroying clerical power makes the Ass Festival also a symbol of what Nietzsche sees as pervasive self-destructive tendencies in Christianity, which ultimately led to the death of God.[22] The fact that the litany in "The
Awakening" is sung by the Ugliest Man, the higher man who allegedly killed
God, further supports this connection.

Third, the reversals involved in the Ass Festival, which Gilhus and T. K.
Seung both emphasize, revalue values along lines that Nietzsche endorses.
Of particular interest for Nietzsche, the Ass Festival rejects the orthodox
Christian view that one must suppress the body and the senses. Seung also
stresses that the Ass Festival rejected the aspiration of trying to become like
God in favor of the goal of being healthy animals.[23]

Fourth, the festival character of the historical feast is something that
Nietzsche would appreciate, which is indicated by his portrayal of Zarathustra praising festival. Zarathustra recovers from his shock and fury at the
higher men and claims that convalescents need festivals. This suggests that
Nietzsche may have seen the participants in the historical Ass Festival as
being convalescents, recovering from Christianity's denigration of the body
and earthly joy. Zarathustra suggests that the Ass Festival is a creative expression of the higher men's spiritual state.[24]

Most important, the higher men's Ass Festival is comical. In the first section of *The Gay Science*, Nietzsche argues that the somber teachers of morality, who insist that some things are too sacred to be laughed at, are always eventually overcome by waves of laughter. The history of religion involves a pendulum swing between the poles of tragic seriousness and comic lightheartedness, and Nietzsche suggests that the latter perspective is the more profound (see GS 1). "The Ass Festival" describes Zarathustra's own spiritual transformation from angry seriousness to light-hearted amusement at the higher men's antics. This shift reflects the religious trajectory that Nietzsche sees as desirable for contemporary Western humanity, and Zarathustra's experience serves as a demonstration of how it can be achieved.

This last point suggests that the ass is an important symbol in Zarathustra's spiritual transformation, as well as in the convalescent stage of the higher men. In order to see how the ass plays this role, we will first observe the interaction that Zarathustra has with the ass-worshipping higher men and then consider the parallels between *Zarathustra* and Apuleius's *The Golden Ass* and their implications. Finally, we will conclude that along with its other symbolic roles, the ass represents both a crucial stage in spiritual development and the folly that is eventually left behind in spiritual maturation.

"The Awakening" and "The Ass Festival"

I am fairly certain that I had read Part 4 of *Zarathustra* numerous times before I fully realized that "The Ass Festival" is not the section in which the higher men worship the ass. That section is called "The Awakening." This title alerts us to Nietzsche's satire of one of the religious movements of his era, one with which he had personal acquaintance. "The Awakening" (*Die Erweckung*) was a term for the Lutheran revivalist movement that attracted both of Nietzsche's parents, as well as Friedrich Wilhelm, the king for whom Nietzsche was named.[25] Carol Diethe describes this movement, which she also calls "neo-Pietism," as involving its adherents in ostentatious confessions of their sins and public conversion. Those in the movement referred to themselves almost obsessively as "children," and they were conservative and chauvinistically nationalistic.[26] Their religious and political tendencies are among those that Nietzsche attacks most stridently. Nietzsche's hostility toward the faith of his childhood is reflected in his titling the section in which the higher men grovel "The Awakening." The reference to the neo-Pietist movement is also evident in the following section, "The Ass Festival," where Zarathustra himself uses the image of the "child" in his remarks to the highest men.

> "How all your hearts wriggled with pleasure and malice that at last you had become again as little children, that is, pious; that at last you did again what children do, namely, prayed, folded your hands, and said, "Dear God!" But now leave *this* nursery, my own cave, where all childishness is at home today! . . . .
>
> "To be sure: except ye become as little children, ye shall not enter into that kingdom of heaven. (And Zarathustra pointed upward with his hands.) But we have no wish whatever to enter into the kingdom of heaven: we have become men—*so we want the [kingdom of the] earth*." (Z:4 "The Ass Festival")

"The Ass Festival," however, does not begin with Zarathustra speaking so calmly. It opens with Zarathustra braying like one of the medieval sub-deacons. "At this point of the litany Zarathustra could no longer control himself and himself shouted Yea-Yuh, even louder than the ass, and he jumped right into the middle of his guests, who had gone mad" (Z:4 "The Ass Festival"). Zarathustra proceeds to chide the higher men, asking how they could have sunk to the point of worshipping an ass. He confronts many of them individually, asking the Retired Pope, for example, "How do you reconcile this with yourself that you adore an ass in this way as a god?" The Retired Pope answers in a way that might have suited the defenders of the medieval Ass Festival: "Better to adore God in this form than in no form at all," the Retired Pope says in his reply. "He who said, 'God is a spirit,' took the biggest step and leap to disbelief that anybody has yet taken on earth."[27]

Several of the higher men make remarks that direct the accusations back at Zarathustra himself. For example, the shadow says in response to Zarathustra's queries of him, "in the case of gods *death* is always a mere prejudice." If Zarathustra is demanding that the higher men adhere to his doctrine that God has died, he himself is asserting a dogmatic prejudice. The higher man identified as "the Conscientious in Spirit" raises the possibility that Zarathustra himself could be an ass. "And whoever has too much spirit might well grow foolishly fond of stupidity and folly itself. Think about yourself, O Zarathustra! You yourself—verily, overabundance and wisdom could easily turn you too into an ass. Is not the perfect sage fond of walking on the most crooked ways? The evidence shows this, O Zarathustra—and *you* are the evidence." The Ugliest Man claims that he, as the murderer of God, is in a better position than Zarathustra to know how dead God is or is not. He also reminds Zarathustra of his own doctrine that laughter kills more decisively than outrage and seriousness.

[The] ugliest man . . . still lay on the ground, . . . raising his arm toward the ass (for he was offering him wine to drink). . . .

"O Zarathustra," replied the ugliest man, "you are a rogue! Whether that one still lives or lives again or is thoroughly dead—which of the two of us knows that best? I ask you. But one thing I do know; it was from you yourself that I learned it once, O Zarathustra. whoever would kill most thoroughly, *laughs.*

"'Not by wrath does one kill, but by laughter'—thus you once spoke." (Z:4 "The Ass Festival")

Salaquarda acknowledges that Nietzsche sometimes presents himself as an ass, but he does not appear to take seriously the suggestion, made in different ways by the Conscientious of Spirit and the Ugliest Man, that Zarathustra might be an ass.[28] In fact, Salaquarda describes Zarathustra and the ass as opposites, with the higher man standing at the midpoint between the two.[29] However, it seems that Zarathustra recognizes his own foolishness by the end of "The Ass Festival." The section concludes with Zarathustra reconsidering the Ass Festival and its significance. He tells the higher men,

Verily, you have all blossomed; it seems to me such flowers as you are require new festivals, a little brave nonsense, some divine service and ass festival, some old gay fool of a Zarathustra, a roaring wind that blows your souls bright.

Do not forget this night and this ass festival, you higher men. *This* you invented when you were with me and I take that for a good sign: such things are invented only by convalescents.

And when you celebrate it again, this ass festival, do it for your own sakes, and also do it for my sake. And in remembrance of *me.* (Z:4 "The Ass Festival")[30]

T. K. Seung takes this parody of Jesus' words at the Last Supper to demonstrate that Zarathustra is seriously consecrating the Ass Festival and instituting a Nature-God religion. He points out that parody originally meant only "imitation," that "parody masses" were a secular version of the Mass composed by many serious composers. Satire and derision were not a part of such parody, and Seung argues that Nietzsche's parody is actually "solemn and reverent."[31] I think Nietzsche is satirizing Christian practices in "The Ass Festival," but I agree with Seung that Zarathustra's praise of the higher men's awakening has serious significance, too. Nietzsche elsewhere praises the externalization of spiritual states through festivals, and the higher men's renewal of the state of mind that provoked the historical Ass Festival represents a stage of spiritual evolution that Nietzsche can positively value.[32]

Still, Nietzsche's allusion to the consecration has a comic element even beyond satire directed at the Christian Church. Zarathustra encourages the higher men to celebrate the ass festival again and says that they should also remember him when they do so. Nietzsche leaves ambiguous what it is about Zarathustra that the higher men should remember. Should they remember Zarathustra's maxim that one who kills thoroughly laughs? Should they remember that even Zarathustra becomes so wedded to his own ideas that he can behave like an ass as a consequence?[33] I think the latter is an idea that *Zarathustra*'s reader, at least, should remember. The book as a whole narrates Zarathustra's spiritual journey, and Zarathustra's failures and follies are important elements of this story.

The end of Zarathustra's evening with the higher men, recounted in "The Drunken Song," draws attention to the ass once again. Taking the tone of a report in the New Testament or a legendary account, it concludes by rejecting the posture of dogmatic authority, the posture that Zarathustra himself abandons in the course of "The Ass Festival."

> But the old soothsayer was dancing with joy; and even if, as some chroniclers think, he was full of sweet wine, he was certainly still fuller of the sweetness of life and he had renounced all weariness. There are even some who relate that the ass danced too, and that it had not been for nothing that the ugliest man had given him wine to drink before. Now it may have been so or otherwise; and if the ass really did not dance that night, yet greater and stranger wonders occurred than the dancing of an ass would have been. In short, as the proverb of Zarathustra says: "What does it matter?" (Z:4 "The Drunken Song")

The Philosophical History of the Ass

I have argued elsewhere that Part 4 of *Thus Spoke Zarathustra* systematically alludes to Apuleius's *The Golden Ass*, a work of the second century BCE.[34] Apuleius based his work on an old Greek story that survived incompletely, the basis for Lucian's "The Story of the Ass," as well. The basic plot of both of these works is quite similar until the end of the story. Some of the details of Apuleius's version in particular, however, recommend considering it to be Nietzsche's model. The story is told by a narrator, Lucius, who takes a trip to Thessaly and stays at the home of a wealthy friend. The friend's wife is reputed to be a powerful witch, and Lucius is curious. With multiple motives, he becomes the lover of the wife's maid, and he describes some of their encounters in considerable detail. However, Lucius does not lose sight of his desire to see her mistress performing a spell. He persuades the maid to let him observe her secretly, and he watches while the witch rubs an ointment on herself and turns into a bird. Fascinated, Lucius tells the maid to rub the same ointment on him so that he can see the world from a bird's viewpoint.

The maid complies, but she grabs the wrong jar. Lucius is not transformed into a bird but into an ass instead. Fortunately, the maid knows the antidote to this spell. If Lucius eats roses, she tells him, he will become a man again. Alas, this is not so easily accomplished. Bandits break into the house, stealing the ass. Lucius suffers through a series of ordeals with miscellaneous owners, most of whom mistreat him. Throughout his adventures, Lucius retains the mind of a man, but as an ass he is allowed glimpses of human beings that he would never have been allowed while in human form. He thereby gains a detached but detailed perspective on human affairs, although not precisely the perspective he had sought.

Ultimately, Lucius is restored to manhood. In Apuleius's story, he has been sold to two brothers who cater for their master. Lucius is therefore often in proximity to delicious food. Being a gourmand if not a glutton, he succumbs to temptation one day when delicacies are in his vicinity, only to be discovered by the brothers. Unlike his previous owners, the brothers do not beat him. Instead, they are amused at the idea of an ass with a refined palate. They give him wine to go with his delectable meal, and they bring their master to see the sight of him dining. The master finds this so hilarious that he decides to have Lucius trained as a performing animal. Lucius has no difficulty with the required stunts until the day when he is supposed to copulate with a woman who has been sentenced to death as part of a major public performance. He had learned the technique from a wanton but wealthy woman, who had been paying for his favors, but he does not want to go public with such an act. Fortunately, he is able to eat some roses before the performance occurs and he becomes a man again. In Lucian's end to the tale, the decadent woman who loved him as an ass rejecting him as a man. He nevertheless goes home and offers sacrifices to the gods. Apuleius, by contrast, has a more mystical ending. The night before the objectionable performance, Lucius receives a prophecy from Isis that rose wreaths will be carried in a procession to her the following day. The prophecy is fulfilled, and Lucius eats from one of these wreaths, becoming a man again. Subsequently, he becomes a devotee of both Isis and Osiris. Apuleius's tale also departs from Lucian's in interpolating a variety of stories that the ass overhears or sees, drawing attention to the insights that Lucius gains by virtue of his experiences as an ass.

Many comparisons can be made between the details of Apuleius's telling of the ass story and the narrative of *Zarathustra*, Part 4. The theme of pity causing disaster is common to both narratives. *The Golden Ass* begins with the story of a merchant named Aristomenes taking pity on a character named Socrates, who has become old and pitiable. The consequence of this pity is that Socrates' bad luck rubs off on the merchant. Zarathustra, similarly, has pity for the higher men, a "sin" that motivates the entirety of Part 4, which is resolved only when he overcomes pity.

Zarathustra's comment about "what gives asses wings" corresponds to the thought of Lucius the ass, while fleeing a pack of wolves, that he is like Pegasus. "It occurred to me that the famous Pegasus must have had a similar experience: the reason they called him 'the winged horse' was doubtless that he was so terrified of being bitten that he buck-jumped right up to the sky."[35] At the festival in which Lucius eats the roses, he also sees an ass that has "wings glued to its shoulders and a doddering old man seated on its rump; you would have laughed like anything at that pair, supposed to be Pegasus and Bellerophon."[36]

The ass song sung by the higher men makes reference to the fact that the ass does not "despise food," certainly a characteristic of Apuleius's ass. The Ugliest Man, like the brothers who see Lucius eating savories, gives the ass wine to drink. The reference to the ass dancing also has its precedent in *The Golden Ass*. Lucius reports, "The tale of my wonderful talents spread in all directions, so that my master became famous on my account. People said: 'Think of it! He has an ass whom he treats like a friend and invites to dinner with him. Believe it or not, that ass can wrestle, and actually dance, and understands what people say to him, and uses a language of signs!'"[37] Apuleius's ass sometimes tries to intervene in human affairs but finds he can only bray. *Zarathustra*'s ass also seems to insert itself into human discussion at times, as when it "said clearly and with evil intent, Yea-Yuh," or when its voice mingles with those of the higher men.

Most obviously, the roses that bring an end to Lucius's misadventures parallel the rose wreaths and roses that Zarathustra mentions in two of his references to asses. The previously cited passage from "On Reading and Writing" contrasts the condition of asses to the delicacy of the "rosebud, which trembles because a drop of dew lies on it." More obviously parallel to Lucius's rose garlands are the rose wreaths that Zarathustra mentions at the end of "The Higher Man" as he describes laughter as the cure for what ails the higher men.

> You higher men, the worst about you is that all of you have not learned to dance as one must dance—dancing away over yourselves! What does it matter that you

are failures? How much is still possible! So *learn* to laugh away over yourselves! Lift up your hearts, you good dancers, high, higher! And do not forget good laughter. This crown of him who laughs, this rose-wreath crown: to you, my brothers, I throw this crown. Laughter I have pronounced holy; you higher men, *learn* to laugh! (Z:4)

The extensive parallels between Nietzsche's text and *The Golden Ass* lead me to conclude that Nietzsche was deliberately alluding to the latter.[38] Even the end of *Zarathustra*, in which Zarathustra enters an apparently mystical state and then decides that the time for his "final sin" is past, resembles the mystical finale of Apuleius's account, in which Lucius leaves his ass condition behind and becomes an initiate into the Mysteries of Isis and Osiris. This final parallel offers a hint, I think, about what Nietzsche means by the allusions to *The Golden Ass*. Like Apuleius's ass, Zarathustra has gained insight through his various experiences, even those in which he has behaved foolishly. The conclusion of both narratives shows the protagonist taking insight with him but moving beyond his days as an ass. The reader may question whether Zarathustra has overcome asinine behavior entirely by the end of the book. Zarathustra returns to his work by descending from his mountain cave, and the rest is unreported. However, what he has resolved at the end of his narrative is that he will no longer consider his folly "sin." "Foolishness, *not* sin!" is Nietzsche's own formulation for the Greek view of human error, which he praises in contradistinction to the Christian interpretation of much human error as sinful.[39] One's follies do not render one guilty; they only make one laughable. By the end of Part 4, this is what Zarathustra has come to understand.

Conclusion

As others have suggested, the ass serves Nietzsche as a symbol of dogmatism and stupidity and also as a positive symbol of the earth, nature, and humanity's animal character. But it is important that the ass also represents laughable folly, both as foolish behavior and as an essential stage in spiritual maturation. In this role, the ass is not merely an image for what Nietzsche rejects. The ass also serves as a symbol of transformation. As asses, Lucius and Zarathustra remain laughable until their metamorphosis is complete. Nevertheless, the asinine stage itself has value, both for the insights gained through it and for the comedy it presents to observers.

The moment of transition, Zarathustra suggests, is the point at which one learns to laugh at oneself. Laughing at oneself, one can recognize the comic aspects of being an ass, even though the detachment from oneself this requires reveals that one is already moving beyond the ass stage. Yet it is through being an ass that one learns to laugh, according to Nietzsche, and laughter redeems our "sin." The only redemption from sin is to move beyond the concept of "sin" itself, restoring to our foolishness the innocence of genuine folly. Innocent foolishness is the condition of the ass. Nietzsche implies that if, as alleged, the early Christians did worship their god through the form of an ass, they would only have been half wrong. The ass, as the symbol of a crucial stage in spiritual development, is ultimately our redeemer.

Notes

1. I rely upon Kaufmann's translations of BGE, EH, GS, and Z; and Hollingdale's translation of TI.

2. Jörg Salaquarda interprets the wine as "Christian ideals," comparable to wine in their negative effects. See Jörg Salaquarda, "Zarathustra und der Esel: Eine Untersuchung der Rolle des Esel im Vierten Teil von Nietzsches 'Also sprach Zarathustra,'" Theological Viatorum 11 (1973): 203.

3. Nietzsche may be following Martin Luther in such usage. See for example Martin Luther, Against Hanswurst, trans. Eric W. Gritsch, in Luther's Works, 55 vols., ed. Jaroslav Pelikan and Helmut T. Lehmann (Philadelphia: Concordia Publishing House, 1955–1986), vol. 41, Church and Ministry III, ed. Eric W. Gritsch, 212; D. Martin Luthers Werke: Kritische Gesamtausgabe (Weimar, 1883–1990), 51, 510, 23–24.

4. Nietzsche frequently makes reference to the fact that he has unusually small ears, typically suggesting that they are an indication of his own refinement. See "Klage der Ariadne" (KSA 6:401). Salaquarda makes much of Nietzsche's self-characterization as "the anti-ass par excellence." See Salaquarda, "Zarathustra und der Esel," 194f., 199, 205.

5. See Nuccio Ordine, Giordano Bruno and the Philosophy of the Ass, trans. Henryk Baranski in collaboration with Arielle Saiber (New Haven, Conn.: Yale University Press, 1996), 11.

6. Friedrich Nietzsche, Sämtliche Briefe, Kritische Studienausgabe, ed. Giogio Colli and Mazzino Montinari (Berlin: De Gruyter, 1975), hereafter cited as "SB-KSA," 6, #429, 390. My thanks to Roger Gathmann for drawing my attention to this passage.

7. See Salaquarda, "Zarathustra und der Esel," 182. Salaquarda refers to G. Naumann, Zarathustra-Commentar (Leipzig, 1899–1901), IV, 24 and 122.

8. Ordine observes that the ass's long ears have been a traditional basis for associating it with wisdom, in that the ass's ears enable it to hear over long distances. See Ordine, Giordano Bruno and the Philosophy of the Ass, 13f.

9. See Salaquarda, "Zarathustra und der Esel," 191–194. See also BGE 239.

10. See E. Louis Backman, *Religious Dances in the Christian Church and in Popular Medicine*, trans. E. Classen (London: George Allen and Unwin, 1952), 54.

11. My thanks to Neil Sinhababu, who first directed my attention to the history of the Ass Festival and some of the literature about it, and to T. K. Seung, who provided me with further information about the practices surrounding the Ass Festival.

12. See Letter to Carl von Gersdorff in Ostrichen, 9 Mai 1885, *SB-KSA* 7, #601, 51.

13. Salaquarda, "Zarathustra und der Esel," 197–198.

14. E. K. Chambers points out that John Huss describes it in the early fifteenth century, remorseful that he himself had participated in his youth. See E. K. Chambers, *The Mediaeval Stage* (Oxford: Oxford University Press, 1903), vol. 1, 320–321. See also Backman, *Religious Dances in the Christian Church*, 51 and 53.

15. Ingvild Salid Gilhus, "Carnival in Religion. The Feast of Fools in France," *Numen* 37, no. 1 (June 1990): 26. Gilhus has compiled a fascinating array of information about the Ass Festival and analyzed its significance in the context of Catholicism. The Ass Festival was also known as the feast of the sub-deacons.

16. Backman, *Religious Dances in the Christian Church*, 54. Backman and Curtis Clark have made English translations of the shorter version of the hymn, and Gilhus translates some stanzas from the longer version. See Gilhus, "Carnival in Religion," 40.

17. Chambers, *The Mediaeval Stage*, 287.

18. Chambers, *The Mediaeval Stage*, 305.

19. Chambers, *The Mediaeval Stage*, 331.

20. Book 4 of *Zarathustra* is framed by references to Zarathustra's "final" sin, identified as his pity for the higher men. This reference to a "final sin" contrasts with the conception of original sin, to which the Theological Faculty appeal in their letter.

21. Gilhus, "Carnival in Religion," 31f., quoted from Mikhail Bakhtin, *Rabelais and His World* (Cambridge, Mass.: Cambridge University Press, 1968), 75.

22. See GS 122, 125, 357, and 377.

23. T. K. Seung, *Nietzsche's Zarathustra: An Epic of Self Love* (forthcoming), ms. 308.

24. The creativity that Zarathustra praises in his higher men's ass festival seems to have been incited by the historical feast as well. Chambers reports on several local innovations. In Tournai, where the feast had been banned for several years, the bourgeois "broke out" in 1498 and kidnapped a chaplain, subjecting him to "baptism," cabaret entertainment, and other mischievous treatment. And in Antibes various antics occurred in the church of the Franciscans until at least 1645.

25. Nietzsche was born on the king's birthday, and his parents named him after the monarch.

26. See Carol Diethe, *Nietzsche's Sister and the Will to Power: A Biography of Elisabeth Förster-Nietzsche* (Champaign: University of Illinois Press, 2002), chap. 1. See also Carol Diethe, *Nietzsche's Women: Beyond the Whip* (Berlin: Walter de Gruyter, 1996), 16 and 21.

27. Gilhus ("Carnival in Religion," 8f.) and others observe that early Christians were reported to have worshipped an ass, an ass's head, or a man with the head of an ass by

Gnostic and pagan sources of 300 CE and earlier. See also Backman, *Rabelais and His World*, 63, who points out that some pagans called the early Christians *asinarii* (ass drivers).

28. Salaquarda, "Zarathustra und der Esel," 196.

29. Salaquarda, "Zarathustra und der Esel," 205.

30. Seung interprets the positive functions of *Zarathustra*'s ass festival as being both the convalescence of the higher men from their earlier despair and their return to reverence. (See Seung, ms. 309.) The latter might seem a dubious function, since "Zarathustra the godless" hardly seems bent on restoring reverence. However, Seung makes a convincing case that Zarathustra himself reveres nature. He sees Zarathustra's goal, in line with Feuerbach's, as the return from a supernatural to a natural religion.

31. Seung, ms. 305f.

32. In GS 89, Nietzsche refers to festivals as a "higher art" than other arts. "Formerly, all works of art adorned the great festival road of humanity to commemorate high and happy moments." Compare GS 144 and see GS 125 and 181.

33. This interpretation of Zarathustra as himself behaving like an ass lends support to Salaquarda's interpretation that the ass symbolizes higher humanity's worship of its own rigidly held convictions, even if Salaquarda does not consider Zarathustra to be himself among the asses. See Salaquarda, "Zarathustra und der Esel," 204.

34. Apuleius, *The Transformations of Lucius, Otherwise Known as the Golden Ass*, trans. Robert Graves (New York: Farrar, Straus and Giroux, 1951), hereafter cited as GA.

35. See GA 182.

36. GA 268.

37. GA 246.

38. For further discussion of the relationship between this work and *Thus Spoke Zarathustra*, see Kathleen Higgins, "*Zarathustra* IV and Apuleius: Who Is *Zarathustra*'s Ass?" *International Studies in Philosophy* 20, no. 3 (1988): 29–53. See also Kathleen Marie Higgins, *Nietzsche's* Zarathustra (Philadelphia: Temple University Press, 1987), 206–232.

39. Compare GM II:23.

PART THREE

BEASTS OF PREY

LION

Zarathustra's Laughing Lions

Paul S. Loeb

Ever since Walter Kaufmann's denazification of Nietzsche's writings, readers of the *Genealogy of Morals* have been routinely reminded that his notorious image of the blond beast (GM I:11, II:16–17) alludes back to his image of the lion in *Thus Spoke Zarathustra*. This reminder helps us to disassociate Nietzsche's *Genealogy* image from his seemingly nostalgic review of past Germanic barbarism and to associate it instead with his abstract and poetic symbolism of the spirit's transformation from camel to lion to child (Z:1 "On The Three Transformations").[1] It is true that some of the controversial aspects of the *Genealogy*'s blond-beast image are to be found as well in *Zarathustra*'s lion image: for example, predation, cruelty, conquest, and destruction. But this would only seem to show that we ought to be more careful when interpreting the blond-beast image. Although Nietzsche's genealogy recalls the barbaric origins of all our culture, this is not to say that he thinks we should, or ever could, return to those origins. Instead, as his future-oriented *Zarathustra* suggests, Nietzsche proposes that we now move forward into a kind of spiritual self-overcoming: our spirit must become a leonine predator and destroyer, not of others, but of all the ascetic traditions and values within us that burden our spirit like a camel. Only then, when our spirit has seized its freedom with a lion's ferocity, shall it become childlike and able to create new values.

I agree that Nietzsche intended his *Genealogy* image of the blond beast to allude back to his *Zarathustra* image of the lion and that we should therefore look to *Zarathustra* when interpreting the former.[2] But I do not think we can begin and end our investigation with Zarathustra's first, and still highly abstract, speech on the three transformations of the spirit. For the figure of the lion introduced in this speech winds its way through the entirety of Nietzsche's book until its final and crucial appearance in the last few pages. Here we are told that Zarathustra has a prolonged vision of a powerful yellow lion with a thick warm mane of hair and a gentle roar. In an allusion back to Nietzsche's famous first image of jungle cats—the tigers and panthers that lie down fawning at the feet of the Dionysian man (*BT* 20)—this lion lies at Zarathustra's feet, lovingly presses his head against his knee, and will not leave him. As in Homer's tale of Odysseus's return home, the lion behaves like a dog that has found his old master again. Fulfilling Zarathustra's announcement that his final descent must wait until he has received the sign of the laughing lion with the flock of doves (Z:3 "On Old and New Tablets" 1), the lion literally laughs in wonder every time one of the newly arrived flocking doves glides across his nose.[3] Although Zarathustra first recognized this lion in the dark through touching and hearing him, he then sees him clearly in the light of dawn and realizes that his sign has arrived. This means that he is now ripe and that he will soon be reunited with the beloved disciples for whom he has longingly been waiting on his mountain (Z:4 "The Greeting"). At this thought, Zarathustra is so overcome with emotion that he begins crying tears, which the shyly growling lion licks off his hands. But upon hearing the higher men approach, the strong lion starts violently, turns away from Zarathustra, and leaps up to the cave roaring fiercely until the frightened higher men flee back inside.

It is surely significant that Nietzsche chooses to conclude his entire book—the book he considered his best and most important—with this extremely vivid and concrete articulation of the schematic lion figure introduced in Zarathustra's first speech. This final emphasis is narratively complex because it includes all at once Zarathustra, his work, and the disciples he calls his children. Most obviously, Nietzsche aims to show us the spiritual transformation within Zarathustra himself. After meditating upon his vision, and like the lion within this vision, the newly hardened and bronze-faced Zarathustra leaps up and shouts out his determination to stop empathizing with the higher men he has been shepherding (finding, gathering, feeding) throughout Part 4.[4] Strong as a lion, and indifferent to his own happiness, Zarathustra cries out his renewed dedication to his arriving children and to the work he must now complete in his dawning great-noon day. This work, we know, consists partly in the lion-spirited assault on the great value-dragon that he had anticipated in his very first speech.[5] And these children, we know, are the disciples he had said would accompany him in this assault and hence be regarded as lion-like predatory robbers and destroyers (Z:P 9). Indeed, since Zarathustra had earlier called his children "laughing lions" (Z: 4 "The Greeting"), and since he takes his vision to be a sign of his childrens' proximity, we may infer that Nietzsche's concluding emphasis on the image of the laughing lion is meant to draw our attention as well to Zarathustra's returning disciples. Like the lion in his vision, these disciples will have grown powerful in their time away but no less devoted and loving to their former master.[6] Also like the lion in his vision, they will spurn and terrify the higher men whom they far surpass.

The significance of Nietzsche's final emphasis on his lion-image is obscured, however, by the notorious inconclusiveness of the book's conclusion. As Robert Gooding-Williams has recently argued, for example, it would seem that Nietzsche ends his book without ever depicting Zarathustra's culminating revaluation of all values. This is because Zarathustra had said he would accomplish this task with his disciples, and yet the book ends without their having arrived:

> Through most of Part Four, Zarathustra anticipates the appearance of the "children" and "right men" in whose company he hopes to become a creator of new values. [. . .] Zarathustra ends, of course, without the appearance of Zarathustra's children (they are said to be "near") and without the creation of new values. The book's conclusion shows Zarathustra believing that a creation of new values is imminent, yet hardly insists that his modernist optimism is well founded. And why should it? Having explained how new values could be created, Zarathustra ultimately leaves unresolved the question of whether what could be will be in the future.[7]

Against this interpretation, however, I would cite Nietzsche's claim that his book already expresses a vision of some stronger future age in which some younger and healthier type, a Zarathustra type, will have the strength to say and do what he himself, belonging to a weak and decadent age, could never say and do (GM II:24–25). So Thus Spoke Zarathustra must itself be the place in which Nietzsche shares with us his prophetic vision of the actual revaluation of all values.

In addition, I have argued elsewhere that Nietzsche designed Part 4 of
Zarathustra as a satyr play that *chronologically precedes* the ending of Part 3.[8]
In that argument, I pointed out that the theme of Zarathustra waiting for his
sign at the start of Part 4 (Z:4 "The Honey Sacrifice") is a direct continuation of the waiting theme at the start of the Part 3 chapter entitled "On Old
and New Tablets." As the narrator notes at the start of Part 4, Zarathustra
has been waiting alone on the mountains for so many years that his hair has
turned white. Indeed, one of the kings in Part 4 recalls his fear that Zarathustra might have died in the metaphorical sense that solitude had swallowed
him up. Nevertheless, the king observes: "Now it happens that solitude itself
becomes brittle and shatters, like a tomb that shatters and can no longer
hold its dead. Everywhere one sees the resurrected" (Z:4 "The Greeting";
cf. also Z:2 "The Tomb Song"). Metaphorically, then, Nietzsche resurrects
Zarathustra for the higher men that he meets throughout the satyr play of
Part 4 and for the disciples whose arrival is imminent at the end of Part 4.
Following the Gospels' account of Jesus's resurrection, Nietzsche depicts the
higher mens' search for signs of Zarathustra, followed by their initial failure
to recognize him and their ensuing shock and adoration. However, Zarathustra has not been waiting alone on the mountains for the higher men and he
will not be going down for the last time with them (Z:4 "The Greeting").
Instead, like Jesus, he has been waiting to appear to the disciples whom he
last saw at the very end of Part 2 (Z:2 "The Stillest Hour"). These disciples,
we find out at the end of Part 4, have also come up the mountain to find
their departed teacher, who has been entombed in the years-long solitude
that began at the start of Part 3's "Tablets" chapter. Nietzsche thus concludes his book with the image of a glowing Zarathustra at last resurrected
from his long wait and departing to meet his disciples in the dawn of his
great-noon day. Following the Gospels, this third-day resurrection ushers in
the day of final judgment and the beginning of a new thousand-year kingdom
(Z:3 "On the Three Evil Things" 2; Z:4 "The Honey Sacrifice").

Thus, at the end of Part 4, Zarathustra finally becomes ripe (which he
wasn't quite yet at the start of Part 4), finally gains a lion's commanding
strength and voice (through overcoming his compassion for the higher men),
and at last sets out to complete his still-unfinished work.[9] But at the start of
the Part 3 chapter entitled "The Convalescent," Zarathustra has *already*
become ripe enough to bring forth his long-ripe most abysmal thought (Z:2
"The Stillest Hour"), and he *already* possesses the lion's strength and voice
needed to command awake his most abysmal thought (Z:2 "The Stillest
Hour"; Z:3 "On Involuntary Bliss"). Moreover, in the second section of this

same chapter, he is resting like God on the seventh day after having *already* completed his creative work. I therefore concluded that all the dramatic and philosophical events narrated in Part 4 (though not the narration itself) are chronologically interposed between the events related at the start of the "Tablets" chapter, on the one hand, and the events related at the start of the "Convalescent" chapter, on the other.[10]

If I am right about this alternative analysis of the structure of *Zarathustra*, then it would follow that Gooding-Williams and others have conflated Nietzsche's *artistic* ending in the concluding chapter of Part 4 with his *chronological* ending in the concluding chapters of Part 3. And among the latter chapters, the one entitled "On Old and New Tablets" stands out right away in the context of our present discussion. For this chapter, the longest one in the book and the one that Nietzsche later called the "decisive" (*entscheidende*) chapter of his book (*EH* "Books" Z:4), depicts Zarathustra as a Moses-like figure who is writing new values and commanding the destruction of the old values. So perhaps this chapter is where we should be looking for the arrival of Zarathustra's laughing lions and their collaborative revaluation of all values. Perhaps this chapter contains the key to understanding Nietzsche's seemingly unresolved final image of the laughing lion. [11]

To be sure, there is no narrative suggestion in the "Tablets" chapter that this is the case. Indeed, except for the ubiquitous signature line "Thus Spoke Zarathustra," there is no narrative voice in this chapter at all. Instead, we hear only Zarathustra's voice, and he begins by saying that he is talking to himself and telling himself to himself. Thus, unlike other chapters (even those in which we hear Zarathustra speak to the sun or to his animals), the long "Tablets" chapter would appear to contain an extended monologue in which Zarathustra simply reviews and summarizes his career and previous speeches.[12] This is why Gooding-Williams writes about this chapter in particular: "As he speaks, however, Zarathustra creates nothing. Where Goethe's Prometheus defiantly creates (forms) men, even as he sits, Zarathustra has deferred his creative action (his going among men with 'new tablets' of values) to an unspecified time in the future ('my hour') that he presently awaits."[13]

Let us suppose, however, as Gooding-Williams convincingly argues, that Nietzsche is here alluding to Goethe's Prometheus. Just as Zarathustra says at the start of the "Tablets" chapter, "Here I sit" (*Hier sitz ich*), so too Goethe's concluding stanza begins with this phrase: "Here I sit [*Hier sitz ich*], forming men / in my own image, / a race to be like me, / to suffer, to weep, / to delight and rejoice, / and to defy you, / as I do."[14] To follow through on this allusion, rather than depart from it, Nietzsche needs to depict Zarathustra's formation of men in his own image, his formation of a race that will be like him. But these men, this race (or at least the ancestors of this race), consist of his disciples (Z:4 "The Greeting"). And this formation is something Zarathustra has worked on each of the times he has been with his disciples, first in Part 1 and next in Part 2. So it is precisely here, in the "Tablets" chapter, that Nietzsche should depict the second reunion and final formation that was promised at the end of Part 1 (Z:2 "On the Gift-Giving Virtue" 3) and that has so far been missing in Part 3. He would thus have artfully constructed his book as a tripartite interaction between Zarathustra and his beloved disciples (leaving the contrasting interaction with the inadequate higher men for the satyr play of Part 4).

Although there is no narrative depiction of this second reunion, and although only Zarathustra speaks in this chapter, I think there is evidence of such a reunion within Zarathustra's speech itself. To begin with, Zarathustra's review of his career and teachings lasts only through the first three sections of the chapter. Toward the end of the third section, Zarathustra reiterates his introductory waiting theme, thus indicating that he has finished telling himself to himself. In the next section, he turns instead to display one of his new tablets of values and asks: "[B]ut where are my brothers, to carry it with me to the valley and into hearts of flesh?" Here Zarathustra refers to his Prologue's realization that he must seek fellow creators who will inscribe new values on new tablets (Z:P 9). This question lets us know that Zarathustra is no longer just telling himself to himself but is instead looking around expectantly for the companions who are supposed to hear this speech in particular. And this expectation in turn sets up the continuation of his speech in section 6, where all of a sudden we hear Zarathustra address his brothers directly and explicitly: "Oh my brothers, whoever is a first-born [Erstling] is always sacrificed. Now, however, we are first-borns." Following this shift, and except for that part in section 30 addressed to his own will, the rest of Zarathustra's speech is addressed entirely to these same brothers (also called "friends"). The reason, Nietzsche's story suggests, is that Zarathustra has now been rejoined by the disciples whose arrival was imminent at the end of the chronologically preceding Part 4.

On this reading, then, Nietzsche ingeniously threads a narrative line into Zarathustra's speech itself—or, more precisely, into that speech's expectation and awareness of its intended audience. But commentators have so far not paid much attention to the hermeneutic question of audience in the "Tablets" chapter. Those who have discussed it, however, all agree that Zarathustra is here speaking *in solitude* to a merely *imagined* audience of brothers that will be arriving sometime in the *future*. Thus, Laurence Lampert writes that, by contrast with the comparable speech in Part 4 ("On the Higher Humans") that is addressed to "actual men who, though superior, are not the longed-for followers," the speech here is addressed to "true but imaginary followers" and to "an imaginary audience of brothers to whom will fall the tasks of the new nobility."[15] And Thomas Pangle observes that Zarathustra is in this chapter "speaking in utter privacy, and addressing only imagined future 'brothers.'"[16] Finally, Anke Bennholdt-Thomsen, whose study is devoted to the question of Zarathustra's audiences, characterizes the speech in this chapter as one of the monologues Zarathustra delivers after his return home. Commenting on Zarathustra's unusual addresses to his brothers and friends, she writes that at this point in his career "there is no other possibility for him as teacher than to anticipate the future pupils in his solitude and to speak with them."[17] Of course, much of the motivation for these scholars' reading of the "Tablets" chapter derives from the standard reading of Part 4 as relating a story that chronologically follows the end of Part 3. On this reading, if Zarathustra's children do not arrive until after the end of Part 4, then they certainly cannot have arrived in Part 3. I would like to ask, however, whether there is evidence within this particular chapter to support this standard reading. It is not enough to cite Zarathura's obviously monologic remarks in the first three sections of the chapter (or his rejoicing at his renewed solitude in the earlier chapter "The Return Home"). For we need to know whether this initial solitude persists through the rest of Zarathustra's obviously public and dialogic speech.

Besides Zarathustra's supposed solitude, then, is there any evidence within the chapter that Zarathustra is speaking to a merely *imagined* or *anticipated* audience of disciples? Writing about the concluding sections of Zarathustra's speech, Lampert alludes to his use of the future tense: "Building with rising intensity to the harshest tablet he will set before his friends (section 27), he imagines their shocked response (section 28) and, granting its legitimacy, shows them how to overcome their initial horror (sections 29–30)."[18] Here, that is, Lampert suggests that Zarathustra is speaking about the tablet that he *will* set before his friends some time in the future and is therefore merely *imagining* his disciples' shocked response. But a close look at the entirety of Zarathustra's speech to his brothers, including the portion cited here by Lampert, shows that he is always speaking to them in the present tense only. Indeed, as the following examples show, Zarathustra seems to go out of his way to emphasize the present moment in which he is speaking to his brothers: "Now, however, we are first-borns." (section 6); "Oh my brothers, is not everything in *flux now?*" (section 8); "And now for the first time the great horror comes to humans. [. . .] Now you shall be seafarers for me, valiant, patient!" (section 28); "This new tablet, oh my brothers, do I set over you: *become hard!*" (section 29).

Nietzsche's tenses in the "Tablets" chapter thus do not support, and they even undermine, the idea that Zarathustra is merely imagining or anticipating his future reunion with his disciples. Moreover, the concluding portion of Zarathustra's speech further undermines this idea by exhibiting not only the presence of his intended audience but also his *interaction* with that audience. Zarathustra does not merely imagine his audience's response to his last words but actually *perceives* and reacts to it: "Oh my brothers, do you understand this word too? [. . .] You flee from me? You are horrified? You tremble before this word?" (sections 27–28). Zarathustra's perception here does not anticipate some future event but rather confirms what he had *already* anticipated at the start of Part 2. In a warning that included the image of the lion for the first time since his first speech, Zarathustra described the violent roaring of his *lioness* wisdom and said: "Yes, even you, my friends, will be horrified by my wild wisdom; and perhaps you will flee from her together with my enemies" (Z:2 "The Child with the Mirror"). Zarathustra's comparable speech in Part 4, "On the Higher Humans," although also a non-narrated monologue, contains the same sort of evidence of his presumably *real* interaction with his audience of *actual* and *present* higher men: "Do you understand this word, oh my brothers? You are horrified: do your hearts fail? Does the abyss here yawn for you? Does the hound of hell here yelp at you?" (Z:4 "On the Higher Humans" 2).[19]

A final problem with the standard reading of Zarathustra's speech in the "Tablets" chapter is that in fact Zarathustra does not speak and interact with just his *disciples*. Having commanded his disciples to shatter the ancient tablets of the pious, Zarathustra turns in section 16 to command them also to shatter a *new* tablet he found hanging in the public markets. This is a tablet that preaches world-weariness, and in section 17 Zarathustra turns directly to the world-weary themselves (obviously not his disciples) and asks who wants to die now. He observes that no one takes up his offer and perceives that their eyes and lips contradict their claim to world-weariness. In the next section, he distinguishes these people, who are merely lazy, from a man lying close by who is genuinely weary. But now Zarathustra has resumed speaking to his disciples, and he asks them to look closely at this man: he points out his languishing position in the dust, his defiant yawning, even the sun beating down on him and the dogs licking his sweat. He tells his disciples to leave the man alone but to scare the dogs away. Later, in section 20, Zarathustra asks his disciples to see how these men of today roll into his depths. And in section 21, he advises his disciples to pass by the rabble who din in their ears, and he asks that they observe closely all the various ways in which the surrounding people behave like shopkeepers. Finally, in section 22, Zarathustra even seems to point as he speaks of some of these people who, according to him, are coarse beasts of prey.

In thus constructing Zarathustra's speech to include references to the valley and the people below, Nietzsche completes his allusion to the biblical narrative in which Moses descends from the top of Mount Sinai in order to consecrate God's chosen people and bring them the covenant and the new commandments (Exodus 32–35).[20] Just as he had said he would do once he received the sign that it was the right time for it, Zarathustra sets out down the mountain to meet his ascending disciples so that together they may carry his new commandments to the valley and into hearts of flesh (Z:3 "Tablets" 1–4; Z:4 "The Honey Sacrifice," "The Greeting").[21] All these details of Zarathustra's speech thus imply the fulfillment of his leave-taking promise that he would be with his disciples a third time in order to celebrate with them the great noon (Z:1 "On the Gift-Giving Virtue" 3)—a promise that was recalled at the very end of Part 4 when Zarathustra recognized the proximity of his disciples and then proceeded to summon up the great noon (Z:4 "The Sign").[22] Hence, besides depicting the second reunion of Zarathustra and his disciples, Nietzsche's "Tablets" chapter should depict the start of this much-anticipated great noon.

Again, commentators typically assume that Nietzsche postpones this great noon until some indefinite future not included in his book. But Nietzsche himself writes retrospectively in Ecce Homo that those who know his Zarathustra will find no mystery (Räthsel-Begriff) in his vision of a great-noon festival where the most select (Auserwähltesten) consecrate (weihen) themselves to the greatest of all tasks (EH "Books" BT 4).[23] This is a vision, he writes, that he first expressed in his untimely essay on Wagner's thought of Bayreuth (RWB 4). In that essay, he argued that Bayreuth signified the morning-consecration (Morgen-Weihe) on the day of battle by those select few who have to fight "against everything that confronts them as a seemingly invincible necessity: against power, law, tradition, convention, and the whole order of things." In order to find the courage to fight, these individuals must consecrate themselves to something above the personal that compensates them for their struggle, eases their worry about their personal inadequacy, and lets them forget their terrible anxiety at the prospect of death. They therefore prepare themselves to die and to sacrifice themselves for the sake of the highest task that is charged to all future human generations—the task of growing together into a single whole with a single common goal.

On the reading I have offered so far, we can indeed find Nietzsche's early vision reiterated in *Zarathustra*. At the end of Part 4, the Zarathustra who knows his disciples are about to arrive is likened to an emerging morning sun, commands the great noon to arise, and proclaims the moment in which he is speaking as his morning and the beginning of his day. Presumably, then, it is still Zarathustra's morning when he is reunited with his disciples in the "Tablets" chapter toward the end of Part 3. If we now turn to Zarathustra's address to his brothers with Nietzsche's Bayreuth allusion in mind, we are led to notice that he begins in section 6 by encouraging his firstborns to sacrifice themselves for their cause. He then spends most of the rest of his address exhorting them to fight against all established tradition, convention, and morality.[24] However, in the middle sections, 11 and 12, Zarathustra articulates a positive suprapersonal task that will justify all of their combat and sacrifice. He consecrates and directs (*weihe und weise*) his brothers to the task of founding a new nobility (*Adel*) that will write the word "noble" (*edel*) on new tablets. This new nobility will not be founded upon that which has previously founded human nobility: wealth, family ancestry, service to royalty, or the fatherland. Nor is Zarathustra's consecration like previous "spiritual" consecrations, such as Moses's consecration of the Israelites as God's chosen people, or King Arthur's consecration of the roundtable knights who sought the Holy Grail. Instead, Zarathustra directs his brothers to become begetters and cultivators and sowers of the future and to found their new nobility upon their love of their children and heirs.[25] For this reason, Zarathustra turns in sections 23 to 25 to write new values for his brothers regarding marriage and family: they should be fit for war and their women should be fit for child-bearing; their marriage should be decided carefully, honestly, and with a trial term if needed; and once decided, their marriage should assist them in propagating not only forward but upward. From such upward propagation, he says, there will ultimately arise a new chosen people (*auserwähltes Volk*)—the same chosen people he had earlier said would be able to yoke together the thousand ancient peoples and goals into a single unified humankind with a single common goal.[26]

Let us turn finally to the central and dominant theme of Zarathustra's speech in the "Tablets" chapter. Alluding often to his earlier speech, "On War and Warrior People," Zarathustra presents himself as a commander and implicitly addresses his disciples as his obedient warriors (see sections 4 and 25). Before he and his disciples can create new values, they must first seize the freedom and the right to do so by killing the great dragon called "thou-shalt" upon whose scales glitter the values of a thousand years and a thousand peoples. Accordingly, speaking to his disciples with his leonine imperative voice, Zarathustra repeatedly commands them to shatter all the old tablets of values. In obeying this command, his disciples will enact their own new role as courageous lions and thieving predators whose power enables them to find illusion and caprice in the old values and commandments they previously considered holy (Z:1 "On the Three Transformations"). Alluding again to Moses's new commandments, Nietzsche has Zarathustra single out especially the ancient commandments "Thou shalt not steal!" and "Thou shalt not kill!" (section 10)—thus indicating that he and his warriors will themselves have to steal and kill in order to be able to create new values. But he counsels his brave swordsmen to let pass the despised rabble and instead spare their hard-cutting swords for a worthier and hated enemy (section 21). These true enemies, Zarathustra announces, are the shepherds and guardians of the rabble who call themselves "the good and the just" (*die Guten und Gerechten*). Accordingly, Zarathustra's entire address to his warrior-disciples culminates in a call to arms against the good and the just:

> Oh my brothers! With whom does the greatest danger for the whole human future lie? Is it not with the good and the just?— [. . .]
> They hate the *creator* most: him who breaks the tablets and old values, the breaker—they call him the law-breaker.
> For the good—*cannot* create: they are always the beginning of the end:—
> They crucify him who writes new values on new tablets, they sacrifice the future *to themselves*—they crucify the whole human future!
> The good—they have always been the beginning of the end.—
> Oh my brothers, have you understood this word too? And what I once said about the "last man"?—
> With whom does the greatest danger to the whole human future lie? Is it not with the good and the just?
> *Shatter, shatter the good and the just for me!*[27]—Oh my brothers, have you understood this word too? (Z:3 "Tablets" 26–27)

Although commentators generally have not paid special attention to this startling peroration, Nietzsche's presentation shows that he himself regarded this passage as the most controversial in his entire book.[28] Just before and just after the sentence in which he commands his disciples to shatter (*zerbrecht*) not just the old tablets but the good and just themselves, Zarathustra asks his audience whether they have understood his "word" (Wort).[29] Nietzsche thus implies that Zarathustra's single brief command is literally incredible to his audience, so much so that they may not even have understood it at first.[30] But then Zarathustra observes the horror and shock that follows their belated comprehension of his word (section 27). As he had anticipated earlier in the book, even his most devoted disciples seem terrified by his wild lioness wisdom, and he worries that some of them might even be driven off by her and join his enemies. Although their return and assembly in this chapter shows that his disciples had indeed passed his earlier tests, Zarathustra implies that he has now begun in earnest the testing he had promised earlier: "Yonder, where storms plunge down into the sea [. . .] / [Each of my children] shall be known and tested, to see whether he is of my race and descent [. . .] / such a one as writes with my will on my tablets" (Z:3 "On Involuntary Bliss"). Alluding back to his stillest hour's prediction that his commanding word, once finally spoken, would bring the storm (Z:2 "The Stillest Hour"), Zarathustra announces that his word has now for the first time embarked humankind upon newly stormy high seas, where it will find no moral compass and where it will experience the great terror, the great nausea, the great seasickness. For this reason, he counsels his disciples: "Straighten up by me in time, oh my brothers, learn to straighten up! The sea storms: many want to straighten themselves up again by your aid. / The sea storms: everything is at sea. Well then! Come on! You old seaman-hearts!" (section 28). Responding to the lack of destiny he sees in his disciples' glances, Zarathustra compares himself to a flashing, cutting diamond and exhorts his noble brothers in war to become hard like him so that they may conquer and create alongside him (section 29).

Thus, at the end of his book's "decisive" chapter, Nietzsche has the lion-voiced Zarathustra finally speak the commanding word, which his stillest hour said belonged to him and which he and his animals call "the Zarathustra-word" (das Zarathustra-Wort) of the great noon of earth and humankind.[31] With this word, Zarathustra begins to fulfill his predictions of a great-noon day of apocalyptic violence and destruction. Alluding to the Bible's book of Revelation, Nietzsche suggests that the final judgment has now begun and that Zarathustra's returned disciples must now begin wielding their "swords of judgments" (Richtschwerten) and fulfill their anticipated role as his hundred sickles and fellow harvesters (Z:3 "On the Three Evil Things" 2).[32] Just as he himself had overcome his compassion at the end of Part 4 and thereby become a lion-spirited bronze-faced commander, Zarathustra now exhorts his newly arrived disciples to overcome their own compassion and to embrace the evil, cruelty, and hardness that will allow them to cut into the living (sections 7, 20, 29).[33]

It is clear enough, then, why Nietzsche portrays Zarathustra and his reunited disciples as lions. But why does he also portray them as laughing? Lions roar, but they do not laugh. So why do Zarathustra and his children laugh rather than roar, especially if they are plotting apocalyptic violence and destruction? Nietzsche's juxtaposition here seems all the more odd if we recall his well-known association of laughter with childlike innocence, cheerfulness, gaiety, levity, playfulness, and joy.[34] As William M. Calder III notes, Nietzsche's remarkable alliterative phrase, *lachende Löwe*, seems to be an oxymoron.[35] On the other hand, this odd juxtaposition should not be unfamiliar to us, since the *Genealogy*'s most notorious blond-beast passage describes the nobles as going back in the wilderness: "to the innocence of the predator's conscience, as rejoicing [*frohlockende*] monsters who perhaps emerge from a horrific procession of murder, arson, desecration, and torture, with high spirits [*Übermuthe*] and equanimity, as if it were nothing more than a student prank, convinced that the poets have something new to sing and celebrate for some time to come" (GM I:11). In the *Zarathustra* passage that clearly anticipates this one, the Wagnerian sorcerer sings seductively of the higher men's secret but unrealizable wild desires. Here Nietzsche explicitly associates laughter with the jungle cat's violence:[36]

> Full of cats' prankishness [*Katzen-Muthwillens*],
> Leaping through every window
> Swish! into every chance,
> Sniffing out every jungle,
> Sniffing with greedy longing,
> That in jungles
> Among colorfully speckled beasts of prey
> You might roam, sinfully healthy and colorful and beautiful,
> With lusting lips,
> Blissfully jeering, blissfully hellish, blissfully blood-thirsty,
> Preying, prowling, lying peering: [. . .]
> You that have seen humans
> As God and sheep—:
> *Rending* the God in humans
> No less than the sheep in humans,
> And while rending *laughing*—
> *That, that* is your bliss [*Seligkeit*]!
> A panther's [bliss]!" (Z:4 "The Song of Melancholy")[37]

Nietzsche's point, in *Zarathustra* as well as in his later *Genealogy*, is that although the victims of the nobles' leonine violence cannot help but blame and demonize their predators, the nobles themselves laugh because they feel no guilt or remorse whatsoever over their naturally predatory deeds. This leonine laughter seems especially horrific and chilling to the victims because it expresses, as Nietzsche puts it, "hair-raising cheerfulness [*Heiterkeit*] and profound joy [*Tiefe der Lust*] in all destruction, in all the voluptuousness of victory and cruelty" (GM I:11).[38]

I do not think we can take much comfort, then, in the fact that Nietzsche's later *Genealogy* image of the rejoicing blond beast alludes back to his *Zarathustra* image of the laughing lion. Indeed, if my interpretation is correct, this allusion raises newly disturbing questions, not about Nietzsche's theoretical concern with the Germanic past but about his practical exhortations to future generations. Given the narrative setting I have outlined above, these exhortations cannot plausibly be read as referring merely to the kind of spiritual self-overcoming usually associated with the Zarathustran lion-spirit. For Zarathustra commands his laughing lions not only to shatter any goodness and justice they may still carry within themselves but also to shatter others who are taken to embody goodness and justice. There is something to be said here for a Straussian suspicion of the author who buries his most explicitly threatening directive in the conclusion of a lengthy and seemingly monologic speech delivered by the fictional protagonist of his most poetic and symbolic book. Yet even Nietzsche commentators working today in the Straussian tradition, and even those directly investigating such issues as Nietzsche's interest in war and revolutionary violence, have so far simply passed over the *Zarathustra* passages I have been concerned to interpret.[39] Nietzsche's esoteric practices thus continue to elude even his most vigilant readers, a fact that is itself worthy of investigation.[40]

Notes

1. See, for example, Kaufmann's commentary to GM 1:11 in his edition of GM; and Robert C. Solomon and Kathleen M. Higgins, *What Nietzsche Really Said* (New York: Schocken Books, 2000), 9, 233. Throughout this chapter, I have consulted Kaufmann and Hollingdale's translation of GM; Richard Gray's translation of *RWB*; Kaufmann's translations of *BT*, *BGE* and Z; and Hollingdale's translation of Z. I am grateful to Robert Gooding-Williams and the editors of this volume for their helpful comments on this chapter.

2. See Nietzsche's image of a desert-dwelling blond-maned lion-monster (*blondgelock-*

ten Löwen-Unthiere) in Z:4 "Among Daughters of the Desert." See also section 3 of Z:4 "The Song of Melancholy" for a clear anticipation of Nietzsche's GM I:11 description of rampaging beasts of prey, as well as of his subsequent GM I:13 description of lamb-hunting birds of prey.

3. One of the participants in Carl Jung's Zarathustra seminar suggests that Nietzsche's image of the laughing lion with the flock of doves (*der lachende Löwe mit dem Tauben-schwarme*) might have been inspired by the Piazza di San Marco in Venice, where doves or pigeons flock about a column topped by the winged-lion symbol of Venice. See C. G. Jung, *Nietzsche's Zarathustra*, ed. James L. Jarrett (Princeton, N.J.: Princeton University Press, 1988), 2:1490. This suggestion is supported by Nietzsche's "*Mein Glück!*" poem in the Appendix to *The Gay Science*.

4. In writing here that Zarathustra, prompted by his vision of the laughing lion, leapt up (*sprang empor*) as he realized that he should no longer shepherd the higher men, Nietzsche specifically recalls Zarathustra's prevision of himself as a young shepherd who bit the head off the serpent and leapt up (*sprang empor*) no longer shepherd, laughing a new and inhuman laughter. For a further discussion of this link, see my essay "The Dwarf, the Dragon, and the Ring of Eternal Recurrence: A Wagnerian Key to the Riddle of Nietzsche's *Zarathustra*," *Nietzsche-Studien* 31 (2002): 91–113, esp. 105–109.

5. Here Nietzsche alludes to the New Testament's book of Revelation, in which the lion of Judah (Christ) ultimately defeats the great dragon Satan.

6. In an alternative version of the ending of Part 4 in his preparatory notes, Nietzsche draws an even tighter link between Zarathustra's vision of the laughing lion and his arriving laughing lions (*KSA* 11:32[14–15]). Of course, the countless flocking doves are also a symbol of Zarathustra's returning disciples. These affectionate doves form a cloud of love that empties itself over a new friend; they are no less eager in their love than the lion, and they sit on Zarathustra's shoulders and caress his white hair and do not weary of tenderness and rejoicing. Here Nietzsche recalls Zarathustra's prevision, in the "Soothsayer" chapter, of being rescued from his solitary mountain entombment by a thousand peals of children's laughter emanating from a thousand child-sized angels and butterflies.

7. *Zarathustra's Dionysian Modernism* (Stanford, Calif.: Stanford University Press, 2001), 19–20; see also 302–304. In his concluding remarks, however, Gooding-Williams suggests that in his next book, *Beyond Good and Evil*, Nietzsche perhaps takes up, or at least hopes to inspire in others, "the child-creator's project of *creating* new values" (307–308).

8. "The Conclusion of Nietzsche's *Zarathustra*," *International Studies in Philosophy* 32 no. 3 (2000): 137–152. In this essay, I discuss the related issue of Nietzsche's unrealized plans to write further parts for his book.

9. Gooding-Williams (*Zarathustra's Dionysian Modernism*, 20, 268, 293ff., 383–386) argues that the last few pages of Part 4 show Zarathustra *overcoming* his leonine spirit. But I think this argument is contradicted by Zarathustra's angry laughter, bronze hardness, and shouted naysaying in relation to the higher men as well as by his renewed, heroic, and self-aggrandizing dedication to his uncompleted work.

10. As this chapter indicates, however, I no longer think that the events narrated in Part 4 have to chronologically follow the *ending* of the "Tablets" chapter. In section 30, Zarathustra is no longer *waiting* to become ripe and ready for the great noon (as he was in section 1). Instead, the thematic continuity of his remarks in this section with his last remarks at the end of Part 4 let us know that he is *already* ripe and wants to preserve this ripeness for the high-noon moment of his great-noon day. This climactic moment is depicted in the next chapter as the moment when Zarathustra summons up his thought of eternal recurrence and hence brings the sun of human knowledge to the peak overhead position, in which the obscuring shadows of God are shortest (Z:1 "On the Gift-Giving Virtue" 3; Z:2 "On the Vision and the Riddle"; KSA 9:11[148]; GS 109; TI "World"). Since Zarathustra's stillest hour told him that this world-guiding thought would come on dove's feet, the flocking doves at the end of Part 4 announce the imminent arrival of this thought, while the flock of doves awaiting the convalescent Zarathustra outside his cave indicates that this thought has already arrived.

11. Notice that this chapter is the only place in the entirety of the book before Part 4 where Nietzsche explicitly mentions the lion-and-doves sign.

12. See, for example, Peter Berkowitz, *Nietzsche: The Ethics of an Immoralist* (Cambridge, Mass.: Harvard University Press, 1995), 202; Gregory Whitlock, *Returning to Sils Maria: A Commentary to Nietzsche's "Also Sprach Zarathustra"* (New York: Peter Lang, 1990), 216; Stanley Rosen, *The Mask of Enlightenment: Nietzsche's Zarathustra* (New York: Cambridge University Press, 1995), 198.

13. Gooding-Williams, *Zarathustra's Dionysian Modernism*, 246.

14. Ibid., 238.

15. *Nietzsche's Teaching: An Interpretation of Thus Spoke Zarathustra* (New Haven, Conn.: Yale University Press, 1986), 300, 204; see also 203–210. Although Lampert describes Zarathustra's "Tablets" speech as "public," he seems to mean only that it is a solitary account *of* his public teaching. For what does it mean to say Zarathustra's speech is "public" if he is alone and knows that he has no audience?

16. "The 'Warrior Spirit' as an Inlet to the Political Philosophy of Nietzsche's Zarathustra," in *Nietzsche: Critical Assessments* ed. Daniel S. Conway with Peter S. Groff (London: Routledge, 1998), 245.

17. *"Also Sprach Zarathustra" als literarisches Phänomen. Eine Revision* (Frankfurt: Athenäum, 1974), 121, see also 120, 126.

18. Lampert, *Nietzsche's Teaching*, 208. But see the very next page, where Lampert inconsistently, but more accurately, paraphrases Zarathustra's speech as delivered in the present tense to a responsive audience.

19. Of course, what Zarathustra says to the deficient higher men is quite different from what he says to his returned disciples. For a good contrast of these two speeches, see Lampert, *Nietzsche's Teaching*, 300–301.

20. Some other Exodus allusions in Zarathustra's speech are to Moses's long wait on the mountains prior to his descent (sections 1–3), to the Israelites' sacrifice of first-born animals (section 6), and to God's instruction to build encircling boundaries around his

mountain (section 19). Nietzsche's other important Exodus allusion, in the Part 4 chapter entitled "The Ass Festival," is to the Israelites' worship of the golden calf after Moses told them his new commandments. On my reading, the allusions are linked: Zarathustra, like Moses, has to deliver his new commandments *twice*—first, in his speech to the higher men who then blaspheme him with their ass-idolatry; and second, in his speech to his returned disciples who (like the select sons of Levi) will end up overwhelming the higher men.

21. On my reading, then, the narrator's mention of Zarathustra's return to the cave (*Rückkehr zur Höhle*) at the start of the "Convalescent" chapter alludes back to the narrator's announcement, at the very end of Part 4, that Zarathustra left his cave (*verliess seine Höhle*) glowing and strong like a morning sun that comes out of dark mountains. Thus, Zarathustra summons up his most abysmal thought one morning "not long" (*nicht lange*) after he and his disciples have returned from their descent into the valley.

22. In his leave-taking promise, Zarathustra had also said that he and his disciples would declare their last will (*letzter Wille*) at the time of the great noon. And, indeed, in the last section of the "Tablets" chapter, when he is presumably still speaking in front of his audience of disciples, Zarathustra declares: "And your last greatness, my will, save for your last—that you may be inexorable in your victory!" For the fulfillment of Zarathustra's prophecy that he will show his disciples a freely chosen, timely, and triumphant death in which he consecrates their solemn vows and oaths (Z:1 "On Free Death"), see my essay "Death and Eternal Recurrence in Nietzsche's *Zarathustra*: A World-Historic Agon with Plato's Socrates" (*New Nietzsche Studies*, forthcoming).

23. Nietzsche writes that *Ecce Homo* is the place where light is first shed upon his *Zarathustra* (letter to Paul Deussen, November 26, 1888), and indeed much of *Ecce Homo* explains, promotes, and quotes *Zarathustra*.

24. In *Richard Wagner in Bayreuth*, of course, Nietzsche is still influenced by Wagner and urges this fight for the ultimate sake of "love and justice" (*RWB* 4).

25. In showing how Nietzsche hoped to inaugurate a new nobility and new noble values, these important *Zarathustra* passages support much that has been written recently about the reasons why Nietzsche does *not* urge our return to the vanished ancient nobility praised in the *Genealogy*. However, the context of these passages, explored below, undermines the usual contention that these reasons *include* the barbarism of the original nobles. See, for example, Aaron Ridley, *Nietzsche's Conscience: Six Character Studies from the Genealogy* (Ithaca, N.Y.: Cornell University Press, 1998), 128–134.

26. See Z:1 "On the Thousand and One Goals"; Z:1 "On the Gift-Giving Virtue" 2; Z:2 "On Redemption,"; Z:3 "On Old and New Tablets" 3. See also *EH* "Books" D:2, where Nietzsche ascribes to himself the task of "preparing a moment of supreme self-examination on the part of humankind, a *great noon*, when it looks back and looks forward, when it steps out from the dominion of accident and priests and for the first time poses, *as a whole*, the question why? To what end?" I discuss Nietzsche's strategy for unifying humankind in my essay "Time, Power, and Superhumanity," *Journal of Nietzsche Studies* 21 (2001): 27–47.

27. Neither Kaufmann nor Hollingdale translates the word "*mir*" in Nietzsche's sentence, "*Zerbrecht, zerbrecht mir die Guten und Gerechten!*"

28. For an exception, see Ofelia Schutte, *Beyond Nihilism: Nietzsche without Masks* (Chicago: University of Chicago Press, 1984), 135–139. But she does not offer a close reading of this passage and even suggests that Zarathustra is here speaking to the higher men (who are spurned by the laughing lion at the end of Part 4).

29. R.J. Hollingdale translates "*Wort*" variously as "word," "saying," and "teaching," thereby obscuring some of Nietzsche's key associations.

30. Nietzsche's language in this passage recalls his own veiled directive in the conclusion of his first book, *The Birth of Tragedy*: "Some day, [the German spirit] will find itself awake in all the morning freshness following a tremendous sleep: then it will slay dragons, destroy vicious dwarfs. [. . .] What is most painful for all of us, however, is—the prolonged degradation in which the German genius has lived, estranged from house and home, in the service of vicious dwarfs. You understand the word [*das Wort*]—as you will also, in conclusion, understand my hopes" (*BT* 24). Although Zarathustra's command does not share the anti-Semitic overtones of Nietzsche's earlier Wagnerian allusion, it is not difficult to see how Zarathustra's identification of the good and the just with the Pharisees who crucified Jesus (section 26) might have attracted the Christian anti-Semitic audience that Nietzsche complained about in his correspondence (see his letters to Theodor Fritsch, March 29, 1887, and to Elisabeth Förster, end of December 1887).

31. See Z:3 "On Old and New Tablets" 3, "The Convalescent" 2; Z:4 "On the Higher Humans" 2. In his later *Genealogy*, Nietzsche mentions the twelve strokes of the noon bell as having awoken him (*GM* P:1), and describes Zarathustra as a "bell-stroke of noon and of the great decision [*Entscheidung*] that liberates the will again and once again gives the earth its goal and humans their hope" (*GM* II:24).

32. See Z:3 "On the Small-Making Virtue" 3 for an allusion to the final harvest; "On Passing By" for an allusion to the pillars of fire that will destroy the great city of Babylon; and "On the Three Evil Things" 2 for an allusion to the revelation itself.

33. It is thus unlikely that Nietzsche intended his final association of the lion and the doves to convey the peaceable expectation that the lion will lie down with the lambs (Isaiah 11:6–9). See, for example, Rosen, *Mask of Enlightenment*, 244; and Lampert, *Nietzsche's Teaching*, 311.

34. For useful discussions of this association, see John Lippitt's essays: "Nietzsche, Zarathustra and the Status of Laughter," *British Journal of Aesthetics* 32, no. 1 (1992): 39–49; and "Laughter: A Tool in Moral Perfectionism?" in *Nietzsche's Futures*, ed. John Lippitt (New York: St. Martin's Press, 1999), 99–125. In the latter essay, Lippitt rightly contrasts Zarathustra's joyful, ecstatic, and triumphant laughter in the conclusion of Part 3 with his mocking, sarcastic, and angry laughter throughout Part 4. However, against his claim that Nietzsche has good reasons for "reducing" Zarathustra's laughter in Part 4, my alternative reading of the relation between Parts 3 and 4 suggests that Zarathustra's laughter builds, increases, and becomes "fuller" as the *chronological* narrative proceeds.

35. "The Lion Laughed," *Nietzsche-Studien* 14 (1985): 357. Notice, however, that in

Nietzsche's writings the lion and laughter are both symbols of courage (which is itself a symptom of strength), e.g. in the face of death.

36. Although Zarathustra succeeds in teaching the higher men how to laugh in their own way, he recognizes that their laughter is not like his own laughter (Z:4 "The Awakening") or like the laughter he will find in his returning leonine disciples (Z:4 "The Greeting").

37. This poem highlights the Dionysian background of Nietzsche's image of the laughing lion, and he includes it in his collection *Dithyrambs of Dionysus*. For a discussion of the role of the joyfully savage panther or lion in the ancient myth and cult of Dionysus, see Walter F. Otto, *Dionysus: Myth and Cult*, trans. Robert B. Palmer (Dallas: Spring Publications, 1993), 109–114.

38. For a discussion of the entirely new and inhuman laughter that terrifies even Zarathustra himself (Z:2 "The Soothsayer," "The Stillest Hour") but in the end allows him to finally slay the spirit of gravity, see my essay "The Dwarf, the Dragon, and the Ring of Eternal Recurrence," 108–109.

39. See, for example, the commentaries by Thomas Pangle and Stanley Rosen cited above.

40. See, for example, Geoff Waite, *Nietzsche's Corps/e: Aesthetics, Politics, Prophecy, or, the Spectacular Technoculture of Everyday Life* (Durham, N.C.: Duke University Press, 1996).

Nietzsche's "Blond Beast": On the Recuperation of a Nietzschean Metaphor

Gerd Schank

The metaphors "beast" and "blond beast" are highly significant in Nietzsche's reflections on the relationship between nature and culture. In his estimation, which he initially presented in *The Birth of Tragedy,* the Greeks succeeded, with Apollo's intervention, in integrating the "wildest beasts" (the barbaric-Dionysian element) into their art and culture. Nietzsche preserves this thesis of the "barbaric" basis of Greek culture even in his later development of his concept of noble Greek culture (*BGE* 257 and *GM* I:11). The productive incorporation of the "beast" into culture and art ended with the decline of Greek tragic culture. Since that time, according to Nietzsche, a similarly productive integration of the "beast,"—that is, "nature"—into "culture" has never been successfully actualized.

Nietzsche's metaphor of the blond beast has proven to be particularly susceptible to misunderstandings and grave misinterpretations, even to the extent of being considered a National Socialist slogan. Thus, a further attempt to reconstruct the meaning Nietzsche likely attributed to this metaphor is merited. Following a brief description of the semantics and metaphorical uses of the word "beast," the various meanings of Nietzsche's blond beast metaphor will be discussed in somewhat more detail and the most salient misconceptions critically tested and refuted.[1]

"Beast"

Exemplary References and Spectrum of Meanings in Nietzsche's Works

Although the word "beast" and its variations (bestial, beastly, bestialized, bestiality, beasts) is evident throughout the entire corpus, it is only present in a total of twenty-seven references (in his published works: a single reference each in *BT*, *D*, *GS*, *BGE*; two references each in *HH* and *TI*; three references in *GM* as "blond beast"; and similarly in his posthumous writings 1875–1888). Depending on the context, the connotations of "beast(s)" are either positive or negative; whereas the forms "bestial/bestiality" (in his posthumous work and in *GM* II:22) always carry negative connotations.

The word "beast" appears in Nietzsche in two different contexts; in one, it refers to the successful integration of the "beast(s)" into Greek culture, and in the other, it refers to the onset of illness in the beast as a result of subjecting it to morality and the attempts to domesticate the beast in the post-Greek era. Neither succeeds in achieving a synthesis of "beast" and culture. Both of these situations can be illuminated by a brief selection of references:

I. The Greeks succeeded on two fronts: (1) "reconciling two opponents": the "wildest Beasts of Nature" and the Apollonian; and (2) incorporating the "beast" into "noble" culture:
    (1) *BT* 2: "The most savage beasts of nature were set free here [at the "Dionysian feasts."] [. . .] But the Greeks were completely safe and protected from the feverish excitements of these festivals [. . .] by the figure of Apollo. [. . .] This resistance became more doubtful, even impossible, when similar impulses finally emerged from the deepest roots of Hellenistic culture. Now, all the Delphic god could do was to disarm the powerful opponent of his destructive weapon with a timely reconciliation." (See also *The Dionysian World View* 1; *KSA* 1:558).
    (2) *BGE* 257 "The noble caste was from the beginning always the bar-

barian caste: their superiority lay, not in their physical strength, but primarily in their psychical—they were more complete human beings (which, on every level, also means as much as 'more complete beasts')."

(3) GM I:11: "One cannot fail to see at the bottom of all of these noble races the beast of prey, the splendid *blond beast* prowling about avidly in search of spoil and victory; this hidden core needs to erupt from time to time, the animal has to get out again and go back to the wilderness: the Roman, Arabian, Germanic, Japanese nobility, the Homeric heroes the Scandinavian Vikings—they all shared this need. It is the noble races that have left behind them the concept 'barbarian' wherever they have gone."

II. Through "morality" and "taming" ("bad conscience") the "beast" is not "improved," but rather made "sick":

(4) *HH* 40: "The beast in us wants to be lied to; morality is a white lie, to keep it from tearing us apart. Without the errors inherent in the postulates of morality, man would have remained an animal. But as it is he has taken himself to be something higher. [. . .] He therefore has a hatred of those stages of man that remain closer to the animal state."

(5) GM II:22: "Oh this insane, pathetic beast—man! What ideas he has, what unnaturalness, what paroxysms of nonsense, what *bestiality of thought* erupts as soon as he is prevented just a little from being a *beast in deed!*"

(6) *TI* "The 'Improvers' of Mankind" 2: "To call the taming of an animal its 'improvement' sounds almost like a joke to our ears. Whoever knows what goes on in menageries doubts that the beasts are 'improved' there. They are weakened, they are made less harmful, and through the depressive effect of fear, through pain, through wounds, and through hunger they become sickly beasts. It is no different with the tamed man whom the priest has 'improved.'" (This passage is followed by an example of unsuccessful "improvement": the "noble Germanic tribes" as allegedly exemplifying an "improvement" of the blonde beast.)

On the Semantic and Connotative History of "Beast"

The word "beast" had a broad spectrum of meanings prior to and during Nietzsche's day, carrying both negative connotations (as a swearword and as a pejorative reference to one's social status),[2] and positive connotations (as, for example, when F. Schlegel uses it to indicate insatiability);[3] and, finally, in a joking manner.[4] "Bestial" referred to a quantification or rather to an intensification (i.e., "very large");[5] but also, when combined with "bestiality," designated "wildness" or even "brute barbarity,"[6] as in Schopenhauer's use of "bestiality."[7] Similarly, the term "beast" is not a connotatively fixed term in Nietzsche's writings, which stands in contrast with the use of "bestial" and "bestiality," which always have negative connotations. Nietzsche therefore had access to a rich history of diverse uses of the word "beast." In addition, he uses the word "beast" metaphorically in new contexts in which it had never before been cited: namely, as a means of interrogating the concepts of "nature" and "culture."

Interpretation

Nietzsche uses the beast metaphor to pose the problem of the relationship of nature to art and culture, which, from the time of *The Birth of Tragedy*, he situates using the Greeks as examples. The "beast" metaphor here reveals, with particular resonance, that he was thinking specifically of wild, untamed nature, which his metaphor of the "beast of prey" also signifies. In *BT* 2, there is even reference to the "wildest beasts of nature," which appears in the context as the "Dionysian," as an image of "sensual pleasure and cruelty"—the "Dionysian double effect of 'loathing' and 'ecstasy.'" A mediation of these "wildest beasts" and artistic creation was supposed to be demonstrated in *The Birth of Tragedy*.[8]

The thesis formulated in *The Birth of Tragedy*, "that human artistic creation is an imitation of natural creation," is explored in relation to Greek art in *BT* 2, where Nietzsche examines "to what extent and to what degree those artistic drives of nature [among the Greeks] have evolved."[9] Nietzsche refers us back to the cult of Dionysus to point out the specifically Greek conception of the intoxifying aspect of the natural artistic drive. Unlike in the case of the "barbarians" (Asians and Orientals), "the artistic potential residing in the intoxified state was only released during the Greek festivals of Dionysius" (*BT* 2). The Greeks owe this "artistic ecstasy" of the Greek orgy to the "influence of the delphic priesthood of Apollo." According to Reibnitz, the "Greek-Dionysian element" is portrayed here as a "transformation of nature into culture, that is, into art." Greek art and culture are thus "basically constituted from the barbaric, and are therefore retroactively [*reaktiv*] bound to the barbaric." The "wildest beasts" (the barbaric-Dionysian aspect) are absorbed into Greek art and culture with Apollo's mediation.[10]

Nietzsche retains this thesis of the "barbaric" basis of Greek culture even when developing his depiction of Greek culture as being a noble culture (*BGE* 257; *GM* I:11), at the heart of which is unmistakably the beast of prey, the blond beast. According to Ottmann, "the tension and 'bestiality' hidden at the core of the Greek soul" means essentially health, innocence, nature free of illness, which has been both transformed by the agon and ennobled in culture.[11]

By the end of Greek tragic culture, this productive incorporation of the beast into culture and art was lost. The church, with its good vs. evil morality and its attempts to domesticate; modern science (e.g., Darwin, Häckel); and political aspirations (e.g., revolution and democracy) were unable, according to Nietzsche, to point out a navigable path toward a renewed, productive integration of the beast (nature) into culture. For Nietzsche, such a route would lead to the "return to health" of culture and individuals according to the Greek model.[12]

Criticism of Darwin and Rée

According to Ottmann, Nietzsche's posthumous work, especially fragment 12[22] (*KSA* 8:259), reveals that for Nietzsche, man's path upward cannot be substantiated "by Darwin's conceptual means," which is why Nietzsche arrives at a reaffirmation of his tragic view of the world in his later philosophy. Furthermore, it reveals Nietzsche's skepticism of the "social Darwinist version of bourgeois social philosophy."[13]

The word "menagerie" as it is used in *TI* "Improvers" 2 may contain a reference to Rée. Compare Nietzsche's text: "Those who know what happens in menageries doubt that the beast is 'improved' there" with Rée's: "Every state community is a great menagerie, in which a fear of punishment [. . .] and of shame prevent the beasts from devouring each other."[14] Nietzsche employs a similar metaphor in *HH* 40, where he states: "Morality is a white lie, to keep it [the beast] from tearing us apart."

However, according to Nietzsche's view (and to his regret), the beast is already so severely weakened that its danger is no longer feared. This is because, as explicitly stated in GM P: 7 in reference to Rée and the "Darwinian beast," it no longer bites. It is now—as it seems evident to Rée—entirely saturated by morality and has become a "moral-weakling."

Summary
Nietzsche uses the word "beast" as a metaphor that carries positive connotations for his idea of the wildness and cruelty of nature (the "Dionysian" element in Nietzsche's works), an aspect of human animals that should not be

permitted to be destroyed in the creation of culture and morality but rather should be regarded as an inherent part of every culture, especially "noble" and "moral" ones. This use of the word and the metaphor "beast" in Nietzsche is original. It also signals a rejection of Rousseau's view of an originally "good" nature, which Nietzsche viewed as based in "hypermoralization" (*KSA* 12:9[146].99).[15]

The positive evaluation of nature in its wildness and cruelty, as expressed by the metaphor of nature as beast, also forms the basis of Nietzsche's metaphor of the blond beast, which can, to some extent, be seen as a special type of the beast metaphor.

"Blond" and "Blond Beast"

Exemplary References and Spectrum of Meanings in Nietzsche's Works

The word "blond" and its associated formulations (blond locks, towhead, blond beast) appear only thirteen times, and of those, all occur in his later works (with the exception of one reference to "blond angel" in an early letter (*KSB* 2:144 July 1866). The references occur between 1885 and 1888 (in Z: 4, *GM*, *TI*, *Dionysus Dithyrambs* II, and in his posthumous writings of 1887 and 1888). The older word "flaxen" occurs once as a synonym for "blond" (*KSA* 13:15[80]).

The terms "blond" and "blond beast" first need to be distinguished with regard to their meanings. Three connotations for the word "blond" are detectable:

(1) It refers, according to the conventional linguistic usage of his day, to a light hair color (*KSB* 2:144 July 1866: the hair color of an actress); (2) It alludes to a criticism of light hair color as a function of "stupidity" and "sensuality," which could perhaps be viewed as an earlier form of today's pervasive cliché of the "dumb blond" (*KSA* 12:9[12] and *KSA* 12:10[36]): "the too blond, too stupid sensuality" of the Viennese waltz; and in *KSA* 13:14[63] and *KSA* 13:15[15], where Wagner's opera heroes are referred to as "blond saints" with "latent [*präexistent*] sensuality"; (3) In one case, it echoes—presumably, critically and in opposition to—the "Aryan myth," when he contrasts the "flaxen heads" and the "blue eyes" of the Germans with the appearance of the "Jews," which Nietzsche perceived to be a blessing (*KSA* 13:15[80]).

The metaphor of the blond beast (and similar formulations) appears in four contexts, which utilize the following meanings of the concept:

(1) The lion as symbol of "might and strength:"[16] "In fear of a grim, yellow, blond-haired lion-monster" (Z:4 "Daughters of the Desert" 3; compare also *Dionysus Dithyrambs* II [KSA 6, p. 386]).

(2) In the context of the hypothesis of two "races" settling "Italian land": settlement of the "Italian land"; first by "pre-Aryan inhabitants"; "*malus/melas*"; the "common man as dark-colored, above all as black-haired"; and, subsequently, "the blond, namely Aryan conqueror-race, that has become the reigning one" (GM I:5).

(3) The blond beast as Nietzsche's image of the "achievers"[17] or as an example of his "ideal of the Greek hero and agon culture"[18]: "It cannot be mistaken that the basis of all of these noble races is the beast of prey, the magnificent *blond beast* roaming lasciviously after prey and victory" (GM I:11); and similarly "the 'improvement' of humans through 'domestication'": "In the early Middle Ages [. . .] one went everywhere in hunt of the most beautiful exemplars of the 'blond beasts'" (*TI* "Improvers" 2);

(4) "A pack of blond beasts of prey" as founders of the state: "the oldest state [was founded by] a pack of blond beasts of prey, a conqueror- and master-race, which [. . .] lays its horrific claws on a populace, which, at least in reference to its numbers, is monstrously superior, but still formless" (GM II:17).

The first meaning can be juxtaposed with the third, and the fourth could be read as a variation on the third, if one understands "pack of blond beasts of prey" (and "claws") to be a paraphrase for blond beast in that use, which is certainly depicted here as a "conqueror- and master-race" (as in the second meaning), but where, however, the image of "animal," of the "blond beast of prey" ("claws") could be predominant. Accordingly, two possible fields of meaning result for "blond beast." On the one hand, we have the nearly synonymous list of metaphors "lion symbol," "blond beast" as "achiever," and "pack of blond beasts of prey" as "founders of the state"; and on the other hand, we find the connection of the word "blond" with the word "race" in the formulation "blond, namely Aryan conqueror-race" (GM I:5), in which case the formulation "blond beast" does not explicitly appear. Above all, it has been this last formulation in GM I:5 ("blond, namely Aryan conqueror-race") which, to the largest extent, has determined the interpretation and reception of the metaphor "blond beast." Therefore it remains most important to verify whether this formulation has any connection to the "Aryan myth" (and to Gobineau, its main spokesman), and, if so, to what extent this formulation expresses Nietzsche's own view.

With the exception of the reference in his early letter (KSB 2:144), all of the references to "blond" listed above have negative connotations. Positive connotations may be assumed, however, in the blond beast references. This seems to suggest that the positive connotation of the blond beast metaphor in this context is primarily traceable back to the overall positive connotation of the beast metaphor in Nietzsche's work (already made apparent in the earlier section on the "beast") but not to those associated with the word "blond." This supports the claim that the adjective "blond" in Nietzsche's works is not to be read against the background of the "Aryan myth" because in this "myth," "blond," without exception, always has a positive connotation.

The meanings of "blond" and "blond beast" can be further elucidated by a selection of additional references:

I. Rejection of the "blond" German with "blue eyes": "What blessing a Jew is among Germans! How much indifference, how flaxen [blond] the head, how blue the eye; the lack of *esprit* in the face, word, attitude; the lazy stretching, the German need for recuperation" (KSA 13:15[80]).

II. The colonization of "Italian lands" by the "black-haired" and the "the blond Aryan conqueror-race, which has become the reigning one": "The Latin *malus* [. . .] may designate the common man as the dark-colored, above all, as the black-haired man [. . .] , as the pre-Aryan occupant of the soil of Italy who was distinguished most obviously from the blond, that is Aryan, conqueror race by his color; Gaelic, at any rate, offers us a precisely similar case—*fin* (for example in the name *Fin-Gal*), the distinguishing word for nobility, finally for the good, noble, pure, originally meant the blond-headed, in contradistinction to the dark, black-haired aboriginal inhabitants" (GM I:5).

III. The "blond beast" "at the bottom of all of these noble races": "One cannot fail to see at the bottom of all of these noble races the beast of prey, the splendid *blond beast* prowling about avidly in search of spoil and victory; this hidden core needs to erupt from time to time, the animal has to get out again and go back to the wilderness: the

Roman, Arabian, Germanic, Japanese nobility, the Homeric heroes the Scandinavian Vikings—they all shared this need. It is the noble races that have left behind them the concept 'barbarian' wherever they have gone" (GM I:11); "The deep and icy mistrust the German still arouses today whenever he gets into a position of power is an echo of the inextinguishable horror with which Europe observed for centuries that raging of the blond Germanic beast (although between the old Germanic tribes and us Germans there exists hardly a conceptual relationship, let alone one of blood)" (GM I:11).

On the Semantic and Connotative History of "Blond" and "Blond Beast"

The German adjective "blond" traces back to the French word "blond." It appears in High German in Gottfried von Strassburg's reference to the "blond Isolde." Since 1688, it has found wide usage in German, above all as a designation for hair color (for the earlier "pale," "flaxen," "golden yellow," etc.).[19] Blond hair color attracted the attention of the Romans, and soon it became the stereotypical depiction of the Germanic tribes as "blond barbarians," a positive connotation because the Germanic people possessed characteristics that the Romans had lost.[20] As early as Ovid's time, "Germanic blond" was considered to be the fashionable hair color for women. The Germanic people were accepted into the Roman army, and, in about 217 CE, troops in Rome were considered "all the more noble, the more barbaric they were"; that is, the more they included people from Germanic tribes. Caracalla introduced the lion as its insignia. The Battle of Adrianople (378 CE), which ushered in the beginning of the end of the Roman Empire, stood in the "astrological constellation of the lion." This could have been the evolution of the "image of the Germanic people as blond lion-beasts." For the Romans, the terms "barbaric," "Germanic," "bestial," "blond," and "lion" were thus considered synonymous.[21]

With the evolution of the "Aryan myth" (after 1800), "blond" became part of the formation of a new stereotype. Blond hair, blue eyes, a longish skull shape, light-colored skin, and spiritual and intellectual superiority were attributed to the "Aryans," the hypothetical Indo-Germanic aborigines. Their original homeland was assumed to be the Orient (in India and the Caucasus), from whence they were said to have conquered Europe.[22] Nietzsche may have come to know of this hypothesis from the work of Poesche, which he had in his library.[23] Gobineau developed the "Aryan myth" into an elaborate theory of race that taught the superiority of the Aryan race, the notion of preserving the purity of the "race" understood biologically, and the belief that the mixing of races was responsible for creating the supposed decline of Europe (via nihilism and the rise of democracy).[24] This racial theory was called into question by R. Virchow, the anthropologist Nietzsche knew and applauded, who ultimately challenged the presence of biologically defined "races" in Europe.[25] There are also remarks in Nietzsche's works that suggest that "race" is to be understood sociologically in terms of "*Volk*" rather than biologically in terms of "race" (as in Gobineau's sense) (*KSA* 11:25[462]). This certainly should be considered with regard to the question of the possible influence of Gobineau on Nietzsche as well as in any attempt to interpret the blond beast metaphor.[26]

The Roman topos of the Germanic people and the "Aryan myth" were taken up and, in part, merged by numerous authors during the nineteenth century; for example, by Richard Wagner, Thomas Fritsch, and H. S. Chamberlain, whose influence on Hitler and the Nazis can hardly be overestimated.[27] Nietzsche distinguishes himself sharply from the Roman *topos* of the Germanic people in his *On the Genealogy of Morals*—between "the Germanic tribes and us Germans" there is "hardly a conceptual relationship, let alone one of blood" (GM I:11)—although at another juncture he nevertheless employs similar formulations—"blond Germanic beast" (GM I:11). For Nietzsche, the Germanic nobility has the same status as the "Roman, Arabian, [. . .] Japanese nobility, Homeric heroes, and the Scandinavian Vikings" (GM I:11). The "blond Germanic tribes" have no particular ranking in Nietzsche's thinking. He also distances himself from the "Aryan myth," as will be apparent below.

Interpretation

According to Brennecke, Nietzsche created "with the slogan of the 'blond beast' a formula, which must have sounded to German ears to be an unmediated exaltation to become overmen themselves," despite the fact that Nietzsche had pointed out that the blond beast was to be found at the "basis of all noble races" and that the Germans of his day hardly had anything in common with the "Germanic tribes."[28] Nietzsche did not intend such a "relationship between the 'blond beast' and Germanic tribes, between Germans and the overman."[29] Nietzsche was much more concerned with the "taming" of the bestial in man, with the undoing of his "hypermoralization"; that is, with the undoing of the process of his "civilization." He also favored a "progression of man beyond himself with the help of pre-human possibilities."[30] The "Darwinian beast, that no longer bites, the ape," should be replaced by the lion as a symbol of the overman.[31] Blondness is to be seen here as a supranational characteristic.[32] Nietzsche's intention, however, has gone unrecognized, since, despite all of his gestures to distance himself from such readings, the "blond beast" was equated with the Germanic people (and with the Germans) as overmen.[33]

Ottmann believes there is merit in Brennecke's "Concordance of concepts": "Germanic people / Barbarians / blond / lion" as put forth by the Romans, but at the same time, he also sees the danger of the assumption that the "racist legend, while conceptually imprecise, was certainly objectively justified."[34] He summarizes his interpretation of Nietzsche's teaching of the blond beast in four theses:[35] The blond beast is "not a concept reserved exclusively for the original Germanic people," since it is found "at the bottom of all noble races" (GM I:11). It is not a "symbol with contemporary meaning": it is not applied to the Germans of modern times. On the contrary, the blond beast is "an image more applicable to the ancient Greeks than to the original Germans" and serves as an example of Nietzsche's "ideal of the Greek hero and agon culture," as described by J. Burckhardt, who interpreted the Greeks' bestiality to be a sign of their health. Additionally, the blond beast sometimes refers to Nietzsche's "Renaissancismus"—that is, his "cult of the Renaissance"—to "health," "innocence," and "virtù." According to Burckhardt, there is not much sense in seeking to examine the meaning of the beast concept with "racist categories." For Nietzsche, Cesare Borgia is the symbol of the "beast of prey-human" and of *virtù*, "virtue free of morals." Both researchers emphasize the supranational quality of the image of the blond beast.[36]

On the Question of Gobineau's Influence on Nietzsche

In the posthumous text already mentioned (*KSA* 13:15[80]), Nietzsche alludes to the Roman-Germanic *topos* of the "blond and blue-eyed German" (as well as perhaps the "Aryan myth," which shares similar attributes) and rejects it. This could already be an indication that attributing references to the "Aryan myth" (and perhaps to Gobineau in GM I:5) to Nietzsche's own view can only be done with caution. Moreover, in the same text, at a later juncture (GM III:12–21), Nietzsche ventures his own interpretation of the sickness and impending downfall of Europe, a notion that he developed completely independently of Gobineau and that makes no reference to Gobineau's biological "races" and "mixture of races."[37] Furthermore, reflections on the significance of Gobineau for Nietzsche up until now have almost

always overlooked the fact that Gobineau's concept of biologically determined races does not appear in Nietzsche's work.[38]

Reception of the Blond Beast Metaphor

Nietzsche's metaphor of the blond beast had become a slogan by 1906, and
it had been already adopted into the political language of the time by 1895.[39]
This was done, to be more precise, in an abbreviated and misinterpreted
manner that was suited to "subverting Nietzschean values."[40] Nietzsche's distancing himself from both the Roman-Germanic *topos* of the blond and barbaric Germanic tribes (and Germans) and from the "Aryan myth"
(including Gobineau's) was ignored in the conflation of "blond beast" and
"Aryan myth." Thus, it became possible for the blond beast to be understood
in this way by the National Socialists, whose racist theoreticians, such as
Thomas Fritsch, Lanz-Liebenfels and H. St. Chamberlain, the stepson of R.
Wagner, prepared and laid the cornerstones of a dogmatic racial theory.[41] In
addition to these impetuses, Richard Wagner also had a very strong and
direct influence on Hitler himself.[42] These vulgarized ideas were granted significant prominence in Hitler's National Socialist "leadership schools" (*Aus-
leseschulen*).[43] Rauschning referred to the epitome of Hitlerian educational
ideals as a "wonderful beast of prey."[44] The leader of the SS Storm regiment
and criminal perpetrator, Reinhard Heydrich, was given the nickname
"Blond Beast" by his party.[45] After the end of the Nazi dictatorship, the racist
interpretation of the term "blond beast" lived on in part in painting and in
popular fiction.[46]

The Marxist Georg Lukàcs saw in the blond beast a symbol of an "ethics
for the bourgeois class struggle and bourgeois imperialistic intelligence."[47]
The influence of Nietzsche's concept of the blond beast on Thomas Mann is
particularly noticeable in Mann's early novella *Tonio Kröger* (1909), in
which, according to Pütz, Tonio's love of blond Ingeborg depended less on
her individuality than on her belonging to the "race" of "blonds and blue-
eyes." According to Pütz's interpretation, all that is left here are the "two
concepts of 'race' and 'blondness,' the 'beasts' have been transformed into
spiritless, but nonetheless dear representatives of normalcy."[48] In his "Leben-
sabriss" (1930), Thomas Mann distanced himself explicitly from the bestiality of the blond beast.[49]

Overall, as might be expected, the reception of the slogan of the "blond
beast," which quickly evolved into its formulaic rendition, was negative and
contributed significantly to an entirely misconstrued image of Nietzsche.

On the "Meaning" of the Metaphors
"Beast" and "Blond Beast"

The misinterpretation of the blond beast metaphor is due to a large extent to the fact that the metaphor is considered to be based on the "Aryan myth" and in that association is misunderstood as a catchword for the notion, derived from biology, of the higher breeding of human beings. This is not at all accurate, since Nietzsche's concept of race can in no way be related to Gobineau's biological concept of race, a fact that, up to now, has not been clarified sufficiently in Nietzsche research (including in Brennecke's contribution, for example). For Nietzsche, the essence of the beast and blond beast metaphors revolves instead around an integration of nature into culture, something already made clear in his early thematic treatments of this matter in *The Birth of Tragedy*.

On the one hand, this suggests a preservation of nature, even a return to nature, but not in the Rousseauean sense, since Nietzsche's and Rousseau's concepts of nature are fundamentally different.[50] Rather, for Nietzsche, it is a question of nature understood in Dionysian terms, and this not only in the context of *The Birth of Tragedy*. Ansell-Pearson formulates it as follows: "The kind of 'return to nature' Nietzsche favors is a Dionysian one in which the fundamentally amoral character of existence is recognized and affirmed and which depends on adopting an attitude towards life that is beyond good and evil." It is a matter of "the triumph of artistic nobility and strength over weakness and resentment."[51]

It is also a matter of preserving Nature in another sense. For Nietzsche, the human is the "as yet undetermined animal [*das noch nicht festgestellte Thier*]" (*BGE* 62). Van Tongeren interprets this notion as follows: "On the one hand the human being is an animal: natural, corporeal, driven by instincts, etc. But, on the other hand, the naturalness of this being is not complete and encompassing. Human beings are not completely determined by their instincts once and for all into one particular pattern. They do not have a fixed and definite identity but maintain many possibilities."[52] Therefore, human beings, as "as yet undetermined," have the task of continually redefining themselves, in order to become that which they should become. In this process of self-realization, there are higher and less-elevated types of self-realization to be achieved. Those on the higher path to self-realization are types, "which most comply with the human being as being undetermined, that is, those who are most open to many possibilities."[53] It is therefore a matter of remaining open despite all inclinations to become fixed;

definitions can only be provisional, specific to a given time. We can now see that all of the above attempts to define the blond beast dogmatically as one particular type are from the start misconceptions of Nietzsche's image of the human.

Both endeavors to "preserve" nature (in Nietzsche's sense of the word) in culture unite in the image of the human, who seeks his self-realization in an agonal struggle of the plurality of opposite drives and instincts of a "Dionysian" nature: in a struggle that never ends and that strives to achieve ever-more-successful—that is, higher—syntheses of "nature" and "culture."[54]

The question as to whether such blond beasts are historically substantiated, whether they ever existed—that is, if "higher" self-realizations of the "as yet undetermined animal" man have been historically realized—has been answered by Nietzsche affirmatively. He makes reference, for example, to the Homeric heroes and to Pericles, just to name a few (GM I:11). Whoever, therefore, is looking for models of blond beasts can refer to these examples, which have no relationship to biological theories of breeding.

Notes

This chapter was translated by Jennifer Ham, excepting translations of Nietzsche's works, for which the following translations are used: Whiteside's translation of BT, Hollingdale's translation of BGE, Kaufmann and Hollingdale's translation of GM, Faber's translation of HH, and Kaufmann's translation of TI.

1. D. Brennecke provides important groundwork for this in "Die blonde Bestie. Vom Missverständnis eines Schlagworts," Nietzsche-Studien 5 (1976): 113–145. My contribution presented here is based on two entries ("beast" and "blond beast") in the Nietzsche Dictionary (volume 1, forthcoming in 2003), revised for the present publication. See also Paul J. M. van Tongeren, Schank, and the Nietzsche Research Group (Nijmegen University), "HORS D'OEUVRE: Nietzsche's Language und Use of Language," Journal of Nietzsche Studies 22 (2001): 5–16.

2. Nietzsche's teacher Ritschl refers to a tour guide in Italy as a "beast" on account of his "cringing soul." F. W. Ribbeck, F. W. Ritschl. Ein Beitrag zur Geschichte der Philologie, 2 vols. (Leipzig, 1879), I:171.

3. On Schlegel's reference to himself as a "beast of friendship," see R. Huch, Die Romantik. Ausbreitung, Blütezeit, Verfall (Tübingen: Rainer Wunderlich Verlag, 1951), 25.

4. Ritschl refers to "false poetic meters" in Plautus as "beasts," which the editor transformed into "well educated, dear house pets" (Ribbeck, F. W. Ritschl, II:124).

5. For the use of "bestial" as an intensification in Grimmelshausen, in the Storm and Stress period, and in Schiller, see H. Paul, Deutsches Wörterbuch 9th completely new edition by Helmut Henne and Georg Objartel in conjunction with Heidrun Kämper-Jensen (Tübingen: Niemeyer, 1992), keyword "beast."

6. On "bestiality" for "brute barbarity" (as early as 1603), see Paul, *Deutsches Wörterbuch*, keyword "beast."

7. In Schopenhauer, "bestiality" appears as a heightened form of "nationalism"; see A. Schopenhauer, *Ueber die vierfache Wurzel des Satzes vom zureichenden Grunde*, 3rd ed. (Leipzig: F. A. Brockhaus, 1864), 122.

8. See B. von Reibnitz, "Die Geburt der Tragödie," in *Ein Kommentar zu Friedrich Nietzsche* (Weimar, 1992), 104–105.

9. For an interpretation of the *Birth of Tragedy* reference, see Reibnitz, "Die Geburt der Tragödie," 90–91.

10. Reibnitz, "Die Geburt der Tragödie," 90–91.

11. See H. Ottmann, *Philosophie und Politik bei Nietzsche* (Berlin, 1987), 257.

12. On the role of morality, see *HH* 40; on Darwin und Rée: *GM* P 7; on the role of "bad conscience": *GM* II:22; on the church's "attempts to tame": *TI* "Improvers" 2; on the contemporary situation and criticism of inappropriate attempts to "improve": Nietzsche's posthumous work *KSA* 8:3[76], *KSA* 13:11[278], and *KSA* 8:12[22]; and *HH* 451.

13. Ottmann, *Philosophie und Politik bei Nietzsche*, 134.

14. P. Rée, *Der Ursprung der moralischen Empfindungen* (Chemnitz, 1877), 45.

15. See also *BGE* 257 and U. Marti, "Der grosse Pöbel- und Sklavenaufstand," in *Nietzsches Auseinandersetzung mit Revolution und Demokratie* (Stuttgart: 1993), 31.

16. Brennecke, "Die blonde Bestie," 136.

17. Brennecke, "Die blonde Bestie," 115–116.

18. Ottmann, *Philosophie und Politik bei Nietzsche*, 257.

19. F. Kluge, *Etymologisches Wörterbuch der deutschen Sprache* (Berlin, 1957), keyword "blond."

20. See Brennecke, "Die blonde Bestie," 135–139.

21. Ottmann, *Philosophie und Politik bei Nietzsche*, 255.

22. For thorough commentary see R. Römer, *Sprachwissenschaft und Rassenideologie in Deutschland*, 2nd ed. (München: Wilhelm Fink Verlag, 1989), 62–84.

23. See Giuliano Campioni, Paolo D'Iorio, Maria Cristina Fornari, Francesco Fronterotta, and Andrea Orsucci in collaboration with Renate MüllerBuck, *Nietzsches Bibliothek* (Berlin: De Gruyter, 2003), 423: no. 1269. Also see Th. Poesche, *Die Arier: Ein Beitrag zur historischen Anthropologie* (Jena: H. Costenoble, 1878).

24. A. de Gobineau, *Essai sur l'inégalité des races humaines* (Paris, 1967 [originally published 1853–1855]). On Gobineau's influence on R. Wagner and on the "Bayreuther Blätter," which he edited, see A. Hein, *"Es ist viel Hitler in Wagner": Rassismus und antisemitischeDeutschtumsideologie in den "Bayreuther Blättern" 1878–1938* (Tübingen: 1996), 139ff.

25. G. Schank, *"Rasse" und "Züchtung" bei Nietzsche* (Berlin: Walter de Gruyter, 2000), 7 ff.

26. See Schank, *"Rasse" und "Züchtung" bei Nietzsche*, 28f. and 426 ff. for a refutation of the influence of Gobineau on Nietzsche.

27. On the reception of the "Aryan Myth," see L. Poliakov, *Der arische Mythos: Zu den*

Quellen von Rassismus und Nationalismus (Vienna, 1977); Hein, *"Es ist viel Hitler in Wagner,"* 110–122; and Schank, *"Rasse" und "Züchtung" bei Nietzsche*, 51–60.

28. Brennecke, "Die blonde Bestie," 140.

29. Brennecke, "Die blonde Bestie," 114.

30. Brennecke, "Die blonde Bestie," 122.

31. Brennecke, "Die blonde Bestie," 122.

32. Brennecke, "Die blonde Bestie," 143.

33. Brennecke, "Die blonde Bestie," 143.

34. Ottmann, *Philosophie und Politik bei Nietzsche*, 255.

35. Ottmann, *Philosophie und Politik bei Nietzsche*, 256–258.

36. Brennecke, "Die blonde Bestie," 143.

37. For thorough commentary see Schank *"Rasse" und "Züchtung" bei Nietzsche*, 150–162.

38. Schank, *"Rasse" und "Züchtung" bei Nietzsche*, 426–441.

39. O. Ladendorf, *Historisches Schlagwörterbuch* (Strassburg/Berlin: 1906), "blond beast"; Brennecke, "Die blonde Bestie," 140; Ottmann, *Philosophie und Politik bei Nietzsche*, 254.

40. See S. Aschheim, *The Nietzsche Legacy in Germany 1890–1990* (Berkeley: University of California Press, 1992), 31, for further references.

41. C. Berning, "Die Sprache des Nationalsozialismus," *Zeitschrift für deutsche Wortforschung* 19 (1963): 98f.; Brennecke, "Die blonde Bestie," 124f.

42. On R. Wagner's influence on Hitler, see W. Santaniello, *Nietzsche, God and the Jews* (Albany: State University of New York Press, 1994), 41f.; and B. Hamann, *Hitler's Wien. Lehrjahre eins Diktators* (München: 1996), 89f.; on Gobineau and Wagner and the "Bayreuther Blätter," see Hein, *"Es ist viel Hitler in Wagner,"* 175–184.

43. See Aschheim, *The Nietzsche Legacy in Germany 1890–1990*, 139.

44. H. Rauschning, *Gespräche mit Hitler* (Zürich/New York: 1940), 237.

45. H. Höhne, *Der Orden unter dem Totenkopf* (Gütersloh, 1983), 154.

46. On painting, see Brennecke, "Die blonde Bestie," 121; on popularized literature (e.g., Ian Fleming's *James Bond* novels): 125.

47. Quoted in Brennecke, "Die blonde Bestie," 127.

48. Both cited by P. Pütz, "Thomas Mann und Nietzsche" in *Nietzsche und die deutsche Literatur II* (Tübingen: B.Hillebrand, 1978), 138.

49. Quoted in Brennecke, "Die blonde Bestie," 142.

50. See *TI* "Skirmishes" 48; and Keith Ansell-Pearson, *Nietzsche Contra Rousseau: A Study of Nietzsche's Moral and Political Thought* (Cambridge: Cambridge University Press, 1991), 30.

51. Ansell-Pearson, *Nietzsche Contra Rousseau*, 31.

52. P. Van Tongeren, *Reinterpreting Modern Culture: An Introduction to Friedrich Nietzsche's Philosophy* (West Lafayette, Ind.: Purdue University Press, 2000), 199f.

53. Van Tongeren, *Reinterpreting Modern Culture*, 201.

54. See Nietzsche's notes at *KSA* 11:27[59]; and Van Tongeren, *Reinterpreting Modern Culture*, 241f.

How We Became What We Are: Tracking the "Beasts of Prey"

Daniel W. Conway

There is, of course, a beast hidden in every man.

—Ivan Karamozov

The beast in me
Is caged by frail and fragile bars.
Restless by day
And by night rants and rages at the stars.
God help the beast in me.

—Johnny Cash

No member of Nietzsche's crowded menagerie has attracted so much attention as the infamous "blond beast" (*blonde Bestie*). The notoriety of this creature persists, moreover, despite only a very few documented sightings. The "blond beast" appears thrice in a single section of *On the Genealogy of Morals* (GM I:11), prowls again in a later section of the same book (GM II:17), and roars one final time in *Twilight of the Idols* (TI "Improvers" 2). [1] Other ani-

156

mals, including the cow, the horse, the ape, the dog, and, of course, Zarathustra's companions, the eagle and the serpent, appear far more frequently in Nietzsche's writings. But it is the rarely glimpsed "blond beast" that fascinates and frightens Nietzsche's readers.

Although some species of lions, tigers, bears, foxes, and dogs qualify quite literally as "blond beasts," it is Nietzsche's practice to reserve the designation for those human (or proto-human) beings who act like wild animals toward other human (or proto-human) beings. The creatures that he so designates, moreover, are not simply referenced and cataloged, as one might expect from a scientific taxonomy of human types. Nietzsche also *admires* the "blond beast," and he does so precisely insofar as it displays a "noble" penchant for predatory behavior toward other human (or proto-human) beings:

> One may be quite justified in continuing to fear the blond beast at the core of all noble races and in being on one's guard against it: but who would not a hundred times sooner fear where one can also admire than *not* fear but be permanently condemned to the repellent sight of the ill-constituted, dwarfed, atrophied, and poisoned? (GM I:11)

Nietzsche furthermore hints that a timely renascence of this type, albeit in dramatically altered form, may yet deliver humankind from the throes of degeneration and the threat of permanent extinction. A renascence of this type is necessary, he explains, because the blond beast did not survive the difficult transition to the modern world. Its impressive reign of terror, as recorded in various epics and circulatory myths of antiquity, ended long before the dawning of the modern age. By the "early middle Ages," he observes, "the most beautiful specimens of the 'blond beast' were hunted down everywhere" and transformed (= "sickened") into Christians (*TI* "Improvers" 2). The blond beast now lives only at the "hidden core" of noble peoples and cultures, its native wildness barely discernible beneath a thick mantle of domestic manners and civilized politesse.

Especially in light of the Nazi appropriation of Nietzsche's philosophy, the controversy surrounding the *blondness* of the blond beast is both understandable and urgent.[2] This controversy has also had the unfortunate effect, however, of diverting attention away from the *beastliness* of this exotic creature. Much to the dismay of many contemporary admirers and champions, in fact, Nietzsche regularly glorifies the violent exploits of predatory peoples and cultures. He maintains, for example, that

> One cannot fail to see at the bottom of all these noble races the beast of prey [*das Raubthier*], the splendid blond beast [*blond Bestie*] prowling about avidly in search

of spoil and victory; this hidden core needs to erupt from time to time, the animal [*das Thier*] has to get out again and go back to the wilderness. . . . It is the noble races that have left behind them the concept "barbarian" wherever they have gone; even their highest culture betrays a consciousness of it and even a pride in it. (GM I:11)

As this passage reveals, Nietzsche treats the "blond beast" as a particular expression or instance of what he more regularly calls a "beast of prey." Like the blond beast, the beast of prey is not so much an animal as it is a *biomorphism*, i.e., a human/hominid type described in terms pertaining more conventionally to non-human animal species. As such, the beast of prey designates any human (or proto-human) being who acts like a wild predator toward other human (or proto-human) beings. Unlike more familiar human/hominid types, the beast of prey is able to enjoy periodic exteriorizations of its "hidden core." It is able to do so, moreover, only at great expense to those weaker human (or proto-human) beings who suffer its "spoil and victory."

Let us now turn our attention to the question that has been obscured by the controversy surrounding pigmentation and other physiognomic markers of ethnic identification: What does Nietzsche mean to convey when he refers, approvingly, to some human beings as "beasts of prey"?

I

It is well known that Nietzsche takes as his task the "translation" of the human being "back into nature" (*BGE* 230).[3] It is also well known that he attempts to accomplish this task by placing the human being on an organic continuum with all other animal species. He consequently locates the human being squarely within the amoral environs of the animal kingdom, which he in turn honors as subordinate to none—including the kingdoms supposedly ruled by "man" and "God." He thus acknowledges no hierarchical index—whether divine, metaphysical, or supernatural—whereby the human animal could be considered to be absolutely superior to other animals or endowed with extra-animalistic powers and privileges. According to Nietzsche, the human animal is neither the acme of natural selection nor the telos of evolutionary development nor the lord of the beasts nor the center of the biotic community nor the steward of the planetary thesaurus. The human animal is distinguished from other animals only by its besetting illness, by its unrivaled capacity to endure self- and other-induced suffering.

Nietzsche thus presents human psychology as a more complicated instance of animal psychology. Like all animals, the human being instinctively seeks above all else to discharge its native energies in outward expenditures of force and power. Like all animals, that is, the human being is a dynamic, surging capacitor of vitality, involuntarily enmeshed in the complex material processes that collectively define the ambit of life itself. Nietzsche thus explains that

> Every animal—therefore la bête philosophe, too—instinctively strives for an optimum of favorable conditions under which it can expend all its strength [Kraft] and achieve its maximal feeling of power [Machtgefühl]; every animal abhors, just as instinctively and with a subtlety of discernment that is "higher than all reason," every kind of intrusion or hindrance that obstructs or could obstruct this path to the optimum. (GM III:7).

According to Nietzsche, human animals differ from wild (or wilder) animals not in kind, only in degree. In particular, he attributes the relative uniqueness of human psychology to its unprecedented degree of internal complexity. Whereas the life activity of a wild (or wilder) animal is characterized by a relatively direct and spontaneous discharge of its native energies, the life activity of human animals is characterized by a relatively indirect and delayed discharge of its native energies. Some human animals are so burdened with internal complexity, in fact, that their "core" vitality can "erupt" only rarely and sporadically, and only under conditions that are carefully scripted and scrupulously policed.[4]

The main problem that Nietzsche faces in pursuing this task is that modern human beings in many respects do not resemble other, wilder animals. We are not obviously reliant upon unconscious drives and impulses to provide us with instinctual patterns of behavior that we then enact in prereflective embodiments of our native vitality. Our possession of conscience and free will, our facility with languages and complex symbolic systems, our creation of cultures and civilization, and our premonition of our own death all seem to place us well outside the animal kingdom. To put it bluntly, the "ultramodern unassuming moral milksop who 'no longer bites'" (GM P:7) is not easily confused with "the splendid blond beast prowling about avidly in search of spoil and victory" (GM I:11). It is therefore incumbent upon the genealogist of morals to explain how it is that we became what we are. In so doing, he must account for the development of the human being from wild predator to domesticated herd animal.

Nietzsche's account of this development is well known to us in its general outline. The domesticated human animal is uniquely characterized by its "bad conscience" (*schlechtes Gewissen*), which Nietzsche diagnoses as an organic affliction that significantly restricts the human animal's capacity to exteriorize its native animal energy.[5] This affliction, he explains, was produced in the human animal by means of an involuntary introjection of its primal drives and impulses. This inward discharge in turn succeeded in forcibly investing the human animal with an unparalleled, if jumbled, expanse of interiority:

> All instincts that do not discharge themselves outwardly *turn inward*—this is what I call the *internalization* of humankind: thus it was that man first developed what was later called his "soul." The entire inner world, originally as thin as if it were stretched between two membranes, expanded and extended itself, acquired depth, breadth, and height, in the same measure as outward discharge was inhibited. (GM II:16)

He furthermore explains this process of "internalization" as a consequence of

> the most fundamental change [man] ever experienced—that change which occurred when he found himself finally enclosed within the walls of society and peace. The situation that faced sea animals when they were compelled to become land animals or perish was the same as that which faced these semi-animals, well adapted to the wilderness, to war, to prowling, to adventure: suddenly all their instincts were disvalued and "suspended." (GM II:16)

This is a powerful and compelling thesis, as confirmed by Freud's extensive reliance on it in *Civilization and Its Discontents*. As an explanation, however, this thesis raises at least as many questions as it answers. How, for example, did this monumental change come about? Who or what is responsible for confining these wild, warlike, prowling semi-animals within the "walls of society and peace"?

Here Nietzsche finds himself in a difficult spot. Much like Hegel, Feuerbach, Marx, Freud, and other practitioners of philosophical anthropology, he must appeal to an event or occurrence that is fully natural (and, so, in principle empirically verifiable), despite having no direct evidence of the event or occurrence in question.[6] This means that he is obliged to speculate on the natural historical processes that have contributed to the domestication of the human animal.[7] The chief danger involved in speculations of this sort is that they encourage historians and anthropologists to appeal to modern human conventions (e.g., founding agreements, social contracts) to explain the origins of human society. If Nietzsche's hypothesis is to avoid a vicious circularity, then it must account for the domestication of the human animal without appealing to any virtues, powers, or capacities that uniquely belong to the modern human beings whose situation it is supposed to explain.

The very next section of GM provides a clarifying expansion of his hypothesis concerning the domestication of the human animal. "Among the presuppositions of this hypothesis," he explains, is the following conjecture:

> The welding of a hitherto unchecked and formless populace [Bevölkerung] into a firm form was not only instituted by an act of violence but also carried to its conclusion by nothing but acts of violence—that the oldest "state" thus appeared as a fearful tyranny, as an oppressive and remorseless machine, and went on working until this raw material of peoples and semi-animals [Rohstoff von Volk und Halbthier] was at last not only thoroughly kneaded and pliant but also formed. (GM II:17)

To be sure, this "presupposition" bears further elaboration. As we have seen, GM II:16 identifies no agents or culprits who might be deemed responsible for the enforced confinement of the formerly wild hominids. There, in fact, we were led to conclude that *all* formerly wild hominids suffered a common fate pertaining to the suspension and devaluation of their instincts.

As Nietzsche asserts in GM II:17, however, this fate was either not suffered, or not suffered uniformly, by all formerly wild hominids. Indeed, GM II:17 alludes to the clash of *two* hominid types, one less and the other more estranged from its native animality. Witness, for example, his unsentimental account of the origins of the "state":

> [S]ome pack of blond beasts of prey [ein Rudel blonder Raubthiere], a conqueror and master race [eine Eroberer- und Herren-Rasse][8] which, organized for war and with the ability to organize, unhesitatingly lays its terrible claws upon a populace [Bevölkerung] perhaps tremendously superior in numbers but still formless and nomadic. (GM II:17)[9]

As this passage reveals, Nietzsche's "presupposition" is apparently meant to explain how the "semi-animals" described in GM II:16 came to find themselves involuntarily immured within civil society. As it turns out, they were forcibly placed there by *other* "semi-animals," who, for reasons as yet unknown, either possessed or retained a greater share of their native wildness and predatory spontaneity.

Nietzsche does not disclose the basis for this stipulated distinction between two types (or sub-species) of wild hominids. He observes only that the aggressor type arrives on the scene much as it appears in the thick of his narrative: suddenly, unpredictably, and without adequate explanation. Relying on a familiar image of the masterful, commanding human types whom he most admires,[10] he compares the arrival of the aggressor type to the onset of an unforeseen natural disaster:

> One does not reckon with such [that is, "masterly"] natures; they come like fate, without reason, consideration, or pretext; they appear as lightning appears, too terrible, too sudden, too convincing, too "different" even to be hated. (GM II:17)

This sort of comparison is convenient not only for the captive hominids, who need not trouble themselves to divine the occult motives of their inscrutable aggressors, but also for Nietzsche, who is freed thereby from the onerous task of explaining the origins, history, and aims of the aggressor type.

What are we to make of this provocative, albeit telegraphic, account of the origins of the "state"? We might understand Nietzsche to be appealing here to the stochastic variations that characterize any species population of sufficient size. It is probable that some identifiable subset of wild hominids would be far more aggressive than the average hominid, and it is plausible that these stochastic outliers might band together and conquer the larger (but less aggressive) subset. Alternately, we might interpret the suddenness with which the aggressor type appears on the scene as suggesting the unprecedented meeting, and subsequent clash, of two separate species of hominid development. Or perhaps Nietzsche helps himself to such an obviously facile distinction in order to mock *any* attempt (including his own) to unearth the historical origins of the "state."[11] Still, one cannot help but wonder if this all-too-convenient distinction between hominid types does not compromise the integrity of his speculative "hypothesis." Did he not originally set out to *explain* (rather than assert or stipulate) the violent capture and enclosure of formerly wild hominids?

In all fairness to Nietzsche, he advances this "presupposition," as well as the "hypothesis" it serves, in the context of a more sweeping anthropological narrative. The text that constitutes GM II:16–17 does not describe the first meeting between rival branches of hominid descent so much as it speculates on the particular kind of meeting that might have led to the establishment of the "state." According to Nietzsche, the hypothetical founding of the "state" was preceded by a lengthy and largely unknown *pre*history, which he describes as the vast era of the "morality of mores" [*die Sittlichkeit der Sitte*], which preceded "world history" as the truly decisive history that determined the character of humankind. (GM III:9)

It was in this prehistoric period, moreover, that "the labor performed by man on himself" attained its most enduring achievement: "with the aid of the morality of mores and the social straitjacket, man was actually *made* calculable" (GM II:2).

Nietzsche furthermore speculates that this prehistoric period of self-directed labor coincided with the heyday of the beasts of prey. Prior to the species-altering moment described in GM II:16–17, he asserts, the beasts of prey enjoyed a long, bloody reign of terror, seizing hominid tribes and inflicting cruelty upon them. Throughout this period, the beasts of prey maintained the purity of their "innocent conscience," dispensing punishment freely, spontaneously, and creatively. Waxing nostalgic for the good old days of natural, manly violence, Nietzsche goes so far as to insist that even the victims and captives of the beasts of prey were better off then, for they were not made to endure—as their fully human progeny soon would be—the suffering of the "bad conscience":

> If we consider those millennia *before* the history of man, we may unhesitatingly assert that it was precisely through punishment that the development of the feeling of guilt was most powerfully *hindered*—at least in the victims upon whom the punitive force was vented. . . . The person upon whom punishment subsequently descended, again like a piece of fate, suffered no "inward pain" other than that induced by the sudden appearance of something unforeseen, a dreadful natural event, a plunging, crashing rock that one cannot fight. (GM II:14)

When placed against the backdrop of this admittedly speculative account, the text that constitutes GM II:16–17 can be seen to describe the founding event of a distinctly human history. From this point forward, "man" became an increasingly interesting animal. He had been made sufficiently calculable, reliable, docile, and adaptable that he might actually survive an enforced estrangement from his natural, instinctual heritage. The "morality of mores," thousands of years in the making, was pressed into service as the largely imperceptible foundation for the kind of morality—inward, reflective, abstract, reactive, and universal—from which Nietzsche traces the descent of "our morality." The text that constitutes GM II:16–17 thus describes the unique historical conditions under which the beasts of prey developed a more settled, place-bound form of community.[12]

The rest, as they say, is history—*human* history, to be precise. Emboldened by the "slave revolt in morality" (GM I:10), which falsely promised captive peoples the freedom to *choose* their enforced domestication, the human animal began to explore the undiscovered country of its inner kingdom, or soul. In order to cope with the meaningless suffering of the "bad conscience," the human animal heaped compensatory fantasy upon compensatory fantasy, culminating in the installation of guilt as the primary motivation for its various endeavors. And so we became what we are: sickly animals precariously converging on the "will to nothingness."

II

But what of the beasts of prey who unwittingly launched the domestication of the human animal along this downbound trajectory? Were they in turn conquered, enslaved, or slaughtered by an even wilder pack of semi-animals? Or did they simply vanish, perhaps as suddenly and unpredictably as they appeared? That such questions are not merely academic is confirmed when Nietzsche surmises that "the *meaning of all culture*" lies in "the reduction of the beast of prey 'man' to a tame and civilized animal" (GM I:11). Let us turn now to consider how this "reduction" might have been accomplished.

It is no coincidence that Nietzsche relegates the formative activity of the beasts of prey to the dim prehistory of the species. In the context of his speculative anthropological narrative, the beasts of prey fill the role of a permanently missing link. They are the shadowy, liminal creatures that connect the domesticated human animal to its wild ancestors in the unbroken chain of evolutionary development. Owing to their unique transitional role in this narrative, the beasts of prey in fact acquire a quasi-mythic status. In what is perhaps his most dubious reference to the beasts of prey, he describes them as partaking equally of both wild predation *and* civilized cultivation:[13]

> Once they [that is, these noble men] go outside, where the strange, the *stranger*, is found, they are not much better than uncaged beasts of prey [*Raubthiere*]. There they savor a freedom from all social constraints, they compensate themselves in the wilderness for the tension engendered by protracted confinement and enclosure within the peace of society, they go back to the innocent conscience of the beast of prey [*Unschuld des Raubthier-Gewissens*], as triumphant monsters [*Ungeheuer*]. (GM I:11)[14]

Although indirectly responsible for the affliction of the "bad conscience" in others,[15] the beasts of prey enjoy the privileges and freedoms pertaining to

an innocent conscience. They can postpone immediate gratification if necessary and without penalty to their capacity to visit primal aggression upon
unlucky nomads. They not only patrol the enclosing walls of civil society but
also scale these walls periodically and return to the wilderness that nourishes
them. These predators operate collectively under an impressive regimen of
self-imposed organization, but they are more similar in their maneuvers to
the wilding of a wolf pack than to the charge of a battalion. Borrowing a
sentence from a related discussion, we might think of the beasts of prey as

> Human beings whose nature was still natural, barbarians in every terrible sense of
> the word, men of prey [*Raubmenschen*] who were still in possession of unbroken
> strength of will and lust for power . . . more *whole* human beings (which also means,
> at every level, "more whole beasts"). (*BGE* 257)

These paradoxical designations of the beasts of prey point to the conceptual problem that exercises Nietzsche in Essay II of GM. Put bluntly, he can
find no fitting analogue in the wild animal kingdom to the organized assault
that his beasts of prey supposedly conduct. Much to our surprise, perhaps, his
beasts of prey do not always mercilessly slaughter their captives. Nor do they
always torture or play with their captives, as a cat will toy with a vole until
(or while) killing it. Unlike the "great birds of prey," who insist that "nothing is more tasty than a tender lamb" (GM I:13), Nietzsche's beasts of prey
occasionally *keep* their captives. They not only put their captives to work but
also impose upon them the order and discipline they need to work efficiently
and productively. These beasts of prey thus exert on their formerly nomadic
captives a distinctly formative influence, which is conducive to the processes
familiarly known to us as "domestication," "cultivation," and "acculturation." In short, Nietzsche's terrible beasts of prey are *also* cultivators and nur-
turers. In this respect, or so it might seem, they depart dramatically from the
practices of the wild predators on whom they are modeled.[16]

Having revealed the softer, gentler side of his beasts of prey, Nietzsche
must now explain how a predatory animal, whose natural orientation to
weaker animals is the dispensation of torture and death, acquires what
appears to be a new orientation to its prey. That is, he must demonstrate
that what we call "predation" and "cultivation" are in fact coeval expressions
of primal animal vitality, such that seemingly uncomplicated beasts of prey
can naturally exhibit predilections for domestication and acculturation. This
is not to suggest, of course, that beasts of prey cannot also be organized and
disciplined. The animal kingdom is replete with creatures that exhibit highly

organized patterns of collective behavior, including those predators that con-tribute unwittingly to the domestication of other animal species. It is to Nietzsche's credit, in fact, that he opposes the popular caricature of "wild-ness" with an expanded and more sophisticated notion that enables him to account for the capacities of complex natural systems for self-organization and self-regulation.

Still, it is certainly fair here to cast a suspicious eye on his evolving por-trait of these surprisingly versatile beasts of prey. In the end, does he not equivocate on the beastliness of the beasts of prey? Has he perhaps baited us with his profile of a bloodthirsty, wild, torture-and-death-dealing predator, only to switch in mid-narrative to an organized, patient, delay-gratifying nur-turer? Has he cleverly trained his beasts of prey to serve their master in the role of *brutus ex machina*?

Nietzsche's most persuasive response to this line of questioning would most likely draw upon his controversial description of the beasts of prey as *artists*.[17] It is their native capacity for artistry, he maintains, that enables them to engage in a kind of predation that is *also* civilizing and nurturing. As he explains,

> Their work is an instinctive creation and imposition of forms; they are the most involuntary, unconscious artists there are—wherever they appear something new soon arises, a ruling structure that *lives*, in which parts and functions are delineated and co-ordinated. . . . They exemplify that terrible artists' egoism that has the look of bronze and knows itself justified to all eternity in its "work," like a mother in her child. (GM II:17)

As this passage confirms, the beasts of prey practice their artistry most con-spicuously in the preferred medium of *other human or hominid beings*. In bring-ing order and purpose to a formerly formless populace, the beasts of prey impart meaning and identity to their captives. They are, in short, givers of new life. Nietzsche thus refers to them, approvingly, as "artists of violence and organizers who build states" (GM II:18).

It is difficult not to find this imagery abhorrent. Nietzsche's cavalier allu-sions to the "molding" and "ordering" of entire tribes and nations—which by no means lack form and culture prior to their capture—are at least as disturbing as his approbatory references to the "blond beast." Many of Nietz-sche's readers have duly registered their disgust with his careless glorifications of violence and with his political naiveté in general.[18] Other readers have attempted to soften his praise for the beasts of prey by focusing on his experimental deployment of potentially defensible rhetorical strategies.[19] Still others have attempted to separate his admiration for innovation and creativity from the retrograde political sentiments it so often serves.[20]

Whatever we may think of it, however, Nietzsche's appeal to the artistry of the beasts of prey is the key to his account of the domestication of the human animal. By characterizing the beasts of prey as artists, he means to draw our attention to the transformative, life-bestowing effects of any outward expenditure of animal vitality. The scene of predation, he apparently wishes to claim, is not limited to the pursuit, capture, and death of the prey organism. Predation more fundamentally produces a multivalent vivification of the surrounding environment. This production is most evident in the predator and prey species, which mutually encourage one another to adapt continually to their shared habitat, but it is by no means restricted to them. Even those outbursts of primal aggression that culminate in the death of the prey organism succeed in reanimating the surrounding environment, for they contribute to the renewal of natural cycles and the maintenance or restoration of growth within the environment as a whole. Although predation invariably eliminates individual members of prey species, it also renews the prey species itself and thereby grants new life to the interdependent configurations of species within a particular habitat.

Predators are therefore always also artists: they continuously re-create the environment that surrounds them, thereby refreshing the dynamism in which its unique beauty lies. They are in fact artists in the highest sense recognized by Nietzsche, for they create and re-create new forms of life. He is quick to emphasize, moreover, that the artistic dimension of these displays of primal aggression is by no means deliberate or intentional, much less malicious or immoral: "Their work is an instinctive creation and imposition of forms; they are the most involuntary, unconscious artists" (GM II:17). In this respect, too, they resemble the swollen river, the bolt of lightning, and the crashing boulder, for they amorally and unintentionally transfigure the environment that surrounds them.

This blind transformation of the surrounding environment is what Nietzsche means by the *artistry* practiced by the beasts of prey. To be sure, beasts of prey cannot help but stalk, maim, torture, and kill their victims, just as birds of prey cannot help but seize tender little lambs (GM I:13). To expect or demand the beasts of prey to do otherwise, after the fashion of the Church, would oblige one to sicken these noble creatures (TI "Improvers" 2). According to Nietzsche, however, the perspective adopted by the Church on the beasts of prey is unfortunately (and typically) narrow. In doing what they do naturally, the beasts of prey do not *merely* stalk, maim, torture, and kill, as if these activities could be neatly abstracted from the larger contexts in which they occur. As predators, the beasts of prey also create something ordered and vital from an otherwise inconsequential mass of formless hominids.

Here, too, we must not be distracted by Nietzsche's offensive imagery. His larger point is that predation in any form contributes to the renewal of life and the reanimation of otherwise moribund natural systems. In the context of his anthropological narrative, this means that the beasts of prey also *elevate* and *improve* the populace upon which they vent their outbursts of primal vitality. Those captives who survive the form-giving wrath of the beasts of prey are ennobled by the assault, for they are then able to partake of "a ruling structure that *lives*, in which parts and functions are delineated and coordinated" (GM II:17).

The specific case of predation thus demonstrates (or reminds us) that the distinction between "wild" and "civilized" is only of limited use to Nietzsche. Any prehistorical event of interest to him, like the founding of the original "state," invariably transpires at (or near) the intersections of "wilderness" and "civilization." As his narrative discloses, what is generally considered "wild" is far more civilized than we initially might have thought, and what is generally considered to be "civilized" is wilder than we are usually inclined to allow. Rather than stray, as suspected, from the model of wild nature to which he appeals, he in fact expands this model and purges it of its moral taint. Rather than equivocate on the beastliness of his beasts of prey, he undertakes a more daring exploration of what beastliness actually entails. He thus encourages us to understand beastliness as always already involving some elements of what we more regularly associate with civilization. As it turns out, in fact, beastliness involves killing *and* cultivating, maiming *and* nurturing, destroying *and* creating. To be a beast of prey is to practice a form of lethal artistry that also nurtures, informs, enriches, and civilizes.

The unintended elevation of this captive populace in turn closed the distance that originally separated it from its captors. As the populace improved, so, presumably, did the quality and quantity of the material products of its enforced labor, upon which the beasts of prey had grown increasingly dependent. When the beasts of prey beheld the fruits of their artistry, as reflected back to them in the structure and definition that had come to inform the nomadic populace upon which they labored, their form-giving artistry eventually fed back upon itself. The perfections mirrored back to the beasts of prey by the products of their primal aggression thus exerted an indirectly civilizing effect on *them*. Inspired by the order, form, and beauty produced by the wrath they had visited upon their helpless captives, the beasts of prey may have unleashed similar regimens of violence against themselves. The ensuing modulations of their artistry may in turn have educed natural capacities for domestication and cultivation from their native complement of drives and impulses. In other words, the evolution of beastly predation into organized domestication may have been a natural, dialogical consequence of the formative artistry practiced by the beasts of prey.

The feedback loop initiated by the artistry of the beasts of prey also enables Nietzsche to account for their eventual disappearance and consequent absence from the historical record. The dialogical process described above also led to the gradual, indirect, and unwitting *self*-domestication of the beasts of prey.[21] Over the course of this process, the acculturation that attends the imposition of form onto matter fed back upon its purveyors, gradually domesticating *them* in accordance with the principles they dictated to their captives.[22] What may have begun as amoral play with their helpless captives—as a prelude, perhaps, to torture or sacrifice—eventually resulted in the beasts of prey *joining* the populace they formerly had terrorized. Although it may be difficult to imagine Nietzsche's beasts of prey blending into the populace of a modern polity, it may not be so difficult to imagine them joining a populace that had been formed, molded, and improved in their own wild image. Perhaps, that is, the beasts of prey need not have fallen very far at all before merging with the elevated populace to which they had given form, shape, and identity.

Yet even the most talented of artists could not have raised a formless nomadic mass to a level commensurate with the wild beasts of prey. Nietzsche must consequently account for a countervailing leveling influence by means of which the beasts of prey were sickened, declawed, and thoroughly domesticated. They were victimized, he conjectures, by none other than the ascetic priest, who effectively poisoned the dialogical relationship that originally obtained between the beasts of prey and the products of their artistry. Owing to the intercession of the ascetic priest, the beasts of prey learned to pity their captives and to loathe the beauty, form, and order that were reflected back to them by the products of their primal aggression.[23] Having become works of art in their own right, the beasts of prey were powerless to refuse the ascetic priest's dispensations of guilt and self-contempt.

III

But why would the noble beasts of prey have made themselves vulnerable to such a dangerous enemy? Nietzsche intimates that they initially may have detected in the priests far more utility than danger. The priestly class originally may have been nothing more than a motley assortment of magicians, seers, shamans, prophets, and healers, from whom the beasts of prey sensed no credible threat to their reign. As we shall see, in fact, the priests became both dangerous and triumphant only as a by-product of their specific use at the hands of the beasts of prey. The ascetic strain of the priestly type emerged fairly late in the reign of the beasts of prey and only as an unforeseen consequence of the organizing disciplines they imparted to their captives.

It seems likely that the beasts of prey would at some point have needed to communicate their organizing principles to the formless populace over which they lorded. If so, then they also may have needed to work closely with a select class or group of mediators, who in turn would have been entrusted to communicate their demands to the populace as a whole. The labor of mediation may have fallen naturally to the priests, whom Nietzsche describes as "neurasthenic" (GM I:6)—and so as naturally (if pathologically) sensitive and empathetic. These early priests, already adept at translating languages, arbitrating disputes, interpreting dreams, divining portents, unlocking prophecies, reading entrails, and generally decoding regnant symbolic systems, presumably would have been indispensable to the organizing activities of the beasts of prey.

As Nietzsche explains, however, the priestly type also possesses a plasticity of soul that naturally manifests itself in a double agency. In political terms, the priest thrives by colonizing the interstitial spaces of a society, mediating between competing classes, strata, and castes. He faces at once in both directions, standing to his flock as the ruling elite stands to him. His mastery of lines and media of communication enables him to reverse the customary downward flow of state power and to disrupt the acknowledged chain of command—even as he honors it. The priest gladly relays the wishes of the ruling elite, but only at great expense to its credibility and authority. With every communication of directives from above, the priest wages from below a silent psychological war. While receiving the commands that are to be disseminated to the populace, the priest also steals secrets, sows the seeds of jealousy and distrust, manipulates language, flatters and ingratiates, and generally subverts the unity and stability of the ruling elite. Nietzsche's beasts of prey may have possessed a sufficiently robust inner life to organize themselves and their prey, perhaps even to cultivate and nurture, but they were no match for the cunning of the ascetic priest.

Nietzsche thus links the disappearance of the beasts of prey to their ill-fated dealings with the priestly class. As he explains, the priest

> must be the natural opponent and despiser of all rude, stormy, unbridled, hard, violent beast-of-prey health and might. The priest is the first form of the more *delicate* animal that despises more readily than it hates. He will not be spared war with the beasts of prey, a war of cunning (of the "spirit") rather than one of force, as goes without saying; *to fight it he will under certain circumstances need to evolve a virtually new type of beast of prey [Raubthier-Typus] out of himself, or at least he will need to* represent *it*—a new kind of animal ferocity in which the polar bear, the supple, cold, and patient tiger, and not least the fox seem to be joined in a unity at once enticing and terrifying. If need compels him, he will walk among the other beasts of prey with bearlike seriousness and feigned superiority, venerable, prudent, and cold, as the herald and mouthpiece of more mysterious powers, determined to sow this soil with misery, discord, and self-contradiction wherever he can and, only too certain of his art, to dominate the *suffering* at all times. (GM III:15, emphasis added)

In this remarkable passage, Nietzsche alleges that the organizing activities of the beasts of prey produced a monstrous mutation of the priestly type. An unintended consequence of their artistry, he speculates, was the empowerment of some priests as "artists" of equal power and surpassing ingenuity.[24] From this "artistic" mutation of the priestly type emerged the arch-villain of Nietzsche's narrative: the ascetic priest.[25]

As the mysterious "law of life" enjoins, "all great things bring about their own destruction through an act of self-overcoming [Selbstaufhebung]" (GM III:27). Such is the fate, presumably, of those "great things" known as beasts of prey. By using the priestly class to propagate their form-giving directives, the beasts of prey unwittingly instructed some of the priests in the strategic deployment of their double agency. Those priests who were not crushed by the artistry of the beasts of prey apparently learned to manipulate the suffering of others to shield themselves from the scrutiny of their captors and to secure the allegiances of their followers.[26] Nietzsche's references to the artistry of the beasts of prey thus enable him to issue a balanced (if fantastic) reckoning of their enduring contributions. Just as he credits them with unconsciously introducing order, discipline, and beauty into the world, so he holds them responsible for unwittingly creating the conditions of the development of the "bad conscience" and the ascetic priest. That the ascetic priest was born of their beastly aggression also furnishes Nietzsche with a possible exit from the otherwise closed and suffocating system of Western morality.

It thus turns out that the form-giving artistry of the beasts of prey served as the model for the cunning machinations of the ascetic priest. What the beasts of prey achieved by means of their physical, outward, overt discharge of animal vitality, the priest achieves through psychological, inward, covert operations. Whereas the beasts of prey seized the external world as their canvas, onto which they spontaneously projected the vibrant hues of their core nobility, the ascetic priest claimed the unexplored inner world as his personal theatre, in which he stages self-serving compensatory spectacles.

As this comparison suggests, in fact, the priest not only learned the principles of animal husbandry from the beasts of prey but also dramatically improved upon their practical application. In particular, the priest discovered the most powerful organizational device known as yet to human history: the *ascetic ideal*, by means of which he turned the tables of domestication on the beasts of prey. Having convinced the beasts of prey to rely ever more heavily on his ministrations, the ascetic priest eventually exploited this dependency and polluted the "innocent" conscience of his captors. Poisoned with guilt, afflicted by the "bad conscience" that they, ironically, had introduced into the world, the wounded beasts of prey finally joined the captive populace they had formerly ruled.

IV

Today the beasts of prey are nowhere to be found (GM I:11). Despite his own fatalistic sympathies, however, Nietzsche resists the conclusion that their disappearance necessarily augurs the collapse of the human species. True, the ominous "will to nothingness" looms just beyond the horizon. True, the mischief of the priestly class continues apace, subjecting all extant vestiges of noble aspiration to its leveling influence. True, the unchecked proliferation of the "maggot-man" threatens to induce pandemic nausea. Nietzsche nevertheless suggests that the animal vitality of the beasts of prey continues to circulate—albeit in dispersed, disaggregated, perhaps even entropic form—throughout the decadent nations, peoples, and cultures of late modern Europe.

When we scour modern polities in search of some residue or trace of Nietzsche's beasts of prey, we need look no further than the priestly classes that preside over our ongoing domestication. In their cunning and cruelty we may discern a grotesque replication of the primal aggression visited upon them by the beasts of prey. This family resemblance should not surprise us. As we have seen, the ascetic priest is a product of the unconscious artistry practiced by the beasts of prey. In fact, it was only in response to their form-giving wrath that the priest "evolve[d] a virtually new type of beast of prey out of himself" (GM III:15). The problem that Nietzsche now faces is not unlike the problem faced by the priestly class at the time of the founding of the original "state"—namely, how can he tap this seemingly inaccessible reservoir of monstrous energy and harness it in the furtherance of his own contrary ends? How can he contribute to the production of a metamorphosis that will supercede, cancel, or neutralize the mutation that ushered the ascetic priest onto the stage of human history?

Not surprisingly, Nietzsche's favored solution to this problem borrows heavily from his account of the ascetic priest's successful campaign to tame the beasts of prey. He pins his dim hopes for the future of humankind on the possibility of another dialectical advance or mutation along the lines of the one he describes in GM. Just as the law of life decreed the destruction of the beasts of prey through an act of self-overcoming, so, presumably, it demands a similar act of self-overcoming on the part of the ascetic priest. In particular, Nietzsche envisions a mutation that would involve a parallel transfer of energy from the ascetic priest to his as-yet-unknown other. This mutation will not yield a simple reincarnation of the beasts of prey, but it may produce an other whose generative powers recall in some respects their form-giving artistry.

Nietzsche may have in mind some such dialectical advance when he alludes to the possible emergence of a "many-colored and dangerous winged creature [Flügelthier]" from the "repulsive and gloomy caterpillar form" of the ascetic priest (GM III:10). He hopefully identifies this emergent "creature" as "the philosopher," who should not be confused with those philosophers who have heretofore disguised themselves in "ascetic wraps and cloaks" (GM III:10). Were this "philosopher" to take wing, carried aloft by a gust of "pride, daring, courage, and self-confidence" unknown since the heyday of the beasts of prey, then the lengthy interregnum of the ascetic priest would be judged to be as natural and appropriate as the caterpillar stage that launches the flight of the glorious butterfly.[27]

In that event, morality itself would appear just as Nietzsche wishes for his readers someday to be able to view it: as a necessary, non-lethal stage in the development of the human spirit. If he has his way, in fact, his preferred readers of a distant posterity will be in a position to regard the moral period of human development as a long, treacherous, comical, but ultimately successful detour to the freedom and strength of will formerly embodied by the beasts of prey.[28]

Notes

1. With the exception of occasional emendations, I rely throughout this chapter on Walter Kaufmann's translations/editions of Nietzsche's writings for Viking Press/Random House.

2. For an illuminating overview of this controversy, see Kaufmann, Nietzsche: Philosopher, Psychologist, Antichrist, 4th ed. (Princeton, N.J.: Princeton University Press, 1974), 224–227. See also Gerd Schank's essay "Nietzsche's 'Blonde Bestie': Zur Wiedergewinnung einer Metapher Nietzsches," which has been translated and reproduced in this volume.

3. For an excellent commentary on this section of BGE, see Laurence Lampert, Nietzsche's Task: An Interpretation of Beyond Good and Evil (New Haven, Conn.: Yale University Press, 2001), 226–231.

4. My understanding of Nietzsche's psychological model is deeply indebted to Graham Parkes, Composing the Soul: Reaches of Nietzsche's Psychology (Chicago: University of Chicago Press, 1994), especially chapter 6, "Animal Procreation."

5. The "bad conscience" is, as he says, "an illness like pregnancy" (GM II:19), from which, presumably, the birth of something new might follow. At this point in his narrative, Nietzsche launches a new account of the origin of the bad conscience, which, as Henry Staten observes, "throws the previous account into confusion"; Nietzsche's Voice (Ithaca, N.Y.: Cornell University Press, 1990), 54.

6. My discussion of Nietzsche's contributions to philosophical anthropology draws extensively from Richard Schacht, Making Sense of Nietzsche (Chicago: University of Illinois Press, 1995), especially chapter 10.

7. For a consideration along these lines of the difficulties involved in Nietzsche's proffered explanation, see Keith Ansell-Pearson, Viroid Life: Perspectives on Nietzsche and the Transhuman Condition (London: Routledge, 1997), 101–103.

8. Nietzsche uses this precise phrase in GM I:5 to describe the Aryan race.

9. Nietzsche offers a similar account of "the origins of an aristocratic society": "Human beings whose nature was still natural, barbarians in every terrible sense of the word, men of prey [Raubmenschen] who were still in possession of unbroken strength of will and lust for power, hurled themselves upon weaker, more civilized, more peaceful races, perhaps traders or cattle raisers, or upon mellow old cultures" (BGE 257).

10. See, for example, TI "Skirmishes" 44, where Nietzsche explains that the "genius, in work and deed, is necessarily a squanderer. . . . He flows out, he overflows, he uses himself up, he does not spare himself—and this is a calamitous, involuntary fatality, no less than a river's flooding the land."

11. See Paul J. M. van Tongeren, *Reinterpreting Modern Culture: An Introduction of Friedrich Nietzsche's Philosophy* (West Lafayette, Ind.: Purdue University Press, 2000), 202–205.

12. It would be interesting to map Nietzsche's anthropological narrative onto the controversial thesis advanced by Paul Shepard. Shepard boldly asserts that "as a species we are Pleistocene, owing little or nothing to the millennia of urban life. . . . The radical implication of this is that we, like other wild forms, may actually be less healthy in the domesticated landscapes than in those places to which our DNA remains most closely tuned"; "Wilderness Is Where My Genome Lives," *Whole Terrain* 4 (1995/1996): 13.

13. Aaron Ridley nicely sums up the problem here by noting that "What Nietzsche is evading in all this, of course, is the recognition that the nobles need a 'bad' conscience themselves even before they can create the conditions required to produce it in others. . . . The nobles need a 'bad' conscience to do what they do": *Nietzsche's Conscience: Six Character Studies from the* Genealogy (Ithaca, N.Y.: Cornell University Press, 1998), 20–21. As I hope to show in Part III of this chapter, it is at least plausible for Nietzsche to claim that the "innocent" conscience of the beasts of prey creates the conditions under which the "bad conscience" arises and develops.

14. Both Staten (*Nietzsche's Voice*, 16–21) and Ridley (*Nietzsche's Conscience*, 20–22) cite this passage as evidence of the internal strain exerted on Nietzsche's hypothesis by his apparent need to maintain his founding dichotomies between "noble" and "slave," "wild" and "cultivated," "active" and "reactive," and so on.

15. As Nietzsche explains, "It is not in *them* [that is, the beasts of prey] that the 'bad conscience' developed, that goes without saying—but it would not have developed *without them*, this ugly growth" (GM II:17). The "inventor of the 'bad conscience,'" he explains, is none other than the "yearning and desperate prisoner" who had no choice but to make an enemy of himself, to redirect inward the animal aggression that he would naturally direct outward (GM II:16). For a detailed and insightful discussion of the emergence of the "bad conscience," see David Owen, *Nietzsche, Politics, and Modernity* (London: Sage), 56–67.

16. Here, it would seem, Nietzsche approaches the limits of his attempt to model the "beast of prey" simultaneously on the instinctual aggression of animal predators and on the self-organizing efficiency of well-crafted artifacts or machines. The more strongly he relies on the latter model, e.g., to account for the organizational predilections of the "beast of prey," the farther he strays from his former model. For a promising account of "machine evolution" that is not restricted (as is Nietzsche's) by an anthropocentric emphasis on machines as human artifacts, see Ansell-Pearson, *Viroid Life*, 138–142.

17. On the unique artistry of the beasts of prey, see Ridley, *Nietzsche's Conscience*, 83–85.

18. See, for example, Mark Warren's catalog of the "limits" of Nietzsche's political thought, *Nietzsche and Political Thought* (Cambridge, Mass.: MIT Press, 1988), 207–248.

19. Richard White thus draws our attention to GM as a "performative critique" that "Nietzsche uses . . . to direct us toward a particular vision of the future"; *Nietzsche and the*

Problem of Sovereignty (Champaign: University of Illinois Press, 1997),138. One result of this "performative critique," apparently, is to free us "to go beyond the fable of a *literal* prehistory" (140). Van Tongeren similarly concludes that Nietzsche does not intend his "myth of descent" to "refer to a specific moment in time." The lesson we should draw from such passages is that "domination, submission, and struggle are not so much the first steps in the development of the human being as they are its continuous principle: from the beginning, human beings are characterized by this distinction"; *Reinterpreting Modern Culture*, 205.

20. Lawrence Hatab maintains, persuasively, that Nietzsche's admiration for creativity and "artistry" actually militates *against* the anti-democratic animus of his political writings. The political regime that would best foster Nietzschean creativity, Hatab proposes, is in fact democracy—provided, of course, that the democracy in question would both honor and enforce a fair, mutually elevating contest between democratic citizens; *A Nietzschean Defense of Democracy: An Experiment in Postmodern Politics* (Chicago: Open Court, 1995), 51–54.

21. Although most domesticated species have been forcibly tamed by other, "stronger" species (usually Homo sapiens or its hominid ancestors), the occurrence of self-domestication is not unknown. Researchers have recently theorized, for example, that some canid species effectively domesticated themselves so that they could live in closer proximity to the edible waste products created by humans/hominids. See Karen E. Lange, "Wolf to Woof: The Evolution of Dogs," *National Geographic* (January 2002): 4–6. According to this account, the human culture or home is an occasion for the domestication of wild canids but not its cause. Could a similar conjecture provide some of the details of Nietzsche's anthropological story? Did early hominids effectively domesticate themselves in order to avail themselves of a promising food supply—perhaps, as Nietzsche apparently prefers, of the stability afforded them by farming (rather than roaming)?

22. My use of the term "domestication" is not meant to imply the kind of change in genetic structure that is produced through standard breeding techniques. As Shepard points out, "if we follow the definition of 'domestic' as a type created by controlled breeding with conscious objectives by humans, then we ourselves are genetically wild"; "Wilderness Is Where My Genome Lives," 13.

23. The unintended self-domestication of the beasts of prey may have prompted Nietzsche's admonition: "[Let us] guard ourselves against two worst contagions that may be reserved just for us—against the *great nausea at man*! against *great pity for man*!" (GM III:14).

24. Staten argues that Nietzsche's account of the ascetic priest as a "delicate" type of "beast of prey" exposes a tension within his own conception of power as primarily physical and outwardly directed; *Nietzsche's Voice*, 57. My own sense is that this passage is meant to explain the emergence of a conception of power that is rooted in an expanded understanding of the physical world. It is not the case that the slaves invented "mental" power to counter the "physical" power of their masters. If that were the case, then nothing would have happened in/to the "physical" world of the masters. What the slaves

accomplished, perhaps unwittingly, was the formulation of a more comprehensive understanding of the physical cosmos, which now must be understood to comprise unseen forces. The slaves do not rule a parallel, "mental" world of their own invention so much as they stumble upon a more complete understanding of the one world, the physical world of visible and invisible forces, over which they and their masters vie for supremacy.

25. That the priests, too, are artists is confirmed by Nietzsche's observation that "the slave revolt in morality begins when *ressentiment* itself becomes creative and gives birth to values" (GM I:10).

26. Nietzsche thus describes this new, mutant species of priest as a "sorcerer and animal-tamer, in whose presence everything healthy necessarily grows sick, and everything sick tame" (GM III:15). He also likens the priest to a "shepherd" caring for his "herd" (GM III:15), a comparison that confirms the formative role of the beasts of prey in the development of the ascetic priest.

27. In fact, if we may associate one *Flügelthier* (the butterfly; KSA 5, p. 361) with another (the honeybee; KSA 5, p. 247), then we are perhaps entitled to read the Preface to GM as introducing Nietzsche and his unknown friends as legitimate claimants to the title of "'philosopher.'"

28. I wish to thank the editors, Ralph and Christa Davis Acampora, for their instructive comments on preliminary drafts of this chapter.

HUMAN ANIMALS
(*UNTER, HALB,* AND *ÜBER*)

Women as Predatory Animals, or Why Nietzsche Philosophized with a Whip

Thomas H. Brobjer

It is well known that Nietzsche, despite his ambivalence toward Darwin and Darwinism, regarded humans as part of the animal kingdom. Not only did he agree with the view of scientific evolutionism (his skepticism in regard to Darwinism concerned mainly the method of selection, which he found too passive), he especially emphasized the animal nature of human beings in his critiques of rationality, Christianity, metaphysics, idealism, human vanity, and overcivilization.

In this chapter I wish to bring forth two dichotomies that are essential for correctly understanding Nietzsche's statements about women. The first one is the belief that human beings biologically contain within them both herd nature and predatory nature, and the second one is his view of humankind as both animal and over-animal. I will use these dichotomies, together with a discussion of some previously little known literary sources for the infamous whip scene in *Thus Spoke Zarathustra*, to illuminate and clarify Nietzsche's view of women.

Nietzsche accepted that humans shared a common ancestor with the apes, but he also had a more specific view of the character of our animal nature that colored his overall view of man, but that, to my knowledge, has not received any attention. Nietzsche regarded our animal nature as a synthesis of herd animal and predatory animal in a rather specific and detailed manner. It is easy and tempting to see this emphasis on both the herd- and prey-animal aspects of human nature as merely rhetorical or as a view having been gained from observations of human beings and then projected onto our early history and evolution. However, that does not appear to have been the case. Instead, Nietzsche encountered a similar view of human evolution and nature in the philosopher and anthropologist Otto Caspari's *Die Urgeschichte der Menschheit: Mit Rücksicht auf die natürliche Entwicklung des frühesten Geistesleben*, which he appears to have read in 1881. Caspari proposed this view from a zoological and evolutionary perspective.[1] It was only after Nietzsche's reading of Caspari that he began classifying humankind in this manner and frequently discussing our herd-like nature.[2] An awareness of this view of the double origin of man's nature, though rarely explicitly referred to in Nietzsche's writings, makes his critique of civilization more comprehensible. The civilizing process, and especially the effect of Christianity, has, at a high cost, favored almost exclusively the herd side of our nature. Nietzsche's description of the last or ultimate men in the prologue to *Thus Spoke Zarathustra* is merely an extrapolation of this development until the herd nature has completely taken over. Nietzsche counters this by claiming that we must better affirm our predatory nature and heritage.

Can an awareness of Nietzsche's belief in this double nature of humankind explain his views of men and women and their relation to one another? Nietzsche strongly emphasizes the difference between man and woman and claims that they therefore inevitably will misunderstand one another, and he sees even love as a terrific battle. In a simplified form, Nietzsche views the woman as mother and the man as discoverer and warrior.

It would perhaps be natural to assume that Nietzsche saw women as more caring and herd-like and men as more predatory, but this does not seem to be the case. An examination of how Nietzsche regarded women as animals and what sorts of animals to which he likens them, as discussed below, seems rather to point in the opposite direction, to his viewing woman as more predatory than man, as more cat-like, with "the tiger's claw beneath the glove" (*BGE* 239).

Let us return to humankind generally for a short while to look at another aspect of Nietzsche's views of man's relation to animals. Humans are, after all, from another perspective, not merely animal (herd and predatory animal), but also the over-animal (*Überthier*) (*HH* 40; *WS* 12; *BGE* 62; *KSA* 12:9[154]), the unfinished animal (*BGE* 62; *KSA* 11:25[428]; *KSA* 12:2[13]), and the most interesting animal, because we have learned to remember and acquired a consciousness (*GM* I:6).[3] Thus, man is not only a synthesis of herd- and prey-animal nature but also a synthesis and delicate balance between animal and god, between instinct and sublimation (or consciousness).[4] This view is visible in that Nietzsche refers to man as both an animal and an over-animal, as half animal (*AOM* 99; *BGE* 61; *GM* II:16), as body and mind, and when he, for example, writes: "Man is a rope, fastened between animal and Superman—a rope over an abyss" (*Z:P* 4).[5]

The fundamental difference between man and woman in this second sense is that woman is *more* animal than man: "The woman is more closely related to nature than man, and remains in all essentials unchanged. Culture is here always something superficial, which does not touch the core which remains eternally faithful to nature" (*KSA* 7:7[122]). Although it is clearly not the *only* source of Nietzsche's misogyny, we shall see below that this belief explains an important part of Nietzsche's hostility toward women.

Nietzsche often compares women to a fairly wide variety of animals: sea animal, snake, hyena, sacrificial beast, cow, bird, and most frequently to a cat, a tiger, a predatory animal and a domestic animal (*Hausthier*). The first three—the woman as sea animal, snake, and hyena—are prominent in the Western tradition and are not original to Nietzsche. The metaphor of woman as a sacrificial beast—as a self-sacrificing beast—is Nietzsche's own, which he explicitly refers to and which echoes much of his thinking about women (compare, for example, his interest in and many comments about woman as mother and about mother-love and his view that it is the nature of women to obey).[6] The woman as cow, bird, and cat occurs in *Thus Spoke Zarathustra*, but also in other places.[7] The most prominent of his similes is the picture of woman as a predatory animal, a tiger, and a cat. To quote but a single example here, Nietzsche claims that "woman is *essentially* unpeaceful, like a cat, however well she may have trained herself to seem peaceable" (*BGE* 131).

Nietzsche's simile of woman as a domestic animal (*Hausthier*) also relates to her as a predatory animal, for the primary domestic animal he seems to be associating with woman is that of the cat or that which is cat-like. In 1879, while writing the third volume of *Human, All Too Human, The Wanderer and His Shadow*, Nietzsche compared woman to a domestic animal from an anthropological perspective and wrote in an early version of section 57: "the *domestic animal* which has succeeded in acquiring rights for herself is the *woman.*" Nietzsche's younger friend Peter Gast, while reading the proofs of the book, strongly objected to the passage as misogynist and mistaken. He argued that Nietzsche should withdraw it, which he did. Nietzsche answered Gast's long letter with the comment:

> Many thanks, dear friend, for the hint. I do not desire the *appearance* of being con-temptuous of women and have withdrawn the complete passage. However, it is *true* that originally men only regarded men as *human, language* proves that still today: the woman was really regarded as animal, the recognition that she belongs to humanity is one of the greatest moral developments. My or *our* present view about "the female" should not be associated with the word "domestic animal."—I follow Huntley's description of the situation of women among primitive peoples.[8]

However, Nietzsche could not get rid of this picture and referred to it repeatedly thereafter. In fact, a belief in the greater animal nature of woman and thus the belief that she had no soul (or a less developed consciousness and ability to sublimate) probably already lay behind an aphorism Nietzsche had published in the first volume of *Human, All Too Human* (1878), although he had then not yet generalized it to apply to all women: "*Masks.*—There are women who, however you may search them, prove to have no content but are purely masks. The man who associates with such almost spectral, nec-essarily unsatisfied beings is to be commiserated with, yet it is precisely they who are able to arouse the desire of the man most strongly: he seeks for her soul—and goes on seeking" (*HH* 405).

By 1888, Nietzsche—again with the help or inspiration of French authors—generalized (and exaggerated) it to the extent that women, like animals, have no soul and no depth at all: "Women are considered deep— why? because one can never discover any bottom to them. Women are not even shallow" (*TI* "Maxims and Arrows" 27).[9]

In the draft to a letter to Lou Salomé from mid-December 1882—that is after she and Paul Rée abandoned Nietzsche—he wrote in pain, disappoint-ment, and anger: "'a brain with the beginnings of soul' The character of the cat—the predatory animal which *pretends* to be a domesticated animal" (*KSB* 6:298).

In *Thus Spoke Zarathustra*, apart from the whip scene discussed below, Nietzsche claims that in women "a slave and a tyrant have all too long been concealed," where the tyrant is associated with being cat-like (*Z*:1 "Of the Friend"), and later in the book he speaks of women as "the most dangerous plaything"—again implying the predatory animal in women. In *Beyond Good and Evil* (1886) he once more portrays and affirms woman as a "strangely wild" domestic animal:

> There is *stupidity* in this movement [women's emancipation], an almost masculine stupidity, of which a real woman—who is always a clever woman—would have to be ashamed from the very heart. To lose her sense for the ground on which she is most sure of victory; to neglect to practice the use of her own proper weapons [. . .] where formerly she kept herself in check and in subtle cunning humility; to seek with virtuous assurance to destroy man's belief that a fundamentally different ideal is *wrapped up* in woman, that there is something eternal, necessarily feminine; emphatically and loquaciously to talk man out of the idea that woman has to be maintained, cared for, protected, indulged like a delicate, strangely wild [*wunderlich wilden*] and often agreeable domestic animal [*Hausthiere*]. [. . .] [W]hat does all this mean if not a crumbling of the feminine instinct, a defeminizing? (*BGE* 239)

Nietzsche is regarded as being hostile and contemptuous toward women, but I have never seen a reasonable attempt to explain why he held such views and values—except the claim that it was in response to the women he knew, which seems to me unlikely. The reasons for Nietzsche's hostility toward women are likely many and complex. Among the influences and causes are: a certain conservatism, the *Zeitgeist,* influences from Greek antiquity, views expressed by Schopenhauer and in other literary works, and possibly his personal encounters with women. In this chapter I am emphasizing only *one* of these reasons or causes.

One must distinguish his hostility as referring to two rather different groups: feminists, modern and emancipated women, on the one hand, and non-feminist women on the other. The cause for his hostility toward the first—which applies equally well to men who are feminists (in Nietzsche's view, for example, Ibsen)—is that feminism is based on the assertion of equality (and the will to make similar) that Nietzsche denies in general and regards as nihilistic and destructive to the highest achievements of humankind. Moreover, he regards feminism as grown out of feelings of resentment. It can be noted that in practice, however, Nietzsche, like Strindberg, was not just hostile to modern women and feminists. He fell in love with (and deeply respected) Lou Salomé, a very strong and modern woman, although she did not sympathize with feminism. Contrary to what is often claimed, Nietzsche's view of women and feminists did not change because of his disappointment and failure with Lou. He expressed the same views before and after his affair with her. Nietzsche also associated with several other modern and feminist women, for example, Meta von Salis, Malwida von Meysenbug, and several female students from Zürich.

Most relevant for us here is Nietzsche's hostility toward women in general (non-feminists). In fact, toward them his hostility is much more limited but still present. This hostility and contempt seems to have two major causes; the first is the so-called natural feeling of contempt and antagonism between the care-taking mother type and the more adventurous father type[10] (and Nietzsche allows himself to speak from a man's perspective, not some attempted objective or neutral in-between position).[11] From this perspective it is likely that Nietzsche would have accepted and regarded as natural that women also felt a certain hostility and contempt toward men. Nietzsche's view of the tension between man and woman and of love—as a mutual war—certainly implies such a view.[12]

The second factor is the requirement that the more sublimated being (male) keeps the more instinctive and animal woman under control (a view that certainly can appear as misogynist and hostile). The woman, as the more natural (and less sublimated), will otherwise, in Nietzsche's view, tempt or tear man down to her level.[13]

This is the background and secret of the whip scene in the section "Of Old and Young Women" in the first book of *Thus Spoke Zarathustra*, where Nietzsche lets an old woman give Zarathustra a little truth: "Are you visiting women? Do not forget the whip!" This episode is perhaps the most well-known (or infamous) of all of Nietzsche's writings, but it has been often misunderstood. The whip does not primarily signal brutality on the part of the man, or sadomasochism, but the necessity for man to be in control. The whip is not a horse whip, or a variant thereof, meant for beating or hitting, but a circus whip (or the lion-tamer's whip), which signals control over the cat and tiger in woman (but which is not used to hit or beat). We know that the whip is a circus whip rather than the more brutal horse whip (although this fact appears not to have been noticed) because when we encounter the whip again in the third book of *Thus Spoke Zarathustra*, "life," personified as a woman, says: "O Zarathustra! Do not crack your whip so terribly! You surely know: noise kills thought" (Z:3 "The Second Dance Song").[14] Furthermore, Nietzsche describes the whip in a letter to Elisabeth: "By the way, I am regarded as *the* 'evil animal' among the group of female students—it seems as if a certain allusion to a noise-making and cracking instrument has had a perfectly enchanting effect!"[15]

Thus Spoke Zarathustra is a poetical and metaphorical book and it is obvious that the whip is referred to metaphorically.[16] Its meaning is thus not brutality but nonetheless one of authority and power—the need of man to be in control (at least from the man's perspective).

To better understand the whip scene, I would like to briefly expand on three aspects of it; Nietzsche's personal experiences, the literary origin of or inspiration for the whip scene, and, finally, its relation to Nietzsche's view of women and the relation between men and women generally.

The first time we encounter the whip, a man, and a woman all together in connection with Nietzsche is *before* he wrote *Thus Spoke Zarathustra*, when Lou Salomé, Paul Rée, and Nietzsche took that famous photograph of the three of them—where, on Nietzsche's suggestion, Rée and he were placed as draft animals before Lou, who is sitting in a small cart with a makeshift whip in her hand.[17] This surely reflects Nietzsche's and their playfulness, but also—again playfully—that men can be made into fools (animals) by women (and love). In fact, one of the contemporary sources regarding Nietzsche's meaning with the whip scene, Resa von Schirnhofer, claims that Nietzsche told her shortly after *Thus Spoke Zarathustra* was published that the scene should not be understood as generally applicable but as referring to a single particular (but not named) person—who is, clearly, Lou Salomé.[18] This picture may well contain part of the truth considering his love of her and his disappointment when she and Rée left him shortly before he wrote the first book of *Thus Spoke Zarathustra*, but is surely far from the complete truth.

More informative is Elisabeth Förster-Nietzsche's account of the origin of the whip scene in her two-volume biography of Nietzsche.[19] She there describes how in early 1882 she read to Nietzsche Ivan Turgenev's short story "First Love," which is about a young man who falls in love with an attractive, capricious, and spoiled woman, Zinaida, some years older than he, who in turn, however, falls in love with his father. In one scene the father hits her (once) with a horse whip, but she continues to love him. Elisabeth claims that Nietzsche reacted negatively to this scene and objected to the father's behavior but that she defended it and argued that some women need to have the threat of a symbolic whip to prevent them from misbehaving. One or two years later she read in Nietzsche's presence *Thus Spoke Zarathustra* for the first time, and, with dismay, called out to him: "Oh, Fritz, I am the old woman," to which Nietzsche laughingly answered that he would not tell anyone.[20]

This account is interesting, for it sheds light on Nietzsche's views of women and of love. There are many similarities between the description of women as femme fatale and of love as both attractive and destructive in Turgenev's "First Love" and in Prosper Mérimée's *Carmen* (which Nietzsche had both read and several times seen in the opera-version with music by Bizet by the time he wrote Z).[21] In Mérimée's *Carmen,* women are also compared to cats, and at two places before the final scene where Don Jose kills Carmen there are descriptions of men mistreating women, but with the effect that the women love the men even more. Later Nietzsche claimed that Mérimée and Bizet describe the highest conception of love:

> Yesterday I heard—would you believe it?—Bizet's masterpiece, for the twentieth time. [. . .] Finally, love—love translated back into nature. Not the love of a "higher virgin"! No Senta-sentimentality! But love as *fatum,* as fatality, cynical, innocent, cruel—and precisely in this a piece of nature. That love which is war in its means, and at bottom the deadly hatred of the sexes!—I know no case where the tragic joke that constitutes the essence of love is expressed so strictly, translated with equal terror into a formula, as in Don Jose's last cry, which concludes the work:
>
> > *"Yes, I have killed her,*
> > *I—my adored Carmen!"*
>
> Such a conception of love (the only one worthy of a philosopher) is rare: it raises a work of art above thousands. (CW 1–3)

These textual influences, together with his own experiences of the "femme fatale" Lou Salomé, all in the year before he wrote the first volume of *Thus Spoke Zarathustra,* are likely to have reinforced his view that women are unfaithful, dangerous, and predatory and that they need to be, metaphorically speaking, kept under control.[22] It is likely that Nietzsche believed that this disciplining and keeping under control was not necessarily oppressive for woman but instead helped her to grow and to bring forth her best side. Nietzsche often claims that mankind has become too civilized, too tame, too much like a herd animal, but his reference to keeping woman under control is not necessarily meant to be oppressive. Human beings need fear, competition, and other pressures in order to develop and to sublimate and to keep them from falling back too much into their more primitive nature. In *On the Genealogy of Morals,* Nietzsche describes the harshness that was required for mankind to acquire memory and consciousness. A fear and respect of man, Nietzsche seems to be arguing, is necessary for woman to develop: "She unlearns *fear* of man: but the woman who 'unlearns fear' sacrifices her most womanly instincts. [. . .] through precisely this fact—woman degenerates" (BGE 239). In Turgenev's story, for example, the young spoiled woman Zinaida could never fall in love, could never develop, without meeting someone whom she respected and feared and who was stronger than herself and to whom she could sacrifice herself.[23]

In *Ecce Homo*, written in November and December 1888, Nietzsche summarizes his final view of woman and again strongly emphasizes her predatory nature, and combines it with her other side, that of being a mother.

> That out of my writings there speaks a *psychologist* who has not his equal, that is perhaps the first thing a good reader will notice. [. . .] Dare I venture in addition to suggest that I *know* these little women? It is part of my dionysian endowment. Who knows? perhaps I am the first psychologist of the eternal-womanly. They all love me—an old story: excepting the *abortive* women, the "emancipated" who lack the stuff for children.—Happily I am not prepared to be torn to pieces: the complete woman tears to pieces when she loves . . . I know these amiable maenads . . . Ah, what a dangerous, creeping, subterranean little beast of prey it is! And so pleasant with it! . . . A little woman chasing after her revenge would over-run fate itself.—The woman is unspeakably more wicked than the man, also cleverer; goodness in a woman is already a form of *degeneration*. [. . .] [T]he state of nature, the eternal *war* between the sexes puts her in a superior position by far.—Have there been ears for my definition of love? it is the only one worthy of a philosopher. Love—in its methods war, in its foundation the moral hatred of the sexes. Has my answer been heard to the question how one cures—"redeems"—a woman? One makes a child for her. The woman has need of children, the man is always only the means: thus spoke Zarathustra. (*EH* "Books" 5)[24]

Notes

1. Nietzsche owned Otto Caspari's *Die Urgeschichte der Menschheit: Mit Rücksicht auf die natürliche Entwicklung des frühesten Geistesleben*, 2nd ed. in two volumes (Leipzig, 1877), but since 1942 it has been lost from his library. The two volumes apparently did not contain annotations (although Nietzsche did possess two other works by Caspari, both of which are annotated), but it is likely that he read it in or near 1881, even though no definite identification of reading-traces has been made. In this work, Caspari argues quite explicitly, using biology, for the view that man has evolved from both herd and prey animals (although he does not refer to herd animals explicitly but to the social apes and rodents, which he describes as "patient," "sympathetic"): "early humans [. . .] stood much closer to the prey-animals than to the apes and rodents, or better, [. . .] *stood between them*; with the animals of prey he shared [. . .] a whole row of properties related to a sharply developed wild self-assurance and egoism [*scharf entwickelter wilder Selbstgefühle*] and with the other main species of related deciduates, the characteristic tolerance towards social family life. Here it is the self-assurance [*Selbstgefühle*], there the sympathy [*Mitgefühle*] which he has taken up and developed. [. . .] [I]t was the *wild nature* of the prey-animal

which by far dominated in the humans. [. . .] In relation to the drives and feelings, [. . .] the human in his nature does not fully belong to any one of [the classes of deciduates], but that he stands in relation to his main properties of character in the middle between the tolerant, sympathetic rodents and species of apes on the one side, and the pride, brave and egoistic prey-animals on the other. [. . .] Both these reminiscences are united and equally distributed in human beings, and they had to unify the good and evil of both parts and develop them to something higher" (Chapter 3: "Die psychischen Charaktärtypen der Deciduaten," 75–79). Caspari repeats this view several times later in the book. Nietzsche began to refer to man as a herd animal in his notes from 1881 and in *The Gay Science* (1882).

2. The view that man is (or is in part) a herd animal was not unusual at this time, and although Caspari appears to have been the triggering source for Nietzsche, he also encountered different aspects of this view in his reading of Oscar Schmidt's *Descendenzlehre und Darwinismus* (1873), W. Bagehot's *Der Ursprung der Nationen* (1874), and F. Galton's *Inquiries into Human Faculty and Its Development* (1883).

3. "Man is the beast [*Unthier*] and over-animal [*Überthier*]." In *KSA* 10:4[163], Nietzsche refers to man as an over-ape (*Überaffe*). Unless otherwise noted, all translations of citations from Nietzsche's works are my own.

4. For example, in *TI* "Maxims and Arrows" 3, Nietzsche writes: "To live alone one must be an animal or a god—says Aristotle. There is yet a third case: one must be both—a *philosopher*." There is a direct parallel to Nietzsche's emphasis on the importance of physiology and the body (the animal) contra the psychological and consciousness (the over-animal). However, Nietzsche nonetheless speaks mostly about, and is most concerned about, psychology (the over-animal, consciousness, or sublimation).

5. R. J. Hollingdale's translation. Other examples of Nietzsche's use of this dichotomy are: "Man is beast and superbeast" (*KSA* 12:9[154] [*WP* 1027]); "In man [*Menschen*], creature and creator are united" (*BGE* 225); and when we realize that there is no God and no moral law "*the wise and the animal* will *become more similar* and a new *type* will arise"(*KSA* 9:11[54]); and "Man . . . is completely nature and carries within him an uncanny double-nature" (*KSA* 1, p. 783 [*HC*]).

6. "Thiere des Meers" in *KSA* 9:7[240]; "Hyäne" in *GM* III:14 and "Schlange" in *A* 48. Women are explicitly described as sacrificial animals in *HH* 430 and *WS* 272. Nietzsche states that it is man's nature to command and woman's to obey in *Z*:1 "Of Old and Young Women" and elsewhere, e.g. *GS* 68. This view seems to go counter to the view of woman as cat or tiger—an inconsistency that Nietzsche does not resolve.

7. *Z*:1 "Of the Friend." "Women are still cats and birds, or, at best, cows." As cow also in *KSA* 10:3[1].133b, as cat also in *BGE* 131, and as bird in *BGE* 237 and *GS* 67.

8. Letter to Gast, November 5, 1879. The source of Nietzsche's statement, a text by Huntley, has never been identified. Gast's letter to Nietzsche, November 2, 1879, is in *KGB* 2:6[2] 1210ff.

9. The text is almost a direct translation of a statement by Gavarni given in *Journal des Goncourts*, 1:325, which Nietzsche read at this time (given in *KSA* 14, p. 412). "We

ask him if he has ever understood a woman? 'A woman, but that is something impenetrable, not because it is deep but because it is empty.' "

10. However, it should be noted that Nietzsche also shows a high degree of respect for the mother-role of women.

11. In *Beyond Good and Evil*, before he expounds about women in several long consecutive sections (231–239), he states,: "Having just paid myself such a deal of pretty compliments I may perhaps be more readily permitted to utter a few truths about 'woman as such': assuming it is now understood from the outset to how great an extent these are only—my truths." In Z:1 "Of Old and Young Women," he claims that "one should speak about women only to men," meaning that *men* should only speak about women to men, thereby implying that there is a fundamental difference between men's and women's perspectives.

12. "Who has fully conceived *how strange* man and woman are to one another!" (Z:3 "Of the Three Evil Things"). See also "We shall have won much for the science of aesthetics, once we have come not only to the logical insight but also to immediate certainty through perception that the continuous development of art is bound up with the duality of the *Apollinian* and *Dionysian*, similar to the way in which procreation depends upon the duality of the sexes, involving perpetual strife [*Kampfe*] with only periodic reconciliations" (*BT* 1). See also "man and woman never cease to misunderstand one another" (*BGE* 85); and "The sexes deceive themselves about one another: the reason being that fundamentally they love and honour only themselves" (*BGE* 131). For further examples, see *BGE* 238, 239, 248; *GS* 363; and *KSA* 10:22[3].

13. There is a serious inconsistency in Nietzsche's argument here, for generally he does not regard taming as an improvement. This inconsistency can be resolved if we accept that he wanted women to accept a lower position either as means rather than ends—which seems to be Paul Deussen's view in his *Erinnerungen an Friedrich Nietzsche* (Leipzig, 1901), 24: "Incidentally, it was never his intention to remain unmarried; according to him, the wife should sacrifice herself in the service and care of the man, and already at Pforta he used to say, half as a joke: I will probably for me alone require three wives"—or that the "taming" in fact implied sublimation and development. Compare the interesting chapter 6, "Husbanding the Soul," in Graham Parkes's *Composing the Soul* (Chicago: University of Chicago Press, 1994).

14. Kathleen Marie Higgins appears also to have noticed that the whip is more like a lion-tamer's whip than a horsewhip in "The Whip Recalled," *Journal of Nietzsche Studies* 12 (Fall 1996): 1–17.

15. Letter to Elisabeth, July 5, 1885: "Übrigens gelte ich, in den Studentinnen-Kreisen, als *das* 'böse Thier'—es scheint, daß eine gewisse Anspielung auf ein lärmmachendes und klatschendes Instrument geradezu bezaubernd gewirkt hat!"

16. That the text should not be understood literally is obvious, apart from the general nature of the book and its narrative, by the fact that the statement about 'not to forget the whip' is also described metaphorically as a "little truth" that is hidden under Zarathustra's cloak, and it is described by both him and the old woman as "a little child" that will cry too loudly if its mouth is not stopped.

17. Partly due to this photograph, and partly for other reasons, it has sometimes been suggested that it is not the man, but the woman, who holds the whip in the Zarathustra scene. This interpretation, however, is clearly false. Zarathustra later in *Thus Spoke Zarathustra* threatens to use the whip against "life" personified as a woman and is thus clearly the possessor of the whip. Furthermore, although Nietzsche sees women as being "dangerous," the danger is not such that it could be symbolized by using a whip—while the whip in the hand of the man fits his view of man and women generally (man as the commanding and active with woman as passive and obeying), and he also on several occasions makes rather similar statements outside of *Thus Spoke Zarathustra* in which the man is the one holding a stick or hitting a woman. For example, in *BGE* 147, Nietzsche reproduces an Italian aphorism he had earlier excerpted with the following content: "buona femmina e mala femmina vuol bastone. Sacchetti Nov. 86." (Good and bad women want a stick.) Nietzsche took this saying from Émile Gebhart, *Les origines de la Renaissance en Italie* (Paris, 1879), which he read in 1885/1886. See also "Quellenforschung mitgeteilt von Thomas H. Brobjer," *Nietzsche-Studien* 28 (1999).

18. "Once he said that I should not take offence at the—later so notorious—whip-passage in *Zarathustra*. This had not occurred to me, since I did not read it as a general indictment of women, but only as a poetic generalization of individual cases. He did not explain to me the original source of this 'advice' as extensively as I later read it in Elisabeth's book, but he did tell me in so many words whom he had meant by it when he was writing *Zarathustra*." Quoted in S. L. Gilman's *Conversations with Nietzsche* (New York/Oxford, 1987), 151 (478, German ed).

19. Surprisingly, I have not encountered any reference or discussion to her account of the whip scene among the many discussions of this passage in *Thus Spoke Zarathustra*.

20. Quoted in Gilman's *Conversations with Nietzsche*, 124f. (429f., German ed.).

21. See letter to Gast, December 8, 1881.

22. In this chapter I have emphasized the literary influence of Turgenev and Mérimée (and Bizet) on Nietzsche's view of women. For a broader examination of literary, mostly non-fictional, influences, see my forthcoming article "Literary Sources and Influences on Nietzsche's Views of Women and Feminism."

23. "No! I cannot love people whom I find that I look down on. I need someone who would himself master me, but then, goodness me, I shall never come across anyone like that. I will never fall into anybody's clutches, never, never" (Turgenev, *op. cit.*, 55).

24. This work has been financially supported by the Bank of Sweden Tercentenary Foundation. I also wish to thank a number of philosophy students at the University of Texas at Austin who read and discussed an earlier version of this chapter during the spring 2000 term. Christa and Ralph Acampora have also suggested a number of useful clarifications.

WOMAN

Circe's Truth: On the Way to Animals and Women

Jennifer Ham

Truth as Circe.—Error has transformed animals into men; is truth perhaps
capable of changing man back into an animal?"

(*HH* 519)

Ah, what a dangerous, creeping, subterranean little beast of prey she is!

(*EH* "Books" 5)

Women and animals are closely linked in Nietzsche's philosophy by their
shared position of alterity beyond and beneath the rationality of the Western
philosophical subject. Both beings, women and animals, are figures of struggle and resistance in Nietzsche's project of overcoming "man." Both are also
frequently misread and misunderstood in Nietzsche's work as caricatures of
blond-beast racism and essentialist misogyny. "If you are going to women,
bring the whip" (*Z*:1 "Women").[1] This infamous aphorism, along with other
sexist remarks, have led to Nietzsche's inclusion on the long list of misogynist

Western philosophers from Aristotle to Schopenhauer. "Woman has much reason for shame; so much pedantry, superficiality, schoolmarmishness, petty presumption, petty licentiousness and immodesty lies concealed in woman" (*BGE* 232). "Everything about woman is a riddle, and everything about woman has one solution: that is pregnancy" (*Z*:1 "Women"). "When a woman has scholarly intentions there is usually something wrong with her sexually" (*BGE* 144). In fact, the virulence of some of Nietzsche's remarks seem to represent a regression within the philosophical tradition when compared to Plato's proposal in the *Republic* that women be included in the elite class of philosopher-kings.

"Ah, what a dangerous, creeping, subterranean little beast of prey she is!" (*EH* "Books" 5). With this last remark, Nietzsche would seem to have achieved the nadir of his misogyny, reducing women to animals. It will be the contention of this study, however, that in grouping women with animals, Nietzsche was arguing vociferously for their liberation within the context of a new posthuman order. Nietzsche's women, while also depicted as domestic animals, notably cows and house pets, most often appear as beasts of prey (like the other fierce animals of Nietzsche's philosophy: Dionysus' panther; Zarathustra's lions, eagle, and serpent; as cat, snake, hyena, tiger, and tarantula), as an energetic destroyer of old values, as a pretender, and as a vital, "pregnant" creator of new sensations and identities. Both women and animals challenge the philosopher on his way to "becoming what he already is": a fully assumed animal, unafraid of the feminine, indifferent to masters, "forgetful" of gender distinctions—open to a limitless, unknown future.

Robbing the Beasts

The beginnings of an understanding of Nietzsche's poetic overstatements about animals and women lie in an appreciation of his overall conception of the animality of the human being, both male and female. In concert with Darwin, who, in Freud's terms, "tore down the barrier that had been arrogantly set up between man and beast," Nietzsche declared repeatedly throughout his philosophy that man was indeed an animal.[2] Man is the "fantastic animal" (*GS* 1), the "most endangered animal" (*GS* 353), the "not yet fixed animal" (*BGE* 62), "the cruelest animal" (*Z*:3 "The Convalescent" 2), "the most courageous animal" (*Z*:3 "Vision and Riddle" 1), "the noble [but also distrusting] animal" (*GS* 346), "the social animal" (*GS* 354), "the resourceful animal" (*BGE* 295), "the sick animal" (*GM* III:13), "the most interesting animal" (A 14), "the absurd animal" (GS 224). Nietzsche clearly underscores the animality of man in his philosophy, yet in view of the contradictory epithets he applies to man ("cruelest," "fantastic," "absurd," "not yet finished," etc.) it is also clear that he does not envision man to be the king of all beasts, as simply the most evolved species atop the evolutionary tree. On the contrary, he asserts that man "does not represent progress in contrast to the animal" (KSA 13:14[133]).

Nietzsche rejected a Darwinian account of the animality of man and the struggle for existence throughout nature as being a reactive, narrow-minded interpretation of life, widely reflective of Victorian and Malthusian values. For Nietzsche, animal life is characterized by a reckless and generous expenditure of energy, a wastefulness without calculation, and an outpouring of unbridled will, not the fearful and defensive strategy of conservation and survival of the species described by Darwin. In Darwinian terms, the most successful animal survives in the greatest numbers. Nietzsche reserved the right to judge the value and nobility of different animal species, not just their success at a kind of Spencerian survival, a notion Nietzsche dismissed as a *bêtise*. His writings are replete with aesthetic judgments about the superiority of some species over others despite their numbers or ability to survive. For Nietzsche, the valiant and worthy animal, or human being, is the one that risks death, not the one that clings strategically to life in the hope of perpetuating its species.

Whereas one version of the Darwinian scientific account depicts a progressive evolution from lower to higher forms of life, culminating in the human being, Nietzsche offers a poetic vision of the animal/human dynamic and his own version of the origin of human nature. In *Thus Spoke Zarathustra*, we learn that man obtained his identity and superiority over the beasts, and thus his human nature, by means of thievery. "He [man] envied the wildest, most courageous animals and robbed them of their virtues: only thus did he become man" (Z:4 "On Science"). "Man is the best beast of prey. Man has already robbed all the beasts of their virtues" (Z:3 "On Tablets" 22). In his healthy state, man is a sum of all beastly virtues, chief among them *courage*—not fear, the emotion that determines all behavior in the Darwinian account: "For courage is the best slayer, courage which attacks; for in every attack there is playing and brass. Man, however, is the most courageous animal: hence he overcame every animal" (Z:3 "Vision and Riddle" 1). The presence of fear is important nonetheless in this animal becoming insofar as its vanquishing by courage is a vehicle of overcoming.

Man is indeed a distinct kind of animal, the concept of the overman also affirms this:

> I teach you the overman. Man is something that shall be overcome. What have you done to overcome him? All beings so far have created something beyond themselves; and do you want to be the ebb of this great flood and even go back to the beasts rather than overcome man? What is the ape to man? A laughingstock or a painful embarrassment. And man shall be just that for the overman: a laughingstock or a painful embarrassment. (Z:P 3)

The overman will thus be entirely animal, but above and beyond the ape or the sick animal, common man. The overman fully recognizes and acknowledges his or her animal nature but uses this aggregate courage, this sum of stolen beastly virtues to go beyond man, the "unfinished" animal. A final metaphor from *Zarathustra* reveals the double nature of the human being: "Man is a rope, tied between beast and overman. A dangerous across, a dangerous on-the-way, a dangerous looking back, a dangerous shuddering and stopping" (Z:P 4). One end of the rope is attached to the animal world, the other to the overman, Nietzsche's extraordinary human. Those who fail to cross the abyss along this rope will go under—engulfed by the chasm. Those who recognize and maintain the bridge's origins in animal passions while striving toward a realization of the extraordinary human will go over— the bridge will be maintained in the very act of crossing it, an act that Margot Norris calls an "animal gesture."[3] It is within Nietzsche's general animal anthropology that his remarks about women must be read. Within this scale of values, courage, lack of self-consciousness, and disregard for the "truth" will turn out to reveal, in most instances, fear, admiration, and respect for women: "The higher woman is a higher type than the perfect man, and also something much more rare" (HH 377).

First Place

To appreciate Nietzsche's capacity to harness the power of animal metaphors to revolutionize woman's status within the discourse of nineteenth-century biology, one can consider a well-known essentialist description of women by Schopenhauer, one of the earliest spokesmen for animals, who describes woman as "undersized, narrow-shouldered, broad-hipped and short-legged. . . . the Number-Two of the human race."[4] This can be compared with Nietzsche's assessment: "What inspires respect for women and often enough even fear, is her *nature* which is more 'natural' than man's, the genuine, cunning suppleness of a beast of prey, the tiger's claw under the glove, the naïveté of her egoism, her uneducability and inner wildness, the incomprehensibility, scope and movement of her desires and virtues . . . this dangerous and beautiful cat" (*BGE* 239). Although there is undoubtedly misogyny in these remarks (e.g., the "uneducability," the "incomprehensibility" of women), it is also clear that the animalization of women in Nietzsche conveys power and respect, even fear of the feminine.[5] A remark from *Ecce Homo* makes obvious that Nietzsche's woman has escaped the Schopenhauerian second place: "Woman, the more she is a woman, resists rights in general hand and foot after all, the state of nature, the eternal war between the sexes, gives her by far the *first rank*" (*EH* "Books" 5).[6]

Dangerous Beasts of Prey

Comparisons between women and dangerous predatory animals were pervasive in turn-of-the-century culture and run throughout Nietzsche's work.[7] The "tiger's claw under the glove" points to woman's duplicitous and dangerous nature. The ability to tear apart and dismember is a threat posed by the beast in general and women in particular. "The beast in us wants to be lied to, morality is a white lie, to keep it from tearing us apart" (*HH* 40). Similarly, Nietzsche fears being torn apart by maenads: "Happily I am not prepared to be torn to pieces: the complete woman tears to pieces . . . I know these amiable maenads" (*EH* "Books" 5). Being torn apart at the hands and teeth of the woman-beast is a fate that Nietzsche simultaneously desires and fears, as will be seen in following the dialectic of this specific theme in *Zarathustra*. This infantile fear may well owe something to Nietzsche's childhood (he lost his father at the age of five and remained heavily influenced by his mother and sister throughout his life) and his troubled, largely unsuccessful relations with women in his adult life.[8]

Whatever the possible biographical roots of this apprehension and loathing for women, this fear is exacerbated and exorcized in his philosophical imagination, particularly in a series of scenes and rhetorical images in *Zarathustra*. Nietzsche stages ever more dangerous and seductive encounters between devouring female felines and various male figures in *Zarathustra* before resolving this strife between the sexes in a final scene of female empowerment, escape, and creativity. The point of departure for this particular transformation of the relationship between the sexes is the infamous aphorism about taking a whip to women. Read simply in isolation, it is certainly a bitter chauvinistic remark, but, as our analysis will show, this remark is but the first move in an argument that concludes in the empowerment of women.

Transvaluing the Whip

In the section "On Little Old and Young Women," an old woman asks Zarathustra to express his thoughts about women since he has not done so in any sustained fashion. The wise man replies with a series of declarations: "A real man wants two things: danger and play. Therefore he wants woman as the most dangerous plaything. Man should be educated for war, and woman for the recreation of the warrior. . . . The happiness of man is: I will. The happiness of woman is: he wills" (Z:1). These statements are, at face value, as sexist and repugnant as many other definitions of women's servile role in Nietzsche's philosophy, reminiscent perhaps of Lou Salomé's remark regarding woman's "amazing stupidity" in rejecting domesticity."[9] For these and other similar remarks, the old woman surprisingly offers Zarathustra a "gift," a parting piece of advice: "You are going to women? Do not forget the whip!'" (Z:1). This aphorism, undoubtedly one of Nietzsche's most famous declarations about women, calls to mind a similarly violent remark that seems to advocate corporal punishment as the best approach to women: "*Buona femmina e mala femmina vuol bastone*" (BGE 147). However strong this language seems, we will see that, ultimately, this agonistic encounter between men and women will lead to a subversion of traditional gender roles, especially the idea of female submission that these passages seem to suggest. Nietzsche wrote that he philosophized with a hammer. The whip and the stick, wielded against women, will, in the end, rouse the woman-animal to fury and creativity. The whip, which, like many other instruments of power and authority in Nietzsche, reminds us of man's distinct identity as Hegelian toolmaker, will be reinterpreted, *transvalued*, changed from a symbol of corporal punishment to one of artistic performance and dance.[10]

This first becomes evident when Zarathustra follows the old woman's advice in the "Other Dancing Song," and brandishes a whip toward a woman. The section is comprised of a hymn addressed to Life, who is personified first as a woman. "Into your eyes I looked recently, O Life: I saw gold blinking in your night-eye; my heart stopped in delight." Life is subsequently characterized in animal terms in the poem: "Away from you I leaped, and from your serpents' ire." "Now you are fleeing from me again, you sweet wild-cat and ingrate!" "Your lovely little white teeth are gnashing at me; out of a curly little mane your evil eyes are flashing at me" (Z:3 "Other Dancing"). The tone mounts, Life is characterized as a "witch," and Zarathustra pro-duces the whip: "Keeping time with my whip, you shall dance and cry! Or have I forgotten the whip? Not I!" This is clearly not a whip of corporal punishment but the whip of animal training, or perhaps simply an instru-ment for marking time in music.

Life attenuates the cruel aspect of the whip further: "Then Life answered me thus, covering up her delicate ears: O Zarathustra don't crack your whip so frightfully! After all, you know that noise murders thought—and just now such tender thoughts are coming to me." The cracking of the whip is similar to the thunderclaps that announce Zarathustra's poetry. The whip is used to bring Life back to herself, away from her thoughts, to awaken her to the present moment, as a lion tamer would use the crack of the whip to get his animals' attention—less out of cruelty or self-defense than as cue to per-formance. This pedagogical and performative use of the whip, as opposed to its punitive dimension, is evident if the context of animal training in the nineteenth century is taken as a backdrop to this scene in *Zarathustra*.

Animal Taming and Training

"Anyone who knows what goes on in menageries has doubts as to whether the beast is 'improved' there" (*TI* "Improvers" 2). Nietzsche was certainly aware of methods of animal taming and training and uses such images to dramatize his thoughts about morality and ultimately philosophy in general. In *The Will to Power* he writes: "Morality is a menagerie, its premise is, that iron bars are more useful than freedom, even for the captive, its other prem-ise, that there are animal tamers who do not shrink from frightful means, who know how to handle red-hot iron. This horrific species, which accepts battle with the wild animal, calls itself 'priest'" (*WP* 397). Similarly, in *Zara-thustra* he argues: "Cursed I call all who have only one choice: to become evil beasts or evil tamers of beasts; among such men I would not build my home" (Z:3 "Spirit of Gravity" 2). For Nietzsche, these facilitators of the "civilizing process" are an even more brutal version of the very beasts they are trying to tame.[11] Because their taming is self-interested, directed, and sadistic, such masters of the ring represent for him "the cruelest animals." This process of "civilizing," taming, is a violent one, one whereby acts of cruelty are transformed into cultural events. Nietzsche states: "Virtually everything we call 'higher culture' rests on the spiritualization and sublimation of cruelty [Grausamkeit]—that is my proposition; the 'wild animal' has not been exterminated at all; it lives, it thrives, it has only become—deified" (BGE 229). Nietzsche rejects such vengeful use of the hot iron, the bastone, and the whip.

Carl Hagenbeck, the famous animal trainer and Nietzsche's contemporary, describes cruel tactics used to train animals in the same language as Nietzsche and also calls for kinder, more humane methods: "I felt a desire to institute a more rational and humane method of training."[12] "Animals are beings like ourselves and their intelligence is only different from ours not in kind but only in degree and strength. They react with cruelty to cruelty and with friendship to friendship. I have found that love, goodness and persistence paired with strictness achieves more from an animal than raw violence. Whoever shares this opinion must be pained to see his dear animal mishandled with the whips, clubs and hot irons."[13] "But these barbarous methods of training animals are now no longer in vogue; they have become obsolete for this reason if for no other: that it is impossible to achieve by ill treatment one one-hundredth of what can be done by humane and intelligent methods."[14] He continues: "What was earlier understood to be training deserves to be called the torture of animals, whereas training today actually should be called schooling. Earlier one relied on the whip, a cane and glowing irons. You can imagine that the animals never developed a trust of their masters, rather, they had only dread and deep hatred for their 'overlords.'"[15] "The secrets of successful tamers of wild beasts may be summed up in three words: Love, Patience, Energy."[16]

In actuality, nineteenth-century animals were subjected to either "wild training" or "tame training"—depending on which aspect of animal essence was desired, its "human" or "non-human" culture. Each pedagogy presented the audience with a different conception of animality, one convincing audiences to perceive animal "distance" from humans. Animals were instructed to either snarl, thrash, claw, and bite the bars (desires to "achieve" animal wildness are seen today in attempts to breed wildness into species, such as broncos, cocks, bulls, or guard dogs) or to ride chariots, bicycles, or even horses; do ball tricks; stage tea parties; and hug circus women. The more successful animal domesticators realized that the animals had their own individual personalities and found those taken directly from the wild and brought into human civilization easier to domesticate than ones born into it. "Tamers find the menagerie-born animal far more unpleasant to deal with than the lion caught in his native wilds, because although the latter is the stronger and more aggressive type he is not so sly and malicious as his degenerate brother that has only known captivity."[17]

Whereas animal vitality fosters power, the process of cultural domestication diminishes the power of the individual and makes sick through the appropriation or imitation of others. The animals (whether human or nonhuman) tamed by what Nietzsche sees as the cruel pedagogy of domestication need to be healed, to recover from the effects of their engulfment by civilization. Nietzsche considered humility, patience, brotherly helpfulness, hope, and love (Christian virtues) to be insidious tools of a domestication that fostered a slave morality concocted by the weak to disarm the strong. Such enslavement forces the subdued weaker being to seek revenge, to be calculative, willful, and hidden in order to resist the dangerous spontaneity of the sadistic and monstrous master.

Turn-of-the-century lion tamers, such as the well-known *dompteurs* Willy Hagenbeck, Herr Schilling, Heinrich Mehrmann, or Tilly Bebe, seemed to be suggesting that by employing the gentler, more subtle, less overt, more "civilized" method, they had succeeded in closing the difference between theirs and the animal's thoughts, if not desires, a moment when the animal forgot itself and did its master's bidding at the expense of its own. One of several female animal tamers, Frau Krone, once described an anthropomorphic moment of identification that resulted ultimately in the compliance of a big cat under training. For Nietzsche, this is the fatal moment of education (*Bildung*) when the Other becomes enthralled by the power and greatness of Another and relinquishes its own. This is the point where Nietzsche's *Raubtiere*, his "blond beasts," risk becoming *Herdentiere*, part of the herd. When their interiors are domesticated, the human animal needs to seek recovery from such an unhealthy and submissive posture. The process of cultural domestication diminishes the power of the individual through the appropriation or imitation of others. Nietzsche refers to this process as the *Dressierbarkeit* of man, his dressage, a performance he incidentally lamented was "gaining popularity in this democratic Europe" (KSA 11:26[449]).

Nietzsche shares Hagenbeck's abhorrence of cruel animal trainers, "the horrific species which . . . calls itself 'priest.'" (WP 397). For Nietzsche, who found life more dangerous among men than among animals, "man is the cruelest animal." For "'it is men,' said he, 'that corrupt women; and all the failings of women should be atoned by and improved in men. For it is man who creates for himself the image of woman, and woman forms herself according to this image.'" (GS 68). Lou Salomé agreed with Nietzsche that women were also capable of thrusting repressive images on women and they both admonished the kind of "breeding" feminists espoused. He exclaims: "One cannot be gentle enough towards women!" (GS 71). Nietzsche draws a parallel here between his warning against cruel animal practices in the circus ring and the similarly violent philosophical gesture of essentializing—in this case, women—and, as we will see later, its consequential corruption (violation) of truth. In Beyond Good and Evil Nietzsche draws out this kind of metaphorical domination. In his words, woman must be "repressed," "kept under control," "locked up lest [she] fly away," and, in a desperate attempt at reversal, "kept afraid of man." When Nietzsche allows us to view the threat of woman's animal strength (i.e., when Nietzsche allows women to move closer and to occupy a traditionally male characteristic), that is the moment when he seems himself to be most cornered—to the extent that he willingly inverts his abhorrence of the cruel master and becomes one himself.

Women, like non-human animals, need to recover. For Nietzsche, the project of recovering oneself does not involve a dubious and highly problematic return to origins as if beneath civilization we would rediscover the persistence of a bestial or primitive humanity. Nor is becoming animal, this restoring to health, a matter of mimicry or representation, neither of which are creative gestures, nor is it a matter of touching base with some subjective reverie of Oedipal beatings. Nietzsche was not impressed with psychological liberations. Recovering means simply forgetting the lesson, becoming culturally innocent, unconcerned with judgments and dangers, and learning to risk spontaneously not mimetically. Nietzsche's practice of Bildung in fact has less to do with building and more to do with a dismantling, a kind of education in reverse (or "reintroduction" program). Only through an erasing of consciousness can all of the contradictory drives and instincts of the organism flourish in uninhibited oblivion. Only by obliterating consciousness, curing oneself of one's enthrallment with others, can natural animal drives exert themselves unfettered, restoring the organism to its natural vigor. Animals, as humans, who are able to recover from this kind of Heideggerian "petting" and to unburden themselves of their pathogenic culture are vitally reclaimed by their instinctual nature.[18] Culture multiplies rather than negates violence by repressing biological force with rational force. The subtitle of Ecce Homo prescribes just such a recuperative process, a cure from culture and return to vitality, a "becoming what one already is," an animal.[19]

Ensphinxed

Nietzsche's final rendition of the encounter between man and women as beast of prey occurs in the wanderer's song in Part 4 of *Zarathustra*, entitled "Among the Daughters of the Wilderness." The wanderer begins by drawing in the new "foreign air in a new country" and sings of two "girl-cats" named Dudu and Suleika, whose names evoke exotic animal performers in a circus. "I lie here, sniffed at / And played about / By little winged bugs—/ Also by still smaller, / More foolish, more sinful / Wishes and notion." Amid roars, howlings, and images of gnawed-off legs, the scenario is taken to its logical end as the wanderer declares himself to be "enveloped by you, / Silent and foreboding / Girl-cats, / Dudu and Suleika—/ *Ensphinxed*, to crowd many feelings into one word" (Z:4).

Faced with this exotic setting and spectacle, the wanderer is pushed to the limits of his European language and sensibility. When he seeks to give vent to his feelings, only moral "roaring" and "virtuous howling" can be produced, hence the need for the neologism "ensphinxed." Of course, the sphinx was a stock figure in fin de siècle misogyny as well, but here again Nietzsche has transvalued this image. The sphinx provokes enchantment, understanding, and delight, not revulsion, violence, and fear, as it has in the West since its origin in Greek mythology.

Another important series of images in the "Daughter of the Wilderness" poem concerns the teeth of the girl cats and the desire to be devoured by them. Just prior to naming Dudu and Suleika, the poet describes himself as a fig or a date. "Brown and sweet through, oozing gold, lusting / For the round mouth of a girl, / But even more for girlish, / Ice-cold, snow-white, cutting / Incisors: for after these / Pants the heart of all hot dates" (Z:4). This language could certainly be interpreted as expressing Nietzsche's own erotic preferences, but, of greater overall significance, the position of cruelty and domineering associated with the whip, and already attenuated in "Dancing Song," gives way here to a stance of complete submission and enchantment on the part of the male spectator. Pushing this scene somewhat, one could say that its underlying logic is one of a zoo-break in which fierce captive animals have been liberated and are free to do what they want. The animal has broken free and devoured the trainer with its "cold white incisors."

This fantasy of pleasurable devouring also rounds out the series of references to maenads in Nietzsche's work. The fear of being devoured is realized and accepted. The encounter has resulted in an engulfment, a simultaneous becoming animal and becoming woman.[20] The Zarathustran seeker has been engulfed by and merged with, transformed into, the feminine, *umsphinxt*, as he says. In the original myth, the sphinx, an inscrutable crouching figure with the head and breast of a woman, the body of a lion, the wings of an eagle, and a serpent's tail, kills herself when Oedipus answers her riddle. In Nietzsche's anti-Oedipal version, the male has joined forces with the female sphinx, the *Halbtier*, not killed her with an essentializing solution to her riddle. Nietzsche's wanderer, unlike Oedipus, prefers to remain enchanted by the sphinx and avoids the deadly finality by resisting any definitive answer to the sphinx's question about which animal walks on four, then two, and finally three legs. The breasted sphinx poses this riddle, the heart of which is the perplexing enigma of animal identity, whose solution is revealed in cryptic poetic language to be man. In the Greek myth, Oedipus answers the question incisively, at once deciphering the sphinx's poetic animalistic language and killing her, thereby intimating the violent difference and superiority of the human being over the animal. In the Nietzschean version, the animal nature of man and woman together is affirmed and understood with neither murder nor separation from the sphinx. This fulfills and completes many of Nietzsche's admonitions about living dangerously in the neighborhood of such fearful animals as panthers, lions, and sphinxes on the way to becoming the overman. The sphinx and the "laughing lions" are fitting animal companions for Zarathustra at the end of his journey, where even the best of human beings, the "higher men," yet instill him with nausea and a need for fresh air. The poetic and revisionary nature of Nietzsche's mythology of women as beasts in *Zarathustra* can be used as a key and provide further insight into Nietzsche's puzzling statements about animal intelligence and truth as woman.

Tierverstand: Animal Genius

Nietzsche stages this scene of animal/woman devouring not as a dignified cultural event, as some practiced act of cruel and humiliating dressage. On the contrary, it is an unscripted animal act, the one all animal tamers dread, one characterized by an absence of rationality, a disregard for all masters. This anti-pedagogical moment requires no whip at all, only a mutual forgetting of all tools. For a moment, the actors are cultural innocents, powerful individuals, now united not by the herd but, as in the riddle, by their shared animal vitality, a kind of unconscious primal truth. Nietzsche termed this truth *Tierverstand* and considered it "of all forms of intelligence discovered up to this point, the most intelligent" (*BGE* 218). Nietzsche is not alone in exploring the agency of interior animal vestiges and traces infiltrating human thought. Freud saw man's unconscious life as a kind of regression back to a primal state, an animality that provided the archaic material of every dreamer. For Derrida, the very language of our thought betrays its animal origins in a "zoon."[21] Nietzsche imagined animals reprimanding man for having allowed his valuable faculty to erode, for having lost "in the most dangerous way its healthy animal sense [*gesunden Tierverstand*]," for having become "the insane animal, the laughing animal, the crying animal, the sad animal" (*GS* 224). He reasons that if "every mistake in every sense is the effect of the degeneration of instinct, of the disintegration of the will: one could almost define what is bad in this way. All that is good is instinct—and hence easy, necessary, free." "Stupidity, basically, the degeneration of instinct, which is today the cause of *all* stupidities" (*TI* "Skirmishes" 40). Like the wanderer, man is inhabited by an animal whose remains, whose survival instincts, rooted in physiology, underlie all human intelligence. All of man's higher faculties, including his creative acts, emanate from his innate animal physiology, whereas his "morality is the herd-instinct in the animal" (*GS* 116). For this philosopher, intelligence is not based in rationality but rather in instinct, which, when fully granted ascendancy, could reveal our true identity.

Truth as a Woman

Men, according to Nietzsche, have lost this animal intelligence, but not women: "The female intellect. Women's intellect is manifested as perfect control, presence of mind, and utilization of all advantages. . . . [W]omen have the intelligence, men the heart and passion" (*HH* 411). Man, unlike woman, is separated from his animal self, trapped in his rationality. He is bereft of his animal innocence and is nostalgic and envious of woman's *Tierverstand*, yet he seeks revenge on the resisting animal in woman for its elusive promise of liberation. Nietzsche suggests freedom from that rational domination with his repeated claims that "truth is a woman" and "wisdom . . . is a woman." The philosopher's gesture is one of *Umwertung*, of placing women and animals on the side of perception and intelligence and putting man outside, desirous of their closer proximity to truth. Zarathustra, the seeker of truth, surrounds himself with animals. The female cats Dudu and Suleika instruct the wanderer brutally; he becomes *umsphinxt* and the half-female sphinx brings her seekers to understanding not by threatening violent punishment but through a more subtle means by engaging and perplexing them with her truth.

What then could Nietzsche mean by this apparently contradictory statement: "Woman does not want truth: what is truth to a woman? From the beginning, nothing has been more alien, repugnant, and hostile to woman than truth—her great art is the lie, her highest concern is mere appearance and beauty" (BGE 232). How is it possible for woman to be truth but for truth also to be foreign and repulsive to her? To attempt to answer this conundrum, we need to reflect on Nietzsche's style, his own mistrust of fixity and finality, which pervades his conception of all three categories—animal, woman, and truth itself.

Animals and women bring to Nietzsche's language a particular kind of silence, a poverty-stricken and inaccessible foreign presence, and it is particularly this shared characteristic, as Derrida points out, that may have attracted Nietzsche to use them as "spurs"—as

> pointed objects, often only a pen, but also a stylet, or even a dagger. With whose help one can certainly cruelly attack what philosophy calls by the name of matter or the matrix, in order to pierce a mark upon it, leave an imprint or a form, but also to repel a menacing force, keep it at a distance, repress it, protect oneself from it—folding oneself or refolding, in flight, behind veils . . . the rostrum, that jut that goes ahead to break up the attack and fend off the adverse surface.[22]

Animals and women serve as challenges, as catalysts of transvaluation, as mediators of truth, yet they are unable to assert their presence on their own. Like Wittgenstein's lion—"If a lion could talk, we would not understand it"—or the hermetic gaze of Rilke's panther or the cryptic animal in Nietzsche's joke:

> A human being may well ask an animal: "Why do you not speak to me of your happiness but only stand and gaze at me?" The animal would like to answer and say: "The reason is I always forget what I was going to say"—but then he forgot this answer too, and stayed silent: so that the human being was left wondering. (HL 1, pp. 60–61)

Nietzsche was intrigued by the unfathomable animal oblivion and the transformative implications that chasm held for humans. Whereas Freud seems to cast animal truth as being within, Zarathustra senses that his animals, the bearers of truth, are also without, beyond, speaking in the "language of the bees." Although animals appear to be clandestine creatures,

Nietzsche presents them, unlike humans, as ironically unable to keep a secret. It is as if this complete and profound openness of animals, their lack of deceit and artifice, were ironically a kind of brute truth yet one that nonetheless confounds.

Nietzsche talks about woman in similar terms, "woman is truth," but also a "veil," hidden. "One should have more respect for the bashfulness with which nature has hidden behind riddles and iridescent uncertainties. Perhaps truth is a woman, who has reasons for not letting us see her reasons" (NCW "Epilogue" 2). He explains that women, like disempowered animals, easily revert to their need to cower and hide, but unlike animals, women are capable of artifice as actresses, as hypnotizers—they wear masks and play roles (GS 361). And like animals, they are a multiplicity of identities, "floating signifiers," "quiet, magical beings gliding past him [man]" (GS 60). Her "great art is the lie, her highest concern is mere appearance and beauty." "All virtue and depth is to them merely a veil over this 'truth.'" "But perhaps that is the most powerful charm [Zauber] of life: it is covered with a gold-wrought veil . . . of beautiful possibilities that grant it a promising, reticent, modest, ironical allure, sympathetic, seductive. Yes, life is a woman!" (GS 339).

Indeed, for Nietzsche truth was as inscrutable as woman. For him, truths were lies, and he found appearances more reliable and much less effective violators of truth than convictions. "Convictions are more dangerous enemies of truth than lies" (HH 483). Again, a reference to Nietzsche's dislike of cruelty, of Grausamkeit, in this case, of the violence done to truth. "Ultimately, it [truth] is a woman: one should not visit violence on her" (BGE 220). "Taking for granted that truth is a woman—what then? Are there not grounds for the suspicion that all philosophers, insofar as they were dogmatists, have had little understanding of women?" (BGE P). Finally, we understand Nietzsche's reference to be directed at truth seekers: "You are going to women? Don't forget the whip!'" (Z:1 "Women"). Dogmatism is the cruel and punitive tamer of truth. Then how do we undo this cruelty done to truth? How can we liberate truth from the domination of her self-interested dompteurs? Nietzsche wonders if perhaps those duplicities (or rather multiplicities), those transient phantoms, animals, and women who convey meaning but are devoid of essence themselves, may provide answers at least to those with ears to hear it. But how can we hear them at such a distance when distance is their power? Although the chasm between animal, (wo)man, and truth cannot be closed, it can be bridged. "Truth as Circe.—Error has transformed animals into men; is truth perhaps capable of changing man back into an animal?" (*HH* 519).

Philosophizing as Circe

In this final rhetorical association of femininity and animality, in the image of the fearful sorceress of antiquity who indeed had the power to transform the companions of Odysseus into swine, Nietzsche states again one of the major projects of his philosophy: to reveal and restore the animal nature of human beings. In a typically hyperbolic and provocative move, Nietzsche describes the activity of Circe as the *truth*. This is the metamorphic truth of becoming, the vision of the human being in a constant state of change. As this truth is revealed, fabricated by the art of Circe, human beings will become animals; they will acquire the eyes, ears, and tastes, the exquisite senses and wisdom of Zarathustra's companions. Nietzsche avails himself of the language and power of the sorceress to obtain this vision of humanity. He philosophizes as Circe bridging the expanse between the human being and her primal past and animal future.

Notes

1. For citations of Nietzsche's works I have utilized the following translations with some modifications: Kaufmann's translations of BGE, EH, GS, NCW, TI, and Z; Faber's translation of HH; and Hollingdale's translation of HL. I also consulted *Joyful Wisdom*, tr. Kurt Reinhardt (New York: Ungar, 1969).

2. Sigmund Freud, "The Resistances to Psycho-Analysis," in *The Standard Edition of the Complete Psychological Works of Sigmund Freud*, ed. and trans. James Strachey, 24 vols. (London: Hogarth 1961), 19:221.

3. Margot Norris, *Beasts of the Modern Imagination: Darwin, Nietzsche, Kafka, Ernst and Lawrence* (Baltimore: Johns Hopkins University Press, 1985).

4. Arthur Schopenhauer, from *Parerga and Paralipomena*, quoted in R. Agonito, ed., "The Weakness of Women," *History of Ideas on Women: A Source Book* (New York: Perigee Books, 1977), 199f.

5. For other work on Nietzsche's relation to the feminine, see Carol Diethe, *Nietzsche's Women: Beyond the Whip* (New York: de Gruyter, 1996); Luce Irigaray, *Marine Lover of Friedrich Nietzsche* (New York: Columbia University Press, 1980); Kelly Oliver and Marilyn Pearsall, *Feminist Interpretations of Freidrich Nietzsche* (University Park: Pennsylvania State University Press, 1999); Paul Patton, *Nietzsche, Feminism and Political Theory* (London: Routledge, 1993); Peter Burgard, *Nietzsche and the Feminine* (London: University of

Virginia Press, 1994); Caroline Picart, *Resentment and the 'Feminine' in Nietzsche's Politico-Aesthetics* (University Park: Pennsylvania State University Press, 1999).

6. Emphasis mine. See Hedwig Dohm's "Nietzsche und die Frauen" *Die Zukunft* 25 (1898) and *Werde, die du bist* (Become the Woman You Are) for a then-contemporary German feminist's critical view of Nietzsche. Other earlier views of this relationship are recounted in Elisabeth Förster-Nietzsche's *Nietzsche und die Frauen seiner Zeit* (Munich· Beck Verlag, 1935) and latei in Henry Walter Braun's *Nietzsche und die Frauen* (Bonn: Bouvier, 1978).

7. A discussion of cultural representations of women as animals in Nietzsche's day is documented by Bram Dijkstra's *Idols of Perversity: Fantasies of Feminine Evil in Fin-de-Siècle Culture* (Oxford: Oxford University Press, 1986).

8. For further interpretations of Nietzsche's biography and his difficult relations with women, see Sarah Kofman and Kelly Oliver, as well as Rudiger Safranski, *Nietzsche: A Philosophical Biography*, trans. Shelley Frisch (New York: Norton, 2002).

9. Quoted in Carol Diethe's *Nietzsche's Women: Beyond the Whip* (New York: de Gruyter, 1996), 59.

10. For a discussion of Nietzsche's notion of transvaluing, see Gilles Deleuze, *Nietzsche and Philosophy*, trans. Hugh Tomlinson (New York: Columbia University Press, 1983).

11. As mentioned in Jennifer Ham and Matthew Senior's edited collection *Animal Acts: Configuring the Human in Western History* (New York: Routledge, 1997) and most recently in Clare Palmer's "Taming the Wild Profusion of Existing Things? A Study of Foucault, Power, and Human/Animal Relationships," *Environmental Ethics* 23 (Winter 2001): 339–358, Nietzsche's mapping of the animal-human power relations is reminiscent of Foucault's discussion of the "civilizing process" in his *Discipline and Punish* (Harmondsworth: Penguin, 1979).

12. Carl Hagenbeck, *Beasts and Men* (New York: Longmans, Green & Co., 1909), 121.

13. Hagenbeck, *Beasts and Men*, 125.

14. Hagenbeck, *Beasts and Men*, 124.

15. Hagenbeck, *Beasts and Men*, 311.

16. A. H. Kober, *Circus Nights and Circus Days*, trans. C. Sykes (New York: W. Morrow, 1931) 118.

17. Kober, *Circus Nights and Circus Days*, 105.

18. For Heidegger, words such as "humanism" gain a firm foothold only when original thinking has already subsided. Humanism, in other words, may represent the greatest obstacle to reinventing the human. Heidegger's rejection of humanism does not rest on a repudiation of the human; on the contrary, "humanism is opposed because it does not set the *humanitas* of man high enough."

19. Nietzsche's thoughts on human education and becoming evolved in part in response to feminists and brutal training methods. He condemned the school system for reducing innate individual life-giving forces to outward general standards of decency and for sacrificing self-affirmation to self-negation: "What the 'higher schools' in Germany really achieve is a brutal training" (*TI* "Germans" 5).

20. The writings of Gilles Deleuze and Felix Guattari have championed Nietzsche as the most important philosopher of becoming, as opposed to the metaphysical tradition, with its insistence on being. In A Thousand Plateaus, they advocate a becoming animal as a means of escaping the subjectivist tendencies of modern politics and philosophy. See Tom Conley, "Pantagruel Animal," in Ham and Senior, eds., Animal Acts for a succinct explanation of becoming animal and its usefulness as applied to a literary text. See also Steve Baker's use of the term as applied to postmodern art in The Postmodern Animal (London: Reaktion Books, 2000).

21. Jacques Derrida, "Plato's Pharmacy," in Dissemination, trans. Barbara Johnson (Chicago: University of Chicago Press, 1981), 79.

22. Jacques Derrida, Spurs: Nietzsche's Styles, trans. Barbara Harlow (Chicago: University of Chicago Press, 1978), 37ff.

SATYR

Human-Animality
In Nietzsche

Lawrence J. Hatab

I am a disciple of the philosopher Dionysus; I should prefer to be even a satyr
to being a saint.

(*EH* P 2)

I estimate the value of men, of races, according to the necessity by which
they cannot conceive the god apart from the satyr.

(*EH* "Clever" 4)

With these references to the satyr in his last published work, Nietzsche
retrieved an image that had figured significantly in his first published work,
The Birth of Tragedy. The satyr was an ancient Greek mythical being that
displayed a combination of animal and human features and that can be taken
to represent an ambiguous confluence of nature and culture. This ambiguity
characteristic of early Greek culture inspired Nietzsche and it can be seen to
mark a fundamental task of his work: how to think human culture and the
forces of animal nature as an indivisible blend that departs from the Western

conception of carnal nature as something to be transcended, mastered, or reformed. Nietzsche advocates the notion of *homo natura* (*BGE* 230), a return of humanity and philosophy to the primal forces of nature (see also *GS* 109, 294; and *TI* "Morality"). Yet Nietzsche's naturalism cannot be called a reductive naturalism according to scientific categories (see *BGE* 22, where he critiques the idea of nature conforming to the "natural laws" of science), nor is it a naturalism that assumes fixed essences or intrinsic purposes (see *BGE* 9), nor is it a romantic "return to nature" that is nostalgic for a precultural harmony (see *GS* 370, where Romanticism is associated with pessimism). Nature, for Nietzsche, is a network of forces that cannot be exhausted by scientific categories or governed by essentialist dreams. Nature, especially in life forms, exhibits indigenous forces of striving, domination, and destruction (captured in Nietzsche's concept of will to power). Yet Nietzsche's naturalism is not a denial or subordination of culture. Forms of culture simply emerge as modifications of natural drives that never fully surpass their base.

A telling account of Nietzsche's nature-culture dyad can be found in an early work, *Homer's Contest* (*KSA* 1, p. 162ff.). Here Nietzsche declares that culture is not something separate from or superceding nature but a modulation of more vicious natural drives into less destructive forms. For example, the Greek preoccupation with contests of all sorts (the agon) transformed a brutal drive to annihilate into a drive to defeat opponents in organized competitions. Cultural contests permitted both a sublimation of cruel instincts and a setting for fostering cultural excellence, since talent unfolds in a struggle with competitors (*KSA* 1, p. 787). Nietzsche's thought abounds with agonistic redescriptions of cultural production. Even consciousness, for Nietzsche, is not the opposite of natural instincts but rather a refined and redirected expression of instincts (*GS* 354). Even the reflective thinking of the philosopher "is secretly guided and formed into certain channels by his instincts" (*BGE* 3).

Against this background, I want to offer some brief remarks on the satyr figure, with the aim of illustrating Nietzsche's cultural naturalism and with the hope of contributing some useful reflections to the present volume on Nietzsche's animals.

In *The Birth of Tragedy*, the satyr is an important figure in Nietzsche's project of demonstrating the Dionysian sources of Greek tragedy. Nietzsche takes the satyr as a synthesis of god and goat (the goat being associated with Dionysus) and as a symbol of Dionysian enthusiasm, a "primal humanity" that experiences the healthy ecstasies of divine madness (*BT* "Attempt at Self-

Criticism" 4). The satyr is an expression of the Greek "longing for what is original and natural," an *Urbild* of nature unmediated by knowledge and reflection, an ecstatic release into the sexual omnipotence of nature driven by the force of the god (*BT* 8). The satyr represents a more dark and wild phenomenon than the modern "idyllic shepherd," and it exposes the delusion of culture taken as the only reality (*BT* 8). The satyr-Dionysus connection, however, is in Nietzsche's estimation a more cultivated dynamic than the "barbaric" expressions of the Dionysian given over to more brutish and licentious forces (*BT* 2).

The satyr chorus and dithyramb in honor of Dionysus are seen by Nietzsche as forerunners of tragic drama. The phenomenon of "drama" (literally, an action) and dramatic impersonation are born in the mimetic enchantment of Dionysian enthusiasts who identify with the satyr celebrants of the god who have identified with Dionysus through ecstatic transformation (*BT* 8).[1] So for Nietzsche, tragedy begins with the satyr, representing a Dionysian experience of exuberant life forces beneath the Apollonian veil of civilization (*BT* 7). And the Dionysian life force behind passing manifestations evokes the positive, celebratory mood that Nietzsche insists be recognized in any account of the Greek phenomenon of tragedy. The undoing of a tragic hero is at the same time the reaffirmation of an undifferentiated natural energy behind cultural forms.

Mention should be made of the "wisdom of Silenus" as it functions in *BT*. The relation between the satyr and Silenus is unclear, although the former has human legs, the latter equine legs. Originally they seem to have been separate fertility daemons, but in time both came to be associated with Dionysus. It is not clear if they were taken as substantively different or if Silenus was a proper name rather than a generic type.[2] Nietzsche seems to conflate satyr and Silenus, although the latter may be a proper name referring to a kind of pessimistic wisdom (It is better never to have been born; next best to die soon) that Nietzsche wants to bring into the picture (*BT* 3). The problem is that the satyr chorus is an affirmative force that saves the Greeks from nihilism and revulsion against life (*BT* 7). It may be that Silenus represents a danger in Dionysian experience wherein the pain of individuation can prompt an ecstatic denial of individuation in favor of annihilation. It is clear that for Nietzsche, the wisdom of tragedy reflects an overcoming of such pessimism through the "reciprocal necessity" of both Dionysian ecstasy and the beauty of Apollonian individuation (*BT* 4). The satyr effect, especially its relation to comedy (*BT* 7), seems to have a life-affirming quality, so the satyr-

Silenus relation would need clarifying on this count. Nietzsche's text, however, does not provide clarification.

What can classical scholarship tell us about Nietzsche's account of the satyr? Nietzsche has been quite influential in opening up concealed or under-developed elements in early Greek culture and tragic drama. Nietzsche was roughly right about tragedy deriving from the satyr chorus and Dionysian worship, and he was prescient in overcoming more prudish scholarship by stressing connections between tragedy, Dionysian passion, and the sexual energy of the satyr.[3] What do we know about the satyr?[4] Satyrs were a race of their own, a hybrid of animal and human traits, depicted as a human form with a horse's tail and ears, sometimes with hooves.[5] Goat features may not be original and seem to be a sixth-century development.[6] Satyrs were usually associated with negative moral traits such as laziness and licentiousness.[7] The relationship between satyrs and other animals was not one of hunting or domesticating but of play, dancing, erotics, and role exchanges. The anatomy, dress, and behavior of the satyr suggest an ambiguous human-animality and an oscillation between barbarian and civilized traits.[8]

The association between the satyr and Dionysus may not be primeval, but there are clear connections in the sixth century. Dionysus's entourage included not males but rather women, nymphs, and satyrs.[9] The behavior of satyrs as companions of Dionysus included drinking, flute playing, dancing, acrobatics, and erotic gestures directed toward maenads and nymphs, all usually presented with comic effects.[10] The leaping and gamboling of the satyrs expressed the joyful delirium of those who follow Dionysus, who call into question established norms, who undo divisions between social roles, sexes, age groups, animals and humans, humans and gods.[11]

Satyrs were on the margins of, but not isolated from, the human world. As servants of Dionysus, who appeared among humans, satyrs performed roles such as artisans, sculptors, and cooks. Yet they were also depicted as wanton drunkards, thieves, and gluttons, beings who could not control or still their desires. At the same time they were shown as "inventing," or better, *discovering* many elements of human culture, usually exhibiting expressions of amazement, astonishment, or an eager gaze. One can surmise that the wildness and marginality of the satyr were given to represent a primal uncovering or renewal of the human world. The "negative" posture, burlesque, and fringe realm of the satyrs can be said to have functioned as an inversion/deforming of human norms that brought both a comic and an exploratory effect. The satyr, then, was an experimentation with alterity that evoked a heightened attention to human culture by exceeding its normalcy and familiarity.[12]

Visual representations of satyrs usually depicted human mimetic performances of these sacred mythical beings in religious rituals and proto-dramas, typically dancing and cavorting around the god Dionysus.[13] They were shown as masked figures with attached animal ears, tail, and phallus. Such a mimetic, masking mode was typical of *thiasoi*, or cult associations where humans achieved identification through imitation of sacred prototypes. In the case of the satyrs, the mimetic identification was with Dionysian ecstasy and latent animality.[14]

Such mimetic performances set the stage for dramatic arts, especially the role of satyr plays in tragic drama.[15] The dithyramb was a mode of poetry sung and danced in honor of Dionysus by choruses of fifty men or boys. Such practices were continued in the satyr play, a short fourth play following a trilogy of tragic dramas. The Dionysian connection was clear to the audience, and they knew during tragic performances that a satyr play was meant to conclude the presentation. In addition, the same performers acted the parts in all four plays. Accordingly, the satyr play was intrinsic to tragedy's cultural function, and the audience anticipation of the satyr play should be kept in mind when trying to understand the effect of tragic drama.[16]

The satyr play involved a chorus of singers and dancers, part human, part animal, engaged in playful, violent, sensual burlesque that was very dissimilar in style and tone from the tragic chorus. Here the heroes and sacred figures of the tragedies were presented in a different, far-from-somber register, and yet the link with tragedy was evident, since the same performers were involved and the vocabulary and metrics of the characters were carried over.

What can we make of the satyr effect in tragedy? The satyr was an antitype (especially compared with male citizens) found on the fringes of the human world. Satyr plays presented exotic locales with fantastic characterizations, often with themes of discovery/invention of something in the human world (wine, music, fire, metallurgy, the first woman). Satyrs, then, represented an inversion/distancing effect creating a scene of surprise and rediscovery of familiar cultural meanings, but always in the setting of a human-animal-nature convergence. With the tragedies portraying somber confrontations with fate, death, the gods, and limits, the satyr effect "played" with culture by way of a disorientation-reorientation structure.

If we consider the Dionysian phenomenon as both a negative and a productive force, given over to both ecstatic abandonment and erotic energies symbolizing the cycle of death and regeneration in nature, the tragic trilogies and satyr play can be understood as a confrontation with limit situations in two registers, one a "serious" expression of loss, the other a "playful" expression of comic juxtapositions, celebration, rediscovery, and reorientation. The intrinsic function of the satyr play in tragic performance lends much credence to Nietzsche's insistence that Greek tragedy was at bottom a life-affirming cultural force, understood by way of the dual nature of Dionysian worship. The function of the satyr was to give presence to the ambiguous commixture in life of animal and human, nature and culture, and to celebrate this ambiguity with a playful modulation of tragic alterity. And Nietzsche would stress the cultural juxtaposition of satyric and tragic drama in distinct performances as an ongoing exchange and as an implicit Greek recognition of the productive tension between the two forms that would be weakened if the two forms were somehow blended together and lost if one form were to overcome or replace the other.

The duality of Dionysian experience can also apply to the historical links between tragedy and comedy and thus to a correlation between pathos and laughter. The buffoonery displayed in satyr plays signal an intermediate genre between tragedy and comedy, with closer affinities to comedy.[17] Comedy can be traced to the Dionysian *komos*, a swarming band of drunken men who threw off social conventions and inhibitions, engaging in boisterous laughter, dancing, and mocking language directed against authority figures. The *komos* can readily be seen as a forerunner of comic theater.[18]

The role of comedy and its Dionysian features were mentioned in passing by Nietzsche but undeveloped in *The Birth of Tragedy*. In later writings, laughter and comedy emerged as significant motifs in Nietzsche's texts, as life-affirming antidotes to the gravity and esoteric nihilism of the Western tradition. In a previous article, I have tried to work out the correlation of the tragic and the comic in Nietzsche's thought by way of the dual Dionysian affirmation of limit conditions, of "negating" states of being through tragic disintegration and comic satire.[19] Clearly the satyr figure stands as a gathering point for the multiform boundary-crossing dynamic of Dionysian religion—with an edge given to restorative comic forces—that so impressed Nietzsche and that in many ways marked his thought and manner of writing.

Nietzsche often refers to the relation between philosophy, comedy, and tragedy, including references to the satyr figure. In an 1888 letter to Ferdinand Avenarius, he says the following:

[T]his year, where a monstrous task, the reevaluation of all values, lies upon me and I literally have to bear the fate of humanity, it belongs to my proof of strength to be something of a buffoon, a satyr, or if you prefer, a "Feuilletonist." . . . That the deepest spirit must also be the most frivolous, this is almost the formula for my philosophy: it could be that I, above all other "greats," have indeed become cheerful in an unlikely manner. (*KGB* 3:5, pp. 516–517)

In *Beyond Good and Evil*, Nietzsche warns against the solemnity of truth and a moral indignation that can ruin one's "philosophical sense of humor." To be a martyr for the truth is a degenerative excess. In fact, philosophy is called a kind of tragedy, but the "fall" of the philosopher is better taken in the spirit of a satyr play, an "epilogue farce" that is the true *end* of any tragedy (*BGE* 25). And a great tragedian shows greatness most in the satyr play, "when he knows how to *laugh* at himself" (*GM* III:3). Indeed, a good case has been made recently that the notorious fourth part of *Thus Spoke Zarathustra*—where the figures and import of the first three parts seem to degenerate into lampoonery—can be read as a satyr play concluding the tragic trilogy of the preceding parts.[20] This helps us make sense out of Nietzsche's reference to *Zarathustra* as both a tragedy and a parody (see *GS* 342 and the first section of the Preface). The satyr connection could also speak well to the wide array of animals that function so prominently in the text.

To conclude, the human-animality of the satyr can stand as a symbol for Nietzsche's exuberant naturalism, his affirmation of a finite, carnal existence. For Nietzsche, human culture is not a transcendence of animal nature but a "sublimation" of natural energies that modulates, but never surpasses, its base. The satyr embodies this ambiguity as an animal-human hybrid who lives on the fringes of the human world, who exhibits astonishment at the unfolding of that world, and whose transgressions and crossings are experienced as comical—which is to say not repulsive but pleasurable, interesting, revelatory, and rejuvenating. Might we say that much of Nietzsche's work, especially its transgressive style and unsettling attacks upon cherished cultural norms by way of startling antipodes, can be seen in the light of a satyr play, in the manner of black comedy, an experiment with inversions and crossovers on the fringe that is meant not so much to destroy as to renew human culture by evoking astonishment before its emergence out of animality and by mocking the gravitas that has marked the West's conception of culture as an overcoming of nature? As Zarathustra put it, the spirit of gravity is killed not by wrath but by laughter (*Z*:1 "On Reading and Writing"). What kind of laughter might we look for in Nietzsche's menacing iconoclasm?

Notes

1. Nietzsche's account and high estimation of the satyr chorus is a function of his early logic of originalism, where a thing's origin displays its nature. So if tragedy is as profound as Nietzsche thinks, its satyric origins must be on that level too. See M. S. Silk and J. P. Stern, *Nietzsche on Tragedy* (Cambridge: Cambridge University Press, 1981), 236–237. Nietzsche's later genealogical method would not necessarily countenance such an originalism.

2. See Timothy Ganz, *Early Greek Myth* (Baltimore, Md.: Johns Hopkins University Press, 1993), 136–137; and Silk and Stern, *Nietzsche on Tragedy*, 148.

3. See Silk and Stern, *Nietzsche on Tragedy*, 142ff.

4. Not much is known from the eighth and seventh centuries BCE. In the sixth century, artistic renderings begin to reveal details. See Ganz, *Early Greek Myth*, 136.

5. François Lissarraque, "On the Wildness of the Satyrs," in *Masks of Dionysus*, ed. Thomas H. Carpenter and Christopher A. Faraone (Ithaca, N.Y.: Cornell University Press, 1993), 208.

6. Ganz, *Early Greek Myth*, 137.

7. Lissarraque, "On the Wildness of the Satyrs," 208.

8. Lissarraque, "On the Wildness of the Satyrs," 208ff.

9. Lissarraque, "On the Wildness of the Satyrs," 207.

10. Ganz, *Early Greek Myth*, 137.

11. Jean-Pierre Vernant and Pierre Vidal-Naquet, *Myth and Tragedy in Ancient Greece*, trans. Janet Lloyd (New York: Zone Books, 1988), 204. This work also notes that the phallus in satyr renderings can be distinguished from erotic and procreative functions, since the maenads always fend off the advances of the satyrs. It may express arousal for its own sake, a symbol of the extraordinary, or a comic effect (195). See also Walter Burkert, *Greek Religion*, trans. John Raffan (Cambridge, Mass.: Harvard University Press, 1985), 166.

12. See Lissarraque, "On the Wildness of the Satyrs," 214ff.

13. Vernant and Vidal-Naquet, *Myth and Tragedy in Ancient Greece*, 183.

14. See Burkert, *Greek Religion*, 104, 173.

15. Most of the following is drawn from P. E. Easterling, "A Show for Dionysus," in *The Cambridge Companion to Greek Tragedy*, ed. P. E. Easterling (Cambridge: Cambridge University Press, 1997), 37–44.

16. For Nietzsche's remarks on the role of the satyr play in Greek tragic drama, see *KSA* 7, pp. 42ff.

17. Vernant and Vidal-Naquet, *Myth and Tragedy in Ancient Greece*, 152. Beginning in the early fifth century, comedy competitions were included in the Athenian Dionysia festival, which devoted one day out of five to comic drama. See E. Csapo and W. J. Slater, *The Context of Ancient Drama* (Ann Arbor: University of Michigan Press, 1994), 103–108.

18. See Carl Kerenyi, *Dionysos*, trans. Ralph Manheim (Princeton, N.J.: Princeton

University Press, 1976), 330–348; and A. W. Pickard-Cambridge, *Dithyramb Tragedy and Comedy*, 2nd ed., revised by T. B. L. Webster (Oxford: Oxford University Press, 1962), 132–162.

19. Lawrence J. Hatab, "Laughter in Nietzsche's Thought: A Philosophical Tragicomedy," *International Studies in Philosophy* 20, no.2 (1988): 67–79.

20. See Paul S. Loeb, "The Conclusion of Nietzsche's *Zarathustra*," *International Studies in Philosophy* 32, no.3 (2000): 137–152. Loeb also makes the interesting suggestion that Part 4 loops back to preceding parts, so it need not be taken as a disconnected departure from the conclusion of Part 3 or as simply an ironic gesture undermining the previous parts.

The Overhuman Animal

Vanessa Lemm

In the following chapter, I argue that the notions of forgetfulness, memory, and promise provide access to Nietzsche's discourse on the animal, human, and overhuman forms of human animal life. The agonistic involvement of these forms with and against each other gives rise to the infinite formations and transformations (*Bildungen*) of human animal nature that are expressed in the becoming of human animal life.[1] Whereas the animal stands at the beginning, the overhuman announces the future of human animal becoming. The future emerges from the self-overcoming of the human. But in Nietzsche, overcoming takes the form of a return to the beginning, to the animal. The forgetfulness of the animal is indispensable to the promise of an overhuman future. The future arises from an affirmation of the continuity between past, present, and future, between animal, human, and overhuman. Their intimate linkage has the peculiarity that the continuity it affirms brings about their discontinuity at the same time. Human animal life grows out of its animal past, not as something from which it derives but as what allows it to spring forward into the future. History is the narrative, the rope, that ties the animal, the human, and the overhuman together. It presupposes a continuity between animal, human, and overhuman that goes counter to the traditional Western understanding of human animal becoming as an emancipation, a sublimation or an overcoming of animality. The animal resists in the human as much as in the overhuman; it withholds the secret of how to bring forth a relation to the past that disrupts and overturns the present in view of its future becoming.

Part 1: Memory and Forgetfulness

The Dissolution of Truth and of Beginning
The becoming of the human animal is fundamentally characterized, throughout all of Nietzsche's work, in terms of the antagonism of culture and civilization.[2] In this antagonism, civilization names the perspective of error that allows to make humans out of animals; culture names the perspective of truth that makes overhuman animals out of humans: "Truth as Circe.—Error has transformed animals into humans; is truth perhaps capable of changing the human back into an animal?" (HH 519).[3] Whereas civilization claims the truth of the human animal to be revealed in its moral and rational nature, culture shows that this truth is part of the set of errors that make humans out of animals. From the perspective of civilization, the forgetfulness of the animals gives rise to error and illusion. Civilization understands itself as the process of improvement of the human animals through the imposition of its truth as a corrective to the forgetfulness of the human animals. From the perspective of culture, this imposition is itself based on error and illusion (GS 121). Nietzsche understands culture as cultivation (Bildung) and opposes it to civilization as taming (Zähmung) and breeding (Züchtung). Whereas the becoming of civilization reflects the domination of the human animal through the imposition of another, supposedly better nature upon it, the becoming of culture reflects the liberation of the human animal from the oppressiveness of civilization and the imposition of its worldview.

The becoming of culture and civilization, of error and truth, of the human and the overhuman animal, takes the form of a question (HH 519). The truth of a question can never be decided once and for all but lends itself to infinite questioning and requestioning. The truth at stake in the question of human animal becoming is not an epistemological or moral truth but takes the form of seduction, of Wahrheit als Circe. Truth seduces the human animal back to its origin where it discovers (sucht und versucht) itself as the one who engenders its life and nature out of dreams, illusions, and irrational passions. What is veiled and unveiled at the origin are dreams and illusions rather than a truth that is entailed in what is to come and evolve out of it. At the beginning there is the dissolution of beginning, the illusion of beginning. From the perspective of the animals, as Nietzsche constructs it, the very idea of there actually existing such a thing as the human being seems highly unlikely, nothing but an illusion: "'Human beings do not exist, for there was no first human being': thus infer the animals" (KSA 10:12[1].95).

When seduced back to the origin, the human animal discovers itself not as a function of what it is but of what it could become if only it keeps on dreaming and inventing illusions.[4] Truth seduces the human animal to the challenging illusion that its truth is to continue inventing its truths, that its nature is to continue inventing its nature: to refine, cultivate, and perfect nature through the means of culture and self-culture.[5] The task of cultural refinement of nature does not confound itself with that of striving for a fusional return to nature, but on the contrary must be understod as the infinite task to keep alive the struggle against the origin, against nature, against the past. It is a struggle for distinction from the origin, for becoming untruthful to it. Only as such can culture and self-culture bring forth the human animal's singularity and genius: its overhuman possibility.

The Forgetfulness of Civilization and the Rise of the All Too Human (Untergang)

The agon between culture and civilization, human and animal, error and truth, takes the form of an agon between memory and forgetfulness:

> The forgetful.—In the outbursts of passion, and in the fantasizing of dreams and insanity, the human being re-discovers its own and the humans' prehistory: animality with its savage grimaces; on these occasions its memory goes sufficiently far back, while its civilized condition evolves out of a forgetting of these primal experiences, that is to say out of a relaxation of its memory. The one who, as a forgetful one on a grand scale, is wholly unfamiliar with all this, does not understand the humans,—but it is to the advantage of all if here and there such forgetful ones appear as those who "do not understand the humans" and who are as it were begotten by divine seeds and born of reason. (D 312)

Whereas culture affirms and holds on to the human animal's continuity with the animals, civilization coincides with the forgetting of animality, the silencing of the animal within the human. The forgetfulness of civilization disrupts the filiation between the humans and the animals; it separates them and set them against each other. Nietzsche argues that civilization's forgetfulness opens up the agon of human animal becoming and thus considers the forgetfulness of civilization to be future promising. It is the forgetfulness of civilization that allows for the transformation of the human animal into something distinctly "human, all too human" and not animal. But this forgetfulness forecloses the possibility of recognizing in the animal and its forgetfulness a source of inspiration and creativity. The forgetfulness of civilization brings with it the risk that the denial of animality will turn into an overly passionate hatred and resentment against animality. If civilization ends up destroying the ground from which it grows, it will unavoidably lead to its own decline (*Untergang*). Once it consumes and lives up its life forces, it perishes and goes under. Nietzsche approves of certain doses of aggression against animality but rejects the aggression of civilization when it turns out to be an overdose. Once one destroys one's opponent, Nietzsche argues, one destroys the one from which one grows and is brought to health, life, and future becoming.[6]

> What in the competition against the animals brought about the humans their victory, at the same time brought about the difficult and dangerous sickness like development of the human being: the human being is the *not yet confirmed animal*. (KSA 11:25[428])

From Nietzsche's perspective, the history of civilization is above all the history of the generation of the most dangerous sickness. Civilization makes the human animal blind to its own animality, to confirming and affirming itself as animal. It keeps the human animal bound to its "all too human" form and thereby forecloses the possibility of its further becoming. Instead of cultivating a future-promising overhuman animal, civilization ends up producing the worst kind of animal: "The domestic animal, the herd animal, the sick animal,—the Christ" (A 3).

Against civilization, Nietzsche defines his own position as inherently pessimistic: true victory and liberation cannot be achieved through the overcoming of animality but only through the overcoming of all-too-human morality and rationality as vehicles of civilization. Nietzsche places the humans amid the other animals (A 14). He overturns the belief in the genius of human animal nature as the crown of evolution and instead hypothesizes whether it is not rather the genius of nature that uses human animal life as a means to its own perfection (AOM 185). Nietzsche resists the belief in "progress," but that does not lead him to call out for a "return to nature" in the sense of a return to a "higher," more "human" origin (TI "Skirmishes" 43, 48). Both positions, the overly optimistic turn to the past and the turn toward the future, are symptomatic of weakness and declining life. They reject life in favor of another life, another world behind and beyond the world. Pessimism instead is revelatory of the strength, health, and overflowing life that results from the embracing of life in all its forms (*BT* P 1).

Morality as a False Overcoming

Since civilization has cut the human animal off its animal beginning, it creates a void that it attempts to fill through the invention of an origin [*arché*], a myth of the beginning, which as an absolute beginning causally determines the future, that toward which it evolves (*telos*). Civilization's construction of the beginning reveals an inherently moral design: the attempt to "improve" life and human animal nature (*TI* "Morality"). According to Nietzsche, this moral interpretation of human animal nature destroys all those forces and instincts within the human animal that are future promising and that are the growing ground of overhuman animal greatness and virtue (*BGE* 62). Nietzsche interprets Christian morality as an example of the hatred and resentment of the animal as much as of the overhuman, the exceptional animal, found in civilization. Christian morality sows the seed for the erroneous belief in the human animal's superiority over the animals and all other forms of life. Christian morality lives off the turning of the human animal against itself, against its animality. But due to the overly aggressive denial of animality, this morality cannot succeed in leading the human animal toward a "higher" form of itself. Its struggle against animality, animal and overhuman, is that of declining life:

> *The over-animal.*—The beast in us wants to be lied to; morality is a necessary lie told so that it shall not tear us to pieces. Without the errors that repose in the assumptions of morality the human being would have remained animal. As it is, it has taken itself for something higher and imposed sterner laws upon itself. That is why it feels a hatred for the grades that have remained closer to animality: which is the explanation of the contempt formally felt for the slave as a non-human, as a thing. (*HH* 40)

Nietzsche turns the prejudices of morality against itself and exposes its "distance" from the animals as pretense. From the perspective of the animals, the illusion of the human animal's moral nature does not make the human animal more moral, it only makes it more prejudiced (*D* 333). Morality does not "improve" human animal life; it only aggravates the human animal's condition. The moral and civilized animal's claim to have surpassed the animals does not reflect a movement of overcoming in the Nietzschean sense of an agonistic encounter with the (overhuman) animals; on the contrary, it signals the escape from such an open and honest competition. The attempt to rise above and beyond the animals, to become overanimal, is revelatory of weakness and lack of courage. The prefix "over" in "overanimal" designates the attempt to establish a hierarchic ordering of the human as superior to the animals. This superiority infinitely distances the human from the animal and thereby forecloses the possibility of their encounter. The idea of the human as an "overanimal" puts an end to the agonistic becoming and overcoming of the human animal. As such, the prefix "over" in "overanimal" has exactly the opposite meaning of "over" in "overhuman" and in "overcoming." Whereas in the first case "over" refers to a vertical movement, in the second it refers to a horizontal movement expressed in the metaphors of the bridge and of the wind (*Über-wind-ung*) blowing over a landscape. In Nietzsche's word "overhuman," the prefix "over" is not used in order to separate the human from the animal but in order to establish just enough of a distance (*Pathos der Distanz*) to open up the space for their agonistic encounter. The agon between the human and the animal within the overhuman animal is an agon of ascending life. The "overhuman" in Nietzsche stands for the courage to surround oneself with animals, for it is only in the eyes of the animals that one can read the decline or the rise of one's life forces (GS 314).

The notion of the "overhuman" in Nietzsche reflects an understanding of human animal nature as what becomes (*Werden*) rather than as what is (*Sein*). The "over" in "overhuman" points to a movement of excess and extension of the human that leads it beyond its "all too human" form. The overhuman is not an overanimal; it is the overcoming of the "all too human" animal. The overhuman is the rise of the exceptional animal against the average mediocrity of the "all too human" herd animal. The overhuman animal becoming points to a movement of overcoming and self-overcoming that is engendered through a return of animality as that force that irrupts the human, exceeds and tears it apart, to open up the space for its future becomings. The future, instead of being reduced to one and only one "all too human" form of life, opens up to an infinity of possible human animal becomings.

The Memory of Culture and the Rise of the
Overhuman Animal (*Übergang*)

Although the aims of culture and civilization are far apart, the question is whether it is not the infinite reversal and overturning of their respective positions that tells the story of the becoming overhuman of the human animal:

> The highpoints of culture and civilization lie far apart: one should not be misled by the abyssal antagonism between culture and civilization. The great moments of culture have always been, morally speaking, times of corruption; and conversely the epochs of willed and forced animal taming ("civilization") of the human being have been times of intolerance of the spiritual and most bold natures. What civilization wants is something different from what culture wants: maybe the opposite [etwas Umgekehrtes]. (KSA 13:16[10])

The story of human animal becoming reveals that the errors of civilization are just as necessary to the rise of the overhuman animal as the truths of culture. Civilization understood as the generation of sickness turns the human animal into an interesting animal, a future-promising animal:

> Since that time, the human being has been included among the most unexpected and exciting throws of dice played by Heraclitus' 'great child," call him Zeus or fate,—it arouses interest, tension, hope, almost a certainty, as though something were being announced through it, were being prepared, as though the human being were not an end but just a path, an episode, a bridge, a great promise. (GM I:16)

The sickness of civilization challenges the becoming of greater health. Civilization, despite itself, leads to its own overcoming. The Untergang of civilization coincides with an Übergang: the rise of the overhuman animal. Nietzsche concedes that civilization contributes to overhuman animal becoming not because of its "higher" reason and "higher" morality but because of its inherent stupidity and immorality as reflections of the forces of life: "this tyranny, this caprice, this rigorous and grandiose stupidity has educated the spirit" (BGE 188).

Culture rekindles the human animal's animality to heal the human animal from its self-denial and life-denial. Against civilization and its forgetfulness, culture stands for the rise of counter-memory as a form of memory that brings back the animal (D 312).[7] Culture reveals that civilization's attempt to tame the animal, to frighten away the ghosts of the past, are in vain, for in the fragile states of dream and illusion the animal returns; it haunts the civilized animal. The memory of culture should not be confused with the voluntary act of bringing back the animal. Memory is not a means of mastery and domination; rather it is animality that irrupts into the face of memory, beyond its control. Remembering is surprised by what exceeds the capacity to remember. Memory becomes a form of attentiveness, a readiness to grasp animality when it comes forward to its encounter.[8] Memory means to encounter the past as much as being encountered by the past. It is a return to the past as much as a return of the past. The encounter of memory and the contingencies of time, as well as the encounter of the human with the animal, calls for the kind of refinement of the senses found in what Nietzsche names the "genius of culture" (HH 241). The genius of culture, as Nietzsche imagines it, is half-animal, half-beast. It reflects the kind of alliance between the animals and the humans that is needed in order to give rise to the future becoming of human animal life. The figure of the genius of culture reveals strong affinities with that of the overhuman animal: both constitute the aim of culture. In the overhuman as well as the genius of culture, the rise of virtue emerges from a return of animality. In view of bringing forth higher virtue, culture thus follows the trace of the animal.

The return of the animal within the human reveals that human animal life not only incorporates the whole past chain of life but, more important, the task of the future of the chain: to go beyond its "all too human" form.

> Superabundant force in spirituality, setting itself new goals; by no means merely commanding and leading on behalf of the lower world or the preservation of the "individual." We are more than the individual: we are the whole chain as well, with the task of all the future of the chain. (WP 687)

Nietzsche privileges the future over the present and the past because the future promises the becoming overhuman of the human animal. The future is brought forth through a movement of overcoming that never attains its aim since the possibility of overcoming always already goes beyond itself.[9] The human animal is neither an end nor a means, but it perfects itself in the infinite becoming and overcoming of itself.

The notion of the promise in Nietzsche points to the beyond and hence destabilizes what is, in view of what shall and will be. The promise announces what is not yet in the present but shall be in the future. The promise is a counter-promise against the imposition of eternal "all too human" identity upon the human animal. The one who makes a counter-promise welcomes the return of animal forgetfulness as that force that allows one to forget one's identities in the name of future possible identities.[10]

Part II: The Promise

The Promise of Civilization as a Means of Domination

Generally speaking, for Nietzsche forgetfulness and memory reflect two different perspectives on the world. Whereas the perspective of forgetfulness is an articulation of singularity as what cannot be shared, the perspective of memory is an articulation of universality as what can only be shared. Whereas forgetfulness gives rise to an equality rooted in difference—that is, in the radical otherness of singulars—memory gives rise to an equality rooted in identity—that is, in the radical sameness of universals. Memory and forgetfulness are involved in an agonistic struggle against each other: whereas memory dissolves singularity into a universal form, forgetfulness disrupts universality in the name of the becoming of singularity.

In *On the Genealogy of Morals*, Nietzsche claims that forgetfulness in the human animal is revelatory of strength and health, whereas memory is symptomatic of weakness and need (GM II:1). According to Nietzsche's genealogical discourse, the human animal could not maintain the great health of the singular and forgetful animal. In order to secure its life and future, the human animal had to transform its life form and become a herd animal, an inherently social and group-oriented animal. The rise of civilization coincides with the rise of the institution of social and political life forms. Civilization forms and preserves the life of the herd in response to a need of human animal life. Not only is the process of civilization necessary to the enhancement of life, but its accomplishments are also acknowledged as praiseworthy.

Civilization accomplishes the transformation of human animal life through the imposition of a *Gedächtnis des Willens*, a memory of the will, on the forgetfulness of the human animal. The *Gedächtnis des Willens* is a promise that civilization employs as a means of domination that provides an answer to the question of how societies keep together and how human animals can be made to dedicate themselves willingly to the welfare of society and the state:

> "How do you give a memory to the animal? How do you impress something on this partly dull, partly idiotic, inattentive mind, this personification of forgetfulness, so that it will stick?" . . . This age-old question was not resolved with gentle solutions and methods, as can be imagined; perhaps there is nothing more terrible and strange in the human prehistory than its *technique of mnemonics*. . . . How much blood and horror lies at the basis of all "good things"! (GM II:3)

Nietzsche dismisses the myth of the foundation of civilization as a social contract between human animals who voluntarily and peacefully agree with each other to submit themselves to the rules of society. In line with Machiavelli, Nietzsche argues that at the beginning of society there is always violence and bloodshed, an illegitimate act of injustice that brings society into rule. The violence and injustice reflected in the way in which a rule comes to rule is always committed toward those over whom it establishes itself as a rule. In the case of the foundation of society, society establishes itself as a rule against the singular forgetful animal. The latter resists the foundation of society and the ongoing process of its civilization and its socialization. If the human animal commits itself to the herd, it is not because it wants to but because it has been made to want to. As such, the institution and execution of political power, according to Nietzsche, always contains an inevitable kernel of tyranny and injustice against singularity and animality.

According to Nietzsche's genealogical discourse, the most effective way to secure the rule of civilization is through the breeding of an animal that strives in the crowd but that would perish on its own; an animal that is docile, tame, predictable, reliable, submissive, and obedient, entirely devoted to the universal good. From the perspective of civilization, the animal that stands on its own manifests a potential threat to the fabric of the group because, by definition, it undermines the universal mediocrity that defines the other herd animals. The animal who can stand on its own is an overhuman animal, a singular and forgetful animal, the antithesis of the "good human being," the one which is inherently non-threatening.[11] Insofar as the overhuman animal resists the leveling process of socialization and herd formation, it becomes the declared enemy of civilization:

> In the fight against *great* human beings lies much reason. These beings are dangerous, accidents, exceptions. Storms, strong enough to question what is patiently-built and—grounded. Human beings who pose question-marks to solidified beliefs. Not only to disarm such explosives, but, if somehow possible, to *prevent* their emergence and multiplication: this is what the instinct of all civilized societies dictates. (KSA 13:16[9])

The process of civilization is directed against the singular and forgetful (overhuman) animal with the goal of making it sick, with the goal of bringing it down. The (overhuman) animal that opposes itself to the herd mentality of the leveled crowd is criminalized and marginalized (*TI* "Skirmishes" 45).

Civilization sees in the human animal's obedience to the rational and moral norms of the herd the achievement of the highest form of responsibility, freedom, and virtue. Civilization undermines not only the freedom of the human animal as the source of new values but also the possibility of bearing full responsibility for them. Civilization always runs the risk of producing an inherently irresponsible and dangerous animal: an overbred herd animal, too obedient and too tame.

The Promise of Culture as a Means of Freedom and Responsibility

From the perspective of culture, the human animal is not an example of the so-called universality of the species but is a unique miracle (*Wunder*), an animal deserving admiration precisely because of its irreducible singularity (*SE* 1). Against civilization, culture engenders a form of sociability that breaks up the totality of the herd. It opens up the space for the becoming of singularity and of animality. The becoming of culture reflects a movement toward greater freedom: a freedom that exceeds the institutionalized limits of civilization. Culture does not reduce sociability to reciprocity and equality but gives rise to friendship understood as a relation based on the respect of the other's irreducible singularity and otherness.[12] Friendship takes the form of unlimited responsibility and self-responsibility. Responsibility is an expression of singular freedom that overcomes the promise of civilization (*Gedächtnis des Willens*) toward a free commitment of the human animal to the other.[13] Responsibility is a privilege, a right given only to those who have qualified themselves as singular and as forgetful animals (GM II:1–2). They are overhuman animals who give and promise themselves to the other and who see in this gift and this promise the greatest extension of their singular freedom.

Nietzsche defines the bringing forth of an animal that can make promises as the highest task of human animal becoming because it provides an answer to the problem posed by singular freedom within the confinements of a social and political form of life. Nietzsche claims that only those who know how to value the forces of forgetfulness—that is, the forces of the animal—can provide an answer to this question:

> To breed an animal *which is able to make promises*—is that not precisely the paradoxical task which nature has set herself with regard to human beings? Is it not the real problem *of human beings?* . . . The fact that this problem has been solved to a large degree must seem all the more surprising to the one who can fully appreciate the countervailing force, *forgetfulness*. (GM II:1)

This task is paradoxical because what the human animal is aiming at is the reversal of its own nature. The human animal, an inherently forgetful animal, has to become the opposite, an inherently reliable animal, an animal that can make promises. The challenge of human animal becoming is to engender a memory that, despite its being directed against forgetfulness, will respect forgetfulness as a force of life, as necessary to life as memory itself (*HL* 1).

Civilization succeeds in making the human animal predictable, but it fails in valorizing forgetfulness, the virtue of the animal, and hence cannot bring forth a truly responsible animal, one that truly deserves the privilege to make promises (*GM* II:2). Civilization, moreover, fails to provide a satisfactory answer to the problem of singular freedom. Its answer to the problem of freedom is socialization, but socialization risks the destruction of singular freedom. For Nietzsche, the freedom of the singular and forgetful animal can never be secured by means of society and the state, only by means of culture:

> The state takes it upon itself to debate, and even decide on the questions of culture: as if the state were not itself a means, a very inferior means of culture! . . . "A German Reich"—how many "German Reichs" do we have to count for one Goethe! . . . All the great times of culture were politically impoverished times. (*KSA* 13:19[11])

The answer to the problem of freedom and responsibility needs to be found in the sphere of culture insofar as culture is the mechanism that brings forth the overhuman animal and the genius of culture as figures of not only free but also responsible animals.

From the perspective of culture, the alliance of animality and singularity is the carrier of future life because it promises to overcome a politics of domination toward the becoming of singular freedom. Singular freedom is typically interpreted as inherently asocial and apolitical because it takes the form of egoism and solitude. Against this prejudice, Nietzsche defends egoism and solitude as the only conditions that allow singular freedom to stand for a relation to the other grounded neither on force and fear, nor on resentment and revenge (*Z* "On the Virtuous"; *AOM* 337). Singular freedom excludes the possibility of domination over the other, of slavery and tyranny, because singular freedom in its highest form is responsibility for oneself:

> For what is freedom! That one has the will to self-responsibility. That one preserves the distance which divides us. That one has become more indifferent to hardship, toil, privation, even to life. That one is ready to sacrifice human beings to one's cause, oneself not excepted. (*TI* "Skirmishes" 38)

Freedom without responsibility and responsibility without freedom are meaningless artifacts (of civilization): they elevate neither the singular nor the herd animal. The project of culture, instead, is that of the bringing forth of the overhuman animal as an exemplar of singular freedom, which constitutes a gain for all. This is possible because in the overhuman animal singular freedom entails the free commitment to the whole that contributes to its bringing forth: "Greatest elevation of the consciousness of strength in man, as he creates the overhuman" (WP 1060).

Freedom in the overhuman animal exceeds the limits of an "I." It flows over to the other beyond calculation. Freedom in the overhuman animal is like the giving virtue, a prodigal, wasteful, dissipating, and forgetful force (Z:1 "Zarathustra's Prologue"). The overhuman animal is like the genius of culture, an animal that cannot but forget itself, spend and waste itself for the sake of the becoming of the other's freedom:

> Of what account is genius if it does not communicate to the one who contemplates and reveres it such freedom and elevation of feeling that one no longer has need of genius!—*Rendering themselves superfluous* [*sich überflüsig machen*]—that is the glory of the great. (AOM 407)

Singular freedom in the overhuman animal (and in the genius of culture) elevates the value of human animal life because it exemplifies human animal life as that kind of life that is free and creative, promising a future and worth living for. The overhuman animal is the gift and the giving that takes the human beyond itself. The overhuman animal is the human animal's offering to life and nature in return for the gift of life (Z:1 "Zarathustra's Prologue").

Nietzsche's notion of singular freedom does not reflect a concern for the individual and its freedom and hence should not, for example, be confused with a liberal understanding of individual freedom as the highest aim of society and the state (WP 687). Singular freedom attains such a high value for Nietzsche only insofar as it elevates the value of all life. Culture attains this aim when the human animal recognizes the privilege of responsibility as the greatest extension of freedom and power. When responsibility has become the "dominant instinct" of the human animal, then the human animals are redeemed from the slavery and tyranny associated with the animal breeding and taming of civilization (GM II:2).

The Economy of Freedom
Nietzsche frames the problem of freedom in terms of an economical problem. He claims that nature is inherently prodigal and extravagant, the opposite of economical and calculating (SE 3). From this perspective, civilization can

appear as a means used by nature to impose a stricter economy on itself. Civilization is the moment of reduction of expenditures, of narrowing down perspectives, of limiting horizons (BGE 188). Nietzsche sees in this "stupidity," this self-imposed restriction, a valuable aspect of the economy of civilization. It shows that civilization is not only a moment of reduced creativity and limited pluralization of forms of life but also a moment of accumulation of life forces. Nietzsche argues that the savings of civilizations should be reinvested in the higher aims of culture, in the bringing forth of the overhuman. Only if the economy of civilization has as its higher aim the luxury of overhuman animal becoming do its repressive and restrictive means against singularity and animality become meaningful and praiseworthy. The economy of civilization simply cannot afford the freedom of the singular and forgetful animal. The economy of culture instead gives expression to the irrepressible desire for the freedom of the singular and forgetful animal. Culture promises, beyond calculation, that the singular and forgetful animal will reclaim its freedom from civilization. This "counter-movement" of culture

> aims to bring to light a stronger species, a higher type that arises and preserves itself under different conditions than those of the average human being. My concept, my metaphor for this type is, as one knows, the word "overhuman." . . . [The] transformation of the human beings into a machine is a precondition, as a base on which it can invent his higher form of being. It needs the opposition to the masses, of the "leveled," a feeling of distance from them! It stands on them, it lives off them. This higher form of aristocracy is that of the future. (WP 866)

The oppressiveness of the machinery of civilization leads to an inevitable counter-movement, an inevitable counter-culture that expresses a strong desire for liberation. Civilization tyrannizes the singular and forgetful animal and in doing so it challenges its "tyrannical" return as the revolutionary one who disrupts, explodes, and overthrows the rule of civilization (TI "Skirmishes" 44).[14] The counter-movement of culture grows against civilization, just as the exceptional and overhuman animal grows against the herd animal. As such, the "all too human" herd animal is indispensable to the overhuman animal's becoming.

Nietzsche does not object to civilization as the inherently violent "transformation of the human beings into a machine" insofar as civilization understands this process as a means toward the bringing forth of a lighter and freer type of human animal. According to Nietzsche, the institution of the modern state so far has failed to attain the goal of using the state (politics, morality, economics) as a means of culture. Nietzsche is particularly critical of modern mass political ideologies—whether socialist, liberalist, or nationalist—of their political as well as their economical doctrines. The reason is that these ideologies appear to him to institute an exploitation that pursues no higher aim beyond itself (WP 866).[15] This lack of cultural aim, together with economical optimism, are symptoms of weakness and declining life. Mass ideologies exemplify the risk that the process of civilization may lead to an increasing expenditure of everybody, which amounts to a "collective loss."[16] Despite their optimistic outlook, despite their promise to bring about "the greatest happiness of the greatest number," mass egalitarian ideologies make the human animal weak, sick, and unfit for freedom.

Against modern mass ideologies, Nietzsche praises the Roman genius for foundation and legislation. He sees the tyrannical aspect of Roman politics as rooted in an affirmation of life. In the Romans, Nietzsche emphasizes the will to authority, tradition, and solidarity over centuries as being particularly life-enhancing, representative of their will to power (TI "Skirmishes" 39). The Romans see no need to hide their politics as inherently exploitative; they affirm exploitation for the sake of the higher aims of culture.

Nietzsche underlines the need for strong institutions not because they secure survival, but because they make for a force against which the human animal can grow. The exceptional, overhuman animal (and the genius of culture) are not engendered in isolation but in the competition against the institution, whether it be in the form of a state, a church, or a university (SE; TI "Skirmishes" 38f., 41, 43f.). The freedom Nietzsche is interested in is neither simply that of the singular and forgetful animal nor that of the institution: the freest institution is the one that engages itself for and against singular freedom, and the freest animal is the one that invests itself in the fight for singular freedom against the institution (BGE 126).

Singular freedom in the overhuman animal is anarchical. It is the kind of freedom that resists the institutionalization of freedom. The overhuman animal refuses to be given the "right" to freedom because freedom is what must be robbed and conquered (Z:3 "Of Old and New Tablets"). It is within this agonistic and revolutionary spirit of the overhuman animal that Nietzsche sees the true guarantor of freedom and responsibility. The promise of the overhuman animal is far more reliable than the power of a "We" that draws its validity and legitimacy from the institutionalization of its agreements. It is a counter-promise, a counter-memory that the overhuman animal has made itself in view of the continuous critical questioning of the legitimacy of the rule of the "We" and of all the social and political configurations that claim eternal and absolute validity for their standards. The promise of the overhuman animal is trustworthy for it is rooted in the overhuman animal's probity as it is brought forth against the imposition of "truth" and " honesty" by civilization.[17] The "privilege to make promises" marks off those whose task it is to reclaim and to contest the freedom of singularity and animality against the destructive forces of civilization and socialization. Nietzsche calls for institutions that see in the overhuman animal's probity their only chance for future becoming because the overhuman animal leads them to their revolution, the becoming other of the institution as the overcoming of itself toward the future. Such institutions challenge the return of the forgetfulness of the animal as that force of the human animal that breaks open the present, the promise of the *"Gedächtnis des Willens"* in the name of its future becoming and overcoming.

The Figure of the *Umgekehrten*

The idea of singular freedom and of the "privilege to make promises" as counter-forces to civilization is expressed by the Nietzschean notion of the *Umgekehrten*: those whose artistic and acrobatic twists and turns are inherently life-enhancing and life-affirming. They are the symbols of culture and counter-culture, of the *Umwertung aller Werte*. The *Umgekehrten* have twisted themselves free from the moral and rational norms of civilization.[18]

> We opposite men [*wir Umgekehrten*] having opened our eyes and conscience to the question where and how the plant "human being" has so far grown most vigorously to a height—we think that this has happened every time under the opposite conditions [*umgekehrten Bedingungen*], that to this end the dangerousness of its situation must first grow to the point of enormity, its power of invention and simulation (its "spirit") had to develop under prolonged pressure and constraint into refinement and audacity, its life-will had to be enhanced into an unconditional power-will. . . . [E]verything in the human being that is kin to beasts of prey and serpents, serves the enhancement of the species "human being" as much as its opposite [*Gegensatz*] does. (*BGE* 44)[19]

The *Umgekehrten*'s subversion of the values of civilization has to be understood as a radical turn. Under attack are not simply some values but all of them. There is no overturning of a value, only an overturning of the entire hierarchy of evaluations. Moreover the *Umgekehrten*'s twists and turns do not simply proclaim a good where the discourses of civilization proclaim an evil or proclaim an evil where these proclaim a good. Rather, they twist free the idea of values from the dualism proper to the moral discourses of civilization that see everywhere either a good or an evil, from its rational discourses that see everywhere either an error or a truth, and finally from its discourse on human animal nature that see everywhere either an animal or a human. In place of the logic of the excluded third, the *Umgekehrten* counter with their logic of the including "and . . . and." *Umkehrung* involves the opposite poles of dualistic evaluations for and against each other, to show that good and evil, error and truth, human and animal are inseparably part of a continuum: the totality of life and becoming.

The *Umgekehrten*'s subversion of the values of civilization provokes the return of the animal. The return of the animal indicates that the *Umgekehrten* have become strong enough to afford the forgetfulness of the animals and to affirm it as life-enhancing (KSA 13:16[7]).[20] The *Umgekehrten* reverse the economy of civilization. They have accumulated so much force that they no longer have a need for the rational and moral memory of civilization:

> One could conceive of the delight and power of self-determination, a *freedom* of the will in which the spirit takes leave of faith and every wish for certainty, practiced as it is in maintaining itself on light ropes and possibilities and dancing even beside abysses. Such a spirit would be the *free spirit* par excellence. (GS 347)

The *Umgekehrten* reject the illusion of a secure and ordered world and the illusion of possessing the means for the prediction of the future and for the mastery of space. These illusions are artifacts provided by the rational and moral discourses of civilization. They renounce the comforts of the herd. Instead they embrace the Dionysian vision of the world as an inherently contingent and uncertain world. The dangers implicit in an abyssal world challenge the *Umgekehrten*'s desire for freedom and self-determination. From the subverted perspective of the *Umgekehrten*, only the one who lives dangerously is capable of bringing forth future life, of opening up new possibilities of human animal becoming.

For Nietzsche, it is a real question whether such free and subverting (*Umgekehrten*) spirits exist any longer (GS 347). He turns to the past for encouragement, for the company of the geniuses of culture: Goethe, Napoleon, Schopenhauer, and all those who promise that the animal cannot be finally tamed and bred, just as forgetfulness and life cannot be finally mastered (D 126). Their example reveals that the life forces of the human animal exceed the rational and moral grids of civilization, that animality resists the mnemotechnics of civilization (BGE 83). That the animal resisted in the past promises its future return. The return of the animal is liberating, it opens up the possibility for the human animal to affirm and confirm itself as singular and as forgetful animal. The thought of the return is an encouraging thought because it calls for the promise to bring forth lighter and freer forms of human animal life. It is this effect that Nietzsche tries to achieve through his own narrative of human animal becoming:

> How natural history should be narrated.—Natural history as the history of the war of the spiritual-moral forces against fear, imaginings, inertia, superstition, foolishness, and their victory over them, ought to be narrated in such a way that everyone who hears it is irresistibly inspired to strive after spiritual and bodily health and vigor, to the glad feeling of being the heir and continuator of the human, and to an ever nobler desire for new undertakings. (AOM 184)

Notes

1. On the notion of becoming and "becoming-animal" see also Gilles Deleuze and Felix Guattari, A Thousand Plateaus: Capitalism and Schizophrenia (Minneapolis: University of Minnesota Press, 1987), ch.10, passim.

2. KSA 13:16[73].

3. With the exception of occasional emendations, I rely throughout this essay on the following translations: Kaufmann's translations of BGE, WP, and Z; Hollingdale's translations of A, AOM, D, HH, TI, and UM; Nauckhoff's translation of GS; Speirs's translation of BT; and Diethe's translations of GM and HC. For KSA, I provide my own translation.

4. Following his inner experience, Nietzsche claims to have discovered himself as a being who continuously reflects a repetition or a variation of an infinity of poetical, logical, aesthetical, and affective becomings of the entire history of life: "I have discovered for myself that the ancient humanity and animality, indeed the whole prehistory and past of all sentient being, continues in me to imagine, to love, to hate, and to infer—I suddenly woke in the middle of this dream, but only to the consciousness that I am dreaming and that I must go on dreaming lest to perish" (GS 54). Nietzsche dissolves the idea of a species, the distinction of one life form from another, just as he disrupts the distinctions between dream and waking, illusion and truth, consciousness and unconsciousness, memory and forgetfulness, human and animal. Consciousness is the awakening into a dream that one needs to dream on in order for life not to consume itself. Nietzsche gains this insight when he awakens within the dream to the consciousness that not only life is illusion and dream but also that dreams and illusions are essential to life. To be alive means

to be dreaming and fantasizing. On the relation between dreams, life, culture, and civilization, see also S. Freud, *Civilization and Its Discontents* (New York: W.W. Norton, 1961).

5. In *Nietzsche et la métaphore* (Paris: Payot, 1972), Sarah Kofman argues that human animal nature does not preexist culture, but that nature imposes itself as the task of culture to form and transform, to interpret and re-interpret nature.

6. In *"Homer's Contest,"* Nietzsche argues that once the Greeks had destroyed their enemies, they brought about the inevitable decline of their culture.

7. On the notion of counter-memory, see M. Foucault, "Nietzsche, la généalogie, l'histoire," in *Hommage à Jean Hyppolite* (Paris: P.U.F., 1971), 145–172.

8. On the art of grasping the moment [*kairos*], see M. Detienne and J.-P. Vernant, *Les ruses de l'intelligence* (Paris: Flammarion, 1974).

9. On this understanding of self-overcoming, see Jean-Luc Nancy, "Notre Probité," in *L'impératif catégorique* (Paris: Flammarion, 1983).

10. Nietzsche's understanding of human animal becoming as a promise has strong affinities with Derrida's notion of the signature; Jacques Derrida, *Otobiographies. L'enseignement de Nietzsche et la politique du nom propre* (Paris: Galilée, 1984). See HL 2; GM P.

11. "The 'good human being' in every stage of civilization, the one who is at the same time useful and innocuous: a kind of middle point, the expression of something that for common sense is not to be feared but that *nevertheless* should not be despised"; (*KSA* 13:16[8]), Frühjahr-Sommer 1888, 16 (8).

12. On friendship in Nietzsche see also Derrida, *Politiques de l'amitié* (Paris: Galilée, 1994).

13. H. Arendt has the merit of having brought back the centrality of the theme of the promise. Nevertheless in her interpretation of Nietzsche in *The Human Condition*, she fails to distinguish between the *Gedächtnis des Willens*, the promise of the civilized animal, and the promise of the sovereign and overhuman animal.

14. "Great men, like *great* epochs, are explosive material in whom tremendous energy has been accumulated; their prerequisite has always been, historically and physiologically, that a protracted assembling, accumulating, economizing, and preserving has preceeded them—that there has been no explosion for a long time. If the tension in the mass has grown too great the merest accidental stimulus suffices to call the 'genius,' the 'deed,' the 'great destiny' into the world (*TI*, "Skirmishes" 44).

15. For an example of exploitation without an aim beyond itself see Foucault's notion of disciplinary power in M. Foucault, *Discipline and Punish* (New York: Vintage Books, 1977).

16. These aspects of Nietzsche's critique of modern economic and political ideologies have been pursued at great length in G. Bataille's work, especially *La part maudite*, vols. I-III (Paris: Les Editions de Minuits, 1970).

17. On the notion of probity, see also Jean-Luc Nancy, "Notre Probité" in *L'impératif catégorique* (Paris: Flammarion, 1983).

18. John Sallis translates *"Selbstüberwindung"* as "twisting oneself free" in *Crossings* (Chicago: University of Chicago Press, 1991).

19. On the notion of "die Pflanze 'Mensch,'" see P. Wotling, *Nietzsche et le problème de la civilisation* (Paris: P.U.F., 1995).

20. "The great human being is great because it opens up a space for the free play of its lusts: the great one is strong enough to make out if these beasts its domestic animals" (KSA 13:16[7]).

PART FIVE

ANIMAL NIETZSCHE

MOLE

On Nietzsche's Moles

Debra B. Bergoffen

The Misunderstood Animal

Much has been made of Nietzsche's self-proclaimed doubled nature, of his rejection of history for genealogy, of his critique of traditional philosophy's notions of truth. Not much has been made of his moles.[1] Perhaps something should—perhaps attention should be paid to the weights these small and secretive creatures carry in Nietzsche's texts.[2]

What did Nietzsche know about moles? Probably no more than the average person. Probably no more than this: the mole is a small animal with strong forefeet, weak eyes, and a large forehead. It is often blind and frequently lacks external ears. During its brief life of about one year, it is active day and night in rapid cycles of work and rest, making elaborate underground nests, shelters, and labyrinths. Above ground the mole's diggings are marked by small mounds of dirt. Their tunneling, which is sometimes damaging to the roots of plants, stirs and aerates the soil and kills noxious organisms. Their molehills annoy gardeners. Rarely seen by humans, and of little if any economic importance, moles are ecologically important as prey for larger mammals and birds, who pursue them despite their noxious odor. They do not carry diseases.

243

An animal with bad eyesight that smells badly. An animal that repels despite the fact that it is harmless. An animal whose underground burrowing refreshes the soil and rids it of unwanted organisms but is only seen by gardeners as an unwelcome creature that uproots plants and ruins their flower-beds with unsightly piles of dirt. A misunderstood animal. An animal whose name is also that of the double agent, the spy who operates undercover, unseen, undermining the rule of established powers. Are we surprised that Nietzsche signs himself mole in the preface to *Daybreak*? Is this not the perfect totem for a genealogist?

But in identifying the mole as his double, Nietzsche marks this difference between them: what is natural for the mole, working in the dark, is a burden to a being whose eyes are highly developed and who craves light and heights. If he is willing to sign himself mole in *Daybreak,* he pulls his pen back in *Human, All Too Human, The Gay Science,* and *Zarathustra.* In *Human, All Too Human,* Nietzsche separates himself from the mole. Named as the organic source of the metaphysical concepts of substance and identity, the mole is now positioned as Nietzsche's adversarial other rather than his double. In *The Gay Science,* Nietzsche continues this distancing. Now he figures the mole as the pathetic figure of modern humanity—a human being whipped by life and devoid of passion who requires the intoxications of music, theater, and culture to sustain him as he crawls back into his hole. In *Zarathustra,* the estrangement is complete. Now the mole is joined to the dwarf and identified as the spirit of gravity, the threat to Zarathustra's over-coming.

As Nietzsche's *Daybreak* double, the mole comes to taunt Nietzsche as his other. It is the nausea of the modern condition, the devotee of the aesthetic ideal, Zarathustra's enemy, the spirit of gravity. Finding it necessary to take up the mole's subversive work, Nietzsche, always ambivalent toward this underground creature, ultimately rejects its dark existence. In *Daybreak,* by accepting the mole as that part of himself that must be simultaneously affirmed and overcome, Nietzsche presents himself as an argument against the metaphysical principle of mole identity. As he links overcoming the mole with destroying the enemy of overcoming in *Zarathustra,* however, Nietzsche seems to be affirming the idea of the self-identical subject. Zarathustra, it seems, cannot tolerate doubles. It may be in this relationship to the mole, rather than (as Heidegger thought) in the affirmation of the eternal recurrence, that Nietzsche succumbs to the metaphysical temptation.

Affirming the Earth But Not the Dark

Following the mole through Nietzsche's thought, I discover that however much contemporary French thought may be indebted to Nietzsche, its current challenges to the visual imperative are not driven by Nietzsche's voice. Following the mole through Nietzsche's thought, I learn that this philosopher who taught me to think through the body was not a philosopher of the earth. I find that his affirmation of life was not an affirmation of dark dwellings, deep abysses, dank wombs. Following the mole through Nietzsche's thought, I see that in rejecting the idea of truth as One, Nietzsche remained caught in the metaphors of light, sun, and sight that fuel the Platonism he found so offensive. Irigaray found Nietzsche fleeing the sea's immemorial waters. Following the mole, I find him averse to the earth's tunnels and caves. In either/both cases, Nietzsche seems to be afraid of the dark.

Were it not for the preface to *Daybreak,* the mole would not be a very interesting critter in Nietzsche's bestiary. Nietzsche's references to this underground digger would constitute little more than a scattering of happenstance references and interesting allusions. But the *Daybreak* preface enjoins us to understand these seemingly disparate citations as indexes to the complexity of an author who, as a fissured subject working out a critique of the modern condition, is himself besieged by a certain blindness.

Nietzsche opens *Daybreak* by telling us that the text is the work of a subterranean man, a solitary mole who "tunnels and mines and undermines"; who goes "forward slowly, cautiously, gently inexorable." Unlike the mole, however, the subterranean man is not at home in the dark. He "needs eyes to work at these depths." Though his work does not betray it, he is in distress, under duress. The "protracted depravation of light and air" of the mole's world does not suit him. It is more than a matter of seeing and breathing. It is also a matter of the necessity of working in obscurity. Despite his love of sunrises and noon times, Nietzsche, in assuming the role of the mole, tells us that he "perhaps desires this prolonged obscurity, desires to be concealed, enigmatic because he knows that he will thereby also acquire his own morning, his own redemption, his own daybreak. . . . [T]his subterranean will return and tell what he is looking for when he has become a man again." Teaching us, through the mole, how to read *Daybreak,* Nietzsche give us, in this sketch of himself as mole, clues for understanding Zarathustra's downgoings and over-comings.

As the image of the genealogist in *Daybreak,* the mole becomes the answer to the riddle of metaphysics posed in *Human, All Too Human* (18). Nietzsche as genealogical mole discovers the mole at the root of the philosophical principles of substance and identity. The irony is unmistakable. Metaphysics, which is enamored of comparing the mind to the eye and its domain of truth to the brilliance of the sun, is charged with perpetuating, as one of its fundamental principles, an idea of a nearly blind creature who lives in the dark. Metaphysics, Nietzsche tells us, has its origin in an organic mole error. The error is twofold. First it is a matter of not seeing the differences; then it is a matter of only allowing for differences so long as each differentiated thing is established as having a single essence. A thing is only allowed to be different from other things insofar as it establishes itself as singular. As self-identical, each substance must remain constant with respect to itself. In this way, organic life, inexpert in the business of seeing, situates itself within its environment according to the principles of pleasure and pain. The organism makes only those distinctions necessary for it to distinguish friend from foe. Nothing more complex is required, needed, or tolerated.

Metaphysics, according to Nietzsche, takes the error common to all organic life, corrects it insofar as it admits of correction at the level of the mole's semi-blindness, and elevates this crude correction to the first truth of being. Despite having evolved with regard to the capacities of seeing, and presumably with regard to the capacities for making nuanced distinctions, we cannot seem to get beyond the idea of identity. We continue to operate at the organic level of pleasure and pain. Dull eyes, not the enlightened eye of reason, justify the philosopher's truth of substance and identity. Perhaps calling the philosopher a mole would wake philosophy from its organic slumber?

Between Nietzsche as the genealogical mole of *Daybreak*, and the *Human, All Too Human* mole identified as the genealogical origin of the philosophical addiction to the idea of substance, there is the story of the archeologist (re)discovering himself at the site of the dig. *The Gay Science* and *Zarathustra's* "The Vision and the Riddle" and "On The Spirit of Gravity" could be read as a continuation of this story of Nietzsche's critique of the principles of identity and substance. For as the genealogist who discovers himself at the origin of his genealogy, Nietzsche becomes, in these texts, the genealogist who discovers that he is, as mole, the modern man he despises, and that he is, as mole, the one who threatens the success of his genealogical project. Nietzsche, however, does not lead us to this reading. Instead, he directs us to take *The Gay Science* and *Zarathustra* references as the beginnings of another story, one that refuses the tensions of the doubled nature for the consistency of a unified self.

Nietzsche's mole references complicate our picture of Nietzsche as the philosopher who recalls us to the body and the instincts; for in these references, the organic earth and the organisms of the earth are figured as undertows that keep us from our destiny. It is the dogmatic philosopher, not the philosopher of the future, who maintains the organic belief in substance. In *Human, All Too Human*, the mole, as organic, is something to be overcome. This is reinforced in *The Gay Science*, where the mole is presented as desiring wings to overcome the passionless life of the hole, and brought to a crisis in *Zarathustra*, where the mole is identified as Nietzsche's devil and archenemy. Now overcoming is a matter of murder. Identifying himself as an eagle in *Zarathustra* (Z:3 "On The Spirit of Gravity"), Nietzsche marks the mole (the Nietzsche of *Daybreak* and the origin of metaphysics of *Human, All Too Human*) as his prey. This mole, now paired with the dwarf as the spirit of gravity, is charged with the crime of alienating us from ourselves. Linking the principles of metaphysics to the dictates of morality, Nietzsche, having found the mole guilty of being the ground of the metaphysical principle of identity, charges it with being responsible for the ethical principle of universality encoded in the morality of good and evil. The spirit of gravity allows only for one good and one evil and insists that all accept this one as their own. It makes us ashamed of our own taste. It bars us from knowing ourselves as singular and forbids self-love. Zarathustra, divesting himself of his enemy (Nietzsche's *Daybreak* double), will find his own way. He will learn to fly. He will seek the heights where his eyes will roam over distances instead of seeing abysses. His ears, larger and better tuned than the mole's, will hear the voice that sings, "Was that life? Well then! Once More! (Z:3 "Vision and Riddle").

But what if Zarathustra is too quick to rid himself of the mole? What if in preying on Nietzsche's double he ends up reaffirming the principle of the one? What if, in his hurry to reach the heights, he repeats the error of Plato's allegory of the cave? What if it is true that we are not destined to live without light? But what if it is also true that overcoming the metaphysics that estranges us from the earthly ground of our being requires acknowledging our debt to the mole's tactile, digging, dark life?

Genealogical Lessons of the Kogi *Mamas*

These questions are provoked by Irigaray's love letter to Nietzsche[3] and by the ways in which the Kogi Indians of Colombia train their *mamas*, holy people charged with caring for the tribe and the earth.[4] Mamas, who are identified at birth or shortly thereafter, spend nine years in semi-darkness hearing only the teachings of the Kogi. When they emerge into the world they find the reality of its beauty beyond anything they could ever imagine. This awe establishes their spiritual relationship to the earth. It inscribes them in their role as caretakers of the earth; for they never take the material splendors of the earth for granted and can never imagine anything superior to it. The mamas, standing Plato on his head, find the abstractions of the world of ideas impoverished and the teeming world of the senses dazzling.

In telling us this story of the mamas, the Kogi acknowledge that it may not be true. It may be a myth. The Kogi are fairly selective in the information they give outsiders. This much, however, seems clear: the Kogi understanding of the relationship between thought and being and between the senses and truth is a radical challenge to the Western philosophical tradition. Listening to the Kogi, I mark the difference between a people that sees itself as responsible for the care of the earth and a people that speaks of itself as having dominion over the earth. I mark the difference between a culture that would sever its ties to the earth for the sake of the sun and a culture that allows its underground experience to inform its life in the light. I mark the difference between a Zarathustra who, in calling the demand "either you or I" his courage, refuses his doubleness and debt to the depths and the mamas, whose courage is a matter of seeing the sunlit world against the backdrop of the opaque lens of the other they once were and still must be. The difference seems to be a matter of memory. It forces the genealogical question: What desires motivate our forgetting and remembering?

The Kogi description of the discipline of the mamas may be read as a deliberate decision to selectively prolong an infant experience for an elite group. For infant life begins, like the life of the mole, like the life of Plato's cave dwellers, and like the early years of the mamas, in the dark. In this life, the sense of touch prevails. As visual beings, we override the tactile experience that blurs the distinction between self and other with the visual experiences of distinct spatial locatedness and bodily integrity. Relying on the visual, we set ourselves apart from each other, develop a sense of our power, and augment our repertoires of bodily "I cans." If we focus on this connection between the role of sight and the experience of establishing a space of our own within which we augment our sense of independence and sovereignty, we can, I think, appreciate our desire to leave behind the dark world from which we came. We can understand the drives that foster the move to establish seeing and light as the metaphors of the mind and its truths. We can begin to explain the endurance of the philosophy of the subject/object distinction. From this perspective, it is not a matter of the fear of the mother's engulfing womb but a fear of losing my space (that space that is me and mine; that place in the world that I carry with me that offers the protections of individuation; that place from which I express the capacities of my lived body to exercise its powers over what is not me/mine) that helps explain Western philosophy's commitment to the paradigm of the allegory of the cave.

Recent philosophical developments and non-philosophical events have undermined this commitment. The subject/object distinction, linked as it is with the idea of the human as subject and nature as object, has been tied to ecological disasters and the ravages of destructive technologies. These non-philosophical realities have had their effect on philosophical thought. There are theoretical rumblings. Nietzsche's genealogy and Husserl's phenomenology have undermined the credibility of the subject/object distinction on straightforward conceptual grounds. Philosophy seems to be taking a second look at an idea of reason and an understanding of subjectivity grounded in paradigms of seeing and light. This rethinking of our allegiance to the categories of sight can and cannot be linked to Nietzsche. On the one hand, his decision to identify Zarathustra with the eagle who takes the mole as his prey maintains the status quo. But as with much else in Nietzsche, this attack on the mole as the spirit of gravity is ambiguous. Nietzsche may have removed the mole from its place as his double. He may have assigned it the role of Zarathustra's enemy. He never, however, renounced his identity as a genealogist, the mole who works undercover, and who, carrying no diseases of his own, rids the earth of its poisons and brings it fresh air. And it is as genealogist that Nietzsche provides us with a method that undercuts dominant subject/object paradigms of truth.

To do genealogy one must accept oneself as part of the field under review. The genealogist cannot assume the subject position of the subject/object relationship. Genealogists know that they cannot be separated from the scrutinized object. There is no space apart, no transcendent position from which to survey the scene. As genealogist, Nietzsche knows that subjects are formed, not given. In turning the mole into Zarathustra's enemy, Nietzsche seems to want to forget that at the origin of our formation there was darkness, not light, and that in this darkness the distinction between subject and object was blurred. Instead of asking how we might retrieve this memory to rework the current genealogy of the subject and its truths, Nietzsche gives us Zarathustra, the one who overcomes his going-under by turning himself into an eagle and preying on his double, the mole. In the end, however, the mole, as double (agent) and as genealogist, threatens Zarathustra's flight. So what shall it be, double or enemy? The answer, I think, is both; for the mole, like other pieces of Nietzsche's thought, if carefully chewed rather than hurriedly digested, teaches us to take up the difficult work of scrutinizing the genealogy of our desire despite being seduced by its blind spot.

Notes

1. *Editors' note:* Only one other commentator, to our knowledge, has worked on this image: David F. Krell, *"Der Maulwurf/*The Mole" in *Infectious Nietzsche* (Bloomington: Indiana University Press, 1996), chapter 5; or "Der Maulwurf: Die philosophische Wühlarbeit bei Kant, Hegel und Nietzsche" ["The Mole: Philosophic Burrowing in Kant, Hegel, and Nietzsche"] in *Why Nietzsche Now?*, edited by Daniel O'Hara (Bloomington: Indiana University Press, 1985), 155–185. These are recommended for those who wish to further pursue this creature.

2. Translations used are R. J. Hollingdale's for *HH* and *D* and Kaufmann's for *GS* and *Z*.

3. Luce Irigaray, *Marine Lover of Friedrich Nietzsche*, translated by Gillian C. Gill (New York: Columbia University Press, 1991).

4. Maxine Sheets-Johnstone, *The Roots of Power: Animated Form and Gendered Bodies* (Chicago: Open Court, 1999).

CAT

The Cat at Play:
Nietzsche's Feline Styles

Martha Kendal Woodruff

Among the many animals populating Nietzsche's bestiary, the cat proves to be a complex creature, recurring in many texts and appearing in different lights. Nietzsche's ambivalence toward the cat reveals tensions central to his philosophy, tensions that in a positive sense sustain the movement of his thought. We may cluster Nietzsche's images of the cat around three central themes: deception, sensuality, and, most important, playfulness. Nietzsche accuses cats of deception, yet he also recognizes the necessity of indirection, veiling, even illusion. He accuses cats of lust, yet he admires feline grace and sensuality as models for an embodied "gay science." Despite his suspicion of things feline, he emulates the feline spirit of play in his own range of styles: his diverse styles move ironically, indirectly, and metaphorically, thus putting all meanings in play.

The cat provides Nietzsche a model of admirable independence: even the housecat still retains an element of wildness. Just as cats insist on independence and refuse herding and training, so too Nietzsche urges us to forge our own paths. Indeed, cats can easily revert to a feral state, between domesticity and wildness, a state Nietzsche advocates for future humanity. Nietzsche praises the one who "like cats and robbers / is at home in the wilderness / and jumps through windows" (KSA 11:28[20]). His use of the image of a cat jumping out a window signifies the transitional space between the domestic and the wild.[1]

In this regard, Nietzsche writes of a "natural opposition" between cats and dogs (KSA 10:3[1].184) and contrasts a "cat-egoism" with a "dog-egoism" (KSA 11:25[515]). More recently domesticated than dogs, cats were never herd animals and have never regarded humans as "masters." So much the better, says Nietzsche, as he disparages the dog as "that lazy, tail-wagging parasite which has become 'dog-like' only through being the slave of man" (WS 350).[2] In rendering animals dog-like, in taming them, we simultaneously tame ourselves. For Nietzsche,

> It is precisely as *tame animals* that we are a shameful sight and in need of the moral disguise. . . . It is not the beast of prey that requires a moral disguise but the herd animal with its profound mediocrity, timidity, and boredom with itself. (GS 352)

To the small-minded, Nietzsche writes elsewhere, "virtue is what makes modest and tame: with it they make the wolf into a dog and man himself into man's best domestic animal" (Z:3 "Of the Virtue That Makes Small"). The cat resists any such taming even when domesticated.

The housecat thus bridges the ferocity of the big cats (lions, tigers, panthers) prominent in Nietzsche's work and the spontaneous playfulness of the child. Zarathustra predicts: "Your wild cats [*Wildkatzen*] must have become tigers" before the Übermensch can appear (Z:2 "Of Human Prudence"). The big cats symbolize the wild energy that belongs to the Dionysian, as portrayed in the vision of the "panthers and tigers" that walk with the chariot of Dionysus (BT 1). Yet, as we shall see, after the fierce power of lions and tigers comes the second innocence of the child; such childlike innocence is exemplified in the animal kingdom by the cat at play.

At times, Nietzsche criticizes the cat for laziness and deceitfulness. Among the frequent references to animals in *Zarathustra*, several associate the cat with deceit. The mention of "the tomcat [*Kater*] on the roofs," for instance, suggests Schopenhauer[3] and other "naysayers" to life, creeping secretly and enviously:

> Every honest man's step speaks out: but the cat steals along over the ground. Behold, the moon comes along catlike [*katzenhaft*] and without honesty. (Z:2 "Of Immaculate Perception")

The moon evokes a feline, nocturnal dishonesty because it has only a reflected light, shunning the warmth and sensuality of the sun's heat.[4] Such a cold light ostensibly seeks a pure perception, without the heat of desire, without procreative eros.[5] However, it too secretly loves the earth, but with a bad conscience: "For he is lustful and jealous, the monk in the moon, lustful for the earth and for the joys of lovers" (Z:2 "Of Immaculate Perception"). Not sexual desire itself but the shame felt over it is lustful. Indeed, Nietzsche redefines innocence as procreative desire: "Where is innocence? Where there is will to begetting . . ." (Z:2 "Of Immaculate Perception").[6] By associating the cat with the moon and with the desire for "immaculate perception," a play on "immaculate conception," Nietzsche uses images of cats to evoke dishonesty, even hypocrisy.

Returning to the image of the sun, Nietzsche contrasts the honesty and openness of the sun and sky with the clouds, called "stealthy cats of prey [Raubkatzen]," who linger with "cautious, uncertain feline repose [Katzen-Ruhe]" (Z:3 "Before Sunrise"). Nietzsche again evokes the thieving nature of cats when he links them to wolves in the famous section on the gift-giving virtue.[7] Zarathustra urges his disciples "to become sacrifices and gifts yourselves," asking them: "What could you have in common with cats and wolves?" (Z:1 "Of the Bestowing Virtue"). An entry from Nietzsche's notebooks helps us understand this brief mention:

> The dog pays back good will with submission. The cat enjoys itself thereby and has a lusty feeling for power [ein wollüstiges Kraftgefühl]: it does not give back. (KSA 10:1[30])

Yet if we remember that the gift-giving virtue itself turns out to be "a thief of all values" and a proud, noble selfishness, it may in the end prove to be closer to such a feline sense of power. Certainly the gift-giving virtue resembles the self-assured pride of cats more than the slavish obedience of dogs.

Further, Nietzsche links feline deceptiveness and graspingness to sensuality. The other side of feline stealth is their fastidious indulgence: "dainty, sneaking lust-cats [Lust-Katzen]" (Z:3 "Tables") is Nietzsche's phrase for those who pretend to be world-weary. Naschkatzen, rendered by Hollingdale as "dainty nibblers," suggests the fussy appetite of the cat (Z:3 "Of the Virtue That Makes Small"). The phrases "full of cat's wantonness [Katzen-Muthwillens]" and "leaping through every window" describe, slightly more positively, those who run "among motley-speckled beasts of prey . . . preying, creeping, lying" (Z:4 "Song of Melancholy"). Even the German word for flatterers,

Schmeichelkatzen, used by Nietzsche in "The Wanderer and his Shadow" (*WS* 252), reinforces the portrayal of the cat as a deceiver, not to be trusted.

Nietzsche's ambivalence toward the feline has a great deal in common with his ambivalence toward the feminine. "Women are still cats and birds," he declares. "Or at best, cows!" (*Z*:1 "Of the Friend"). Women resemble cats in that they are, in his estimate, incapable of the true friendship and self-overcoming that herald the coming of the *Übermensch*. As Nietzsche remarks in his journals: "what do I care for the purring of one who cannot love, like the cat?" (*KSA* 10:5[1].122). In his many strikingly misogynist remarks, Nietzsche often compares women to cats: "You silent girl-kittens [*Mädchen-Katzen*]," he writes, calling them "more foolish and more sinful" wishes and thoughts (*Z*:4 "Daughters of the Desert"). In *Beyond Good and Evil*, Nietzsche asserts: "Woman is essentially unpeaceful, like a cat," speaking also of "this dangerous and beautiful cat 'woman' [*Katze 'Weib'*]" who conceals "the tiger's claw under the glove" (*BGE* 131, 239). Given the conflict between an inherent catlike wildness and a socially imposed domestication, it is no wonder that Nietzsche describes woman as "more condemned to disappointment than any other animal" (*BGE* 239).

Yet if Nietzsche at times condemns "feline" sensuality, deception, and femininity, at other times he affirms and esteems these very qualities. Indeed, the traits Nietzsche attributes to cats he also seeks for his own life-affirming laughter, embodiment, and artistry. Such critiques reveal a central tension within Nietzsche's own project, an anxiety about the mysteries he has uncovered. Thus Nietzsche's criticisms of cats, and all they represent, should not lead us to dismiss their value for him. Sensuality, although in some cases dismissed as fastidiously "feminine" and "feline," can lead to a liberating celebration of human embodiment: "The body is a great intelligence, a multiplicity with one sense," as Zarathustra puts it (*Z*:1 "Of the Despisers of the Body"). The purring cat at play serves for Nietzsche as an emblem of joy in such embodiment. What is more, deception has as its other side the artistic illusions we create to make life worth living. As Nietzsche asserts: "life is no argument; the conditions for life might include error" (*GS* 121). Error can be positively construed as a healthy illusion, as a necessary fiction. For as the Greeks realized, *pseudos* means both "lie" and "fiction."[8] The cat as a Nietzschean metaphor, I believe, lives in the tension between these two sides of deception.

Nietzsche's lifelong questioning of the distinction between truth and error belongs to his understanding of the human being *as an animal*, of the perspectives and appetites of its physiology, and of its long-repressed life instinct. In his early essays, for example, Nietzsche praises the "unhistorical sense" of animals that frees them from the burden of memory to live in the full present tense; we "cannot help envying them their happiness" and regarding this state as a "lost paradise" (HL 1). Nietzsche further contrasts the "mood of pious illusion" that affirms life with the paralyzing, overly analytical historical awareness (HL 7). Anticipating much poststructuralist thought, he famously deconstructs the distinction between truth and illusion:

> What then is truth? A moveable host of metaphors, metonymies, and anthropomorphisms. . . . Truths are illusions which we have forgotten are illusions; they are metaphors that have become worn out and have been drained of sensuous force, coins which have lost their embossing and are now considered as metal and no longer as coins. (TL, p. 84)[9]

In his early works on tragedy, Nietzsche understands illusion as an Apollinian dream world, a veil of *maya*, layered over an unbearable Dionysian truth: "one must even *will illusion*—that is what is tragic" (PT "The Philosopher," p. 37).

In his middle period, Nietzsche incorporates "error, deception, simulation, delusion, self-delusion" into his "joyous wisdom" that seeks to restore our animal nature to the "great health" (GS 344). Irony, one of Nietzsche's many rhetorical tools, also counts as a form of dissimulation.[10] In later works, Nietzsche continues to ask: "What forces us at all to suppose that there is an essential opposition of 'true' and 'false'? . . . Why couldn't the world *that concerns us*—be a fiction?" (BGE 34). The human animal *needs* illusions and deceptions; it is "a manifold, mendacious, artificial and opaque animal, uncanny to the other animals" (BGE 291). Nietzsche goes so far as to assert that the human animal is one that "knowingly, willfully has to lie" (Z:4 "Song of Melancholy"). If we contrast this position with the charge discussed above, "catlike and without honesty," we must consider whether such "feline" deception in the end proves necessary to the Nietzschean project of science in the service of life. To the extent that the cat captures for Nietzsche the spirit of play, it exemplifies the life-affirming forgetfulness and spontaneity that make the pure present possible.

Similarly, the "feminine wiles" that Nietzsche so often dismisses prove to be part of his own project. Despite his blatant misogyny, Nietzsche's own thought evokes a womanly center of artistry, fertility, and animality.[11]

"Woman is so artistic," he writes (GS 361); in such artistry, I suggest, Nietzsche himself resembles a woman. Nietzsche famously asks: "Supposing truth is a woman—what then?" (BGE P). Instead of the traditional methods of "clumsy obtrusiveness" for courting this elusive woman, Nietzsche employs the same woman's ways he criticizes: covert artistry, veils, and surfaces, with the ironic realization that truth might consist of necessary illusions. Indeed, life itself proves to be a woman—as mysterious as a cat:

> But perhaps this is the most powerful magic of life: it is covered by a veil inter-woven with gold, a veil of beautiful possibilities, sparkling with promise, resistance, bashfulness, mockery, pity, and seduction. Yes, life is a woman. (GS 339)[12]

The Dionysian, as the mysterious source of life, proves to be gendered feminine: Nietzsche connects Dionysian artistry to "the eternally primordial mother" and to the "exuberant fertility of the universal will" (BT 16).

Nietzsche's frequent use of pregnancy as a metaphor for creativity shows his affirmation of female animality, despite his own troubles with women (and "Woman"). In striking contrast to the earlier use of the cat to evoke a monastic celibacy (Z:2 "Of Immaculate Perception," discussed above), Nietzsche represents Zarathustra's wisdom with an image that combines both female and feline traits, namely the pregnant lioness (meine Löwin Weisheit): "My wild Wisdom became pregnant upon lonely mountains" (Z:2 "Child with Mirror"). Elsewhere Nietzsche asks, "Is there a more holy condition than that of pregnancy?" and calls it a state of "ideal selfishness" (D 552).[13] Nietzsche praises the Greeks for recognizing, as Plato does in the Symposium, both the joy and the pain of giving birth: "Every element of the act of repro-duction, of pregnancy and birth, awoke the highest and most festive feelings" (TI "Ancients" 4). A state of "creative androgyny" (to borrow Virginia Woolf's phrase), which remarkably combines mother, father, and child in one, serves as Nietzsche's model: "For the creator himself to be the child new-born he must also be willing to be the mother and endure the mother's pain" (Z:2 "Blissful Islands").

Further gendering nature as feminine, Nietzsche associates women with cats in the in-between space of the window: "To be at home in the wilderness like cats and women, and to jump through windows" (KSA 11:29[1]).[14] While full discussions of Nietzsche's misogyny, his own paradoxically "femi-nine" ways of writing, and his use of gender roles all go beyond the scope of this essay, suffice it to say that feminist interpreters have found many resources to salvage from Nietzsche's thought.[15] If Nietzsche deems woman a cat because of her will to deception, then we can reply that Nietzsche himself employs such "feminine/feline" artistry.[16]

If deception is made knowingly, with a good conscience, it is art. Unlike positivist science that remains unaware of its own fictions, art is honest about its own necessary dishonesty: "thus art treats *illusion as illusion*; therefore it does not wish to deceive; it *is true*" (*TL*, p. 96). Without art, Nietzsche warns, "the realization that delusion and error are conditions of human knowledge and sensation—would be utterly unbearable" (GS 107). Art is defined as "the *good* will to appearance," and for that we owe it "our ultimate gratitude" (GS 107). In Nietzsche's use of language, an insistence on metaphor recognizes the need for illusions and images since literal language, like the "pure truth," proves impossible. The question then becomes how one employs illusions: Nietzsche praises actors for demonstrating "falseness with a good conscience; the delight in simulation . . . the inner craving for a role and a mask, for *appearance*" (GS 361). Having goodwill toward masks, appearances, and illusions means having goodwill toward our animal natures, our tendency toward error and forgetting. Thus Nietzsche can affirm the vulgarity of popular art in southern Europe as a way of saying:

> "The animal has as much right as any human being: let it run about freely. And you, my dear fellow man, are also still an animal in spite of everything!" (GS 77)

Illusion in this positive sense thus affirms our animal nature, our need to forget, to overcome, and to re-create meanings for life.

Such re-creation involves *play*, and the cat, for Nietzsche and other thinkers alike, serves as a paradigm of such play. Nietzsche, described by one recent interpreter as "the arch-philosopher of play,"[17] realizes that play has its serious side: "A man's maturity consists—in having found again the seriousness one had as a child, at play" (BGE 94). We engage in such significant play not only in art and sport but also in re-creating our own identities, in viewing life "as a playful exchange of masks," in another critic's words.[18] Depth of character *needs* the play of surfaces: "Every profound spirit needs a mask" (BGE 40).

In the well-known section in *Zarathustra* on the three metamorphoses of spirit, the endurance of the camel as "beast of burden" turns into the fierceness of the lion as destructive energy, only to overcome itself again and become the child at play:

> The child is innocence and forgetfulness, a new beginning, a sport [*Spiel*], a self-
> propelling wheel, a first motion, a sacred Yes. Yes, a sacred Yes is needed . . . for the
> sport of creation [*zum Spiele des Schaffens*]. (Z:1 "Of the Three Metamorphoses")

Spiel, meaning sport, play, or game, thus captures the spirit of creativity. It ranges from human creations, especially the play as drama, to the world itself regarded as perpetual play. *Spiel* thus encompasses the play of appearances and surfaces that for Nietzsche constitutes the "real" world, a world that necessarily includes illusions.[19] Nietzsche praises Heraclitus's "sublime metaphor" of the world as eternal play, "play as artists and children engage in it" (*PTA* 7). He repeatedly affirms the Heraclitean sense of "the playful [*spielende*] construction and destruction of the individual world," in which "even the ugly and disharmonic are part of an artistic game [*Spiel*]" (*BT* 24).[20] Nietzsche even refers to his beloved Greeks as "eternal children" because of their love of play (*BT* 17); at the same time, he recognizes that even among this "most humane" people of the ancient world there exists "a trait of cruelty, a tigerish lust to annihilate" (*HC* 32).

The cat exemplifies such playful creativity and serves as a transitional figure between tigers and lions as beasts of prey, on the one hand, and the child as innocence at play, on the other. Play among animals functions in part as practice for hunting, and Nietzsche's philosophical play likewise hunts its prey and sharpens its claws on those who try to tame it. Yet play can also become a self-fulfilling experience of sheer pleasure; witness the delight of kittens at play. Other philosophers from diverse traditions have drawn similar interpretations from the cat at play. Montaigne famously asks: "When I play with my cat, who knows if I am not a pastime to her more than she is to me?"[21] The intelligence, independence, and mystery of cats challenge any attitude of mastery we might have over them; they resist training; they play with our assumptions. Montaigne, of course, wielded a deep influence on Nietzsche, prompting him to exclaim: "that such a man wrote has truly augmented the joy of living on this earth" (*SE* 2).[22] Through his close readings of the *Essays*, Nietzsche would have known Montaigne's respect for cats at play and for animals in general.

In his hermeneutic discussion of play, Gadamer also seizes upon the cat as a model of the "movement to-and-fro" essential to play: "Thus the cat at play chooses the ball of wool because it responds to play."[23] As in the play of interpretations, so too in the philosophical trope of cats' play, both resistance and flexibility are key. Nietzsche too uses the cat to represent play and laughter:

All good things approach their goal crookedly [*krumm*]. Like cats [*gleich Katzen*] they arch their backs, they purr inwardly at their approaching happiness—all good things laugh. (Z:4 "Of the Higher Man")

In this striking passage, Nietzsche's admiration for cats hints that he too approaches his goals crookedly and indirectly, curving around meanings, arching his back in the "archness" of irony, purring with secret pleasure.

Nietzsche himself achieves catlike artistic play, I want to suggest, through his diverse *styles*—his ways of putting established meanings in question and engaging the reader in the play of plural interpretations.[24] Stylistically, Nietzsche imitates cats by writing "crookedly," that is, metaphorically and obliquely, while "purring inwardly," while showing us how to laugh. Nietzsche's styles range from his diverse genres (poetry, genealogy, tragicomic drama) to his shifting tones (irony, parody, hyperbole) to his use of diction and punctuation (italics, question marks, dashes, and other flourishes). As Sarah Kofman writes, even Nietzsche's prose is unlike any other in philosophy, "exclamatory, interrogative, filled with metaphors, with terms in italics or inverted commas . . . unplaceable, atopic."[25]

As a metaphor for Nietzsche's interest in the play of styles, the cat may also serve as an emblem for what is perhaps most distinctive about his approach to philosophy. Style for Nietzsche goes beyond the merely verbal level and takes on ethical significance, in the broadest sense of ethical (relating to character, *ethos*): "One thing is needful—To 'give style' to one's character—a great and rare art!" (GS 290). The distinction between form and content, style and sense, breaks down for Nietzsche: "one is an artist at the cost of regarding that which all non-artists call 'form' as content, as 'the matter itself'" (WP 818). For Nietzsche, then, style is not an arbitrary choice but is necessitated by the way the world speaks to us. Thus, figurative language is not merely decorative but disclosive; it seems "as if the things themselves approached and offered themselves as metaphors" (EH "Books" Z:3). Or as Zarathustra puts it: "on every metaphor you ride to every truth. . . . [H]ere all being wishes to become word, all becoming wishes to learn from me how to speak" (Z:3 "Return Home").

Hence, Nietzsche's feline stylistic play makes a serious point[26]: his insistence on a range of unique styles evokes the plurality of the creative self and encourages us to find our *own* style(s) that might serve as "the signature(s) of the self." Just as Zarathustra says to his disciples, "This—is now *my* way; where is yours?" (Z:3 "Spirit of Gravity"), Nietzsche says to his readers, "This—is now *my* style; where is yours?" One's own style should be as proud and independent as the cat, resisting any doglike obedience or imitation. The play of styles thus communicates what a direct thesis could not. As Derrida writes: "[W]ithout a writing strategy, without a difference or divergence of pens, without style . . . the reversal would simply amount to a noisy declaration of the antithesis."[27] Nietzsche plays with styles in the name of opening up interpretations and reminding us that science should serve life, not vice versa. As Karsten Harries puts it:

> Nietzsche's style is a tearing of language in the service of life. . . . Life overflows every interpretation . . . .To open philosophy to life, to the sea, Nietzsche's discourse challenges ossified and taken-for-granted ways of speaking; semantic oppositions and collisions deny us the security of what is expected and accepted, opening up the horizon of the questionable.[28]

While Harries uses the metaphor of the philosopher at sea, we could also use the metaphor of the supple jumping cat as a challenge to rigid structures of thought.

Indeed, Nietzsche's association of the cat with a playful style indicates that his language partly serves our *animal* life. There is something animalistic about that most civilized of things, style: Nietzsche associates the tempo of a written style with the tempo of a people's metabolism (*BGE* 28).[29] The sensuous images of Nietzsche's language, especially his frequent evocations of taste and smell, vividly remind us of our own animal natures. So too does his emphasis on perspectives. Nietzsche's styles make us *feel* the force of his perspectivism without turning it into an abstract, and questionable, dogma. As Alexander Nehemas writes,

> [Nietzsche's] many styles . . . show his perspectivism without saying anything about it, and to that extent they prevent the view that there are only interpretations from undermining itself.[30]

Along different lines, Derrida links Nietzsche's styles to a pluralizing movement: "If there is going to be style, there can only be more than one."[31] As Nietzsche puts it: "Good style *in itself*—a pure folly, mere 'idealism'" (*EH* "Books" 4).

Since style, like emotion, has often been devalued as "merely feminine" in contrast to the "masculine" language of argument and abstraction, Nietzsche's catlike emphasis on style also involves a play of gender identities, such that David Krell, following Derrida, proposes that Nietzsche writes with "the hand of woman."[32] In spite of his dismissals of women as cats, Nietzsche himself becomes surprisingly "feminine" and feline with his playful, poetic styles, with his veiled, covert double meanings. As Derrida notes,[33] immediately after Nietzsche boasts that he possesses "the most multifarious art of style that has ever been at the disposal of one man," he asserts that he knows women as part of his "Dionysian dowry": "Perhaps I am the first psychologist of the eternally feminine" (EH "Books" 4). Thus the question of style, often dismissed as marginal to the (male) philosopher's discourse, becomes central to Nietzsche's project of a "gay science" that knows how to appreciate beautiful surfaces.[34] Like Nietzsche's vision of the Greeks as "eternal children," his emblem of the cat affirms the spirit of play—what is "superficial—*out of profundity*" (GS P), what turns substance into style, and what makes the serious project of life into art.[35]

Notes

1. Nietzsche uses this image more than once, in fact. See my discussion below of the following: "To be at home in the wilderness like cats and women, and to jump through windows" (KSA 11:29[1]; see also KSA 11:25[92], quoted below). I used the following translations of Nietzsche's texts: Kaufmann's BGE, BT, GS, and HC; Hollingdale's D, SE, WS, and Z; and Breazeale's PT. For HL, I used "On the Advantage and Disadvantage of History for Life," trans. Peter Preuss (Hackett, 1980). Translations of KSA citations are my own.

2. For more on this topic, see Gary Shapiro's chapter, "Dogs, Domestication, and the Ego," in this collection.

3. In this context, consider Nietzsche's analysis of Schopenhauer as one who "treated sexuality as his personal enemy (including its tool, woman)" and likewise of Kant, whose notion of a non-erotic, "disinterested interest" in beauty shows "the naiveté of a country parson" (GM III:6).

4. Of course cats also love sunning themselves, but since they are active at night, they span the distance between "high noon" and nighttime.

5. For more on this theme, see Karsten Harries, "Light without Love," in The Broken Frame (Washington, D.C.: Catholic University of America Press, 1989). Harries links such cold light to what Nietzsche calls our "ill will against time": "It is the spirit of revenge that bids us think beauty against time and separate light from love" (32).

6. In such passages, Nietzsche harks back to Plato's vision of spiritual pregnancy and "giving birth in the realm of the beautiful" (Symposium 206C ff.). As Graham Parkes notes, "If one substitutes (will to) power for eros, Zarathustra's subsequent characterization of beauty can be read as a play on the central image of the Symposium" (Composing the Soul: Reaches of Nietzsche's Psychology [Chicago: University of Chicago Press, 1994], 221). My reading of procreation and pregnancy in Nietzsche is indebted to Parkes's study.

7. For more on the paradoxes of the gift-giving virtue, see my essay "The Ethics of

Generosity and Friendship: Aristotle's Gift to Nietzsche?" in *The Question of the Gift*, ed. Mark Osteen (New York: Routledge, 2002), 118–131. See also *The Logic of the Gift*, ed. Alan D. Schrift (New York: Routledge, 1997).

8. Homer combines both aspects of *pseudos* in Odysseus, in whom, according to Nietzsche, the Greeks admired most of all "his capacity for lying" (*D* 306).

9. See Derrida's influential reading of metaphor, with special reference to this passage, in "White Mythology: Metaphor in the Text of Philosophy," in *Margins of Philosophy*, trans. Alan Bass (Chicago: University of Chicago Press, 1982).

10. As Ernst Behler says, "ironic dissimulation, configurative thinking and writing, double-edged communication, and artistry of living and philosophizing were his response to the universal irony of the world"; "Nietzsche's Conception of Irony," in *Nietzsche, Philosophy and the Arts*, ed. Salim Kemal, Ivan Gaskell, and Daniel Conway (Cambridge: Cambridge University Press, 1998).

11. For more on the these topics, see Thomas Brobjer's "Women as Predatory Animals" and Debra Bergoffen's "On Nietzsche's Moles" in this collection.

12. As Eric Blondel writes, "As the privileged metaphor of life, woman is thus enigma and appearance"; "Nietzsche: Life as Metaphor," in *The New Nietzsche*, ed. David B. Allison (Cambridge, Mass.: MIT Press, 1997), 156.

13. On pregnancy as a central metaphor for philosophers, especially Plato and Nietzsche, see Amy Mullin, "Pregnant Bodies, Pregnant Minds," *Feminist Theory* 3, no. 1 (April 2002): 27–44.

14. Consider also the passage quoted by Nietzsche in his notebooks: "Women are always less civilized than men: fundamentally wild in their soul; they live in the state as cats do in the house, always ready to jump out the door or the window and to return to their element" (*KSA* 11:25[92]).

15. Such readings include the following: Peter Burgard, ed., *Nietzsche and the Feminine* (Charlottesville: University Press of Virginia, 1994); Carol Diethe, *Nietzsche's Women: Beyond the Whip* (Berlin: de Gruyter, 1996); Luce Irigaray, *Marine Lover of Freidrich Nietzsche*, trans. Gillian Gill (New York: Columbia University Press, 1991); David Krell, *Postponements: Woman, Sensuality and Death in Nietzsche* (Bloomington: Indiana University Press, 1986); Kelly Oliver, *Womanizing Nietzsche* (New York: Routledge, 1995); Caroline Picart, *Resentment and the "Feminine" in Nietzsche's Politico-Aesthetics* (University Park: Pennsylvania State University Press, 1999); and Kelly Oliver and Marilyn Pearsall, eds., *Feminist Interpretations of Friedrich Nietzsche* (University Park: Pennsylvania State University Press, 1998).

16. As Derrida writes, beyond Nietzsche's complex negations, "woman is recognized, affirmed, as an affirmative, dissimulating, artistic, and Dionysian power" ("The Question of Style," in *The New Nietzsche*, ed. David B. Allison [Cambridge: MIT Press, 1997], 185).

17. Catherine Bates, *Play in a Godless World* (London: Open Gate Press, 1999), iii.

18. James Hans, *The Play of the World* (Amherst: University of Massachusetts Press, 1981), x.

19. Our word "illusion" itself stems from *in ludere* [in play]. For this reference I acknowledge Catherine Bates's *Play in a Godless World*, 51.

20. Consider for instance Heraclitus's fragment 52: "Time is a child playing a game of draughts; the kingship is in the hands of a child" (*Ancilla to the Pre-Socratic Philosophers*, trans. Kathleen Freeman [Cambridge, Mass.: Harvard University Press, 1983]).

21. "Apology for Raimond Sebond," in *Essays* II, bilingual edition, ed. Donald Frame (New York: Columbia University Press, 1963), 221. Montaigne's affirmation of our closeness to animals, and his condemnation of cruelty to animals (*Essays* II "On Cruelty"), invites comparison with Nietzsche's statements such as: "he who is cruel towards animals . . . counts as ignoble, as lacking refinement in pride" (*WS* 57).

22. See Brendan Donnellan, "Nietzsche and Montaigne," *Colloquia Germanica* 19, no. 1 (1986): 1–20; Dorothea B. Heitsch, "Nietzsche and Montaigne: Concepts of Style," *Rhetorica* 18, no. 4 (1999): 411–431; and David Molner, "The Influence of Montaigne on Nietzsche: A Raison d'Etre in the Sun," *Nietzsche-Studien* 22 (1993): 80–93.

23. *Truth and Method*, trans. Sheed and Ward (New York: Crossroad, 1982), 95.

24. As Bernd Magnus, Stanley Stewart, and Jean-Pierre Mileur write, "all of [Nietzsche's] writings evoke the feeling that their author places every reader's interpretation in scare quotes, is always undermining an interpretation in the very act of suggesting it" (*Nietzsche's Case: Philosophy as/and Literature* [New York: Routledge, 1993], 19). The authors focus on five traits of Nietzsche's style (or range of styles): hyperbole, undecidability, resistance to paraphrase, self-reference, and self-consuming activity (16).

25. *Nietzsche and Metaphor*, trans. Duncan Large (Stanford, Calif.: Stanford University Press, 1993), 5.

26. So too does his use of metaphor. As Sarah Kofman writes, "The philosopher does not just 'play' with metaphors: his play is of a 'formidable seriousness,' for it is designed to oppose modernity's hatred of art, to obliterate precisely the opposition between play and seriousness, dream and reality, to show that [in Nietzsche's words] 'mathematical expression is not part of the essence of philosophy' (*PT* "The Philosopher," p. 53)"; *Nietzsche and Metaphor*, 18.

27. Derrida, "The Question of Style," 185.

28. "The Philosopher at Sea," in *Nietzsche's New Seas*, ed. Michael Gillespie and Tracy Strong (Chicago: University of Chicago Press, 1988), 33.

29. Nietzsche further asserts: "it is not improper to describe the entire phenomenon of morality as animal" (*D* 26).

30. *Nietzsche: Life as Literature* (Cambridge, Mass.: Harvard University Press, 1985), 40.

31. *Spurs: Nietzsche's Styles*, trans. Barbara Harlow (Chicago: University of Chicago Press, 1979), 139.

32. Krell, *Postponements*, 85.

33. Derrida, "The Question of Style," 187.

34. As Eric Blondel writes: "To be wise in a Dionysian way would be to stay near the surface, to 'adore the epidermis' of the *vita femina*"; "Nietzsche: Life as Metaphor," 161.

35. For valuable help with this chapter, I would like to thank Christa Davis Acampora, Ralph Acampora, James Berg, Daniel Conway, Alan Schrift, Gary Shapiro, and Marc Witkin.

Nietzsche's *göttliche Eidechsen*: "Divine Lizards," "Greene Lyons," and Music

Babette E. Babich

This *Lyon* maketh the *Sun* sith soone
To be joyned to hys Sister the *Moone*:
By way of wedding a wonderous thing,
Thys *Lyon* should cause hem to begett a King:
And tis as strange that thys Kings food,
Can be nothing but thys *Lyons* Blood;
And tis as true that thys ys none other,
Than ys it the Kings Father and Mother.

—*The Hunting of the Green Lyon*, 1652

On Nietzsche and Animals

In what follows, I ask what Nietzsche knew about animals. I then raise the question of Nietzsche's specifically esoteric style as his own private alchemy—not the "alchymical" Lyon forged above; this stylistic alchemy was Nietzsche's writer's art. Following a central reflection on music, words, and writing, I raise the question of Nietzsche's "divine lizards."

Like his rather better-known metaphors of the lion or the eagle, Nietzsche's choice and use of the lizard (*Eidechse*) betrays a complex constellation of metonymically interlaced ideas. And beginning with his earliest writings, Nietzsche called on animal totems. Thus, Nietzsche's animals seem creatures of the same invention that brought Zarathustra to life. But running true enough to observational or "real" life, Nietzsche's animals strike the reader as accurate accounts—if it is also true that at times these same accounts can attend a set of mistaken associations, as in the case of the tarantula and the infectious dance of a similar name. With all his multifarious imagery, Nietzsche is able to philosophize through his writing, adding philosophical thought to the many things one can do with style or rhetoric.

Writing on "Zarathustra's Animals," Martin Heidegger poses the question of the context of Nietzsche's images in terms of the specific force of those same ideas. Thus he invokes Nietzsche's declaration of an affective relationship to animals—"*His love of animals*—men have always recognized the solitary by means of this trait"[1]—as the identifying characteristic of the hermit. This would also be the mark of the saint, as in the case of St. Francis or St. Jerome, the last with his emblematic lion and characteristic asceticism an even more appropriate comparison with Nietzsche's Zarathustra.[2] Different from such saintly familiars, Zarathustra's animals are not symbolically "ornamental" companions. Rather, Heidegger argues, these animals are themselves the sign of Zarathustra's reflexivity. "Their essence is an image of Zarathustra's proper essence, i.e., an image of his task—which is to be the teacher of the eternal return."[3] Thus, for Heidegger, an inquiry into what it is that "the animals themselves" are is not to be confused with "romanticizing" them but is rather "to possess the force that will enable one to remain true to oneself in their proximity and to prevent them from fleeing."[4] To stay them from fleeing is to say that one is able to keep them, holding them present as needful. Reflecting on Zarathustra as convalescent, i.e., Zarathustra as he becomes the one he is and as he affirms himself as such, Heidegger will explain this same exigence as attending to the essential truth of Zarathustra's animals: "a matter of bringing to the light of wakeful day, in purest solitude, what the animals symbolize."[5]

We know that Nietzsche loved the real flesh-and-blood horses he cared for, not just horses as symbolic images. Yet we also know that in every case, Nietzsche's expression of such solicitude was a societal affair; privately,

Nietzsche kept no pets. He did not *live* among animals—that is, he did not have them as companions—and he certainly did not live with Zarathustra's animals, that is with snakes or eagles or lions, let alone camels and doves. Nevertheless, he knew dogs and cats, as he knew squirrels and lizards, from direct experience. And if Nietzsche had some familiarity with horses and dogs, both protypically German domestic animals, his most compelling animals, Zarathustra's companion animals, the eagle, the serpent, and the lion are exactly non-domesticated animals, charged with symbolism.[6] To talk about Nietzsche's lizard invites us to such traditionally symbolic accounts.

Nietzsche's Esoteric "Alchemy": Laughter and Transfiguration

"The Hunting of the Greene Lyon" cited as epigraph above, refers to the practice of alchemy, one of the central preoccupations not of Nietzsche's life but that of Sir Isaac Newton. As Newton is usually identified with the triumph of modern scientific reason over premodern superstition, founding scientific physics, precisely in its modern mathematical form, Newton was also centrally concerned with alchemy—the arch-signifier of anti-science and superstition, indeed, the paradigmatic pseudo-science.[7]

I suggest that we see a connection between Newton's esoteric studies and Nietzsche not because I mean to argue that Nietzsche was an alchemical adept—Nietzsche claims to reject the literal premises of alchemy: "I deny morality," he wrote, "as I deny alchemy" (D 103). But as Nietzsche speaks of what he typically names "Alchymie" metaphorically, I point to the importance of two aspects of Nietzsche's philosophical work of an esoteric kind. The first is the importance of the image of transformation (and indeed of transfiguration) in Nietzsche's writing.[8] The second corresponds to Nietzsche's patently esoteric style—Nietzsche himself makes a distinction between writings of exoteric and esoteric kinds (see BGE 30). For my purposes here, speaking of a metaphorical alchemy, I refer to Nietzsche's esoteric style. And if it is well known that Nietzsche wrote exoteric books—as he "spoke to all," he would write, he "also spoke to none," as in his famous subtitle to *Thus Spoke Zarathustra*—we also know that he wrote *esoterically*: "whoever has ears to hear, let him hear!" (GS 234).

If the exoteric sees things from the extern's or outsider's point of view, Nietzsche claims the esoteric as the elevated perspective: "the esoteric sees them *from above*!" (BGE 30). In the penultimate section of *On the Genealogy* of Morals, Nietzsche identifies the *ascetic* or religious ideal par excellence as the veritable ideal of spirituality: "esoteric through and through." On such esoteric terms, in terms, that is to say, of what Nietzsche here names the "will to truth," he is able to represent "unconditional, honest atheism" not as the antithesis to the spiritual ideal but "only one of the latest phases of its evolution" (GM III:27). In the same way, Nietzsche condemned the naïveté of the opposition between scientific and religious ideals that still governs popular and academic opinion: "Don't come to me with science when I ask for the natural antagonist of the ascetic ideal" (GM III:25). Concluding a self-declared polemic against ascetic ideals as such, Nietzsche reminds us that "science"—by which he means modern science in its most rational or "scientific" form—"is not the opposite of the ascetic ideal but rather *the latest and noblest form of it*" (GM III:23). We note the backward movement of these comments as the progression of a concern that only works its artistry retroactively upon the reader.

In the context of the aftermath of the triumphs and failures of Nietzsche's relationship with Lou Salomé, Nietzsche writes in a letter to Overbeck of the urgency of spiritual transformation. This is, of his need to "invent" the "alchemical artistry" for transmuting the perceived backwater of his life into gold.[9] In this way, Nietzsche addresses himself to alchemy's primary aim, that of the transformation of the highest gold that is the soul. This we otherwise call Nietzsche's self-overcoming. Examples of such transformation run throughout his work. The chorus and then the audience in his *Birth of Tragedy* sees itself transformed; it becomes the god, and it itself in this transformation takes on the suffering of Dionysus. Perhaps most famous of all such examples is his invocation of the metamorphosis of the spirit. In *Zarathustra* in "Of the Three Transformations," to the camel and the lion, Nietzsche adds the strangest animal of all: the child, as Oedipus recalled the human infant as an animal of the four-footed kind to solve the ambiguously footed animal of the riddle posed by the sphinx (Z:1).

The ultimate image of transfiguration, however, appears in Zarathustra's dream image. This is the shepherd's laughter, expressing a transformation of spirit. Such a transfigured being invokes the experiential moment that could so transform the soul in the alternative response of joy, blessing (rather than cursing) the demon who disturbs one in one's deepest solitude with the proclamation of the eternal return of the same. We recall one of Nietzsche's notes from 1883, seemingly written in the same spirit of transformation: "And he knew not how to conquer his virtue: the lion rent the child within him: and finally the lion consumed itself" (KSA 10:4[218]). As Zarathustra's third animal that follows the classic imagery of eagle and snake, Nietzsche characterizes the lion, regarded "as Zarathustra's maturity and mellowing" (*KSA* 10:16[51]), as the apotheosis of the "I will," the resolute consummation of will itself. As the hymn of the convalescent and the triumphant, Nietzsche speaks of the "laughing lion."[10] In fact, Nietzsche, *pars pro toto*, will name all of his totem animals as his "children" (Z:4 "The Sign"). In "The Old and New Tablets" he pronounces as the signs of the coming of his hour—"for once more will I go unto men"—"the laughing lion with the flock of doves" (Z:3). Laughter thus accompanies Zarathustra's psychologically unnerving image of the transformation of the shepherd, which David B. Allison analyzes for us as none other than Zarathustra himself,[11] ecstatically positioned, fantastically beside himself: "into whose throat the serpent had crawled," but now transformed, following his own, Zarathustra's, admonishment "Its head off! Bite!" and becoming in that moment a "transfigured being [*ein Verwandelter*], a light surrounded being that laughed!" (Z:3 "On the Vision and the Riddle" 2).

Laughter is not only an esoteric device, it is also a gnostic signifier. In an early note, Nietzsche aspires to go one better than the "doubled laughter" of Epictetus, thereby inviting his readers to take amusement in one's own circumstance without the mirror of an external point of view—i.e., not merely to laugh with the world laughing against you (this is Epictetus's co-opted recommendation), Nietzsche proposes that one go even farther. Laughing at oneself, as a reflexive modality of conscious generosity ("out of the whole truth"), is opposed to the more serious solicitude of love for others as for oneself traditionally attributed to Christ (see *KSA* 9:6[352]).

Accordingly, in his late-written attempt at a self-criticism to his *The Birth of Tragedy*, Nietzsche would advise his readers to "learn laughter" (*BT* P:7). In *The Gay Science* (a book that can perhaps be claimed to be dedicated to the art of laughter), the joy of the titled *Joyful Science* is presented as self-transforming in the wake of its "alliance with wisdom." For Nietzsche does not only suggest that the reader learn to laugh "at oneself as one would have to laugh in order to laugh out of the whole truth," but contends that laughter itself might (thereby) be transfigured: "laughter *may* have a future" (*GS* 1). Earlier, Nietzsche had pointed to the cruelty of the human being in comparison to the relative sobriety of animal savagery (*HH* 553), while identifying the human as the affectively insane or "laughing animal" (*GS* 224). And finally we note Nietzsche's arch German invocation of those whose laughter contains the dawn itself: "for those of golden laughter" (*KSA* 12:1[229]).

The thematics of Nietzsche and laughter are of course well known.

Indeed, even in the context of esotericism, numerous scholars, ranging from Laurence Lampert to Barry Allen to Graham Parkes, have explored themes of laughter, usually with the aid of Straussian courage.[12] One may well connect Nietzsche's reflections on Homeric or "Olympian laughter"—that is, the laughter of the Homeric gods as we hear it in the *Iliad*, ringing over the cries of the suffering and the piled bodies of the dead on a wasted battlefield: in Pope's translation "And unextinguish'd laughter shakes the skies" (*Iliad* Bk. I, l. 771)—to be compared both to the "waves of uncountable laughter" Nietzsche attributes to Aeschylus (GS 1) as well as to Nietzsche's recurrent image of occasionally just juvenile but ideally prophylactic laughter. A connection between laughter and cruelty is patent in *The Poet's Vocation*, one of the poems included among Nietzsche's appendix of rhymes to *The Gay Science*. Describing the vitals of the lizard (*Lazertenleibchen*) and the torments of its anguish, pierced by the arrow or the pen of his verse, Nietzsche's ticktock rhyme affirms the paradox of what is called poetry: its innocence and its cruel compulsions. And in the conclusion of the third book of *Zarathustra*, Nietzsche combines cruelty *and* laughter—as laughter is *always* cruel—writing, "my wickedness is a laughing wickedness, at home among rose bowers and hedges of lilies: for in laughter all evil is present, but sanctified and absolved through its own happiness" (Z:3 "The Seven Seals" 6).

The laughter in which all malice is present but transformed as such would be the laughter of the gay or joyful science in the wake of its proposed "alliance with wisdom" (GS 1). We shall return to both the "golden laughter" of the Zarathustran shepherd exulting in his transfiguration and the lizard after a reflection on Nietzsche's rhetorical alchemy and the question of music.

To Have Ears for the Music of the Text: Nietzsche's Rhetoric for All—and None

If one can speak of tragedy as the offspring ("at once Antigone and Cassandra") born of the "mysterious marriage" (BT 5) between Apollo and Dionysus (see BT 22 and 25), this same union constitutes Nietzsche's most important alchemical image. Beyond popular accounts of alchemy as it may be counted among what Nietzsche names the "preludes to science" (GS 300) and just as prototypically associated with the vulgar desire for gold or the image of spiritual transformation evident in an allegorical reading of *Zarathustra*, Nietzsche's primary reference to the image of alchemy corresponds to its manifestation in *The Birth of Tragedy* as the precisely, perfectly, alchemical "wedding" between Apollo and Dionysus. This particular union is so com-plete that subsequent discussions of Dionysus in Nietzsche's text are refer-ences to the fulfilled consummate assimilation of Apollo to Dionysus. Commingled with Apollo in the mysterious wedding bond of Nietzsche's account of the genesis of ancient tragedy, even after tragedy's decline, Nietz-sche's Dionysus acquires formative powers, becoming a deity of transformed energies and the orgy itself a means of life perpetuation and the assurance of fertility, and birth the sanctification of pain.

Today, almost everything to nearly everyone, Nietzsche seems less and less the antipodal or "rare" philosopher he liked to think he was. But, and this reflection is key to the question of Nietzsche's "divine lizard," might an author who wrote such books as he did, reflecting in *Ecce Homo* on his work with reference to his early book *Daybreak: Thoughts about Morality as a Preju-dice*, be thought to have been aware of the effects of his books on those who read them?

For his own part, Nietzsche characterizes the text that will draw forth his expression of what he calls his *divine lizards* in terms of his assault against the convictions and practices of morality, alluding here to the subtitle of GM: "With this book begins my campaign against *morality*. Not that it smells in the slightest of gunpowder—quite other and more pleasant odours will be perceived in it, provided one has some subtlety in one's nostrils" (*EH* "Books" D 1).The reference to smell is important for Nietzsche, as he liked sensual metaphors, especially (and particularly dissonantly for modern read-ers) those of smell, but such an odor is also significant of the alchemical domain of the present metaphor. The odor of evil (rather than sanctity) recalls the lizard as it appears in *Zarathustra*, at the conclusion of the section entitled "Immaculate Conception" or un-bespattered knowledge (*Von der unbefleckten Erkenntniss*), where Nietzsche writes of subterranean odors and sensibilities: "Distance concealed from me the serpent filth and the evil odour, and that a lizard's cunning was prowling lustfully around."[13] Thus this same reference emphasizes his (esoteric) appeal to the uncommon reader.

What I am calling to attention here in the context of the present review of Nietzsche's use of the word "lizard" is Nietzsche's writerly style as his prow-ess as rhetorician and hence as a modern master of an otherwise rarely achieved *alchemical* art. Not merely a writer, not merely a stylist, Nietzsche wrote for particular readers and he wrote to ensure that he be read in a cer-tain way. So far, so good. Here I want to emphasize to what unprecedented extent this effort would exceed other instances of rhetorical achievement—unprecedented enough to change—and this should be alchemy enough—the character of a language itself.

Language scholars count Nietzsche as one of the great stylistic masters of German, ranking him with Luther and Goethe. Such a ranking calls for the question What *did* he do as a writer? *How* did he do it? As Nietzsche conceived his own achievement, his invention was a matter of *rhythm* and *style*: "Before me one did not know what can be done with the German language—what can be done with language as such. The art of *grand* rhythm, the *grand style* of phrasing, as the expression of a tremendous rise and fall of sublime, or superhuman passion, was first discovered by me" (*EH* "Books" 4). A student of the art of language, Nietzsche achieved not only a *theoretical* but also and remarkably—for it is this accession that remains rare—a *practical* mastery of the art of written composition or style.[14] In fact, this mastery does not necessarily make Nietzsche easier to read. However, it does mean that much more is going on in his texts than is manifest at a first encounter or even after many such encounters. In part this has to do with Nietzsche, in part this has to do with his audience.

As Nietzsche taught his own students at Basel, an understanding of the classical (Greek and Latin) art of rhetoric included a review of the meaning of and the workings of metaphor, metonymy, and every trope of language written precisely for a given or specific *and not and never* for a general audience. One cannot write a "universal" book, and here Nietzsche invokes the example of the Bible (*AOM* 98), without also writing a book for no one in particular, as Nietzsche himself would *affect* (or pretend to parody) writing such a book with his *Thus Spoke Zarathustra*. There is no universal or objectively transparent mode of expression. The limitations of such "all-wordly" books are not to be attributed to some fundamentally undemocratic or anti-enlightenment tone generic to Nietzsche (or else the rhetoricians of antiquity) but just and exactly because no book can be written for a general audience without being quite inherently addressed to no one. In another expression of this inherent stylistic limitation of specialty or esoteric texts, the problem with classical philosophy in its quite specific context. Philosophy in its origins and as a way of life is not quite an open book, but its special dialogical forms, its confessions and meditations, are *practices* of a very particular kind: practices in some part lost to us, who quite literally do not and cannot know how to understand or *hear* what we read.[15]

Music and Words: Rhythm and Measure

A more than merely metaphorical but rather literal modality is to be heard at the start of Nietzsche's *Zarathustra*, where he thunders in Zarathustra's mouth: "There they stand (he said to his heart), there they laugh: they do not understand me, I am not the mouth for these ears. Must one first shatter their ears to teach them to hear with their eyes?" (Z:P 5). Nietzsche's rhetorical power is thus coincident with the singular and singularizing, even isolating, and still today insufficiently attested (critically studied) discovery of his formative philological career.

When Nietzsche cries that one needs to "shatter their ears to teach them to hear with their eyes" scholars routinely read such talk of "shattering" ears, "hearing" with one's eyes, as effectively figurative language. These are metaphors, such as the image of Zarathustra speaking "to his heart." But the metaphor conveys a particularly literal and key insight here. The young Nietzsche had argued in his first book that the phonetic texts of the past do more than merely preserve written markings but—and he regarded this discovery as his great insight—the texts, especially lyric poetry, are the "sediment" preserving the music of the folksong (see KSA 8:6[9]). In the folksong, in the lyric, Nietzsche argued, word and music come together. In the case of the written texts of ancient Greek (using a phonetically voiced alphabet and a rhythmic language of highly formalized metric rhyme), we encounter nothing less literal than "recordings": a frozen but still and barely decipherable or readable repository of lost sound.[16]

We do not have the music of ancient tragic drama, so Nietzsche would argue, hence we have only the barest part of what would be needed to understand ancient Greek tragedy and yet we are not without a clue to this art. If we regard it from its originations in the folk song, the spirit of the same music that can be heard (not merely read) in lyric poetry. "We lack competence with regard to a Greek tragedy," Nietzsche would declare in his first Basel lecture, Greek Musical-Drama, "because its major impact resided in great measure in an element that has been lost to us: the music" (KSA 1, p. 528).

If we emphasize the origins of The Birth of Tragedy as Nietzsche traces it out of what he called the Spirit of Music, the key to the tragic dramas of antiquity would be the folk voice of lyric poetry, once distinguished, as Nietzsche insisted, from its modern literary rendering as "subjective" expression. Cast as the opposition between epic and lyric poetry, the opposition between Homer and Archilochus thus provides the missing link to tragedy interpreted as ancient Greek "music-drama." This poetic contrast, Nietzsche claimed, "indicated the only possible relation between poetry and music, between word and tone" (BT 6). The score of this music was lyric poetry; its pathic expression, the music of the written word.

Nietzsche argued that by means of philology he had uncovered the lost music of the ancient tragic art in the metric rhythm of the past (KSA 1, p.

515). Thus, what Nietzsche proposed to teach us as the possibility he claimed he had himself achieved was the point of the protracted title of his study of Greek tragedy—*Out of the Spirit of Music*—that is, literally to "hear" with one's eyes. Ultimately, Nietzsche took his inspiration for an understanding of the Greek music-drama (as he would later attempt to comprehend *The Birth of Tragedy*) out of the text itself (philology, we have noted, must be conceded as the *only* archaeological means for this inquiry), but he found it only by cultivating the art of reading musically: attending to the music of the text (see *BT* 17). Where Nietzsche differs from other exponents of this same conviction is in his dedication to taking his metrical studies as music, parsed as a music exactly alien to modern or contemporary ears. Ancient texts were characterized by music, but one lacking the interpretive/emotive stress or emphasis (*ictus*) preferred by modern ears, as Nietzsche claims and also as attested by scholarship ancient and ultramodern.[17] What kind of music would this be, what would such verses "sound like"? Of one thing Nietzsche was certain: they would resonate in an utterly different manner from what we today call music. As a music available only in time, in fixed or masked time, and thus set or measured only in accord with a certain metric interpretation, it could only be conveyed through tradition and was consequently profoundly unstable.[18]

It is intriguing to point out that a close parallel to this musical tradition is found in a tradition otherwise wholly associated with the written word: the tradition of Torah instruction; that is, the transmission of the law of the fathers from teacher to son, *bar mitzvah*, as this tradition has with fits and starts, interruptions and restorations, come down to us.

Nietzsche's insight here is not a matter of mistaking the libretto *for* the opera, or indeed (to use the opposition Wagner preferred), of relegating the music beneath the total work of art, as Wagner himself conceived the music as only part of the whole. Rather, in the case of antiquity there is *only* the text, and what is here invoked as the lack of music (the failure of "musical" reading in Nietzsche's sense) does not ground the assumption that we are lacking what *would have been* the music (as we could hear such music *as* music). It is not that we lack the "score" or the sounds as they would be available if we had at our disposal a recorded version of truly genuine or originally authentic Greek music. The music we are missing cannot be restored by a reconstruction of likely instruments and of what bare traces of such late musical scores as have come down to us in historical transmission.

For an understanding of the Greek music-drama, as for an account of *The Birth of Tragedy Out of the Spirit of Music*, Nietzsche turns to the residue preserved in the words that remain as the evidence of lyric and tragic poetry. Nietzsche's strange and radical claim then was that the text itself *was* the music, a music that can no longer be heard. Thus, just as we do not know how to scan ancient Greek, we do not exactly know, although Nietzsche felt that he could intimate on the terms of an utterly alien measure, the limits of that "music," and in the same way, today's scholars, at once more distant from and closer to the problematic than Nietzsche was, similarly suppose how Greek verse might be declaimed. For Nietzsche, such modern suppositions had intrinsic dangers.

Sounding very much like Heidegger here as he mourns the inception of what is from the start already lost in its first aletheic beginning, Nietzsche claims that the tragic music from which tragedy had its origins was elided almost from its inception. Even at its height, even in its most accomplished instaurations, there is *already* in Aeschylus and *already* in Sophocles an unequivocal understanding (familiarity with) the experiential, ecstatic practice of music that had already begun to give way to another more readerly, declamatory, and logically rational expression that would culminate in Euripides (see KSA 7:1[1]).

Literally born of music in its origins from folk song, tragedy was always embodied in music (see KSA 1, p. 529), and born and borne, it would be as a result of the loss of that same ecstatic or Dionysian musical spirit that tragedy would suffer its own death at its own hand, which subtext (the death of the tragic art form) was of course the explicit subject of *The Birth of Tragedy* (see BT 11 and 16). For Nietzsche, "Tragedy went to ground on the basis of an optimistic dialectic and ethics, that is to say: music drama went to ground owing to a lack of music" (KSA 1, p. 533; see KSA 7:1[15]).

Writing of the consequences of the lack of orchestral accompaniment where, Nietzsche notes, the Greeks lacked instrumental accompaniment of the modern, melodic musical kind, the ancient world depended to a far greater extent than we can imagine (and this imaginative limitation was Nietzsche's scholarly point in his book on tragedy) on a purity and rigor of traditional form. Deviation from that earlier tradition, the kind of deviation that is inevitable over the course of time, means only that such a tradition had to be lost to itself almost from the start except that it sound *each time* and recover itself in itself in song. This μέλος was the poet's art as a singer of tales; this was the rhapsode's art knotted into that same tradition. For if the music of the artwork had nothing to do (so Nietzsche charges, as the emphasis of expression had nothing to do) with the sensible or intellectual meaning of the verse expressed in words, then no kind of literary analysis or interpretation can restore the music. It is revealing less of simplicity than of an unbridgeable distance that, Nietzsche argues, we can only approach the lost art of Greek culture by the meanest of techniques. The instrument required demands neither art nor skill: just "beating a drum" offers us our only conduit to such a lost art of "music appreciation." In other, more exact words, the song tradition is ineluctably lost to us *as* a tradition. The words remain—if on the terms of antique music we can learn to read them musically, i.e., metrically, if we conscientiously restrain our all-too-modern musical intuitions, attending to another framework of measure and time.

Nietzsche offered the comparison to the Middle Ages, a time when taste and convention had fallen into such disparity that one could no longer, failing suitable conventions, compose music for the ear but only for the eye. The result yielded brilliantly "illuminated" scores, to what seems the absurd extreme of matching "notes to something's color: like green in the case of plants, or purple for vineyard fields" (*KSA* 1, p. 517). With regard to the spoken texts of ancient music drama, and like the medieval scholiast so charmingly absorbed by color, we are confined to signs we scan rather than read in the case of ancient texts, because we cannot hear with our eyes.

By merely reading a score, by contrast here, the musically trained reader *hears* what an untrained reader can only see. Because the tradition of the tragic age is lost, "we are condemned to misprision regarding Pindar, Aeschylus, and Sophocles" (*KSA* 1, p. 517). And because we cannot (as it were) "sight-read" ancient tragic drama, because we *literally* fail to "hear" with our eyes, we are worlds of silence away from any comprehension of ancient tragedy. Not because ancient tragedy was performed in the open light of day (rather than in today's darkened theaters) or because it lacked the surprise factor of a novel plot but because it does not resound for us as music does: "We are incompetent with respect to Greek tragedy because its central influence was in great measure founded on an aspect which has been lost, namely music" (*KSA* 1, p. 528). Because we fail to hear the tragic myth *as we hear music*, a comprehension of the ancient art form can only elude us. Thus (and at best) preoccupied only with the role of the actor or else the audience, we cannot but misconstrue the reflective centrality of the chorus (the community) as the vehicle of the work as a whole. This same lost possibility for music is also the key to the essence of ancient tragedy. Recognizing tragedy as adumbrated in terms of *pathos*, the feelings of tragedy would be sentiments of a thoroughly musical kind, and tragic dissonance would be a literal word for musical dissonance (see *D* 142). But the kind of music, the sound of it, would be nothing we can know or even suppose. Thus Nietzsche writes of the ancient world as a world lost; "to touch even the hem of which," he writes, would be the rarest joy. The only means to the past, the only means to Nietzsche's insight into the musical essence of tragedy is through philology. The philologist's tools are what Nietzsche brings to every problem, just as, *word for word*, his "polemic" on the origins of morality details the ultimate consequences of nothing other than a philologically driven *etymological* analysis.[19] Returning to the level of the word itself, we return to the question of the skittering, glitteringly divine lizard: Nietzsche's *Eidechese*.

Spearing the Divine Lizard, or How One Becomes What One Is

In *Ecce Homo*, a book Nietzsche wrote to tell the story of his books, if not quite the story of his life ("I am one thing, my writings are another"), Nietzsche looks back upon a lifetime by reviewing his achievement as a writer writing wise, clever, and, above all, *such* "good books" (*EH*). What is important in the midst of this self-assertion is his claim that he "never had any choice" (*EH* "Books" Z:3). "Thoughts," Nietzsche argued, simply came to him—washing over him, catching him up with their own rhythm and movement. Correspondingly, the art of writing would be the art of catching his thoughts as they flashed by, ideas as they came to him, the art of freezing—impaling—such "godlike" moments. The best metaphor for that would seem to be a recording device, writing itself. And for the German-speaking author (the non-authorizing author, or *Schriftsteller*) who mused upon himself as only a poet, taking dictation from a source that came from without, over which he had no choice, a mere enthusiast, ecstatic poetologue, *"nur Narr, nur Dichter"*—only a mindless fool, only a poet—writing, like poetry itself, is inspiration: *Dichtung*. Nietzsche is here concerned with the functioning of thought itself for the thinking, knowing subject, capable of as much reflection as observation and capable of writing, indeed, as an art. The metaphor he finds for the quick object of that art is the lizard—Nietzsche's *Eidechse* is a metaphor for his insights: for lapidary, illuminated insights, *fleeting* insights.

Like Nietzsche's other metaphors, the *Eidechse* thus works in more than metaphoric fashion in his text but has exactly metonymic resonance. In sound, *Eidechse* invokes "idea" along with the iconic philosophical associations that are thought together in the idea as such (*Idee, eidolon*). In addition, the lizard, the signified animal itself, has a characteristic brilliance in appearance, particularly as Nietzsche describes it. Small and clean, clear and precise, the scales of a lizard are increasingly variegated or detailed in complexity the closer one looks at it. Yet in spite of the reptile's prototypical association with stolidity (such as turtles or as exemplified by the nineteenth-century invention of the dinosaur), the lizard moves with striking speed. And its movement is reactively directed, always in patent response to the viewer. The lizard's movement is so very much a response to consciousness that the viewer is inspired to hold him or herself magically still to prevent the lizard from taking flight. The reptilian dimension, the cool, the cold, is always clear to Nietzsche and in its connection with transfiguration would seem to be related, at least in the metonymic order, with the amphibian salamander and thereby and once again to alchemy.[20]

Reflecting on his book *Daybreak*, Nietzsche develops his claim that the ultimate poetic (or musical, writerly task) is to learn to see out of a thousand eyes and—"shuddering with recollection"—to be able to catch the moments he calls "divine lizards," flashing, slithering moments, as they change and transform the thinker. In this context, the art of the book as a whole (and by the same token, the core of aphoristic achievement, which has as its goal to say what others do not say in a book) is described as the extraordinary art of freezing such elusive insights: "making things which easily slip by without a sound, moments which I call divine lizards, stay still for a little—not with the cruelty of that young Greek god who simply impaled the poor little lizard, but nonetheless still with something sharp, with the pen" (*EH* "Books" D 1).

Apollo, we will need to recall when Nietzsche speaks of young Greek gods, casual in their cruelty, was also celebrated for playing with reptiles—the god was said to have received the gift of the first lyre when Hermes chanced upon the shell of a dead turtle, upended, a shallow vessel tautly strung with dried tendons. The invention of the lyre is thus attributed to Apollo, or, maybe more likely, to Hermes, and one may imagine that the lyre would have been made from the shallow shell of a sea turtle—thus explaining Nietzsche's reference to a sea animal—but the lyre could just as well have been fashioned out of the shell of the box turtles that one can still find by the heights of certain Greek temples, animals in either case with dimensions that could serve a god for a lyre. And, again, we recall Marcel Detienne's manifold studies of Apollo in all his aspects, aspects including cruelty, and "soaked in blood," to use a Nietzschean metaphor.[21] The pure rationality of the Apollinian, which Nietzsche named a dream image, is an image that endures in spite of dissonant mythological associations.

Nietzsche here characterizes his *Daybreak* as a book of clear peace and calm: presenting the quiet demeanor of an animal "lying in the sun, round, happy, like a sea-beast sunning itself among rocks" (EH "Books" D 1). Nietzsche will confess that ultimately "it was I myself was that sea-beast." Here, with the same metonymic resonance, we find another word for Nietzsche's claims that his writings are so many fishhooks.[22] In this case, he speaks of his writing like Apollo's fisher's lance: "a spike with which I again draw something incomparable out of the depths: its entire skin trembles with tender shudders of recollection" (EH "Books" D1). But who is speared, who does the spearing? One is almost compelled to imagine that as the author, as the wielder of pen or spear, Nietzsche considered himself almost on the terms of his youthful reflection as he writes in a Nachlass note from the winter of 1880–1881, "joyful [fröhlich] and acute [schlau], like a lizard in the sun" (KSA 9:8[23]). And certainly his commentators, most enthusiastically Joachim Köhler, have made this association one of a prurient certainty, speculating on the mystery of Nietzsche's sexual preferences. The lizard for Köhler turns out to be a phallus. But the image in Daybreak, according to Nietzsche's own account in Human, All Too Human, is the story of convalescence or alchemical regeneration. To amplify the same image, Nietzsche recollects the lizard's power to regrow, in contrast with human beings, a lost finger (BGE 276).

Nietzsche had earlier compared the lizard with the convalescent (which we do read as speaking of himself) in his introduction to Human, All Too Human: recalling the needfulness of all and every means of knowledge, spoken of as a "fish-hook," "which may not dispense with wickedness." This is the time when the convalescent truly convalesces, the moment of a turning that begins to return to health. In this sense, this is a time that is grateful for the patience of the course of recovery and the small comforts of the same, as the convalescent comes to himself, as if for the first time: "Only now does he see himself—and what surprises he experiences as he does so! What unprecedented shudders! What happiness even in the weariness, the old sickness, the relapses of the convalescent! How he loves to sit sadly still, to spin out patience, to lie in the sun!" Like a lizard, Nietzsche continues, "Who understands as he does the happiness that comes in winter, the spots of sunlight on the wall! They are the most grateful animals in the world, also the most modest! these convalescents and lizards again half turned towards life" (HH P:5). Like the poikilotherm, the ectothermic lizard, stilting to regulate its body temperature, the convalescent himself moderates his return to health.

If the image of inspiration, the absence of any subject for and of thought itself, points to the vulnerability of the idea that, as Nietzsche says, glances away when one looks directly at it, this is opposed to his example of philistine creativity, which is precisely productive for the sake of appearances and *so that* (this is the feminized aspect of bourgeois invention) it may be seen (i.e., *TI* "Maxims" 20; see *BGE* 148). By contrast, because the thought comes when it wants, the idea of the writer, as an idea, is falsified almost immediately: it is a consummation that is maculate or spoiled in every sense of the word.

This image of flawed conception and maculate inspiration—which is, for Nietzsche, another word for writing in blood—compares productively with Heinrich von Kleist's archly doubled reflection upon reflexivity in his short-story parable on the life of puppets, "Über das Marrionetten-Theater." The story Kleist tells details the dynamics of the way in which awareness, consciousness as such, undercuts the life of beauty, the mien of grace caught as a fleeting vision that one glimpses and just as quickly loses, expressed via its corollary in terms of an animal antipode of unfaltering grace: the bear's inability to be fooled or to respond to the trained fencer's feint.[23] As Kleist moves in his account from the frustration of vanity lost to itself at the same moment that it glimpses itself as such, both recognizing and vainly sacrificing grace in its every attempt to recall it, he trains his own and therewith the reader's attention to the devastation wreaked by consciousness. The parabolic high point of Kleist's story is that same grace in the moment of recognition *and* sullying, in Kleist's recourse to the affected danger that is the "sport" of bear-baiting, where the fencer's skills fail him as the animal responds only to the one thrust that has to be bodily parried, so that the fencer cannot, by sleight or illusion, catch the animal any more off guard than the already captive bear must be said to be, to the practiced fencer's awkward disadvantage. Despite his captivity, the bear, exactly brute, is always on its guard. Complete grace: the beauty of being without seeming. The progression as Kleist details it calls for mechanization or else deification, and perhaps in his day and in ours, the two come down to the same technical ambition: "in the world of organic matter, as self-consciousness becomes dimmer and weaker, so does grace shine more and more radiantly and dominantly." In human beings, of course, reflexivity is such that rather than grace, growth tends toward consciousness. By contrast, grace is only to be regained at the end of such an evolution that, for Kleist, must pass through such an infinity that it can only reappear in two equivalent guises, both of which are regarded from the standpoint of consummate grace: "either framed in the human form which lacks all consciousness or in that which is infinite—that is to say, in the marionette or in God."[24]

Music and Happiness: Bagpipes
and the Smallest Joy

As a writer, Nietzsche's procreative sensibility wants the kind of differences he calls musical—not in the sense of the lost music painstakingly measured out of the lyric texts of antiquity, not in the sense of the contemporary music he himself attempted to compose, but the kind of music he also claimed to have written, precisely where such wild aspects could be regarded as the children of eternity for his metaphorical vision, his own texts. In this sense, he claimed in his *Ecce Homo* that one could count "the entirety of *Zarathustra* under music" (*EH* "Books" Z:1). The musical thoughts in question would call for a "rebirth in the art of hearing" and have only the value of seeming, and here Nietzsche repeats his reptilian image. They are "the values of the briefest and most transient, the seductive flash of gold on the belly of the serpent *vita*—" (*KSA* 12:9[26]). It is indispensable to an understanding of the meaning of these fleeting values, of thoughts that flash by unremarkably, to underscore them as values of appearance. Only poetry or the music of artistic invention can mark such flashing values as the highest will to power: marking *becoming* with the character of being, the seeming of being.

Another note captures this same reflection as a reflection on happiness. In a list of titles, between "Beyond Yes and No" and "The Last Virtue" we come upon " 'We Lizards of Happiness:' Thoughts of a Thankful Man" (*KSA* 12:1[143]). We are invited to reflect on Nietzsche's happiness, the happiness that he later characterizes as specifically his own: the happiness that should correspond to a love of fate, of divine blessing. And here too the image of the lizard recurs as a gliding allusion. Thus the parodic fourth movement or "act" appended to his *Zarathustra* prefigures images recalled in his *Ecce Homo* to write of music and happiness in a transposed time. Here in his song—not to night but to noontide, but still with a word for the burnished and "brown" reflections he will later recollect—now, when the day forgets its morning, it beats out a certain still point in time:

> Take care! Hot noontide sleeps upon the fields! Do not sing! Still! The world is perfect.
> Do not sing you grass bird, oh my soul, O my soul! Do not even whisper! Just see—still!
> Old noontide sleeps, it moves its mouth: has it not just drunk a drop of happiness —an ancient brown drop of golden happiness, of golden wine?
> Something glides across it, its happiness laughs. Thus—does a god laugh. Still! (Z:4 "At Noon")[25]

What, as "its happiness laughs," "glides across" the sleeping noontide, what fleeting movement catches the eye of the midday lover, would seem to be the lizard or its kin: "Precisely the least thing, the gentlest, lightest, the rustling of a lizard, a breath, a moment, a twinkling of the eye—*little* makes up the quality of the *best* happiness. Still!" (Z:4 "At Noon"). This littlest of things, the little it takes to make us happy, is music, Nietzsche writes. We hear the merest note of a bagpipe and we are transported—evidence for him of how little one needs for real joy. The French say there is no happiness, only small or lesser happiness (*il n'y a de bonheur que le petit bonheur*), and Nietzsche recalls this when he speaks of the small woman he imagines to himself in *Ecce Homo*, a woman of the south, a woman who is a metaphor for music.

Writing a passage-poem, a poetic array of mixed titles and observations or "Halcyonic Expressions" and beginning with "Caesar Among the Pirates," Nietzsche explains his thoughts of gratitude, lizards of happiness, as the happiness that, finding itself among what we descry as all-too-Wagnerian companionship (*Zwergen*), wishes for and embraces misunderstanding. This happiness is not merely a quiet, small happiness but the thankfulness of a convalescent grateful for the spots of sun in winter, like a lizard, a chance to stilt into the warmth: this Pindarian gratitude is thankful for being misunderstood—as it finds itself among dwarves, as among children.

> *Halykonische Reden.*
> *Cäsar unter Seeräubern*
> *Die Stunde, wo die Sonne hinunter ist—*
> *Die Menschen zu lieben um Gottes willen—*
> *Für die, welche golden lachen.*
> *Dankbar für das Mißverstanden werden—*
> *Am goldenen Gitter.*
> *Wir Eidechsen des Glücks—*
> *Unter Kindern und Zwergen. . . .*
> —Nietzsche (KSA 12:1[229])

Notes

1. Martin Heidegger, *Nietzsche: Volume II*, trans. D. F. Krell (San Francisco: Harper & Row 1984), 45.

2. If David B. Allison is right in tracing the ultimate design of Nietzsche's Zarathustra through the labyrinth of Nietzsche's highly charged and fatal relationship with Lou Salomé, the icon of Saint Jerome emblematized by his lion, *and* his deliberately ascetic

existence, this last image may well be more significant than it is usually thought to be. See David B. Allison, *Reading the New Nietzsche* (Lanham: Rowman & Littlefield, 2001), pp. 112f and 154f.

3. Heidegger, *Nietzsche II*, 45.

4. Heidegger, *Nietzsche II*, 46, 48.

5. Heidegger, *Nietzsche II*, 50.

6. Heidegger, *Nietzsche II*, 50.

7. B. J. T. Dobbs, *The Foundations of Newton's Alchemy: or, "The Hunting of the Greene Lyon"* (Cambridge: Cambridge University Press, 1975), 6.

8. For recent discussions of this theme in addition to the titled discussion in Tracy B. Strong, *Friedrich Nietzsche and the Politics of Transfiguration* (1975; reprint, Urbana: University of Illinois Press, 2000), see Gary Shapiro's extended analysis of Nietzsche's reading of Raphael's *Transfiguration* in *Archaeologies of Vision: Foucault and Nietzsche on Seeing and Saying* (Chicago: University of Chicago Press, 2003), chapter 3, and David B. Allison, *Reading the New Nietzsche* (Lanham: Rowman & Littlefield, 2000), who reads Nietzsche's writing especially *Thus Spoke Zarathustra* as a veritable art of self-transfiguration, pp. 115ff.

9. Letter from Nietzsche to Overbeck, Christmas 1883. See also Allison, *Reading the New Nietzsche*.

10. Nietzsche used the image frequently, and notes in this context; "im Lachen nämlich werden alle bösen Triebe heilig" (*KSA* 10:19[6]). See *KSA* 11:31[11] for an indication of the function of the laughing lion. It is an esoteric image to the extent that willing is thereby transformed by means of laughter.

11. Allison, *Reading the New Nietzsche*, 163f.

12. See Graham Parkes, "The Wandering Dance: Chuang Tzu and Zarathustra," *Philosophy East and West* 33:3 (July 1983); Laurence Lampert, *Nietzsche's Teaching: An Interpretation of "Thus Spoke Zarathustra"* (New Haven, Conn.: Yale University Press, 1986); Barry Allen, "Forbidding Knowledge," *The Monist* 79 (1996): 294–310; and John Lippitt, "Nietzsche, Zarathustra and the Status of Laughter," *British Journal of Aesthetics* 32, no. 1 (1992).

13. Hollingdale's translation.

14. In this context, Nietzsche's reading of Gustave Gerber's *Kunst der Sprache*, so much of which would find its way into Nietzsche's own (unpublished) *TL*, is less a case of suppressed influence, as some scholars have argued, than taking for granted a handbook and presumptive referential context, more rather than less so, given that it was the era of the exactly non-mechanical (non-photocopy based) means of reproduction.

15. See for a discussion of this tradition and its complexities Pierre Hadot, *Philosophy as a Way of Life: Spiritual Exercises from Socrates to Foucault*, trans. Michael Chase (Cambridge: Blackwell, 1995).

16. For an account of the signal discoveries of Milman Parry and Albert Lord in the early part of the twentieth century, see Albert Lord, *A Singer of Tales* (Cambridge: Belknap Press, 1960) and Adam Parry, ed., *The Making of Homeric Verse: The Collected Papers of Milman Parry* (Oxford: Oxford University Press, 1987).

17. See Michael S. Silk and Joseph Stern, *Nietzsche on Tragedy* (Cambridge: Cambridge University Press, 1981); Barbara von Reibnitz, *Ein Kommentar zu Friedrich Nietzsche, "Geburt der Tragödie aus dem Geiste der Musik" (Kapitel 1–12)* (Stuttgart: Metzler, 1992); Martin West, *Ancient Greek Music* (Oxford: Clarendon, 1992); James Porter, *Nietzsche and the Philology of the Future* (Stanford: Stanford University Press, 2000); and Christopher Middleton, "Nietzsche on Music and Metre," *Arion* 6 (1967): 58–65.

18. For a discussion of such a fixed or masked time, see my discussion of Thrasyboulos Georgiades and other commentators on ancient Greek music in Babich, "*Mousiké techné*: The Philosophical Practice of Music in Plato, Nietzsche, Heidegger," in *Between Philosophy and Poetry: Writing, Rhythm, History*, ed. Massimo Verdicchio and Robert Burch (London: Continuum, 2002), 171–180. See especially my notes on this point on 200–201.

19. This same methodic focus appears in the discussion of the "noble"—or the "blond beast" or else the "slave"—in Nietzsche's GM. Working as a stumbling block to scholars seeking to pry his ethics from its manifestly incendiary associations with Nazi imagery, Nietzsche himself does not claim to retrieve supposedly historical facts (it was not news to Nietzsche; it was much rather his very stylistic conceit that there never was an ancient world peopled by great blond marauding "beasts" and craven downtrodden "slaves")—nor does his voice, as is so often interpreted to psychoanalytic excess, express his deeper personal fantasies or dark desires.

20. Thus, in the section entitled "Of Immaculate Conception/Knowledge [*Erkenntnis*]," Nietzsche describes the lizard's lascivious cunning, employing an image that Ernst Bertram and Angéle Kremer-Marietti long ago reminded us to count as an engagement with Wagner's ring mythos. This is hardly the worst allusion. Nietzsche's drafts in May-June 1883 take the metaphor from reptile to insect (*KSA* 10:9[16]); the allusive association appears to trade upon the transformational quality of the lizard as a pupal form. "Einer Eidechse List schlich mit göttlicher Larve herum!" (*KSA* 10:13[1].422).

21. Marcel Detienne, *Apollo le couteau à la main* (Paris: Gallimard, 1998). See also his earlier *Dionysos mis à mort* (Paris: Gallimard, 1977).

22. It must be said that another sort of metonymy is at work here as David Farrell Krell reads Nietzsche as sunning himself, lizard like, drawing the association to criticize Heidegger's notorious charge of the animal's putative world-indigence. Krell, *Daimon Life: Heidegger and Life Philosophy* (Bloomington: Indiana University Press, 1992). Thus Joachim Köhler, in his *Zarathustra's Secret: The Interior Life of Friedrich Nietzsche*, trans. (New Haven, Conn.: Yale University Press, 2002), reminds us of the ancient metaphor for a lover's penis. And in the realm of popular metonymy, Jim Morrison, a music star of a past era who conscientiously identified with Nietzsche, happened also to have proclaimed himself the "lizard king." Yet one does not need to go so far afield. The lizard in the sun is the one who stilts and in this way maximizes the heat of his physiological life: lizards are poikilothermic, and to the degree that the heat they absorb exceeds the ambient air temperature, to that same degree they have an advantage.

23. See Heinrich von Kleist's marvelous vanity parable: "Über das Marionettentheater," in *Sämtliche Werke in zwei Bänden* (Stuttgart: Parkland Verlag, 1975), 339–345.

24. Kleist, "Über das Marionettentheater," 344, 345.

25. Hollingdale's translation, with alteration.

AFTERWORD

~

Paws, Claws, Jaws, and Such: Interpretation and Metaphoric Modalities

Christa Davis Acampora

Nietzsche's bestiary includes not only whole animate forms but also hundreds of references to different animal parts. Unlike Aristotle's interest in the parts of animals, Nietzsche's concern is not, of course, to ascertain their function in a fixed form but rather to discover and recover the variety of resources—domesticated, wild, and feral—upon which humans draw (or to which they resort), particularly in the context of interacting with other human beings. I wish to focus on some ontological aspects of Nietzsche's use of animal parts as they have a bearing on the possibilities of human existence. In so doing, I shall make observations about Nietzsche's conception of metaphor generally, the use of metaphor in interpretation, and how interpretive matters have ontological import in Nietzsche's work. In particular, I shall amplify a theme that resounds throughout the volume, namely, that Nietzsche's animal metaphors play a role in his diagnoses of the decadence of the human animal but also that they play a crucial role in his project to devise a therapeutic remedy utilizing metaphoric modalities. In other words, I shall claim that Nietzsche's uses of animal metaphors are not just intended to rhetorically deliver us to a new conception of the relation between nature and culture—Nietzsche's "parts of animals" play a significant role in his *treatment* of the sickness of morality. More than just rhetorically powerful descrip-

285

tions, metaphoric modalities, I suggest, are intended as *treatments* or remedies that potentially bring about metamorphic and metabolic transformations in the beings to which they are applied.

Paws, Claws, and Jaws

Let us begin with some Nietzschean physiology. "Claws" are frequently mentioned in Nietzsche's works. A passage discussed by several other contributors recalls their role as tools in the formation of the state:

> I employed the word "state": it is obvious what is meant—some pack of blond beasts of prey, a conqueror and master race which, organized for war and with the ability to organize, unhesitatingly lays its terrible *claws* upon a populace perhaps tremendously superior in numbers but still formless and nomad. That is after all how the "state" began on earth: I think that sentimentalism which would have it begin with a "contract" has been disposed of. (GM II:17)[1]

Nietzsche associates the appeal to moral goodness with a kind of compensation for those who lack claws. Zarathustra counsels his audience, "Verily, I have often laughed at the weaklings who thought themselves good because they had no *claws*. You shall strive after the virtue of the column: it grows more and more beautiful and gentle, but internally harder and more enduring, as it ascends" (Z:2 "On Those Who Are Sublime"). Zarathustra does not rally those possessing claws to use them to rip to shreds those who are weaker than they or even to bear them as a way of putting others in their place. Rather, he advises acquiring a fortifying refinement—*beautiful, gentle, but harder and more enduring*—to counteract the effects of a morality that aims to soften and tame. But it would be beneficial to acquire some claws, Nietzsche thinks, as protection against those who would exploit us with open hands. Thus warns Zarathustra: "And beware also of the attacks of your love! The lonely one offers his hand too quickly to whomever he encounters. To some people you may not give your hand, only a *paw*: and I desire that your *paw* should also have *claws*" (Z:1 "On the Way of the Creator"). Those who would manipulate others using the guise of love might very well need to be warded off by a display of the means of self-defense.

Fingers also have multiple meanings in Nietzsche's texts. On the one hand, Nietzsche recognizes their significance in figuring the human as primarily rational (read: calculating and clever), as industrious (read: busy and routinized), and as honest (read: weak and pliable). On the other hand, properly trained and employed, they can be utilized for the kind of probing and careful examination characteristic of the readers Nietzsche anticipates. In an account of the decay of taste resulting from Socratic-Platonic philosophy, Nietzsche writes in *Twilight of the Idols*:

> With Socrates, Greek taste changes in favor of dialectics. What really happened there? Above all, a *noble* taste is thus vanquished; with dialectics the plebs come to the top. Before Socrates, dialectic manners were repudiated in good society: they were considered bad manners, they were compromising. The young warned against them. Furthermore, all such presentations of one's reasons were distrusted. Honest things, like honest men, do not carry their reasons in their hands like that. It is indecent to show all five fingers. What must first be proved is worth little. (*TI* "Socrates" 5)

Dialectic seeks to secure its force through the enumeration of reasons. For Nietzsche, it is "*self-defense* for those who no longer have other weapons" (*TI* "Socrates" 6). But fingers can also bring with them refinement: they exhibit a kind of cultivation Nietzsche praises when they are exercised in pursuit of the art of philology or the kind of probing involved in reading well. In the context of discussing philology as "a goldsmith's art and connoisseurship of the *word*," the fingers play a role in reading. Nietzsche asks readers to approach his works with an art does not so easily get anything done, "with delicate eyes and fingers" (*D* P:5). Fingers are also specifically mentioned in the context of discussing the free spirits. There, they serve the free spirits inasmuch as they become "investigators to the point of cruelty, with uninhibited fingers for the unfathomable" (*BGE* 44).

In *Thus Spoke Zarathustra*, in the section "On Virtue That Makes Small" (*Z*:3), Nietzsche writes: "They are clever, their virtues, and have clever fingers. But they lack fists, their fingers do not know how to hide behind fists. Virtue to them is that which makes modest and tame: with that they have turned the wolf into a dog and man himself into man's best domestic animal [*den Menschen selber zu des Menschen bestem Hausthiere*]." Again, Zarathustra's counsel here does not seem to be going to blows with the virtuous clever ones. The antidote to the condition he laments appears to be borne out by Zarathustra's example: keeping company with animals that are not commonly domesticated, such as serpents, eagles, and the like. I am not suggesting that Nietzsche's conception of the detrimental effects of domestication necessarily implies that one ought to resort to primitivism or that what we should do is strive to recapture a kind of nobility that was at its base savage and brutal. The human animal, in Nietzsche's view, has been *tamed* (brutally incapacitating various aspects of human animality through techniques of shaming), but that does not mean that *training* is out of order. Very generally speaking, it seems that Nietzsche conceives of taming, or the kind of domestication that turns a wolf into an obedient dog, as a process that endeavors to extirpate various essential aspects of the species. Training, on the other hand, does not endeavor to kill off basic or prominent drives but rather cultivates, redirects, or rearranges their order.[2] In the course of that process, some drives may whither, die off, or "go to ruin," as Zarathustra describes the kind of destruction he believes underlies creativity. But training, as I am describing it here, does not achieve its aim by specifically seeking the destruction of the most vital or lively aspects of its subject.

In *Beyond Good and Evil*, the "prelude to a philosophy of the future" that Nietzsche addresses to those who constitute the "we" who inherit the strength marshaled in the overcoming of "Plato's invention of the pure spirit and the good as such" (*BGE* P), he asserts that it is his aim, in part, to "translate humankind back into nature" (*BGE* 230). How did we get out of nature? In the same work, at least, Nietzsche's answer seems to be that we *got out of nature* when we got what was "natural" but deemed "savage" *out of us*— namely, bestial cruelty. In the process of crafting "humanity," "the savage cruel beast" in the human was "finally 'mortified'" (*BGE* 229). It is Nietzsche's contention, of course, that that pest has not really been exterminated and that, instead, we have spiritualized it or made it divine. Savage cruelty lives on in self-torture and spiritualized suffering. It is just that we now act as artists and transfigurers of cruelty inasmuch as we are inheritors of and participants in the denial of drives and human wants of which the human animal is made. The domestication processes of (all-too-)humanization have not produced the transcendence of animality that they aimed to achieve. Our breeding (for "Goodness") might have begotten animals that are *seemingly* more docile, but it has not cultivated us into creatures that are superior to all others. If anything, the result of the taming of human animality, Nietzsche suggests, has been that we have become, on the one hand, more stupid and less elegant and, on the other hand, more brutal and less compassionate animals than we were before.

Bad conscience, for example, disciplines our physical being as it aims to produce a certain type of spirit. This results in the rather curious phenomenon of the human becoming the animal that *makes itself wild*. Ripped from the world in which he is an animal among others (in which case the "natural drives" find their expression in a vast economy of other constitutions), the man of bad conscience—in response to the effort to make him what is supposed to be most truly human—creates opportunities for wilderness gaming within himself. At the same time the human beast was asked to trade *paws* for (neighborly) *hands,* and as the function of *claws* was replaced by the clutches of the moral law, the caged animal transfigured himself into a host of monstrous brutes more dangerous than ever before.

As one more example of how Nietzsche views the perverting effects of domestication on the moral meanings and lived possibilities of human *physis,* particularly the visceral, consider the following:

> On his way to becoming an "angel" (to employ no uglier word) man has evolved that *queasy stomach and coated tongue [jenen verdorbenen Magen und jene belegte Zunge]* through which not only the joy and innocence of all the animals but life itself has become repugnant to him—so that he sometimes holds his nose in his own presence and, with Pope Innocent the Third, disapprovingly catalogues his own repellent aspects ("impure begetting, disgusting means of nutrition in his mother's womb, baseness of the matter out of which man evolves, hideous stink, secretion of saliva, urine, and filth"). (GM II:7)

In pursuit of the *supernaturalization* of human being, the body becomes a site of decadence and degradation. Sex, nutrition, digestion, and our very materiality become offensive, despicable, and vile.

The fatality of this kind of breaking lies in the fact that it robs us of our sense of ourselves as animate, living creatures, of the creative function of the body in making meanings and pursuing other possible forms of life. Not only morality but also (hyper)rationality has had the effect of stripping away our experiences of our animal selves. The domestic reconfiguration of animalic possibilities does not so much as create a new being as it disjoints, disembowels, and disintegrates the human. If it does not turn us into angels, then it transforms us into machines:

> Here I am, disintegrated and fragmented, my whole nature almost mechanically split into interior and exterior, sown with concepts like so many dragon's teeth [*Drachenzähnen*], breeding conceptual dragons [*Begriffs-Drachen*], suffering also from the disease of words and lacking faith in any feeling which has not yet been stamped with words. Being what I am, this lifeless but incredibly busy factory of words and concepts, I may perhaps have the right to say of myself, "Cogito, ergo sum," but not "*Vivo, ergo cogito.*" Empty "being" is granted to me, not full, fresh life; my most personal awareness merely assures me I am a thinking, not a living,

being; that *I am not an animal*, but at best some sort of *cogital"* [*dass ich kein animal, sondern höchstens ein cogital bin*]. (HL 10, p. 142)

Such complaints against the purportedly Cartesian conception of human embodiment are fairly familiar to us today. What is of special interest in the context under consideration here is the fact that Nietzsche sees rehabilitating animality not as a retreat from cultivation and culture as such, but as essential for the possibility of having any real culture at all. In the same passage, he writes, "To this day we still do not have even the basis for a culture because we ourselves are not convinced that an authentic life is ours. . . . 'First give me life, and from it I will then create a culture for you!'—that is the cry of every individual of this generation, and we all recognize each other by virtue of that cry" (HL 10, p. 142). This raises the questions—What kind of animal *is* the human? What kind of animal *can* the human possibly *become?*

Human Speciation

In his notebooks from the period of his *Beyond Good and Evil*, Nietzsche suggests that he writes for "a species that does not yet exist" (WP 958), and yet earlier he questions whether species themselves exist rather than just differing individuals (KSA 9:11[178]). Around the same time that he questions speciation as such, Nietzsche writes of animals in *Daybreak*: "animals learn to master themselves and alter their form so that many, for example, adapt their colouring to the colouring of their surroundings, . . . pretend to be dead or assume the forms and colours of another animal. . . . Thus the individual hides himself in the general concept 'man'" (D 26). A few years later, Nietzsche writes in his notes that "the experience of the transposition of values produces 'new weapons, pigments, colours, and forms, above all, new movements, new rhythms, new love calls and seductions. It is not different in the case of man.'"[3] As the foregoing discussion of animal parts suggests, Nietzsche conceives the human animal as, at least, a shape-shifting animal, one that with a new set of values fashions new weapons, delineates its parts differently, and transforms its *physis* to meet its new demands or to establish new goals. In the *Genealogy*, Nietzsche even suggests that the acquisition of this very capability of metamorphosis is what distinguished the animal "man" as "interesting," that it is what, perhaps, constitutes the advent of the human as a distinctive animal. The creation of slave morality, the very morality that produced the debilitating transformative effects described above, nevertheless resulted in the condition for the possibility of the human becoming "an interesting animal," an animal with the prospect of self-cultivation, in which "human soul in a higher sense [acquired] depth and [became] evil—and these are the two basic respects in which man has hitherto been superior to other beasts!" (GM I:6).

So, returning to the specific focus of this chapter—the role of Nietzsche's discussion of parts in his philosophical anthropology, his conception of interpretation, and the ontological ramifications of these views—let us consider how the problem that Nietzsche diagnoses might possibly respond to a therapeutic interpretative practice. Nietzsche's animal metaphors generally, and his discussion of parts specifically, do not merely play with or prey upon familiar images. Nietzsche is not simply massaging the nature/culture distinction to lure the human to some kind of new state of nature; his is not just a call to wilding. The animal imagery in Nietzsche's work appears, instead, to have ontological import by endeavoring to open different possibilities for being, for possibly becoming a different kind of animal from that which we have become.

Beyond Simile; or
The Transfiguration of Interpretation

Sarah Kofman's well-known *Nietzsche and Metaphor* elaborates how Nietzsche challenges the distinction between the metaphorical and conceptual uses of language as they relate to truth.[4] Drawing largely upon Nietzsche's notebooks and plans for the essay commonly called "On Truth and Lies in a Non-moral Sense," Kofman notices that Nietzsche conceives of all language as artistic and inventive, all naming and describing as metaphoric. Casting things in terms of concepts is merely a specialized form of metaphorical thinking. A distinctive feature of this kind of thought, however, is that we have forgotten its metaphorical nature. Kofman writes, "[T]hanks to the concept, man arranges the whole universe into well-ordered logical categories without realizing that he is thus continuing the most archaic metaphorical activity."[5] Moreover, in tying the conceptual to the true and the real, the recognized metaphor has been, by contrast, cast aside as less desirable, less pure, derivative, and ultimately less powerful, a pale imitation or image of what truly is.

Kofman makes much of Nietzsche's claim that the specialized language and conceptualization that philosophy utilizes is metaphorical, which we have forgotten is metaphorical:

Because of this fetishization of value, the fact that value is the product of evaluation gets forgotten, and the latter is now measured against the former; the fact that
the concept results from a metaphorical activity gets forgotten, and it is taken for
a transcendent model, with all specific things and actions being simply degraded
copies or simulacra of it. The phantasmatic construction of a transcendent world
means that the genesis of the measuring standard gets forgotten.[6]

The concept is based on metaphor, a metaphor of a metaphor, but it is judged
as the standard and, therefore, as superior in relation to the metaphoric process from which it is derived, as itself *proper*. It forgets and denigrates its origin. The concept is based upon forgetting in another respect, too, insofar as
its insistence on sameness, regularity, and identity amount to an active forgetting of differences.[7] Thus, the process of conceptualization is itself a *secondary* metaphoric process, itself derived from the original metaphoric
grasping that characterizes human understanding and description of its experience. And this derivative or secondary metaphoric transformation works in
such a way that it "forgets," extracts, or refuses to recognize as significant
many differences, distinctions, and other possible features that might be further explored or otherwise emphasized. Therefore, what we generally take to
be the legitimate scrutiny of the world is actually a willful blindness to many
different aspects of our experience.

Kofman emphasizes that Nietzsche replaces the image of humankind as
rational animals with the idea of the human as the metaphorical animal.[8] It
is not that Nietzsche is tossing rationality to the wind or denying that rationalizing is a useful function of human cognitive activity. He is rather claiming
that what we identify as *reason* is but one, and a very specialized and at times
narrow, kind of metaphorical activity. It is the capacity to engage in metaphorical thinking generally, and to direct our actions in light of such, that is
characteristic of human being for Nietzsche. Moreover, Nietzsche suggests,
we share this interpretative activity with other animals as well. All animals,
it is suggested by Zarathustra, are involved in a process of development that
is driven by the reinterpretation of their aims and goals. But the human—
committed as it is to its conception of *humanity*, the *good* as such, and the
relentless reduction of all existence to the *rational*—is currently experiencing
a kind of stasis, what Zarathustra describes as the "ebb of the great flood" in
which "all beings have so far created something beyond themselves" (Z:P 3).
What must we do in order to create something beyond ourselves, and what
would it mean to "overcome man," as Zarathustra puts it and as Nietzsche as
author of *On the Genealogy of Morals* further describes it?

Our overcoming "man" seems to involve the continuation and further development of the process that made us human in the first place, specifically the activity of metaphorically interpreting our environment and adapting and redirecting our goals in that light. But it might seem that this is a fairly aimless process. What would be accomplished by expanding our metaphoric range? Even if rationality is, in fact, a specialization of our metaphorical pow-ers, what would be had by giving up the notion that truth, as we presently conceive it, is itself a product of metaphorical activity? If we diminished or at least interrogated the status of that kind of metaphor, what would we really stand to gain? I think these are some of the most significant questions this volume raises, and so I wish to consider more precisely how Nietzsche appears to think about the relationship between metaphor, interpretation, and our possible ways of being. Before addressing these pressing questions directly, it is necessary to say more about interpretation and the ways in which it might bear on ontological issues.

Numerous scholars writing on Nietzsche and philosophy more generally have noted how metaphoric structures shape forms of thought, redefine lim-its, and open new possibilities. These features of metaphor are obviously cru-cial for Nietzsche's predominant interest in giving birth to new values. But I am interested not only in the axiological possibilities of metaphor but also the cognitive and ontological ones. In this chapter, I focus only on the lat-ter.[9] Specifically, I think that Nietzsche entertains an idea, developed at much greater length by Heidegger,[10] that the reconfiguration and reconstitu-tion of the constellation of relations that is possible through metaphoric transformation, in disclosing different possibilities for us to pursue, creates different possible realities.[11] The possibilities that interpretations illuminate provide entrées to different courses of action, different ways of conceiving the world, different orders of significance and desirable elements, and these give shape to different forms of life. Nietzsche's appeal to the overcoming of humanity and its relation to ascetic ideals in GM conveys such an interest.

Such a prospect is not limited to his later writings. In the second Untimely Meditation, Nietzsche casts the idea of using different modes of historical interpretation—critical, monumental, and antiquarian—to create for our-selves a "second nature," one that would reconstitute the past and redirect the aims of the future:

> We plant in ourselves a new habit, a new instinct, a second nature, so that the first nature withers. It is an attempt to give ourselves a past a posteriori, as it were, a past from which we prefer to be descended, as opposed to the past from which we did

descend—always a risky task since it is so difficult to set limits to this rejection of the past, and because second natures are generally weaker than first natures. Too often we know the good but fail to do it because we also know the better but are incapable of doing it. But now and then a victory does occur, and for those who struggle, for those who use critical history in the service of life, there is significant consolation in knowing that even this first nature was once a second nature, and that every victorious second nature will become a first. (HL 3, p. 103)

In constituting a "second nature" through the activity of exercising critical history, we engage in an interpretive enterprise that calls together aspects of the past in order to challenge and ultimately condemn them. To engage in nothing but critical history is to diminish our own power; it is "lack of self-mastery, . . . what the Romans call *impotentia*" (HL 5). Once the needs that generate critical history have been dissolved, we must employ a creative form of history if we are to redeem the past and create a history of which we want to be worthy. Such interpretative activity reveals or discloses the resources of the past that enable one to claim the future that one desires.

Interpretation, for Nietzsche, takes place not only in our uses of language: it is an activity in which the entire world seems to be engaged. In Nietzsche's physics of interpretation and incorporation, human beings are conceived as pluralities of affects that are essentially relational.[12] Each affect has its own perspective in relation to the other affects, and each seeks to have its particular view become the vantage. All action changes the constitution of the relations we are and the others in which we participate. By living—by taking any action at all—we play a role, though not an exclusive one, in creating reality. Given this, Nietzsche appears to wonder whether it is possible that human beings could actively affect the course of their organic development, give themselves "a new . . . physis" (HL 10). And, if so, could they, in effect, bring about a new species? These questions are at once tantalizing, if also bizarre and perhaps somewhat romantic.

For Nietzsche, the concept "species" is as much a human invention as the concept "individual." Wolfgang Müller-Lauter discusses Nietzsche's conception of speciation, engaging it partly in the context of addressing the issue of whether or not there are species-specific perspectives or interpretations, in his "On Judging in a World of Becoming: A Reflection on the 'Great Change' in Nietzsche's Philosophy."[13] Müller-Lauter argues that, for Nietzsche, what defines and sustains a species are its *habitual* interpretations that have become conditions of existence (i.e., the "perspectival seeing and judgment of all things for the purpose of self-preservation" particular to the organism seeking its advantage).[14] Thus, it would seem that when Nietzsche mentions a particular species he is also calling attention to the habit that sustains it *as* that species. In this way we might consider being human as essentially sustained by the practice of a habit, one we conceivably might overcome on the way toward becoming something else. I recognize that this is not a conclusion that Müller-Lauter pursues, but I think it is worthy of exploration. Is this anticipated overcoming of the habit of the human intended to introduce a new habit, or, in the course of overcoming the habit of being human, does one strive to overcome habituation itself? If the latter, the *Übermensch* as the form of life on the developmental horizon would not be a new species, but it would not be properly human either.

Rather than pursuing a science that investigates what are hypothesized as automatic adaptive responses to changes in the environment governed by laws, Nietzsche questions whether and how one might bring about an advance in the human species as such. He does not advocate a eugenics that aims to improve the same and directs change along the lines of what is considered to be better relative to current prevailing norms and values. Instead, Nietzsche's project can be described as a kind pragmatic axiology that potentially has ontological import. How does "human being" acquire its value? How can that value be transformed and maximized? What would constitute an advance in the meaning of human existence as such? And if such an "advance" were pursued, would we still recognize that form of life as human? The answers to these questions remain largely undetermined for Nietzsche, but his gay science aims to replace the concept of development as adaptation with that of shaping orientations—new goals and ends—by the creation of new interpretations, and his animal metaphors play a significant role in that process.

Ultimately, what Nietzsche envisages is an integrative mode of philosophizing in which the language of evolutionary science (for example, adaptation, development, etc.) is mapped onto and appropriated for Nietzsche's project of the poetic transformation of both the meaning and future constitution of humanity.[15] He imagines transformative conceptual unification as wedding the fruits of various scientific disciplines and approaches. Such conceptual development—the creation and offering of "many kinds of causality," as Nietzsche puts it in *Beyond Good and Evil*—is what philosophy brings to the table. Nietzsche conceives this process as having its hand in poetry or art because it issues not merely from the empirical sciences themselves—although it is, as Nietzsche's own efforts attest, informed by them—but rather from a kind of speculative projection. Nietzsche's future philosophy as gay science advances a kind of poetry of metaphors whereby scientific inquiry is *oriented* in such a way as to promote integrative understanding. It is animated by a spirit of invention that creates concepts that deliver the forms of thinking and conceptual formations that set scientific researches in motion and that supply the paradigms that make new discoveries possible. The deployment of metaphor in the context of gay science thus conceived as an art of transfiguration (GS "Second Preface" 3) potentially plays a role in *reshaping* (reforming or reconstituting, not merely redescribing) both the objects of its inquiry and the inquirers themselves.

Zarathustra's Transphysis and Future Animality

In a remarkable set of passages in *Thus Spoke Zarathustra* (Z:3 "On the Spirit of Gravity" 1–2), which nearly constitute a bestiary in brief, Nietzsche describes Zarathustra's transformation of his human-animal *physis*. The work of his mouth (*Mundwerk*) speaks in ways that are rough to those who, like silky rabbits (*Seidenhasen*), are cultivated for dainty things, and it is alien to those who merely spew forth ink like squid (*Tinten-Fischen*) or produce little more than clever trash in the manner of a fox with quills (*Feder-Füchsen*). His hand is a playful, unpredictable "fool's hand"; nothing might escape its scrawl. His foot is cloven (*ein Pferdefuss*), enabling him to trot, trample, and run, thereby turning the obstacles of difficult terrain into child's (or devil's) play. Being fleet of foot like the ostrich (*Vogel Strauss*), who can outrun the horse (*Pferd*), is not enough—one must learn to fly in order to avoid the spirit of gravity. His stomach (*Magen*) is compared with that of an eagle, who has a palate for the flesh of lambs (*Lammfleisch*). His bird-stomach requires little to be nourished and has a taste for what is innocent. Such a stomach is choosy, unlike the stomach of the swine (*Schweine*), and his tongue (*Zungen*) and stomach are able to say "no," unlike the ass (*Esel*). His arms are like wings, enabling him to take flight. In his bird-like qualities he is the primordial enemy (*Urfiend*) of the spirit of gravity.

What lends the human form the capability to fly? Love, Zarathustra claims. Love, particularly love for oneself, leavens. And it is in the context of leavening the burdens of what is alien to us and what burdens us about ourselves that the camel (*Kameel*) reappears in the passages under consideration. This suggests, in contrast with how Nietzsche's famous account of the metamorphosis is ordinarily conceived, that love and reverence, and not merely brash rebellion, somehow play a role in the transformation from camel to lion, from burden-bearing camel to beast-of-prey lion who also shares a nature much like that of the eagle.

It is worth ruminating about the nature and predilections of Zarathustra's stomach, how it might be eagle- and/or bird-like and why it might have a preference for things innocent. In most organized religions, the killing of innocents (much less eating them!) is the ultimate act of evil. It is easily conceived in terms of predation and moral reprobation. But if we are to endeavor to think non-morally, what might this mean? Considered beyond the axis of good and evil, a desire to devour innocence need not *necessarily* exemplify a wanton lust for cruelty. The stomach digests and serves as the primary site of the breakdown of that which is ingested. It is the place, so to speak, of *incorporation*, of the transformation of what is eaten into the body of that which eats. Given that we must eat, that we must nourish ourselves, which is preferable: indigestible moral stones or vibrant life forms that are free of the lead and poison of morality?[16] I take it that the preference for what is described as "innocent" is bound up in this dilemma. And the kind of predation of the innocent described in this particular context in *Zarathustra* is soon contrasted with the brutality of the spirit of gravity. That spirit, "suffering little children," starves innocents by "[forbidding] them betimes to love themselves" (Z:3 "On the Spirit of Gravity" 2), somewhat like, we might imagine, the Giant Water Bug, which injects its prey with a corrosive poison that kills it from the inside out leaving nothing but a hollow husk of the animal that once was.

Even skin is transformed from vulnerable flesh to protective outer casing. It is needed to contain and protect the interests of the human's inner "oyster" (*Auster*), which is "nauseating and slippery and hard to grasp." To have one's shell (*Schale*) in order to create a beautiful appearance and to practice clever blindness[17] rather than using it as a fortification or a hovel into which one retreats is an art that needs to be learned.[18] But skin is not merely a decorative covering. In the book immediately preceding *Zarathustra*, Nietzsche describes the overcoming of truths as like shedding skin (GS 307): as one comes to have a different life, to pursue different possibilities that give one's life different orientations and directions, one's perspective changes and the beliefs that gave shape to an earlier life might be said to no longer "fit." This is more like shedding skin "that concealed and covered a great deal that you were not yet permitted to see." Cast thus, it is living, not the triumph of something we might call "Reason," that prompts the shedding of former belief.

Zarathustra embodies all of these animalic possibilities. He is not (unlike those among whom he would not live) limited so as to have only the choice of being either the "evil animal" (böse Thier) or the "evil animal-tamer" (böse Thierbändiger). And yet what I have described as a prospective inter-pretative therapeutic practice of transforming our physical being by meta-phoric affiliations and identifications with other animal possibilities is precisely what Nietzsche thinks the animal-taming ascetic priest does—he evolves "a virtually new type of preying animal out of himself" (GM III:15). He becomes part polar bear (Eisbär), part tiger (Tigerkatze), and part fox (Fuchs) to meet his foe, the "healthy" beast of prey. Nietzsche's suggestion appears to be that if we desire to overcome the ascetic ideal, we must simi-larly draw upon animal potencies to produce a new zoomorph.

Equipped with "depth of soul" and having "become evil," Nietzsche's genealogy suggests, the human animal at this stage literally incorporates a monumental transformation of values that realizes a capacity to shape-shift or to transfigure the meaning of the human body and what it conceives as its own most wants and needs. Metaphors are not merely symbols or signs for something else that could, if they were really significant, be described more clearly, more specifically in another, more literal way. Nietzsche's objective through the application and use of animal metaphors is a transfigured physis, which involves not merely mimicking other animals but drawing on the ideas of speciation as relevant to a habit as described above; actually becoming (insofar as one assumes the habits of) the animal described. Such becoming-other is metamorphosis, not fanciful imitation. When the Iroquois dance the Eagle Dance, for example, they are not merely mimicking eagle gestures or depicting or representing the eagle; rather, by virtue of the fact that they are sharing in the bodily movements and ways of being typical of the eagle, they are becoming eagle. The Nietzschean bestiary draws us toward such possibili-ties as a way of transforming both the meaning and possible ways of being human.

If philosophy is the art of transfiguration (e.g., GS P), then the very muta-tion that allows for our development as moral animals also puts us on the way to becoming philosophical animals. Whether becoming the latter—that is, the beast that has acquired philosophy—enables us to cultivate that spe-cies for which Nietzsche writes, or any overhuman, transhuman,[19] and/or newly human species, and precisely in what that would consist are questions experimentally addressed along with and against Nietzsche in the preceding chapters. The tentative conclusion I think that does follow from what is traced here is that at least one of Nietzsche's aims seems to be the perform-ance of a certain taxis that seeks not only to rearrange parts that have ceased to perform their natural (or unnatural) functions but to call into question human limbation as such, or the process through which human boundaries have been determined and codified. Nietzsche conceives of human speciation as neither fixed and static (as Linnean conceptions would have it) nor sheerly the product of natural selection (as "ultra-Darwinists" believe) but a *potentially* deliberate experimentation with the characteristics and relationships that define us as "human" (and that differentiate us from non-human animals). In other words, conceived from a Nietzschean perspective, the human is the animal that explores and ranges across taxonomic borders. Blurring and bending the biological boundaries of human animality—paws, claws, jaws, and such, Nietzsche extends both the moral meanings and possible ways of being of human physiology.

Notes

1. Kaufmann and Hollingdale's translation; emphasis here and in the following two citations is mine. Unless otherwise noted, I use Kaufmann and Hollingdale's translations of GM and WP; Hollingdale's translation of D; Kaufmann's translations of BGE, GS, TI, and Z; and Arrowsmith's edition of UM.

2. Graham Parkes discusses related issues in ways that illuminate interesting similarities and differences in the works of Plato and Nietzsche in his *Composing the Soul: Reaches of Nietzsche's Psychology* (Chicago: University of Chicago Press, 1994), 215–225. Compare GS 304, in which Nietzsche contrasts "negative virtues," which negate and deny, with a morality that promotes doing something well in course of which "what does not belong to such a life drops off."

3. WP 808 as cited in Keith Ansell-Pearson, *Viroid Life* (London: Routledge, 1997), 121–122. I am indebted to Ansell-Pearson's work for furthering my understanding of Nietzsche's thoughts on speciation.

4. Sarah Kofman, *Nietzsche and Metaphor*, trans. Duncan Large (Palo Alto, Calif.: Stanford University Press, 1993).

5. Kofman, *Nietzsche and Metaphor*, 35.

6. Kofman, *Nietzsche and Metaphor*, 44.

7. See Kofman, *Nietzsche and Metaphor*, chapter 3 "The Forgetting of Metaphor."

8. See Kofman, *Nietzsche and Metaphor*, 25ff.

9. What is today described as "analytic philosophy" appears to have "discovered" a link between metaphor and cognition in recent years, but thus far the research on metaphor does not yet cross the so-called continental divide between philosophy that looks to Kant's critical philosophy as its origin and philosophy that traces its roots—if and when it recognizes that it too has roots—from Cartesian rationalism to Frege's theory of meaning and more recently to models of cognition supplied by cognitive science. Shared interest in the significance of metaphor ought to make possible a rapprochement between these different philosophical orientations. On metaphor, see, for example, George Lakoff

and Mark Johnson, *Philosophy in the Flesh: The Embodied Mind and Its Challenge to Western Thought* (New York: Basic Books, 1999); Eva Feder Kittay, *Metaphor: Its Cognitive Force and Linguistic Structure* (Oxford: Oxford University Press, 1987); and Paul Ricœur, *The Rule of Metaphor: Multi-Disciplinary Studies of the Creation of Meaning in Language*, trans. Robert Czerny (Toronto: University of Toronto Press, 1977).

10. See especially *Being and Time*, Division I, Part 5.

11. The metaphysical and ontological implications of interpretation are much more elaborately explored in Christoph Cox, *Nietzsche: Naturalism and Interpretation* (Berkeley: University of California Press, 1999). Cox's book is highly recommended for those wishing to further develop the ideas and themes introduced in this book.

12. This paragraph and the several that follow include revised portions of several paragraphs that appear in my "Between Mechanism and Teleology: Will to Power and Nietzsche's 'Gay' Science," forthcoming in *Nietzsche and Science*, ed. Gregory Moore and Thomas H. Brobjer (Aldershot, Hants, U.K.: Ashgate, 2003).

13. Wolfgang Müller-Lauter, "On Judging in a World of Becoming: A Reflection on the 'Great Change' in Nietzsche's Philosophy," in *Nietzsche, Theories of Knowledge, and Critical Theory*, ed. Babette E. Babich and Robert S. Cohen (Boston: Kluwer, 1999).

14. Müller-Lauter, "On Judging in a World of Becoming," 174.

15. On the topic of how Nietzsche appropriates the language of biology and medicine, see M. Pasley, "Nietzsche's Use of Medical Terms" in *Nietzsche: Imagery and Thought—A Collection of Essays*, ed. M. Pasley (Berkeley: University of California Press, 1978), 123–158; and Scott Podolsky and Alfred I. Tauber, "Nietzsche's Conception of Health: The Idealization of Struggle" in *Nietzsche, Epistemology, and Philosophy of Science*, ed. Babette E. Babich and Robert S. Cohen (Boston: Kluwer, 1999), 299–311.

16. Nietzsche uses the image of a stomach full of stones in the context of discussing education, conceived as stuffing one full of historical facts in *HL* 2.

17. And this sort of blindness should be contrasted with that of the mole, who is mentioned later in the same section in connection with the dwarf.

18. Note the contrast between this use of skin/encasing with the "Stoic hedgehog skin" described in *GS* 306.

19. For further exploration of transhuman possibilities, see Keith Ansell-Pearson, *Viroid Life* and his *Germinal Life: The Difference and Repetition of Deleuze* (London: Routledge, 1999).

~

Traces of the Beast:
Becoming Nietzsche,
Becoming Animal, and the
Figure of the Transhuman

Jami Weinstein

In this essay, I propose a historical foundation, rooted in Nietzsche's implementation of animal references, for the trajectory ending in the recent philosophic understandings of human and non-human animals.[1] The primary aim is to document the ways in which Nietzsche's menagerie has been drawn toward the future in contemporary theory. To illustrate this, the essay focuses on how modern theorists are indebted to Nietzsche for their understanding of animal and human ontologies, subjectivities, and bodies. This unfolds into a conception of human-animal relations that looks substantially different from the one Nietzsche originally held. It is abundantly clear that Nietzsche encouraged humans to live and not deny their animal instincts. But despite this view, he did not necessarily think that we should collapse the categories of human and animal into one comprehensive classification. Although Nietzsche made contradictory claims about these relations throughout his works, one abiding theme is that humans have greatly misjudged their status with regard to animals and nature. Hence, the third of the four great errors according to Nietzsche, is that man "placed himself in a false order of rank in relation to animals and nature." He asserted that, "[I]f we removed the effects of [this] error, we should also remove humanity, humanness, and 'human dignity'" (GS 115).[2] To develop this latter trans-humanist point to the fullest extent, contemporary theorists have launched a critique of the binary and hierarchical split between humans and animals and have extended their resulting more fluid ontological understanding of the human to incorporate animals.[3] Thus, the goal here is to track the traces of the beast in recent philosophy and elucidate the ultimate erosion of the boundaries between human and animal.[4]

Exploring the various creatures in Nietzsche's zoo and their intersection with humans has transformed our understanding of human experience/experiment and has fostered the overcoming of man he advocated.[5] I shall now show how this experimentalism with animal nature and, in turn, human nature, rhizomatically germinated in some of the many theorists profoundly influenced by Nietzsche's work. This study highlights the motif of *becoming animal* advanced by Deleuze and Guattari, which serves as the fulcrum upon which analysis of the works by Heidegger, Foucault, and Irigaray balance. The notion of becoming animal possesses the richness and profundity necessary to portray the ideas explored here as continuous with the Nietzschean project. For, in a sense, each of the theorists under consideration has had to become animal in order to achieve the novel perspectives for which her or his work is celebrated. By becoming animal, the agent engages in a praxis of experimentation; the strategy is to propel the subject beyond her humanity to experience an encounter with animal others and simultaneously unveil the beast within. Along this path, each has paused momentarily for a stint at becoming Nietzsche; each has experimented with, experienced, and formed assemblages with Nietzsche that have created new lines of flight. That process freed each of them from the grip of the enlightenment project long enough to breed becoming-animals and to spawn multiplicities of new perspectives on human subjectivity and animality. Consider first the already becoming-animal that is Nietzsche.

The Nietzschean Subject: Nietzsche's Own Becoming-Animal

In sketching his account of the human subject, Nietzsche extended two post-Enlightenment challenges to his readers: embrace "(1) the absolute loss of transcendence (God is dead); and (2) the dethroning of reason as man's most characteristic and cherished faculty."[6] One could claim that they each constituted a tine of the divining rod that ushered in the flows of trans-humanism and the work on animality at play in the work of Deleuze and Guattari.

Nietzsche was trying to disentangle himself from the paradigm of the modern subject still holding sway; this is the vision of the subject as a unified, static, rational, self-identical, and interior with mental substance free from instinct, animality, flux, exteriority, and bodily nature. This classic paradigm defined the human in negation to other animals and distanced the human being from its animal being. It was this very model that justified the rejection of the evolutionary schema that located human being as continuous with animal being. Hence, Nietzsche endorsed evolutionary theory's central tenet, often insisting upon animal traces in human beings, while he rejected the teleological component of natural selection that he believed placed humans atop the hierarchy as natural perfections. For him, there was no fixed human being or even a set course of human becoming; instead, he focused his attention on human *becomings*. Schrift notes the resemblance between Nietzsche and Deleuze on teleology: "whereas evolutionary language focuses our attention on the beginning and endpoint of a process in a way that obscures the passage between them, the language of compound becoming draws our attention to what happens *between* these ever-receding endpoints. Becomings take place *between* poles; they are the in-betweens that pass only and always along a middle without origin or destination."[7]

Deleuze and Guattari offer a faithful Nietzschean reading (with a touch of Spinoza thrown in for good measure) of the idea of transcendence as "*what man does*; or, rather, has never yet done but *could do*. 'Man is something that has to be surpassed.'"[8] They claim "we know nothing about a body until we know what it can do, in other words, what its affects are, how they can or cannot enter into composition with other affects, with the affects of another body."[9] Emphasis on *doing* is further evident when Nietzsche mocked, "'I,' you say, and are proud of the word. But greater is that in which you do not wish to have faith—your body and its great reason: that does not say "I," but does 'I'" (Z:1 "On the Despisers of the Body"). Most famously, he rebuked the metaphysics of substance: "there is no 'being' behind doing, effecting, becoming; 'the doer' is merely a fiction added to the deed—the deed is everything" (GM I:13). These references all point to a general theory of the material subject founded on praxis and becoming, which affects a radical deterritorialization of the modern subject.

If it could be said that Deleuze has one underlying theme in his work, perhaps it is his emphasis on praxis. He seeks to "invent an experimentalism, which, instead of asking for conditions of possible experience, would look for the conditions under which something new, as yet unthought, arises."[10] Undoubtedly, this experimentalism is Humean in character, but it also most vividly heralds the influence of Nietzsche's bestiary and the method under which Deleuze and Guattari elect to engage it. The enchanting interplay of creatures appearing and often multiply re-entering Nietzsche's work call upon us to re-envision what we habitually call human nature and human experience. Their presence is an appeal for us to attend to issues of our ontology by emphasizing becoming over being, uncovering the flux and impermanence of the self, elevating the status of our bodily nature, rethinking the status of humankind with respect to animals, meting out new relationships between and conceptions of human beings and nature, and obtaining a more profound insight into our psychology and emotions. It is also a plea to reconfigure the many problems that have plagued philosophy in domains such as metaphysics, epistemology, and ethics. In short, the aim is to unleash the previously unforeseen, to give birth to the novel, through experiment/experience.

By employing animal imagery, Nietzsche was certainly building a case for a materialist view of the self. If humans are animals and not defined in opposition to them, a wholesale recasting of human ontology needs to be executed: "Nietzsche, who was quite aware of the permeability of the division [between Man and nature], saw a need to 'consider where the beast ends and the man begins.'"[11] In Zarathustra's cryptic words, "man is a rope, tied between beast and overman" (Z:P 4). By this, Nietzsche intended that the human is the essential bridge between the animal and the over- (trans-) human or, at the very least, an integral link in the chain. It is as if Nietzsche presaged the work of Deleuze and Guattari when he asserted that in order to get beyond humanism, we must uphold our elemental association to animals, we must become animal. It is thus that Deleuze and Guattari's notion of becoming animal summons Nietzsche to the next level; in order not to be encaged by the Enlightenment, we must extrapolate upon Nietzsche's ontological foundations.

Thus we arrive at a robustly *human* trans-humanism to which Nietzsche alluded in is figure of the Übermensch. But caution must be exercised, for Nietzsche himself would have fervently opposed an utter blurring of the boundaries of humans and animals. Despite countless intersections peppered throughout his work, Nietzsche would no more advocate placing animals on an equal plane with humans than he would sanction a blanket preference for animals over humans. Nevertheless, Deleuze and Guattari do advance the former ontology in their conceptualization of becoming-animal. Revisiting Nietzsche from this renewed vantage point, Deleuze and Guattari find novel lines, extensions, dynamics, relations, ontologies, traces, possibilities, and openings that help locate the efforts of the other theorists included in this study. Before wandering into the territory of the post-Nietzschean tropes of animality, humanity, and their intersection, we should first unpack the crucial concept of becoming-animal.

Deleuze and Guattari's Becoming-Animal

By way of introduction, allow me to cull the essential features of becoming as rendered by Deleuze and Guattari themselves in A *Thousand Plateaus*:

> A becoming is not a correspondence between relations. But neither is it a resemblance, an imitation, or, at the limit, an identification. . . . [Becomings] are perfectly real. . . . [I]t is clear that the human being does not "really" become an animal any more than the animal "really" becomes something else. Becoming produces nothing other than itself. . . . [A] becoming lacks a subject distinct from itself. . . . [B]ecoming is not an evolution. . . . [B]ecoming is involutionary, involution is creative. . . . Becoming is a verb with a consistency all its own; it does not reduce to, or lead back to, "appearing," "being," "equaling," or "producing."[12]

It is important that Deleuze and Guattari do not simply erect the usual binary clash between being and becoming. They direct us to slip altogether beyond the dualism and beyond teleological interpretations. Becoming always includes being in that it enters a variety of states of being on its nomadic path of continual experimentation. There is nothing other than becoming according to their blueprint, and becoming only gives rise to itself, to more becoming. The point of this process of becoming is not to transform into another pure entity or being but rather to become other and ultimately become imperceptible. For example, in becoming animal, we are not trying to achieve a state of pure animality but rather we are asymptotically navigating toward some sort of a crossbreed that mingles animal with human. Deleuze and Guattari's own model of becoming dog is the following:

> [H]ow [should we do this]? This will not involve imitating a dog, nor an analogy of relations. I must succeed in endowing the parts of my body with relations of speeds and slownesses that will make it become dog, in an original assemblage proceeding neither by resemblance nor by analogy. For I cannot become dog without the dog itself becoming something else. . . . [E]lements will enter into a new relation, resulting in the affect or becoming I seek. . . . [One should not] compare two organs but place elements or materials in a relation that uproots the organ from its specificity, making it "become" with the other organ.[13]

Thus, "there is a reality to becoming-animal, even though one does not in reality become animal."[14] The reality is that there is a certain animality, "*an inhumanity experienced in the body as such.*"[15] Therein lies the key—there must be a shared experience/experiment such that the difference between the beings reads as imperceptible.

It is only in this way that humans can become trans-human and in doing so paradoxically maximize human potential. In any becoming, including becoming human, the self is deterritorialized and, in the case of humans, dehumanized. The plateau reached from the deterritorialization of becoming human can be depicted as "a new notion of freedom: not the freedom of a human self who can be disengaged from the force of life, but a freedom gained by no longer seeing ourselves as a point of view detached from life. We become *free from the human*, open to the event of becoming."[16] Accordingly, becoming animal is not mimetic. It is not becoming *like* an animal. It is becoming some novel hybrid, always a heterogeneous multiplicity without an origin or genesis. As multiplicity is constitutive to animal Being, in becoming animal, the human is embedded in a dynamic connection with multiplicity. This relation becoming-animal is an assemblage, since "becomings, and especially becoming-animal, involve a mediating third term, a relation to something else, neither animal nor human, through which the subject enters into connections with the animal."[17] Deleuze and Guattari accordingly proclaim: "[B]ecoming and multiplicity are the same thing. [I]ts variations and dimensions are immanent to it."[18]

Deleuze and Guattari open up the possibility of many types of becoming that, according to their schema, all flow toward a becoming-imperceptible of the human. The becoming through which all becomings must pass to arrive there, they argue, is becoming woman. It is worth mentioning at this stage that all trans-human subjects began the process of becoming-other by first performing a molecular becoming-woman. All becomings are already molecular. By this, they intend becoming as a process that takes place at the level of shared particles within a dynamic zone of nearness to the object of becoming. In this zone, relationships of movement and rest, speeds and slownesses, are parsed out and transmuted. This experience is pitted against the molar, which reads more like the traditional notions of self and identity. In other words, the molar woman must still become woman, blacks must become black, Jews must become Jewish. This entails the controversial claim that "[b]ecoming-woman necessarily affects men as much as women."[19]

What makes this schema so relevant to the present study is that it transports Nietzsche beyond Nietzsche; the self emerging from this Deleuze-Guattarian picture "is only a threshold, a door, a becoming between two multiplicities. . . . [a] fiber stretched from a human to an animal, from a human or an animal to molecules, from molecules to particles, and so on to the imperceptible. Every fiber is a Universe fiber. A fiber strung across borderlines constitutes a line of flight or of deterritorialization."[20] The fiber recalls Nietzsche's rope, and the human it represents, now extrapolated and unsedimented, liberated and rhizomatic, nomadic, imperceptible, beyond (trans-) human, a Body without Organs. But, to achieve this result, we do not simply become animal, we must "engage in an animal relation with animals."[21]

Becoming-animal is real and thus should never be taken as metaphor; that tack simply reduces becoming to imitation or analogy, which was ruled out above. Like all becomings-other, the other should be "taken in its radical immanence as a field of forces, a quantity of speed and intensity."[22] Instead, human experience/experiment commingles with that of animal-becoming to generate a new organization of perspective. In other words, human Being opens up to animal Being. This is not entirely voluntary and, once performed or initiated, it is irreversible:

> [T]hese becomings are not simply a matter of choice, not simply a decision, but always involve a substantial remaking of the subject, a major risk to the subject's integration and social functioning. One cannot become-animal at will and then cease and function normally. It is not something that can be put on or taken off at will like a cloak or an activity.[23]

One will never be the same once on the track to becoming animal, or becoming other more generally.

The schizophrenic, nomadic body proposed by Deleuze and Guattari, what Braidotti describes as "enfleshed materialism," issues from the novel perspective on human and animal ontology developed from Nietzsche's critique of the modern idea of the self and his musings on animality and humanity. The Body without Organs is situated well within the Nietzschean corpus as witnessed in the remark that, in respect to the Nietzschean body,

> [T]here is no quantity of reality, for all reality is already a quantity of force. There are nothing but quantities of force "in a relation of tension" between one another [WP 635]. What defines a body is this relation between dominating and dominated forces. Whether chemical, biological, social, or political, every relation of forces constitutes a body. Composed of a plurality of irreducible forces, the body is a mul-

tiple phenomenon; its unity is that of a multiple phenomenon, "the unity of domination."[24]

This emphasis on multiplicity promotes a more accurate ontological perspective of the body than that of the traditional enlightenment view, because
human animals live in symbiosis with thousands of anaerobic bacteria—600
species in our mouths that neutralize the toxins all plants produce to ward
off their enemies, 400 species in our intestines, without which we could not
digest and absorb the food we ingest. The number of microbes that colonize
our bodies exceeds the number of cells in our bodies by up to a hundredfold.[25]
Given the biological reality that without the constant dynamic interaction
between human bodies and the autonomous bodies of other living organisms
human bodies would not survive, the economy of the independent, unitary,
fixed, stable, whole body (or animal) becomes a fantasy (or a fiction of science). It is thus that symbiosis and trans-species interdependence emerge as
the reality of human being so much so that animals cannot be deemed properly other.

Becomings-Nietzsche, Becomings-Animal

As indicated above, the essential feature of becomings-other, and in particular of becoming-animal, is the emergence of novel perspectives. In the case of
the commingling of animal and human intensities, these novel assemblages
encourage us to generally refigure human and animal ontologies and to recast
the human subject. The Nietzschean project on many levels appears to be an
exercise of becoming-animal. Deleuze and Guattari's experimentation with
Nietzsche and his conceptions of the animal and the human, their "becoming Nietzsche," as it were, has opened up lines of flight that have provided
the fodder for the present analysis of Heidegger, Foucault, and Irigaray. Each
of these theorists performs a becoming-Nietzsche en route to becoming-animal. In what follows, I pinpoint their novel articulations of human and animal ontologies (their becomings-animal) and the ways in which these
articulations might have been implicitly heralded by a previous experimentation with, or becoming, Nietzsche.

Heidegger

It is perhaps strange to include Heidegger among the theorists said to be participating in becoming-animal, because among the others under consider-

ation here he had the most restrictive scope of animality; his contribution to fleshing out Nietzsche's becoming-animal might actually lie more in the tensions and failures of his project than in its affirmative conclusions. However, his four-volume study of Nietzsche's work certainly attests to his dogged experimentation with Nietzsche. And his becoming Nietzsche in this manner did help to issue new interpretive possibilities of the human experiment and a large-scale refiguration of human ontology.

In *The Fundamental Concepts of Metaphysics: World, Finitude, Solitude*, Heidegger struggles to locate the animal somewhere between two poles of Being: that of non-living material entities and that of Dasein. The schema he advocates holds that "the stone is worldless, the animal is poor in world, man is world-forming."[26] So what is the character of animal essence? Heidegger claims that the animal:

> somehow possesses less . . . in respect of what is accessible to it, of whatever as an animal it can deal with, of whatever it can be affected by as an animal, of whatever it can relate to as living beings. Less as against more, namely as against the richness of all those relationships that human Dasein has at its disposal.[27]

Briefly put, animals are in deprivation or lack of world. They possess 'world,' but only in the mode of *not-having*. They have the possibility of world, unlike a stone, but cannot access beings in the world as being. They are not worldless but rather are world impoverished. But, Heidegger cautions, "this comparison between man and animal . . . allows no evaluative ranking or assessment with respect to completeness or incompleteness. . . . However ready we are to rank man as a higher being with respect to the animal, such an assessment is deeply questionable. . . . May we talk of a 'higher' and a 'lower' at all in the realm of the essential?"[28] Nietzsche had already warned us against these sorts of normative hierarchical arrangements. Similarly, Deleuze and Guattari make it abundantly evident that all ontological planes, all becomings, were equal to all others insofar as they were all temporary assemblages, multiplicities without originariness.

The key to unlocking the Heideggerian storehouse of human Being, to forming world, is language, which many hold that animals conspicuously lack. If the many are correct, this entails that animals do not possess Being, at least not in its full spectrum. Heidegger states, "Where there is no language, as in the being of stone, plant, and animal, there is also no openness either of that which is not and of the empty."[29] Another essential difference between human and animal rests on Dasein's capacity to stand outside itself, to be ecstatic, and to open up the space of the world to itself. This is a brand of trans-humanism; the human is, by virtue of its humanity, beyond or out-side humanity. Lingis points to the paradoxical nature of this mode of Being; it is "an ex-sistence that is simultaneously a transcendence toward the being of the world and toward the nothingness of death, a world that is simultane-ously the array of possibility and the immanence of impossibility."[30] Heideg-ger in fact demarcates three discrete types of death depending on the nature of the being experiencing it. His tripartite schema places Dasein either authentically being toward death or inauthentically undergoing demise, while animals simply perish, they physiologically cease.[31] Once again, the human emerges as essentially different from animals and as apart from ani-mal nature. For even in its physiological end, Dasein never perishes.

Ultimately Heidegger acknowledges that "this characterization of animal-ity . . . is not a genuine one, not drawn from animality itself and maintained within the limit of animality, since the character of poverty of world is being conceived by comparison with man. It is only from the human perspective that the animal is poor with respect to world, yet animal being in itself is not in deprivation of world."[32] By his own admission, then, animal essence remained problematic within his anthropocentric corpus. His question of whether it is coherent to even ascribe the thesis of world poverty to animals from the perspective of animals qua animals should give us all pause. Further, though his theory allows that we not only can but that it is constitutive of Dasein to be able to "transpose" ourselves into other Dasein, we cannot fully do this with animals. The intersubjective character inherent in Dasein thus does not reach the level of our animality. Nonetheless, the inquiry does pro-duce a more profound account of the fundamental Being of Dasein as an ecstatic being-toward-death, in possession of language, and world-forming. This shift in the conception of the subject to an inherently intersubjective Being that is always already projected beyond itself certainly demonstrates that he has been freed his becoming-Nietzsche to arrive at a trans-human picture of subjectivity; he has thought the unthought—Being—however imperfect his account remains.

Because Heidegger's human Being still flows through a negation to ani-mality, he fails to escape the anthropocentrism plaguing the metaphysics from which his project evoked its future. Perhaps by superimposing becoming animal onto his work, we could move to interpret world poverty as alterity rather than lack and elude the trap. Doing so would decenter the inherent humanism in his theory. Heidegger himself hints at this possibility in the last section, in which he suggests that perhaps animals just have *other* worlds. If we follow his lead, we might be inclined to elevate the status of his warning against erecting a normative hierarchy of essences and place animal qua animal on par with human qua human, as Deleuze and Guattari promote. Heidegger's becoming animal could thus engender an even richer deterritorialization of human Being.

Foucault

The traces of the beast in Foucault's corpus lie in his use of Nietzsche's genealogies of the concept of humanity. Foucault holds that "[b]efore the end of the 18th century, man did not exist. . . . He is a quite recent creature, . . . fabricated. . . . [L]ess than two hundred years ago . . . there was no epistemological consciousness of man as such."[33] This advances his theory that the species man qua man as an epistemological and scientific category, in contrast to other animals, was bred at that time. Foucault's model of animality, or the practice of superimposing the animal onto certain human bodies, follows from his treatment of biopower and its relation to the production of the subject. Biopower is the primary disciplinary and regulatory instrument of institutions; it seeks to control people and bodies through discourses developed to classify and paradoxically multiply identities. Institutions are erected to attend to the business of describing and analyzing. The concept of the normal subject emerges as a result of the efforts of these technologies of signification, which steadfastly monitor and discipline bodies through and by these regulatory regimes and institutions. The norm does not emerge alone, however. Determinations of the abnormal emerge simultaneously with the naming and classification of the normal. Biopower thus has the effect of creating identities and truths. It constructs tropes of the normal while it identifies, formulates, organizes, and then seeks to suppress the multiple abnormalities or deviances that are concomitantly spawned. Animality is produced through the same discourses of power, regulatory regimes, and institutions that seek to insure that rationality continues to be upheld as the sine qua non of human being.

In trying to retrace Nietzsche's bestial disruptions through Foucault, we are drawn to the passages in *Madness and Civilization* that vividly evoke the historically entrenched relationship between madness and animality. In it, we find that "animality . . . reveals the dark rage, the sterile madness that lie in men's hearts"[34] and that, "[t]he animality that rages in madness dispossesses man of what is specifically human in him."[35] Madness was thus "an animal with strange mechanisms, a bestiality from which man had long been suppressed."[36] It was the deeply entrenched belief that people deemed mentally ill were more like animals than humans that justified centuries of mistreatment and inequities. Foucault notes that "[t]he model of animality prevailed in the asylums and gave them their cagelike aspect, their look of the menagerie. At the hospital of Nantes, the menagerie appears to consist of individual cages for wild beasts."[37] Configured in this way, the becoming-animal associated with madness neglects to provide openings to novel subjectivities; rather it absolves the crimes against humanity committed by those who control the institutions and disciplinary regimes. It is here that Foucault puts his finger on the pulse of becoming-animal in the transformative sense: we must become aware of and strive to remove the element of domination that figures in this schema of animality. For, he claims, we can never escape the discursive-productive power immanent to all relations. The best hope is to reconfigure the dynamic such that we sanction the minimal possible quotient of hegemonic domination. In metamorphosizing and reterritorializing the human in conjunction with so many dehumanized, animalized others throughout his work (the prisoner, the medical patient, the homosexual, the mentally ill), Foucault uncovers a novel trans-human species. He submits that "madness did not disclose a mechanism, but revealed a liberty raging in the monstrous forms of animality."[38] Thus Foucault begins his transcendence of the epistemological man, the rational animal, through a becoming-animal that undermines the anthropocentric, ahistorical, privileged positionality of the view of humanity previously advanced.

Irigaray

One final departure from the Nietzschean bestiary remains. In *Marine Lover of Friedrich Nietzsche*, Irigaray experiments with Nietzsche in the context of a critique of his silence on woman. She dubbed it "a book not on Nietzsche, but with Nietzsche."[39] Under the guise of a transformative mimesis, she enters a zone of proximity with Nietzsche in which she draws herself as the figure of his lover and intimately engages his work in a dialogue about what remains unrepresented. She listens to his silence and from it tries construct a representation of the female subject she calls *le féminin*. Her fundamental critique is that Nietzsche privileged sameness and repetition over difference by maintaining the traditional status of woman as other to the male subject. Correspondingly, she faults him for not escaping the binary structures of the metaphysics he alleged to repudiate. Her subject, *le féminin*, is different from the feminine in that it does not operate within the matrix of the human with its attendant binary masculine-feminine; it is the unthinkable feminine *subject*, not the feminine *other* to the masculine subject. Thus, *le féminin* is a trope of trans-humanity. This female subject, her vision of the trans-human, is "already two but not divisible into one(s)."[40] She counsels that though "we haven't been taught, nor allowed, to express multiplicity,"[41] we should not allow ourselves to be "fixed, stabilized, immobilized."[42] Recall that Deleuze and Guattari, following Nietzsche, also advocate a multiplicity of the subject.

Irigaray's work epitomizes the becoming-woman that undergirds all other becoming-others, including becoming-animal.[43] She strives to speak the deterritorialization of the human, to, "[f]ree the subject woman from the subjugated position of the other (and) express a 'different difference,' a pure difference released from the hegemonic framework of oppositional binary thinking."[44] Her radical version of subjectivity is minimally carved out by the thirty-odd animal references in *Marine Lover*. While Nietzsche's Zarathustra has animal companions that are either decidedly terrestrial or airborne, Irigaray conjures the more fluid aquatic beasts. Asking Nietzsche, "Are you a fish or eagle . . . when you announce the decline of man? Do you seek to sink or climb? Flow out or fly up?" she wonders whether his thought embodies fluid animalic becomings or the universalist "eagle-eye" perspective of the bird of prey.[45] Observing that "as companion [Zarathustra] never chose a sea creature. Camel, snake, lion, eagle, and doves, monkey and ass . . . Yes. But no to anything that moves in the water. Why this persistent wish for legs, or wings? And never gills?"[46] she reiterates the glaring lack of beasts of flux accompanying Nietzsche's vision of the human subject. Nietzsche's investment in land rovers paralleled his lack of true feminine subjectivity, which, Irigaray hints, is founded on a material fluidity.

Irigaray asserts that in order to conceptualize and articulate an autonomous specific feminine subject, we must step outside the human and embrace our animality. She claims this not because she affirms the classical configuration of the essence of woman as closer to nature, as animal,[47] but rather because she thinks the very notion of humanity entails the traditional metaphysical binary masculine subject/feminine other. For this reason, Irigaray is ambivalent about Nietzsche's invocation of the figure of Dionysus. Her Dionysus is "clad in animal skin, instead of divine appearance";[48] he is "put to death as (both) animal (and) god."[49] Nevertheless, whereas he embodies desire and represents the subject that reunites the bodily with the conceptual, he is at best an adumbration of the feminine. He continues to appropriate woman as other and thus fortifies the metaphysical binary subject/object. Though Dionysus "embraces the becoming that dissolves stable forms, he wants to be that becoming. He thus displaces the totalization of masculine subjectivity to the totalization of becoming."[50] Despite the ultimate failure of Dionysus to reap the true feminine subjectivity, he remains a promising figure in that his desirous material subjectivity offers a possible portal to le féminin.

Through her becoming-Nietzsche as becoming-woman, Irigaray welcomes a becoming-animal. Her subject, le féminin, is situated outside the human, outside the metaphysical binary rubric man-woman that has heretofore constituted humanity. Embarking on her line of flight, she endeavors to think the unthought, perhaps even the impossible. She strives to provide the building blocks of le féminin, who has remained for so long linguistically, symbolically, materially, and conceptually homeless. By most accounts, she has merely cleared a via negativa to her trans-human figure, but her identification and critique of the structures that prevent us from accessing feminine Being has been integral to the feminist project of defining the specific and autonomous female subject.

Conclusion

Each of the theorists of this study has dared to unveil the beast within her or his version of the human subject; each has released the line of flight known as becoming animal. All of them have as a point of departure an experimentation, a commingling of intensities, with Nietzsche. And along the way to becoming animal, each has, at least momentarily, paused to reflect on his or her own becoming-Nietzsche. In the case of Deleuze and Guattari, becoming Nietzsche means embodying and discovering the creative possibilities of becoming. For Heidegger, it is summoning forth the post-metaphysical future of historically forgotten Being. For Foucault, it manifests in his shift in thinking about the nature of power and its influence on human bodies. And for Irigaray, it is the attempt to think the historical silence, le féminin. All four trans-human figures issuing from this sojourn into becoming Nietzsche—the nomadic subject, Dasein, the genealogical subject, and le féminin—require the additional performance of a becoming-animal to reach their tectonic profundity, to which the Nietzschean meditations on animality and human nature certainly were a dress rehearsal. Like Nietzsche, each of the theorists of this study repudiates the metaphysics of substance; each ventures to replace traditional versions of the hegemonic subject (the rational animal) with a decentered, material, trans-human subject, which included in some sense both human and non-human animal intersubjectivity.

One last consideration should give us pause before concluding. David Wood provocatively stresses that "there are no animals 'as such,' rather [a list of] extraordinary variety."[51] If he is right, can we coherently talk about becoming animal in a non-specific way? Perhaps we can take "animal" to represent something like "other," insofar as the construction of an other is a form of dehumanization that can manifest as an "animaling." If interpreted in this manner, this extraordinarily varied list could include such minoritarian subjectivities as women, "the native," "the negro," "the poor," "the pervert," "the Jew," "the insane," etc., each of which has been historically perceived as animal. Consequently, the recognition of the animal as multiple and an acknowledgment that we are always in a dynamic relation to animals under the guise of our becoming animal bestows life to the trans-human with its concomitant multiplicity and flux. Deleuze concurs when he writes that "what is involved is no longer the affirmation of a single substance, but rather the laying out of a *common plane of immanence* on which all bodies, all minds, and all individuals are situated."[52] This plane includes both animals and humans. Because these becomings deterritorialize both human and animal subjectivities in the process, we must develop a new language with which, and a new people with whom, we can articulate this interspecies intersubjective world. As we have seen, Irigaray has not yet completed her quest to articulate *le féminin* because she still lacks the appropriate non-metaphysical language in which to do so. She also recognizes that if such a figure were to be drawn, the risk to the organizational structures of language and society might be colossal. Similarly, in wondering about the consequences for Dasein in "transposing" itself into animal (becoming animal), Heidegger recognizes this problem and thus remarks, "*we find ourselves forced to adopt another language because of a fundamental transformation of existence.*"[53] Deleuze, unconcerned about the risk of enacting becomings, counsels that we actively undertake "to create a foreign language within our language to be spoken by a people that does not yet exist."[54] Perhaps, if nothing else, this essay has confirmed that we have already begun the process of populating the trans-human world with these multilingual figures.

Notes

1. Hereafter referred to as "human" and "animal."

2. I consulted the following English translations of Nietzsche's works: *The Will to Power*, trans. Walter Kaufmann and R.J. Hollingdale (New York: Vintage Books, 1968); *The Gay Science*, trans. Walter Kaufmann (New York: Vintage Books, 1974); *The Portable*

Nietzsche, ed. and trans. Walter Kaufmann (New York: Penguin Books, 1982); *On The Genealogy of Morals* and *Ecce Homo*, trans. Walter Kaufmann (New York: Vintage Books, 1989).

3. Many terms can evoke transcending the human: post-human, anti-human, meta-human, trans-human, overman, superman, and *Übermensch*. In keeping with the numerous interpretations that figure the *Übermensch* as becoming, a process, not a super-subject, not a higher kind of man in (ultra-)Darwinistic evolutionary fashion, I opt for trans-human.

4. *Editor's Note*: Not unlike the self-safari Jacques Derrida has recently thematized: "No one has ever denied the animal this capacity to track itself, to trace itself or retrace a path of itself," which is all the more challenging philosophically, because "an animal's signature might yet be able to erase or cover its traces"; "The Animal That Therefore I Am (More to Follow)," *Critical Inquiry* 28 (Winter 2002): 417, 401.

5. It is useful to underscore that in French, the word for experiment is *expérience*. The dual register of this term puts a Deleuzian spin on the notion of human experience that is helpful when thinking about human ontology. If we characterize "human experience" more like "human experiment," perhaps it could free us from some of the anthropocentric and static portraits of being and engender freer lines of flight, more fruitful becomings.

6. Joan Stambaugh, *The Other Nietzsche* (Albany: State University of New York Press, 1994), 3.

7. Alan D. Schrift, *Nietzsche's French Legacy: A Genealogy of Poststructuralism* (New York: Routledge, 1995), 70. Also see Gilles Deleuze and Félix Guattari, *A Thousand Plateaus: Capitalism and Schizophrenia*, trans. Brian Massumi (Minneapolis: University of Minnesota Press, 1987), 256–257; hereafter *ATP*.

8. Joan Stambaugh, *The Other Nietzsche*, 4.

9. *ATP*, 256–257.

10. John Rajchman, *The Deleuze Connections* (Cambridge, Mass.: MIT Press, 2000), 17.

11. Jennifer Ham, "Taming the Beast: Animality in Wedekind and Nietzsche," in *Animal Acts*, ed. Jennifer Ham and Matthew Senior (New York: Routledge, 1997), 156.

12. *ATP*, 237–239.

13. *ATP*, 258–259.

14. *ATP*, 273.

15. *ATP*, 273, italics original.

16. Claire Colebrook, *Gilles Deleuze* (London: Routledge, 2002), 129.

17. Elizabeth Grosz, *Volatile Bodies: Toward a Corporeal Feminism* (Bloomington: Indiana University Press, 1994), 174.

18. *ATP*, 249.

19. Many feminists question this, citing that Deleuze and Guattari do not make it clear that individual becomings-woman are cast in different lights insofar as there is a molar gender difference prior to becoming. Notice, too, that there is no becoming-man on their map because it is what they call majoritarian, or molar in the most profound sense. Since

all becomings are molecular—minoritarian—and becoming-other, becoming-man is a logical impossibility. (See *ATP*, 291–292.)

20. *ATP*, 249.

21. Rosi Braidotti, *Metamorphoses: Towards a Materialist Theory of Becoming* (Cambridge: Polity, 2002), 121.

22. Braidotti, *Metamorphoses*, 126.

23. Grosz, *Volatile Bodies*, 174.

24. Gilles Deleuze, "Active and Reactive," in *The New Nietzsche: Contemporary Styles of Interpretation*, ed. David B. Allison (Cambridge, Mass.: MIT Press, 1992), 80f.

25. Alphonso Lingis "Satyrs and Centaurs: Miscegenation and the Master Race," in *Why Nietzsche Still?*, ed. Alan D. Schrift (Berkeley: University of California Press, 2000), 167.

26. Martin Heidegger, *The Fundamental Concepts of Metaphysics: World, Finitude, Solitude*, trans. William McNeill and Nicholas Walker (Bloomington: Indiana University Press, 1995), II:3, 185. Hereafter *FC*.

27. *FC* II:3 §46, 193.

28. *FC* II:3 §46, 194.

29. Martin Heidegger, "The Origin of the Work of Art," in *Poetry, Language, Thought*, trans. Albert Hofstadter (New York: Harper Colophon Books, 1971),7 3.

30. Alphonso Lingis, *Foreign Bodies* (New York: Routledge, 1994), 217.

31. Martin Heidegger, *Being and Time: A Translation of Sein und Zeit*, trans. Joan Stambaugh (Albany: State University of New York Press, 1996), II.1 §49, 229.

32. *FC* II:3 §63, 270–271.

33. Michel Foucault, *The Order of Things: An Archaeology of the Human Sciences, A Translation of Les Mots et les choses*, ed. R. D. Laing, (New York: Vintage Books, 1973), 308.

34. Michel Foucault, *Madness and Civilization: A History of Insanity in the Age of Reason* (New York: Vintage Books, 1973), 21.

35. Foucault, *Madness and Civilization*, 74.

36. Foucault, *Madness and Civilization*, 70.

37. Foucault, *Madness and Civilization*, 72f.

38. Foucault, *Madness and Civilization*, 83.

39. Irigaray as cited in Tamsin Lorraine, *Irigaray and Deleuze: Experiments in Visceral Philosophy* (Ithaca, N.Y.: Cornell University Press, 1999), 49.

40. Luce Irigaray, *This Sex Which Is Not One*, trans. Catherine Porter (Ithaca, N.Y.: Cornell University Press, 1985), 24.

41. Irigaray, *This Sex Which Is Not One*, 210.

42. Irigaray, *This Sex Which Is Not One*, 216.

43. For brevity's sake, I refrain from foregrounding Irigaray's critique of becoming-woman except to mention that, according to her economy of sexual difference, since it can be practiced equally by molar men and women, becoming-woman cements the already entrenched absence of woman as an organism. It fails to recognize the historical

and cultural situation of women and the difficulty of locating a female subject. Deleuze and Guattari do attempt to address this in *ATP*, 276 but feminists such as Irigaray remain skeptical about the potential benefits of their strategy.

44. Rosi Braidotti, "Of Bugs and Women: Irigaray and Deleuze on the Becoming-Woman," in *Engaging with Irigaray*, ed. Carolyn Burke, Naomi Shor, and Margaret Whitford (New York: Columbia University Press, 1994), 112.

45. Luce Irigaray, *Marine Lover of Friedrich Nietzsche*, trans. Gillian C. Gill (New York: Columbia University Press, 1991), 13; see also 46, 48, 62, 146.

46. Irigaray, *Marine Lover*, 13.

47. In *Marine Lover*, Irigaray explores this through Artemis, who "subsists between the animal and the divine kingdoms," and because she lacks "an identity of her own, [is] kept within ambiguity" (153); "she is abandoned to the animal kingdom: wild, indomitable nature, excluded" (157).

48. Irigaray, *Marine Lover*, 129.

49. Irigaray, *Marine Lover*, 131.

50. Tamsin Lorraine, *Irigaray and Deleuze: Experiments in Visceral Philosophy* (Ithaca, N.Y.: Cornell University Press, 1999), 56.

51. David Wood, "*Comment ne pas Manger*—Deconstruction and Humanism," in *Animal Others: On Ethics, Ontology and Animal Life*, ed. H. Peter Steeves (Albany: State University of New York Press, 1999), 29.

52. Gilles Deleuze, *Spinoza: Practical Philosophy*, trans. Robert Hurley (San Francisco: City Lights Books, 1988), 122.

53. *FC* II:3 §49, 203.

54. Proust via Deleuze, as quoted in Rajchman, *The Deleuze Connections*, 10.

Sources for the Metamorphoses: The Ages of Man and the Three Metamorphoses of the Spirit

Richard Perkins

He must also be a consummate animal who wishes to become a consummate man.

(KSA 10:4[94])[1]

"What is the ape to man?" chides Zarathustra, trying to get a point across to the thronging crowd gathering in the marketplace. "What is the ape to man? A laughingstock or a painful embarrassment" (Z:P 3). Here we have a proportional analogy, a comparison owing its resonance to Heraclitus as well as to Darwin, which pictures superhuman nature as being as much superior to humanity as humankind is to its prehistoric simian ancestors.[2] As an associative counterpoint to the superman, the ape is an interesting contrast, especially when we take Zarathustra's continuing remarks into consideration—"Once you were apes, and even now man is more ape than any ape"—a sad verdict anticipated at *HH* I 247. It entertains a curious possibility involving a "circular orbit" shaping human history: "Perhaps humanity as a whole is merely a phase in the evolutionary development of a certain animal species of limited duration: so that man once originated in the ape and will again return to the ape, while no one will be around to take any interest at all in this strange comic conclusion." As the aphorism ends, Nietzsche strikes a more positive note regarding this forecast: "Precisely because we can envision this prospect, we might possibly be in a position to avert it." As

319

Nietzsche famously insists in *Beyond Good and Evil*, the human being is an as-yet-undetermined animal. How we are to end up remains uncertain. One possibility is that we will revert to the ape. The other is that we will consciously avert this outcome. There is a choice to be made.

Since *ape* is to *man* as *man* is to *superman*, perhaps we might be able to trade on the variance between "ape" and "man" to gauge the distance separating "man" and "superman." A note dating to late 1880 suggests a convenient way to measure and to assess these increments, taking *man*, the middle term in the analogy, as a pivot possibility that can either turn, through regressive descent, into a semi-human laughingstock and embarrassment or, through progressive ascent, into a superhuman redeemer and creator who gives meaning to existence. Nietzsche made the following short entry in a notebook: "'At 40 years one is a camel, at 70 an ape'—Spaniard" (*KSA* 9:7[4]). His cryptic remark is an allusion to Schopenhauer's most beloved author, Baltasar Gracián, a Spanish prose writer and Jesuit priest who, in his *Oráculo Manual*, divides human existence into seven zoomorphic stages: "At twenty years we are peacocks, at thirty, lions, at forty, camels, at fifty, serpents, at sixty, dogs, at seventy, apes, and at eighty, nothing at all."[3] Two stages interest Nietzsche. He ignores all the rest, focusing on decisive turning points in our lives when we become servile camels and senile apes, leaving out the other mutations. His selective allusion suggests familiarity with an earlier narrative tradition serving Gracián as an immediate source and extending back into ancient Hellenic, Aesopic, and Haggadic materials. Gracián points to this source in *El Discreto* (originally published in 1646): "One discusses it gracefully and the other sweetly sings it, the Falcón who turns into a swan—Man is given thirty years of his own, for enjoying and pleasing; afterwards twenty borrowed years of the ass, for working; as many years again of the dog, for barking; and finally twenty of the ape, for doting; an excellent parable of the truth."[4] The reference to Falcón is to Jaime Juan Falcón (1522–1594), whose work is discussed below. The image pictures us past our prime as living lives absorbed successively in *working* (as a toiling ass), in *barking* (as a snarling dog), and in *doting* (as a clowning ape), having lost our native capacity to realize our human nature in *enjoying* ourselves and *pleasing* others.

Nietzsche's Zarathustra portrays a living rainbow bridge and staircase to the superman in his famous opening discourse to his disciples, a parabolic apologue depicting three zoomorphic metamorphoses shaping our creative and re-creative spirits, spirits ultimately giving themselves the right to live and act in this world as superior beings—loving, knowing, and creating wills that will themselves into all eternity.[5] It is a winding staircase, a discontinuous passage ascending through three alternating flights and delineating the stages we pass through as we turn our all-too-human devaluations into super-human transvaluations, transcending our immature sumpter and predator natures and becoming innocent, independent, and strong children, playing with the values that guide and support our lives. Through its circulating exercise in transmutative negations and double negations, we emerge as playing children, realizing in our newborn attitudes to existence the divine attributes that Nietzsche prizes most highly among all our inchoate possibilities as human beings.

First, we become laboring camels. Creative energies within us slowly grow in reverence, obedience, and love, assuming as willingly as camels all the gravely ascetic prescriptions and proscriptions that our supreme values place upon us. We discipline ourselves, training and restraining our rambunctious, ambiguous impulses and dedicating our lives to a single unremitting aim. Once we are true, unswerving servants, however, something happens to change us into bloodthirsty monsters bent on destroying the very virtues that master our loving wills. We become raving lions, rejecting what we love and honor most, overthrowing the draconic moral principles that weigh us down, and liberating our own remorseless creative spirits. Following this crisis and axis point where sumpter turns into predator, we at long last overcome even our own overcoming and emerge as children playing with divine possibilities, willing our own restless ludic wills and transmuting our own nihilistic terrors into ultimate values. It is in this parable that Nietzsche indicates how it is that we conquer our human, all-too-human natures and replace man with superman.

At this point—and as a backdrop to what is to come—it is worth mentioning Erich Heller's reaction to this triple metamorphosis and the strange shapes its changing spirit assumes. He regards it as a close approximation to "allegorical disaster."[6] How could the spirit submit to turning into a camel without feeling degraded? How could the lion submit to turning into so helpless a human shape without offering resistance? Heller wonders whether it is possible to imagine such incongruous guises in such close proximity to one another. Consequently, he tends to dispense with the ponderous "allegorical equipment" impeding access to Nietzsche's message in this section and succeeds quite well in articulating its autobiographical meaning. This approach possesses certain advantages. But what he loses in the process is at least as important as what he gains.

In earlier articles dealing with this issue, I have assembled basic documents and arguments disclosing and illuminating literary source materials underlying and patterning those peculiar animal phases appearing in Zarathustra's address "On the Three Metamorphoses."[7] There is no doubt, it seems to me, that Nietzsche generates his transmutative tale as a parodic counterpoint to a satiric fable that Jaime Juan Falcón introduces into European literature and folklore in the late sixteenth century.[8] Falcón, in "De partibus vitae," relates how, once upon a time, when everything was new, God summoned all living creatures to come to him to receive their destinies and their allotted years. He granted thirty years to the ass, the dog, and the ape, in turn, but because their lives were too tedious, too contentious, or too ridiculous to bear, they earnestly begged him to reduce their spans. God was gracious and answered their petitions. When man appeared to learn his fate, however, he thought the thirty years God allotted him too little, and he complained to God, asking him to prolong his time on earth by giving him the excess years cast aside by the other lower animals. God relented and granted him his request, providing only that as he lives their years he also lives according to their destinies. So, as a bitter result, surpassing our true and proper limits as we outlive our thirty human years and leave our pleasures and rewards in genuine human existence to the past, we enter into three subhuman metamorphoses, enduring the burdens that weigh down the toiling ass, the animosities that provoke the snarling dog, and the humiliations that reduce the clowning ape to a laughingstock and a miserable caricature, deforming, degrading, and discrediting all our human ambitions and values.

This is human, all-too-human existence. Even our most enviable human specimens betray these ignoble and subhuman characters. Our artists are merely feeble simian pretenders, imitating nature and aping human emotions, while our philosophers are merely scavenging canine cynics and our saints are suffering asinine porters who take up the poverty, the guilt, and the loneliness that depress man but are as yet unable to make it over into something glowing with promise. The saint can never seem to turn his yielding forbearance into pure love. Neither can the philosopher turn his disillusionment and his tightening skepticism into knowledge. He is caught up in a swirling abyss, reeling with a sudden disorienting, dissipating awareness that nothing is true and all is in vain. The artist does no better than the others. He can never turn his simulation and dissimulation into genuine creation, into creation that produces or reproduces something possessing ultimate value where nothing at all or, worse yet, where something detested and despised beyond everything else still hangs in empty abeyance. For these purposes, we require a new and superior type, a superhuman being who integrates the lover, the knower, and the creator into a single divine character.

By assembling an elevating, constructive parody to revalue the satiric prototype he discovers in Falcón, Nietzsche generates a new tripartite dialectic to illustrate the radical victories we win over ourselves as we overcome these three popular images and so give rise in our own crucibles to the superhuman trinity we desire with all our creative and procreative will. The resulting dialectic preserves the basic patterns marking its prototype, including successive mutations that force the human spirit to serve time as a beast of burden and a beast of prey as it makes its way to its second childhood. Yet at the same time it employs new symbols to distinguish its own stages, turning the ass into a camel, the dog into a lion, and the ape into a child, much as similar substitutions turn the saint into a lover, the philosopher into a knower, and the artist into a creator. It also replaces the negative satiric theme. Nietzsche rewrites the nihilistic fable, describing man and his degenerating decline through three subhuman animal phases, as a ludic parable, prescribing the parallel phases he must experience as he makes his regenerating ascent to superhuman being.

My main thesis is that recognizing its source in earlier satiric fable makes Zarathustra's speech concerning these three metamorphoses inestimably more accessible to probing readers. We can clearly see how it is that the parable comes to mean what it does. Structuralist techniques in analysis uncover basic articulations along its syntagmatic and paradigmatic axes, showing generative mechanisms through which it produces meanings.[9] A single glance comparing Nietzsche's parable with Falcón's fable is sufficient to establish that their syntagmatic narrative sequences are equivalent and that their contrasting paradigmatic terms can be deployed into a systematic relationship involving a transformative inversion. Humanity loses its innocence. As a necessary result, our human precursor must become, in turn, a sumpter, a predator, and a quasihuman culminator representing our second childhood. As an expedient, we may designate this culminator as a jester, recalling the jester (*Possenreißer*) who leaps over the tightrope walker (*Seiltanzer*) and threatens Zarathustra in the prologue to Z. The tightrope episode and the three metamorphoses represent alternative expressions illustrating the same dramatic process.[10]

The satiric fable depicts the sumpter beast as an ass, a laboring pack animal on whose weary back heavy burdens are heaped, a mistreated, ignoble servant toiling under duress. It pictures the predator as a beleaguered watchdog standing guard over its useless possessions and gives us a ridiculous ape to illustrate the pathetic jester, an impotent embarrassment and an incompetent laughingstock and dupe to poke fun at the infirmity and senility marking our second childhood in advancing old age. During our thirty human years, we are creatures at play, knowing neither seriousness nor boredom, as Hage-dorn puts it, and experiencing our lives as a joyous delight.[11] Pure and simple humanity, given shape at the creation *in imago dei*, masters the world and rules the animals as *homo ludens*. But man is seduced by his own intemperate will to live. His impious desire to stretch out his existence on earth beyond the proper limits set by Jupiter yields, in its fulfillment, its own poetic justice, divine retribution in a satiric mode, one visited on all succeeding human generations. Having lost our innocence, we are driven into three metamor-phoses. With our asinine years, we assume the unaccustomed responsibilities attaching to marriage, business, and our standing in the community. We give up our independence and live as saddled drudges. Later, with our canine years, we give up our power, our generative and creative capacities. We are neither producers nor consumers but rather nervous watchmen and accoun-tants protecting our valuables, snarling as dogs do at strangers. So at last, sans innocence, sans strength, sans everything, we wind up as miserable, atavistic caricatures derisively mocking our former selves. During our simian years, we are no longer players, we are involuntary playthings. These are the three syn-tagmatic units demarcating what we might conveniently call the ages of man, and the stages making up the three metamorphoses of the spirit follow this generic outline precisely.

Zarathustra tells how it is that the spirit, overcoming morality, becomes a sumpter, a predator, and a quasi-human redeemer, a culminating jester repre-senting our second childhood. The human spirit loses its innocence. Moral-ity brings man to embarrassment, shame, and guilt. Imposing a moral world order onto existence, man loses contact with the Dionysian innocence of becoming. At length, the youngest and most unrelenting of all moral impera-tives voices its commandments to mankind, the unconditional will to truth. Like Oedipus, whose heroic drive to knowledge drew him into unspeakable crimes against nature, parricide and maternal incest, we, too, must be brought, by our stern unwillingness to deceive ourselves, to an involuntary murderous assault on the moral resentment fathering our passionate and unbridled lust to uncover, penetrate, and know the truth as well as to an incestuous assault on the artistic illusions mothering it.[12] Knowledge turns us into animals (see *HH* 519). As camels, we gladly assume the gravest and most demanding burdens, burdens that might easily crush others lacking our strength and reverence. We patiently, lovingly, obediently submit ourselves to trying labors, testing our loyalty and disciplining our characters into wholeness. As true ascetics, we deny ourselves any indulgence in indepen-dent cognitions, volitions, or actions, and we bind ourselves as tightly as possible to our servitude. We accept our moral responsibility to the truth, and, doing so, we regain our innocence. As lions we rise up in violent rebellion against our absolute master, one we knelt down to in love as perfect servants. Renouncing any power to create, we strike out in destructive frenzy, declaring autonomous, arbitrary independence. We struggle against our moral obligations, refusing to believe in their sacred inviolability, hence summoning their ultimate origins and values into question. We even dare to be honest about what honesty actually means, insisting on knowing the ugly, unseemly truth about truth, and, as a result, we finally overthrow our draconic master and assert our freedom. As children, we rediscover our ability to be and to become the truth, willing our own wills and giving ourselves the right to act in an innocent style, playing as children play, without expecting unity, reality, absolute veracity, or any other moral attribute to rule our lives. Hence our creative energy returns, the strength and force that makes us gods, the power to create new values, superhuman meaning. At this stage, our ludic virtues are complete. We are as innocent, as independent, and as strong as children at play. We have lived as consummate animals as a means to overcoming, integrating, and elevating ourselves as consummate humanity—"superhumans."

We are now in a position to draw some conclusions. Mechanical articulations along their syntagmatic and paradigmatic axes generate whatever meanings we might discover within the three metamorphoses. We may regard Nietzsche's parable, literally and quite specifically, as a transformation of the satiric fable it takes as its prototype and source. It converts its source fable, even inverts, subverts, and contraverts it, into a new narrative text by employing a simple method—ignoble sumpter, predator, and jester figures are deleted and noble ones are substituted. The camel is the noblest sumpter and the lion the noblest predator, the ship of the desert and the king of the beasts. There is no question. Alongside them the ass and the dog resemble inferior types, even opposites. The camel is the supreme beast of burden, the sumpter that surpasses all other pack animals and carries its servile nature to the absolute limit, the extreme boundary where it exhausts its possibilities and discovers no recourse but to overcome its submission. Likewise, the lion is the ultimate beast of prey, the predator that masters even preying dragons and pursues its heroic spirit to the turning point where it conquers even its conquering violence. The perfect beast of burden excels all others in obeying orders and the prefect beast of prey excels all others in commanding obedience, but neither is complete. The camel knows nothing about giving orders, and the lion knows nothing about carrying them out. The child alone has the power both to rule and to serve, to obey and to command, and so it is the child who yokes the beast of burden to the beast of prey and, by mastering his own liberating conquests, assumes the right to will his own will.

In this allegorical dramatization, Nietzsche depicts the spirit's determination to choose earthly vitality over otherworldly morality, superman over the last man, the playing child over the doting ape. He represents man's progressive transformations toward superhumanity (camel, lion, and child) as an alternative to his regressive deformations toward bestiality (ass, dog, and ape). He portrays the movements required to avert the dim prospect that an as-yet-undetermined human species whose origins are in the ape will renounce its possibilities and return to the ape once again. It is a parodic revision reworking its underlying substrate and making it over into precisely its opposite.

The address Zarathustra delivers "On the Three Metamorphoses" takes as its primary source the discouraging prototype it discovers in early satiric fable. Beside the original Latin version appearing in Falcón, there are also derivative Spanish, French, German, and Hebrew variants as well as examples in numerous other Western and Eastern European languages. A popular version, certainly familiar to Nietzsche, is given by Jakob Grimm in the *Kinder und Hausmärchen*. The literary roots supplying and anchoring this modern tradition may be traced back to ancient Aespoic and Haggadic sources and may even be detected in Sophocles. The third stasimon in *Oedipus Coloneus* laments our human inclination to want to live longer than the span appointed to us and passes judgment against any man who clings to this unrestrained will to live. The chorus repeats the pessimistic wisdom Midas finally forces Silenus to divulge, the tragic knowledge that what is best above all else is never to be born into the world, while the next best thing is to die away as quickly as possible (see *BT* 3). Moreover, it mentions the toilsome troubles, the strife, and the solitary, estranged old age that awaits him once he loses his youth, laying preliminary groundwork structures, perhaps, to support the asinine, canine, and simian personalities concluding the Haggadic commentaries in *Midrash Kohelet* and *Midrash Tanhuma* and constituting the modern satiric tradition. The basic meanings attaching to ass, dog, and ape are already present in these tragic woes.

The Haggadic versions present a heptadic sequence to illustrate our common human destinies. We start out our lives as newborn kings but with the passing years come more to resemble pigs, kids, horses, asses, dogs, and apes as old age finally torments us with infirmity and senility. Falcón seems to derive his symbolic animals from this Judaic tradition. His triadic series, however, as well as the idea about transferring years from various animals to man seems to originate with an Aesopic fable surviving in two variant forms, one Babrian and the other Augustanan. In this tale, man, either through extortion or through gratitude, receives years given to him by a horse, an ox, and a dog. As a result, he becomes as rambunctious as a horse in mature age, as industrious as an ox in middle age, and as contentious as a dog in old age.

Later emblematic apologues abandon the triple stages patterning this Aesopic scheme and its satiric derivatives and adopt various multiple stages in their place. Voltaire, in his article on man in the *Dictionaire Philosophique*, gives a six-stage sequence, including caterpillar, butterfly, peacock, horse, fox, and ape personality; and Gracián, in the *Oráculo Manual*, gives a seven-stage progression already noted. It seems to me that the camel and the lion in Zarathustra's discourse on the three metamorphoses might well have their origins in this version, but whatever their source, their meaning becomes clear when we see them as the ultimate beasts bearing burdens and seeking prey.

"There is a danger that we will return to *bestiality*" (KSA 10:4[84]). As Zarathustra's parable would have it, the means to averting this "strange comic conclusion" to which our *circular orbit* would lead us is to go under to our own going-over and to enter into our own three metamorphoses. Our aim is the regenerate child rather than the degenerate ape, the superman rather than the last man, a ludic transfiguration rather than a nihilistic disfiguration. Having come to recognize what Nietzsche is up to in reworking Falcón's satiric fable and in channeling its Hellenic, Aesopic, and Haggadic roots into his own parodic revision, we come at the same time to appreciate the extent to which his apologue "On the Three Metamorphoses" achieves an allegorical integrity and consistency that Erich Heller entirely misses. "He must also be a consummate animal who wishes to become a consummate man" (*KSA* 10:4[94]). The camel must displace the ass, the lion the dog, and the child the ape. These three movements are the spirit's means to transvaluation.

Notes

1. Compare KSA 10:5[1]: "One should also be a consummate animal—said Zarathustra." Unless otherwise indicated, translations of citations of Nietzsche's works are my own.

2. Although this proportion and extrapolation, placing man in relation to superman as ape is to man, owes its impact in large part to Darwin and evolutionary theories con-

cerning human descent, it seems more specifically to echo a comparison attributed to Heraclitus by Plato at *Hippias Major* 289a-b. See also Peter Groff's discussion of the connection to Heraclitus in his contribution to this volume.

3. Baltasar Gracián y Morales, *Oráculo manual y arte de prudencia* (Huesca, 1647), aph. 276.

4. Gracián y Morales, *El Discreto*, ed. Arturo del Hoyo (Madrid, 1963), 140 (sec. 25).

5. For the grounds supporting an interpretive approach to Nietzsche's *Übermensch* sensitive to its tripartite structure (a model combining the lover, the knower, and the creator in a single superhuman personality), see Richard Perkins, "The Genius and the Better Player: Superman and the Elements of Play," *International Studies in Philosophy* 15, no. 2 (Summer 1983): 13–23. An important indication pointing to this triadic synthesis appears at *KSA* 10:16[11]: "To become artist (creator), saint (lover), and philosopher (knower) *in a single person—my practical goal!*" The insertions enclosed in parentheses were later additions written above their corresponding terms. See *KGW* 7 4/1, 228, in Montinari's commentary on 16[11], 29f.

6. Heller's comments on the "extreme zoological and spiritual discomfort" involved in making an attempt to imagine the virtually "unimaginable transformations" have been reproduced in several formats. See Heller's *The Disinterested Mind* (New York: Harcourt Brace Jovanovich, 1975), 303–326; *The Importance of Nietzsche* (Chicago: University of Chicago Press, 1988), 70–86; and *The Poet's Self and the Poem* (London: Athlone, 1976), 28–50.

7. See "Metamorphosis in Nietzsche and its Sources in Satiric Fable," *Comparative Literature Studies* 22, no. 4 (Winter 1985): 472–496; and "How the Ape Becomes a Superman: Notes on a Parodic Metamorphosis in Nietzsche," *Nietzsche-Studien* 15 (1986): 180–183.

8. *Operum poeticorum Iacobi Falconis Valentini* (Mantuae: Carpetanorum, 1600), folio 60 verso.

9. Concerning syntagmatic and paradigmatic relationships in linguistic theory, see Roland Barthes, *Elements of Semiology*, trans. A. Lavers and C. Smith (New York: Hill & Wang, 1977/84), 58–88.

10. See Richard Perkins, *Between a Fool and a Corpse: Zarathustra and the Overcoming of Man* (Mt. Pleasant, Mich.: Enigma Press, 1980).

11. See "Jupiter, *die Tiere und der Mensch*" in Friedrich von Hagedorn, *Poetische Werke*, 3 vols., (Hamburg, 1757), vol. 1.

12. The opening section in *BGE* employs the heroic contest between Oedipus and the strangling sphinx as a mythic paradigm illustrating a crisis in *Selbst-in-Fragestellung* occurring once the truth-seeking drive to knowledge gains insight into its own questionable origin and value. For other relevant 1885 notes bearing on this image, see *KSA* 11, pp. 497, 498, 579, 667, 693; and *KSA* 12, p. 71. Earlier references appear at *KSA* 7, pp. 11, 37, 99, 141, 156, 201, 228, 460, 461, and 572; and *KSA* 9, pp. 574, 622, 664, and 668.

~

Index to Animals in
Nietzsche's Corpus

Brian Crowley

Note: The original plan for the book called for what would be a comprehensive index of animal references in Nietzsche's works. Because an exhaustive index would far outstrip the present work's scope, the decision was made to limit the index to the animals treated in the volume and, as often as possible, to include related phrases and activities (e.g., "spinning" with spider). Entries for the lizard and polyp were forgone as Nietzsche's references to those creatures are very few, and the authors of those essays cite the immediately relevant passages. Gerd Schank's essay, drawn from the forthcoming Nietzsche Dictionary, admirably gathers the passages for the "blond beast" and "beast of prey." A list of the generic "animal" proved too extensive to be helpful. One creature found its way into the index without an appearance in the bestiary proper, namely der Wurm, since it intersects in many interesting ways with animals that do appear in the book, such as the mole and the snake. The entries here are intended to supplement rather than substitute for the chapters in the volume. While the preparer's prefatory remarks to entries occasionally overlap with those made by authors of chapters, they generally underscore dominant or deviant uses. Finally, the list of literature cited herein does not aim at being comprehensive. It provides helpful direction for those who wish to pursue these matters further.—Eds.

This section is intended to indexically gather passages from the *KSA* collection of Nietzsche's works. Sections or fragments cited that are not followed by a modifying word represent a site for the main entry word (in any grammatical variation of case or number); those followed by a modifying word built upon or related to the head word represent Nietzsche's usages of that word (or those words). If the citation is followed by "incl.," the section includes both the head word and the variants listed after "incl." Parenthetical remarks within a citation are intended to give context to that passage (with a paraphrase, quotation reference, etc.), or to direct the reader to its drafts or closely related passages. I have cited page numbers to long sections in the following works: *UM*, *FEI*, *TL*, and "The Greek State." All other instances of page numbers refer to the relevant volume of the *KSA*. Cited translations include: Kaufmann's *A*, *BGE*, *BT*, *CW*, *EH*, *GS*, *NCW*, *TI*, and *Z*; Hollingdale's translations of *D* and *HH*; Hollingdale and Kaufmann's translation of *GM*; Gray's *UM*; and "The Greek State" as translated by Mügge.

I would like to thank those essayists with whom I have corresponded about the various animals, especially Paul S. Loeb and Nickolas Pappas. The members of the Nietzsche Research Group in Nijmegen, Netherlands, deserve thanks for providing me with advice and expertise in this project's early stages. Finally, I wish to thank the editors, especially Christa Davis Acampora, for providing this opportunity and consultative assistance.

Ape

The human's origin in the ape figures in several ways: sometimes as a return to its nature (e.g., *Z*:1 "New Idol" [from being in the city] and *BT* 2), which is sometimes brutal (cf. *GM* II:6); as part of a mixed nature (e.g., *BGE* 26 both crude body and higher intelligence); and sometimes the ape is even better than the human (e.g., *KSA* 10:1[38], and *KSA* 11:25[235]). The idea that humans may still be traveling on an evolutionary trajectory from ape to man and beyond, and thus bringing a transvaluation (of the sort intimated by Heraclitus' frag. 83), is present already in *HH* 247 and resurfaces in *Z*:P 3. Nietzsche gives some discussion in *BT* 8 as to what it means to have different archetypal origin animals (for instance ape or satyr).

Most frequently Nietzsche plays on the derivative expression "to ape." Mimicry of this sort, he tells us, is endemic to European culture; indeed, "to take joy in a strange originality without becoming its ape, perhaps one day will be the sign of a new culture" (*KSA* 9:3[151], see also *KSA* 9:3[34]). The genealogies of our bodies and morality branch from the root of being an ape. Nietzsche theorizes aping to be a means of early value learning as when children mimic parents' inclinations in their actions, establishing what ought be done (*D* 34). At *KSA* 9:3[34], compassion is called "an involuntary, inner mimicking," and at *KSA* 11:26[460] aping is a manner of giving way to the trained values "good," "evil," and "praiseworthy." Having been made in

God's image (i.e., making ourselves in his image), humans also ape Him; but as merely mimicking, we do not create morals, values, etc. (WS 14, KSA 10:22[3], p. 620, and KSA 13:20[28]).

That humans are "more ape than any ape" only appears published at Z:P 3, (but see also KSA 9:3[34] where man is more ape than the apes because of mimicry, and KSA 10:3[1].403). If the worm is to indicate our hidden, only remembered instincts (see the worm's index entry for some discussion of this) and the ape our ability to mimic the perceived world, then the human may be more of a (mimicking) ape than the instinctual ape—instincts that evolved it into humanity and perhaps one day beyond. (This is but one plau-sible interpretation of this brief, many layered passage.) Perhaps similarly, Nietzsche is appalled that the Germans would renounce their natural dispo-sition in order to acquire talents that are merely entertaining, in other words, they renounce their true nature in order to be apes (SE 6, p. 222).

BT 2; BT 8; BT 10 (Hercules' ape, cf. "Socrates and Tragedy," p. 549); DS 7, p. 39 incl. ape genealogists; DS 9, p. 58; DS 12, p. 80 primal monkey (Uraffe) (partially quoting D. Strauss); HL 9, p. 154 aping (Nachäfferei); SE 6, p. 222 (cf. KSA 7:35[12]); "Greek Music Drama," p. 515 aping (Nachäffung) (cf. KSA 7:1[1]); HH 99; HH 247 incl. apishness; WS 14 (God's apes; cf. Heraclitus frag. 83 and Gen. 1:27); D 34; D 49 (ape and other beasts at human's origins); D 241 apishness; D 324; GS A "In the South" aped (äffte); GS 86 aping (Nachäffung); GS 316; Z:P 3 (cf. the drafts KSA 10:3[1].403, 10:4[181], 10:5[1].255, and also KSA 10:4[163]); Z:1 "New Idol"; Z:3"Passing By" Zarathustra's Ape; Z:3 "Other Dancing Song" ape (äffen; also means "to confound"); BGE 26 incl. ape's body (cf. KSA 11:40[35]); BGE 222; BGE 253; GM II:6; CW 14; TI "Max-ims" 39; AC 39; KSA 7:23[11]; KSA 7:26[2] (partial quote of Heraclitus 83, cf. KSA 7:27[67]); KSA 7:37[6] apelike; KSA 8:21[79] girl-ape; KSA 9:3[34] incl. the apish; KSA 9:3[151]; KSA 9:3[158]; KSA 9:7[4] (from Gracián, see Perkins' essay herein); KSA 9:11[130] ape-herds; KSA 9:11[177]; KSA 10:1[38]; KSA 10:4[163] overape; KSA 10:4[181] (cf. KSA 10:5[1].255); KSA 10:22[3], p. 620 (cf. KSA 13:20[28]); KSA 11:25[235]; KSA 11:26[460]; KSA 11:29[1] spider monkeys (cf. KSA 11:31[50] and 32[8]); KSA 11:41[2], p. 676 (draft for a new UM, Wagner, Paganini, and Liszt are between "God" and "ape"); KSA 12:10[142] ("pes-simists of today, these lean apes"); KSA 13:11[27]; KSA 13:11[61] ("such a lean ape as Hartmann"; cf. KSA 12:10[142] and KSA 13:11[101]).

Ass

Although known for its endurance and sure-footedness, but also its stubborn-ness, many ancient proverbs utilize the donkey as a figure for a lesser kind of horse, showing foolish envy, clumsiness, nondiscrimination, and follies of all kinds. It can represent the rabble as hard-working, enduring, yet stupid (e.g., KSA 12:1[170]). Primarily with Nietzsche, the ass stands for someone with a poor ability to judge, be it from naïveté, ignorance, stupidity, or indiscretion. Most Aesopian fables involving the ass show it either misjudging its own capabilities or those of others, leading to its downfall. The "yea-yuh" in Z:3 "Spirit of Gravity" 2 indicates an indiscriminate nature, lacking standards and measures by which to choose. On this lack of acumen see also BGE 239, BGE 264, BGE 283, KSA 7:29[91], and KSA 12:10[150], and on its associa-tion with a lack of suspicion or skepticism see GS 350, KSA 10:18[53], and KSA 12:5[44]. Nietzsche draws on the biblical scene of riding into town on a donkey (Zech. 9:9 and Matt. 21:4–5) at AOM 313, KSA 9:10[D80], KSA 10:12[1].37, and KSA 13:11[288]. There are probably traces of this scene in Z:2 "Famous Wise Men."

Nietzsche also employs the ridiculousness of the donkey. Once, the apos-tates believed and heard the laughter in Zarathustra's wisdom (Z:3 "Apos-tates" 2), but now Zarathustra laughs painfully at those returning to the faith, those with a reawakened but weakened religiousness. Zarathustra announces that he would die of laughter to see such drunken asses and weak-ened pious ones. Here Nietzsche draws on the account of the death of Chrys-sipus the Stoic, who dies of laughter upon seeing a donkey eat figs and drink wine, in Diogones Laertius's *Lives of the Eminent Philosophers*. This foreshad-ows events with the higher men insofar as corrupted laughter, being "pious again," and an alcohol-drinking ass return latter in Z:4 "Awakening" and in Z:4 "Ass Festival." (On the ridiculousness of the festival see also Aesop fable 266 "The Ass Carrying a Statue of a God.") In "The Awakening" Zarathus-tra is pleased by the good cheer of the higher men, but recognizes that they laugh differently from him (cf. GS 381 as well as KSA 9:6[337]). For more on the meaning of the ass festival see Kathleen Marie Higgins's works in this collection and in her *Nietzsche's Zarathustra*, pp. 211–232.

Several passages elaborate on the burden carrying of certain donkeys. Zar-athustra proclaims (Z:1 "Reading and Writing") that we are all "fair burden-able asses and she-asses" and that there is a certain kind of pack animal that can carry its load out of a love that lightens the load. However, even if the ass could unfetter itself and carry its burden in the desert it would still not be a "strong spirit" (GM III:7), perhaps because it cannot laugh or smile at existence, perhaps because it does not take an enemy (both are discussed here, cf. KSA 12:7[13]). This may also reference the 'higher men' in *Zara-thustra*, who made their way up to the mountain cave, but forgot how to hear the laughter in Zaratustra's wisdom and became like the ass they brought with them. *TI* "Maxims" 11 asks, "Can an ass be tragic?—That one perishes under a burden one can neither carry nor throw off? The case of the philosopher."

In German, *Langohr* is an alternate expression for the ass and "lange Ohren machen" means 'to attentively listen in with curiosity', 'to prick up one's ears.' Nietzsche sometimes combines these two to critique moralists—the "long ear" eagerly perceives moral maxims and their transgressions. At KSA 13:18[8] such "an ideologue of virtue" is called "Lord Long-ear and Virtuous" (cf. *KSA* 12:10[83]). The deaf father confessor of GS 223 still has these long ears. Seeing his followers straining for doctrines (Z:3 "Apostates" 1), Zarathustra asks, "Did their ears perhaps listen longingly long, in vain, for me and my trumpet and herald's calls?" Nietzsche even notes his own small ears and amoral, non-doctrinal thought, calling himself the Anti-ass in *EH* "Books" 2. (See also *KSA* 10:18[53], and Z:4 "Higher Men" 1.)

DS 11, p. 69; *SE* 7, p. 236 incl. mule driver; *PTG* 7 (quoting Heraclitus 9B); *AOM* 313; *WS* 92; *GS* 223 the longest ears; *GS* 350; *GS* 381; Z:1 "Reading and Writing," incl. she-donkeys (cf. 10:5[1].21, and *KSA* 10:4[73]); Z:1 "New Idol" long-eared; Z:2 "Famous Wise Men" incl. little donkey (cf. *KSA* 10:13[1], p. 421 and *KSA* 10:13[14]); Z:3 "Apostates" 2; Z:3 "Spirit of Gravity" 2; Z:4 "Conversation with the Kings" 1; Z:4 "The Greeting"; Z:4 "Last Supper" (cf. *KSA* 11:30[7]); Z:4 "Higher Men" 1 long mob ears; Z:4 "Higher Men" 20 (cf. as drafts *KSA* 11:29[11], *KSA* 11:29[13], *KSA* 11:31[50], and *KSA* 11:31[64], see also *GS* 68 as a precursor to the image of giving an animal wings); Z:4 "Awakening"; Z:4 "Ass Festival" 1,3 incl. theo-asininities (*Götter-Eseleien*) and ass festival; Z:4 "Drunken Song" 1,2; *BGE* 8, *asine* (cf. *KSA* 11:24[466]); *BGE* 237 she-donkey; *BGE* 239; *BGE* 264; *BGE* 283 incl. asinine;

BGE 284; *GM* III:7; *TI* "Maxims" 11; *EH* "Books" 2 long ear and anti-ass; *KSA* 7:29[91]; *KSA* 8:2[4] *asine* (quoting Cicero); *KSA* 8:41[23] (quoting H. C. Carey's *Lehrbuch der Volkswirtschaft und Sozialwissenschaft*); *KSA* 9:6[337]; *KSA* 9:10[D80] she-donkey and donkey foal; *KSA* 10:10[46], *KSA* 10:13[3], p. 448, *KSA* 11:29[39], *KSA* 11:31[5] (fragments of ass with kings); *KSA* 10:12[1].37; *KSA* 10:18[53] donkey ears; *KSA* 11:25[462]; *KSA* 11:28[45] (poem fragment "The German Ass"); *KSA* 11:32[13]; *KSA* 11:32[14]; *KSA* 11:34[45] and *KSA* 11:38[6] (V. Hugo as "ass of genius," coined by Baudelaire); *KSA* 11:34[154] (Heine knew the gray donkey "German"); *KSA* 11:37[5]; *KSA* 11:41[3]; *KSA* 12:1[170]; *KSA* 12:5[44]; *KSA* 12:7[13]; *KSA* 12:10[83] moral-ass; *KSA* 12:10[150]; *KSA* 13:11[288]; *KSA* 13:14[120]; *KSA* 13:18[8] long ear; *KSA* 13:20[88].

Bird

The bird is far and away the most populous animal in Nietzsche's writings, with sightings in over 140 passages (and to thoroughly index flying, wings, feathers, eggs, subspecies, etc., would add several hundred more entries). As an important figure in the corpus, it appears in the prefatory remarks to *Human, All Too Human*, as well as the culminating sections of *Daybreak*, *Thus Spoke Zarathustra*, and *Beyond Good and Evil*. Nietzsche, of course, mostly utilizes birds' abilities of flight, like those described of eagles, condors, and albatrosses at KSA 10:8[2]. The apparent ease and grace of flight, its heights and solitude influence most, if not all, of the citations indexed here. This and more assist his ornithomorphizing of humans; for instance, Nietzsche asserts that humans have already inherited many of the mental pleasures (now sought in art) from the animals, such as the joy in (birds') songs (KSA 8:23[81]). In Z:3 "Old and New Tablets" 22, one reads that humans have taken on the characteristics of many animals in order to adapt to hard times, yet they could still learn from the birds, learn to fly and take their rapaciousness (*Raublust*) to new regions.

The preface of 1886 (sections 4 and 5) to Nietzsche's "book for free spirits" (*HH*) describes this audience as convalescing, having been through deserts of isolation from old values and evaluations, as learning to live as avian free spirits. Traveling along lofty paths in such expanses affords one a "bird's view of contemplation" from which to grasp "everything as it *should go* and actually goes" (KSA 13:11[30]; cf. WS 138), however, this difference of imperfection causes suffering, is difficult, and may indicate why birds are best for gazing into abysses (cf. Z:2 "Famous Wise Men" and *EH* "Books" 3). However, these spirits have the ability to experiment and take adventures with their values and lives, independent of morals and concerns. Thus they can survive such trammels. In the common opinion these avian thinkers are "banned under outlawry" (*Vogelfreiheit*) (D 164), but occasionally they congregate for brief repose on small yet solid ground (D 314).

Not only the thinker, but thoughts themselves, their content and expression, become ornithomorphic for Nietzsche. As singers of songs and signs of changing weather, birds have long been thought to carry ideas; presumably, Greek augury partially stems from this (an activity specifically referenced e.g., at Z:2 "Tomb Song"). Socrates, in Plato's *Theatetus*, likens thinking to a dove-cot full of birds that one must grab to have one's idea immediately (197c); this is a direct influence on GS 298, Z:2 "Poets," and BGE 296, where Nietzsche highlights the negative implications of this way of thinking, writing, and speaking ideas. By prioritizing the flight of the bird, as essential to an idea's forcefulness, *liveliness*, and accuracy, as opposed to its being held, he is also inverting the German proverb that it is "better to have a bird in the hand than ten in the air" (*besser ein Vogel in der Hand als zehn in der Luft*).

That thoughts are best left in flight is an early concern in Nietzsche's works, perhaps dating back to 1872's "The Philosopher: Reflections on the Struggle between Art and Knowledge" (in Breazeale's *Philosophy and Truth*, p. 42): "The philosopher caught in the nets of *language*." That singing would be a better representation than theater and a better relation to audiences' imaginations (*D* 265) is due to the rhapsodist's art being more like bird flight and winged. Poetic idiom, in its avian mimicry, overcomes some of these linguistic challenges as expressed in several of Nietzsche's poems (e.g., *IM* "Prinz Vogelfrei": "Reason and tongue often stumble!"). In a fragment from 1880, Nietzsche describes the poets' representation of metaphorical reality and their drive to knowledge as playing and hopping from branch to branch, singing in their colored feathers (*KSA* 9:3[108]).

Perhaps combining these uses, Zarathustra praises the bird's virtues of lightness and liveliness as countermeasures against the spirit of gravity (*Z*:3 "Spirit of Gravity"). Indeed, "all that is body [should become] dancer; all that is spirit, bird" (*Z*:3 "Seven Seals" 6, see also *Z*:4 "Higher Men" 18 on dancing) and the bird-wisdom says "Sing! Speak no more! Are not all words made for the grave and heavy? Are not all words lies for those who are light?" (*Z*:3 "Seven Seals" 7). As another difference between thinking and singing, the narrator in *GS* A "In the South" proclaims, "To think in solitude is wise / Singing in solitude is silly" (cf. *Z*:3 "Spirit of Gravity" 1). (For more on the musicality of birds' songs and on becoming avian see Gary Shapiro's essay in this collection.)

On deterring birds, however, Nietzsche is of two minds. Sometimes it is a consequence of his type of philosophizing (*HH* P 1 and cf. *Z*:4 "Honey Sacrifice") that some incautious birds (and their values) are caught in his nets, or that cautious ones are caught by birds of prey. However, some birds are lured in by metaphysicians' trickery (*Z*:4 "Science" and *BGE* 230) others scared away by scarecrows such as Kant (*KSA* 11:26[417]) and Plato (and other ancient dialecticians) (*KSA* 13:14[111]). Yet it is sometimes necessary for even the free spirit to be a scarecrow of a bird (*BGE* 44).

As a final note, regarding the enigmatic image of the doves and lion concluding *Zarathustra*, if one focuses on this lion's behaving like a domesticated dog as it is described, one may recall the same animal pairing (dog and bird) in *Z*:1 "Enjoying and Suffering the Passions." In this earlier chapter, the birds "and lovely singers" represent the expression and transformation of the passionate wild dogs "in one's cellar"; but to consider them (and thus the doves in the later chapter) also as words would draw further connections to Schiller's dove and lion pairing (discussed in the lion's index below), since words are precisely what Schiller's characters are discussing.

DS 8, p. 50 *vogelfrei*; *TL* 1, p. 86–87; *BT* P 7; *BT* 24 birds' voices (refers to music: Wagner's); *HL* 7, p. 134; *HH* P 1 incl. bird catcher (*Vogelsteller*) (cf. preface draft at *KSA* 11:40[59]); *HH* P 4 and 5 incl. bird-like freedom, altitude, and exuberance, and bird flights (cf. *KSA* 11:40[65] and *KSA* 11:41[9]; both incl. birdlike circumspection [*Vogel-Umsicht*]); *HH* 133 phoenix; *HH* 426 (free spirits likened to augury birds in their flying alone, i.e., not marrying); *AOM* 172 (poets today, not being good teachers, grow up right away into temple ruins and caves dwelt in or haunted by snakes, worms, spiders and birds); *AOM* 390 song bird (adherents singing praise, cf. *KSA* 10:12[1].28); *WS* 138 incl. bird's eye view (*Vogelperspective*); *WS* 171 incl. nests; *WS* 269 bird song; *D* 164 outlawry (*Vogelfreiheit*); *D* 193 little bird; *D* 202 (quoting from Ludwig Uhland's *Kurze Biographie und Proben aus seinen Werken*, cf. *KSA* 7:1[30] and *KSA* 8:18[1]); *D* 265 bird flight and wings; *D* 314 birds of passage (*Wandervögel*); *D* 470 incl. beak; *D* 482 (cf. *KSA* 9:9[3]); *D* 568 incl. phoenix (a phoenix's daybreak, cf. *KSA* 7:19[199]); *D* 575 incl. flock; *GS* "Prelude" 53 incl. eagle and Minerva's favorite (i.e., the owl); *GS* 107 scarecrow (moral monsters and scarecrows); *GS* 184 scarecrows; *GS* 294 (cf. *GM* I:13); *GS* 298; *GS* 378 (dirty birds); *GS* A "Poet's Call" incl. woodpecker (cf. *IM* "Vogel-Urtheil"); *GS* A "In the South" incl. bird's nest and little bird (cf. *IM* "Prinz Vogelfrei"); *GS* A "Declaration of Love" (cf. *IM* "Albatros"); *Z*:P 2; *Z*:1 "Enjoying and Suffering the Passions" incl. nest and egg (virtue is this bird laying golden eggs, cf. *D* 568); *Z*:1 "Friend" (women as birds, cats, or cows; cf. the unidentified quote at *KSA* 10:3[1].133 and

BGE 237 where women are birds because exotic to men, who lock them up); *Z*:2 "Famous Wise Men" incl. eagle (cf. draft at *KSA* 10:10[6]); *Z*:2 "Tomb Song" incl. bird signs, song birds, and owl-monster; *Z*:2 "Land of Education"; *Z*:2 "Poets" incl. dovecot (cf. *Theatetus* 197c); *Z*:2 "Soothsayer" incl. owl and wings (of dream's meaning, cf. *KSA* 10:10[12] and *KSA* 10:13[3], p. 452); *Z*:3 "Passing By" (sending up warning birds against despising); *Z*:3 "Apostates" 2 nocturnal birds (*Nachtvögel*); *Z*:3 "Return Home" incl. nest and egg (refers back to *Z*:P 6–10, cf. *KSA* 10:19[2]); *Z*:3 "Spirit of Gravity" 1 and 2 incl. bird's manner (*Vogel-Art*), eagle, and ostrich (cf. *KSA* 10:20[15]); *Z*:3 "Old and New Tablets" 2 scarecrow; *Z*:3 "Old and New Tablets" 22; *Z*:3 "Convelescent" 2 incl. songbirds and dove swarms (*Taubenschwärmen*); *Z*:3 "Seven Seals" 6 and 7 incl. bird-wisdom and wings; *Z*:4 "Honey Sacrifice"; *Z*:4 "Ugliest Man" bird voices; *Z*:4 "Higher Men" 9 (before scholars' eyes all birds lie deplumed); *Z*:4 "Higher Men" 18 incl. wings and flight-ready (cf. *KSA* 11:31[64] and 33[1]); *Z*:4 "Science"; *Z*:4 "The Sign" incl. wings and doves; *BGE* 44 scarecrows (new, free spirits need to be these sometimes); *BGE* 230 bird catchers; *BGE* 296; *BGE* "From High Mountains" bird's eye view (*Vogel-Schau*); *GM* I:13 birds of prey; *GM* II:9 *vogelfreien*; *DD* "Zwischen Raubvögeln" birds of prey and wing; *EH* "Books" 3; *KSA* 7:1[35] bird's voice ("the ability of the bird's voice to wake the hero's spirit"); *KSA* 7:5[44] bird's voices; *KSA* 7:12[1], p. 368; *KSA* 7:15[1] (poem, "An die Melancholie"); *KSA* 7:19[199] phoenix; *KSA* 7:29[73]; *KSA* 7:32[5] (plan for work involving Aristophanes' *Birds*); *KSA* 7:38[4] *Unglücksvogel*; *KSA* 8:13[1]; *KSA*

8:23[81] song birds; KSA 9:3[108] incl. little feathers; KSA 9:4[112] little song birds; KSA 9:19[9] *Vogelfrei* (poem entitled "Desperat"); KSA 10:9[24] eagle and bird of prey (cf. KSA 10:13[1], p. 431); KSA 10:5[1].111; KSA 10:5[1].198 incl. flight ("This one loves the bird in its flight and that one sees only dawns and seas"); KSA 10:7[244] (notes to Alfred Espinas' *Die tierischen Gesellschaften. Eine vergleichend-psychologishce Untersuchung* [1879]); KSA 10:8[2] incl. eagle, albatross, condor, and wings; KSA 10:13[1], p. 426; KSA 10:13[15]; KSA 10:18[8] song bird; KSA 10:18[38]; KSA 10:22[1], p. 605 incl. birds' voices (as warning signs); KSA 11:25[29] (unidentified quote about Stendhal, who "writes like the birds sing"); KSA 11:25[339] scarecrow (Priapus as scarecrow); KSA 11:26[116] scarecrow (criminal as scarecrow); KSA 11:26[417] scarecrow; KSA 11:28[42] incl. phoenix (poem entitled "An Hafis"); KSA 11 28[58] (poem entitled "Der Wanderer," cf. KSA 8:17[31]); KSA 11:28[60] (poem entitled "Am Gletscher"); KSA 11:28[64] incl. crow, flight, and wild-bird-tone (poem entitled "Freigeist"); KSA 11:31[39] incl. egg ("—he broods with right so long upon his mishap: in this ugly egg a beautiful bird hides itself"); KSA 11:31[45]; KSA 11:35[46] a joker (*Spaaßvogel*); KSA 11:37[13]; KSA 11:40[59] Prince Vogelfrei; KSA 11:41[12]; KSA 12:1[183]; KSA 12:9[120] *Vogelfreiheit*; KSA 13:4[1]; KSA 13:11[30] bird's eye view; KSA 13:14[111] scarecrow; KSA 13:16[65] little bird; KSA 13:19[7] bird's voice (the voice of *Zarathustra*).

Camel

Although beasts of burden, camels are less domesticated than the donkey and at least more exotic to the Westerner as denizens of deserts and wastelands. They also lack most of the ridiculous characteristics associated with the donkey. This difference plays out in *Zarathustra* and GM III:8 when discussing what kinds of burdens can be taken up and in what ways. Some academic labors, for Nietzsche, represent one way. The specialist in some science becomes a camel, by deforming itself in its work, giving itself humps (KSA 9:11[299], for more on gaining humps see SE 2, p. 177, KSA 7:29[204], and, positively, AOM 132). These camels of education have a "frog's nose wisdom" (*Froschnasen-Weisheit*) with their narrow frog's perspective on the world; they lack a "feeling for universal existence [*eine Empfindung für das allgemeine Dasein*]," the bigger picture, and are therefore "cold." When Zarathustra asks in Z:1 "Three Metamorphoses," "what is most difficult . . . stepping into filthy waters when they are the waters of truth, and not repulsing cold frogs and hot toads?" he is making a distinction between the waters and wells of truth dirtied by deformed, specialist academics and those more difficult ones "dirtied" because they are difficult truths. Such difficult well water would be found away from the narrow-minded academics, such as the "famous wise men," who have the rabble to drive them on and lead them in certain directions. The solitary camel, however, lacks such "dirty" goading and drivers (Z:2 "Rabble"). Zarathustra laments those beasts burdened by what is given to them and even derides those that willingly accept all loads such as the ass (Z:3 "Spirit of Gravity" 2). For more on what it means to have to take up one's own burden (value or creation) independently, with discrimination, and on the camel's way of carrying a burden see Charles S. Taylor's essay herein.

TL 1, p. 85; WS P; KSA 9:12[138] (see Hamlet act 3, scene 2); Z:1 "Three Metamorphoses" (cf. KSA 10:4[242]); Z:2 "Rabble" camel drivers; Z:3 "Spirit of Gravity" 2; GM III:8; KSA 9:7[4]; KSA 9:11[299] incl. camels of education (Bildungskamele) and humps (Höckern); KSA 11:26[312] Camel drivers (smoking hashish).

Cat

There are several figurative idiomatic phrases in German that lend the cat to some of Nietzsche's usages. Some associate the cat with being flattered, but also to being flattering, particularly katzenfreundlich, meaning outwardly (but insincerely) friendly, and also the proverbial: "hüte dich vor den Katzen, die vorne lecken und hinten kratzen" (beware of false friends, or literally: guard yourself from cats, who up front lick and from behind scratch). The cat (die Katze) can be used to mean shrew (or, generally, one's quarrelsome or treacherous character), a prejudice Nietzsche trades on in the more misogynist passages. Nietzsche uses the tomcat far less frequently and it always appears associated with jealousy (Eifersucht), and twice with a monk figure (IM "Die kleine Hexe" [cf. GS A "Pious Beppa"] and Z:2 "Immaculate Perception").

The most frequent application of the cat describes the semi-feral in humans (women especially), their occupying the liminal place between house and wilderness. This usage likely derives from an unidentified quote about women being "less civilized than men, essentially of a wild soul; they live in the state as cats in a house, always ready to spring out through the door or window and to return to their element" (KSA 11:25[92]). Z:4 "Song of Melancholy" 3 continues this theme. Having there introduced the opposition of a cat's not "being at home" before temples (as moral centers), Nietzsche may carry this into Z:4 "Daughters of the Wilderness" 2, as the wanderer calls the "moral lion" to roar before the two girl-cats. These cats, Dudu and Suleika, are named after two of Lord Byron's characters in "Don

Juan" and "The Bride of Abydos," respectively (Köhler, p. 41; and for more on the connection between the wanderer, his shadow, and Lord Byron see forthcoming work by Paul S. Loeb). Nietzsche calls women "strangely wild" and "more 'natural' than man's" nature (BGE 239). Part of this feral nature is dangerous and if pent up will find new means of venting its inclinations (KSA 11.29[64] and the drafts noted below).

Another theme for the cat is friendship and the related issue of giving. Z:1 "Friend" (and its draft noted below) likens "woman" to birds, cows, and cats while arguing that they are not yet capable of friendship. Z:1 "Gift-giving Virtue" 1, KSA 10:4[100], and KSA 10:5[1].110 each describe as cats (and wolves) those who never give (and would prefer to take or steal). Similar to the pleasure cats of Z:3 "Old and New Tablets" 17, the question is asked (KSA 10 5[1].122): "What matters to me, the purring of those who can not love, like the cat?"

These last two sections may concern themselves more with a feline relationship of coming to and conveying knowledge. The cat's independent, slow, pleasure-finding approach is lauded at Z:4 "Higher Men" 17 (and its drafts noted below) and its similarities to the laughing and cat's prankishness of Z:4 "Song of Melancholy" 3 make an interesting contrast between the cat in the first passage and the panther in the second. However, the audible "step of everything honest" is placed in stark contrast to the sneaking cat of Z:2 "Immaculate Perception."

Lastly, there are several interesting cat passages on feline egoism. In a draft for Z (KSA 10:4[234]), "the cat and the wolf should be a model for me: they hold their self tighter"; here, not wanting to give of oneself is praised unlike the discussion above. Similarly, "the dog repays goodwill with subjugation. The cat takes pleasure in the same and has a lascivious feeling of power: it gives nothing in return" (KSA 10:1[30]); the cat knows how not to give itself away in self-subjugation and, in addition, takes pleasure in seeing the canine type fail at this. "That the cat, human, always falls back on its four legs—I would prefer to say on its *one* leg 'I'—is only a symptom of his *psychological* 'unity,' more correctly 'union': no reason to believe in a mental [*seelische*] unity" (KSA 12:1[72]).

IM "Die kleine Hexe" tomcat ("often like the grayest cat"); GS A "Pious Beppa" ("often despite the grayest hangover [*Kater*]"); Z:1 "Friend" (cf. KSA 10: 3[1].133); Z:1 "Gift-giving Virtue" 1 (cf. KSA 10:4[100], KSA 5[1].110 but also KSA 4[234]); Z:2 "Immaculate Perception" incl. cat-like and tomcat (on the latter cf. KSA 10:9[6] and KSA 10:13[1], p. 425); Z:3 "Before Sunrise" preying cats and cat's calm; Z:3 "Old and New Tablets" 17 pleasure cats; Z:4 "Higher Men" 17 (cf. KSA

11:31[37], 31[64], and 32[13]); Z:4 "Song of Melancholy" 3 cat's prankishness (*Katzen-Muthwillens*) (cf. *DD* "Nurr Narr! Nur Dichter!"; *KSA* 11:28[21] wild-cat's-prankishness; *KSA* 11:31[31], *KSA* 11:28[20] (poem fragment "Die Bösen liebend"); and on springing cats cf. *KSA* 11:25[92] and 29[1]); Z:4 "Daughters of the Wilderness" 2 girl-cats; *BGE* 131; *BGE* 239 (cf. *KSA* 11:25[92]); *DD* "Among Daughters of the Wilderness" girl-cats; *KSA* 7:1[30]; *KSA* 7:1[41]; *KSA* 8:17[98]; *KSA* 9:4[268]; *KSA* 9:6[133] tomcat; *KSA* 9:12[118] (cf. *KSA* 9:15[57]); *KSA* 10:1[30]; *KSA* 10:3[1].184;

KSA 10:4[234]; *KSA* 10:5[1].122; *KSA* 10:7[42]; *KSA* 10:13[3], p. 450 cat steps; *KSA* 10:18[52]; *KSA* 11:25[92] (unidentified quote); *KSA* 11:25[516] cat-egoism; *KSA* 11:28[5] cat feet; *KSA* 11:29[64] scratch-cat (cf. *KSA* 11:31[35] and 32[10] draft entitled "Voluntary Beggar"); *KSA* 11:31[51] ("heavy granite cats, the values out of primeval times"; cf. *KSA* 11:32[9], *KSA* 12:9[59] and, in verse, *KSA* 13:20[29]); *KSA* 11:40[35] (cat opposed to ape; on Galiani and d'Epinay, cf. *BGE* 26 and 222); *KSA* 12:1[72] (cf. *KSA* 11:25[516]).

Cow

The primary cow attribute applied by Nietzsche in his writings is its lazy, quiet lifestyle, for example, in *AOM* 107 a work of art should lie like a cow in a field (imagery that returns in *TI* "Morality" 3) and have something easy going in it. The cow's glossy stare as a sign of stupidity is commonly employed as well, for example, *WS* 313: cows (in opposition to the higher intelligence) wear an expression of "wonderment halted on the way to a *question*." Similarly, in a fragment on the meaning of possessing a language (*KSA* 7:37[6]), Nietzsche writes that cows (seals and horses, too) have small souls from lacking language and "humans of entire ages do, in fact, have something of the cow about them." Also, he owes some of his thinking on cows to his readings on the Hindu tradition: *DS* 11, p. 70 quotes an Indian proverb; *AC* 56, *KSA* 13:14[176], *KSA* 13:14[178], and *KSA* 13:14[177] each cites some Hindu ritual prescription involving cows.

Perhaps Nietzsche's best-known cow is "The Motley Cow." There is some indication that the narration does not actually *use* Zarathustra's town's proper name, rather we are told that it "is called" or that the "name sounds of [*die Stadt . . . deren Name lautet*]" the motley cow, emphasizing an evaluation of the place and its inhabitants. Moreover, the name itself is placed in quotation marks (except in the first chapter). The name is only mentioned during moments of transition into or out of the town or in contrast to being alone, as on a mountainside; they are: Z:1 "Three Metamorphoses," Z:1 "Tree on the Mountainside," Z:1 "Gift-giving Virtue," and Z:3 "On Apostates." For more on this name and its relation to Cadmus and Thebes see

David Allison's *Reading the New Nietzsche* (pp. 128–129) and Tracey Stark's chapter in this collection.

There is an unusually enduring image throughout Nietzsche's productive life; that of milking adversity. It begins with *HH* 292: the difficult life of becoming a necessary catalyst for the future can be borne well when (perhaps sometime in the future) the knowledge required is regarded as honey and the strife involved as refreshing milk. Later, in *Z*:1 "Enjoying and Suffering of the Passions," the passions become sufferable, even enjoyable, when a goal is placed before them. In both, melancholy (or affliction) becomes something nourishing and plentiful—a cow bearing milk. It is not explicitly melancholy that is being milked in *DD* "Von der Armut des Reichsten" (and the same poem in publication at *NCW* "Epilogue" 3) but dark clouds (as in *HH* 292) yielding "milk-warm wisdom." Lightning may be this milk of dark clouds. We find the same inversion of value here as in the others—from an immediate source of displeasure to its becoming a source of something better, particularly some bit of knowledge or wisdom. Milk as a figurative term for something nourishing for the mind or soul is very old in both German and English, and may originate in Exodus 3:8 (land flowing with milk and honey) and Joel 3:18 (here coupled with wine). Some older and more famous such uses include Chaucer's *The Parson's Tale* line 613, "norrissen his children with Milk of losengerie"; Shakespeare's *Macbeth* act 1, scene 5 and act 4, scene 3; *Romeo and Juliet* act 3, scene 3, "I'll give armour to keep off that word; / Adversity's sweet milk, philosophy, / to comfort thee though thou art banished"; and lastly Schiller's *Wilhelm Tell* act 4, scene 3, "*die Milch der frommen Denkart*." Again at *Z*:2 "Night Song" and *Z*:3 "Old and New Tablets" 30, the imagery continues (including refreshment and lightning clouds) as does its inverting power, while *Z*:3 "Great Longing" follows the same metaphor.

Nietzsche's explicit association of women and cows begins with *GS* 67 (cf. *KSA* 9:6[193], which is very similar, yet refers to Italians instead of women) and claims that they have an ill-founded calm confidence (*ein ruhiges Vertrauen*) in their relationships. In *Z*:1 "On the Friend" Zarathustra proclaims woman is incapable of friendship. Later (*KSA* 13:15[83]), one finds that women severely brought up, of sterling character, (*stark gerathen, von altem Schrot und Korn*), having the temperament of a cow, understand their good fortune to come from trust in god (*Gottvertrauen*) but should really see their own constitution as the cause. Focusing on George Sand (*TI* "Skirmishes" 1, *TI* "Skirmishes" 6, and *KSA* 13:11[24]), Nietzsche trades on the use of 'cow' as a derogatory term for women (cf. *KSA* 13:19[1]).

The lazy, bovine life takes on a moral-psychological usage in the later works. The moralistic cow (*TI* "Morality" 3), desirous of "peace of the soul," of no internal opposition, is antithetical to "the *great* life" with its war and "spiritualized hostility." In *TI* "Skirmishes" 38, cows (as well as other types) want well-being without struggles, war, and resistances. At *AC* 52 the moralistic cow returns as part of the "pietists and other cows from Swabia" who interpret all events as acts of grace, without contention or skepticism; the Swabian in mind seems to be "*Hegel:* something of the Swabian faith in God, of bovine optimism" (*KSA* 13:18[14], see also *KSA* 13:15[83] on bovine faith in God). Nietzsche opposes two religious types at *KSA* 13:11[297], each dealing with an internal split between good and evil while attempting to cease inner, opposing value-drives (*Werth-Antrieben*). The "consistent type" or "the Buddhist type: or the complete cow" overcomes evil by overflowing the peaceful, helpful, loving conditions as a constant praxis and does not hate evil for its own sake, but because it causes harmful conditions. This is opposed to the Christian type ("the inconsistent" type or the "complete mosquito"), which must feed its hate of evil and war against it to survive as the type that denounces evil, hate, and war. The cow's inactivity would here be its lack of war both internally and externally; it "lives wholly in the positive feelings." For an early sign of this usage see *GS* 351, where both bovine piety and peace of mind (*Gemüthsstille*) are at play.

In Nietzsche's early epistemological writings, he calls thought's relation to reality "a piecemeal ruminating", and the will a "ruminating of experiences in conscious thought" (*KSA* 7:5[80]). Purposes arise from the ruminating of experiences (*KSA* 7:5[83]). The point seems to be that given the nature of human thinking purposes, actions, and thoughts are not necessitated, for example, by nature. From the time of the second *Untimely Meditation*, rumination focuses on stultification in various ways: *HL* 1, p. 89 and *KSA* 7:29[32]. Scholarly thinking or studying, as rumination, needs to stop periodically (either to forget some of the past or to place standards and feelings on the subject) in order to result in action or valuation (see also *EH* "The Untimely Ones" 3 and *KSA* 9:6[342]; cf. *KSA* 8:23[29], *KSA* 9:1[122], and esp. *KSA* 8:5[148] where the right rumination of history can lead to advances). Inhibiting rumination returns later on in *CW* 3 and its draft *KSA* 13:16[36]. One of the few entirely positive uses of rumination is Nietzsche's well-known call for a ruminative (re)reading of his works (*GM* P:8).

DS 11, p. 70 cow horn; *HL* 1, p. 89 ruminating; *HH* 292 utter; *AOM* 107; *WS* 57; *WS* 295; *WS* 313; *GS* 67 (cf. *KSA* 9:6[193] paraphrasing Stendhal); *GS* 128 ruminating; *GS* 351 bovine, ruminating; *Z*:1 "Three Metamorphoses"; *Z*:1 "Teachers of Virtue" incl. ruminating; *Z*:1 "Enjoying and Suffering of the Passions"; *EH* "Books"

Z:5; *KSA* 10:4[6] and *KSA* 10:5[1].102 utter of melancholy; Z:1 "Tree on the Mountainside"; Z:1 "New Idol" ruminated; Z:1 "Friend" (cf. *KSA* 10:3[1].133); Z:1 "Gift-giving Virtue" 1; Z:2 "Night Song" utter; Z:3 "On Apostates" 2; Z:3 "Old and New Tablets" 30 milk-utter; Z:4 "Voluntary Beggar" incl. ruminating; Z:3 "Great Longing" utter; GM P:8 incl. ruminating; *CW* 3 ruminating (cf. *KSA* 13:16[36]); *TI* "Morality" 3 moral-cow; *TI* "Skirmishes" 1 milk cow; *TI* "Skirmishes" 6 writing-cow; *TI* "Skirmishes" 38; AC 52; AC 56; EH "Books" UM:3 ruminating; *EH* "Books" Z:5 cow herd; *EH* "Books" Z:7; *NCW* Epilogue 3 and *DD* "Von der Armut des Reichsten" incl. utter; *KSA* 7:5[80] ruminating; *KSA* 7:5[83] ruminating; *KSA*

7:7[124] ruminating; *KSA* 7:13[2], *Kuhreigen*; *KSA* 7:17[3]; *KSA* 7:29[32] ruminating; *KSA* 7:37[6]; *KSA* 8:5[148] ruminating; *KSA* 8:10[2] *kuhwarme Liebe*; *KSA* 8:23[29] ruminating; *KSA* 9:1[122] ruminating; *KSA* 9:6[342] ruminated; *KSA* 9:11[260] and *KSA* 12:4[5] milking the cow of the night; *KSA* 11:28[19] (cf. *KSA* 11:29[1]; *KSA* 11:30[13] cow herdsmen; *KSA* 12:5[44] and *KSA* 12:5[48] (refer to German youths), *KSA* 13:11[40] and *KSA* 13:20[68] lukewarm milksops (*kuhwarme Milchherzen*); *KSA* 13:11[24]; *KSA* 13:11[297]; *KSA* 13:18[14] bovine; *KSA* 13:14[176] (section titled "Alcoholism"); *KSA* 13:14[177]; *KSA* 13:14[178], incl. cow herdsmen (section titled "Priests"); *KSA* 13:15[83]; *KSA* 13:19[1].

Dog

Generally speaking, Nietzsche uses *hündisch* to indicate something domesticated to the point of being utterly servile or shamelessly fawning; that which waits obediently (e.g., *KSA* 10:1[30]: "The dog pays for goodwill with subjugation . . ."). He often associates such images with what is parasitic and sponge-like and also with those who are mere flatterers (e.g., D 158) or followers. The image of rolling over like a dog is used in reference to religious devotion (e.g., *KSA* 11:34[141] in which Augustine is described as "rolling over" in his *Confessions*); and the dog is described as having something like religious feelings for the human (also cf. *KSA* 11:26[242] and 31[32]). *Hund* is also used as a curse (as in "you dog!" e.g., HH 111), to indicate poor treatment (e.g., AOM 256) or a pitiful creature (e.g., D 135), as an object of scorn (e.g., D 369), as an indication of something lowly (e.g., "a dog of a man [*Hund von Menschen*]" as in GS 40; or that which is lowest (*Hundemässigeres*) (as in D 199), and as a degenerate beast of prey (*Raubtier*) (e.g., *KSA* 10:7[42]). However, notice that when the lion at the conclusion of *Zarathustra* is characterized by his great love, he is described as acting "like a dog that finds its old master again" (Z:4 "The Sign"). This is immediately followed by the image of doves flying over the nose of the lion to show their affection, and so it might be compared with the image of the wild dogs in one's cellar being transformed into birds (Z:1 "Enjoying and Suffering Passions"). The cry of the dog as pitiful in D 135 might be usefully compared with the dog in Z:3 "Vision and Riddle" 2, which is discussed by Shapiro in this volume. See also Kathleen Marie Higgins's discussion of Nietzsche's dog and its association with pain in GS 312 (Higgins, *Comic Relief: Nietzsche's Gay Science*). There are also occasional references to dogs in relation to herding and hunting.

Several interesting deviations from these dominant associations are noteworthy. At least two other kinds of dogs make their appearance in Nietzsche's works, including one that is frighteningly brutal and deadly, as in the common association of *hündisch* with *Angst* (e.g., SE 4) and the "philosophical dog," which is obviously a reference to Diogenes (e.g., WS Epilogue), whom Nietzsche admired for his deflation of hollow values. The image of the dog as domesticated stands in contrast with the wild or ravenous dog, which is a common association but one that Nietzsche uses less frequently. This use is relevant for those interested in the kind of transformation that Nietzsche describes in GM and that Zarathustra envisages in Z. Compare the passages linked below that describe human beings as having wild dogs in their cellars, and how Nietzsche describes the ascetic priests as pressing these into service, releasing one and then another in order to jar their flocks from melancholy through the production of "an orgy of feeling" (GM III:20). Nietzsche might be said to combine the wild and the philosophical dogs in a single passage in *Zarathustra* in the section "On Great Events." It is the passage in which Zarathustra confronts the fire hound (in earlier drafts as the "hell hound"). Nietzsche wrote numerous lengthy drafts of this section, and for some time anticipated including an entire section to be titled "On the Firehound." It begins with Zarathustra describing the earth as having a skin that suffers from two diseases: "man" and "fire hound." The latter seeks to frighten and force submission by "bellowing smoke" like the Church or the State, which Zarathustra likens to a "hypocritical hound." Zarathustra describes the Church as striving to be the most important animal on earth. This makes the fire hound crazed with envy, and Zarathustra then threatens him with another (more philosophical) fire hound who *actually* "speaks out of the heart of the earth" rather than merely *pretending* to speak from the "belly of reality." Upon hearing this, the fire hound is shamed and reduced to a mere whimpering dog that crawls away. The former, the wild fire hound, Nietzsche connects with "scum- and overthrowing-devils"; it likes to bellow about freedom and is always found with mud.

The *philosophical* dog, Diogenes, appears in a passage in the form of a dialogue at the end of WS. It follows WS 350, which discusses the chains of "heavy and pregnant errors contained in the conceptions of morality, religion and metaphysics" laid upon the human animal to make it less like an animal, and which have successfully made the human "become gentler, more spiritual, more joyful, more reflective than any animal is." Thus, these chains can be thought of as necessary. They might be seen as supporting the distinc-tion, drawn by several contributors, between taming and training, in which case, training is a necessary cultivation of animal potencies rather than the sheer domestication to which taming amounts. In WS 350, Nietzsche suggests the chains have been worn too long, though, and now seem to have a deleterious effect. Recovery from the sickness brought about by wearing the chains for too long will finally accomplish the goal that the chains instigated: "the separation of man from the animals," which at this point Nietzsche seems to think admirable and worthy. He also ties this goal's accomplishment to achieving "Peace on earth and goodwill to men." Until such time, however, we have the "age of the individual." Again, interested readers are directed to Shapiro's discussion of the association of the dog with the concept of the ego in this volume, and how this bears on the common view that Nietzsche advocates a kind of radical individualism or so-called sovereignty of the individual.

BT 20; SE 3, pp. 186, 192; SE 4, p. 200; FEI 1, p. 22; FEI 4, pp. 99–101; "The Greek State" p. 15 (ref. to Iliad, bk 1: slaying of mules and dogs; cf. KSA 7:10[1]); PTA 7 (paraphrase of Heraclitus frag. 97: "Dogs bark at everyone they do not recognize"); HH 34 (on chained dogs; cf. Taylor's and Shapiro's essays in this volume; cf. WS 140 and WS 350); HH 111; HH 372 ("learned how to laugh but forgotten how to bite"); AOM 256; WS "Epilogue" incl. canine; D 24; D 91; D 135; D 158 canine; D 194; D 199 the doggish (Hundemässig-eres); D 227 dog kennel; D 258; D 273; D 369; IM "Song of the Goatherd" (cf. GS A "Song of a Theoretical Goatherd"); GS "Rhymes" 39 ("Dog Star"); GS 40; GS 146 ("Tartars"); GS 312; Z: P 8 (fig. for corpse) and Z: P 9; Z:1 "Enjoying and Suffering Passions" (wild dogs in cellar, cf. GM III:8,

KSA 8:25[2], and the drafts at KSA 10:4[86] and 5[1].141); Z:1 "Tree on Mountainside" (dogs in cellar); Z:1 "Chastity" bitch (Hündin); Z:2 "Famous Wise Men"; Z:2 "On Immaculate Perception"; Z:2 "Great Events" incl. fire hound; Z:3 "Vision and Riddle" 2; Z:3 "Virtue that Makes Small" 2 (wolf makes himself into a dog as man makes himself into his best domestic animal; cf. GS 314 and the drafts at KSA 10:17[25] and 22[5]); Z:3 "Three Evils" 1, 2 canine monster (Hunds-Ungethüm) and doglike (hündisch); Z:3 "Old and New Tablets" 18; Z:3 "Other Dancing Song" 1; Z:4 "Cry of Distress"; Z:4 "Conversation with the Kings" 1; Z:4 "Leech"; Z:4 "Magician" 1; Z:4 "Ugliest Human" (cf. drafts at KSA 11:29[1], 31[49], 32[9], and 32[10]); Z:4 "Higher Men" 2 hell hound, and "Higher Man" 13

(*Pöble-Schwindhunde*) (cf. drafts of the latter at *KSA* 11:29[1], 31[50], and 31[64]); *Z*:4 "Drunken Song" 4, and 8; *Z*:4 "The Sign"; *BGE* 45 including tracking dogs (*Spürhunde*); *BGE* 202 anarchist-dogs (*Anarchisten-Hunde*), *BGE* 260 doglike people (*Hunde-Art von Menschen*) (doggish way of permitting others to harm them); *GM* I:14; *GM* III:8 (cf. *Z*:1 "On Enjoying and Suffering the Passions" and *KSA* 8 25[2]); *GM* III:14; *GM* III:20; *CW* 3 (going to the dogs); *EH*, "Clever" 1; *DD* "Ariadne"; *KSA* 7:1[30] (citation possibly from Uhland); *KSA* 7:17[3]; *KSA* 7:21[13]; *KSA* 7:23[11]; *KSA* 8:25[2] (cf. *KSA* 11:40[65] and notes for *HH* 34); *KSA* 8:42[12]; *KSA* 9:3[158]; *KSA* 9:4[48]; *KSA* 9:19[6] (from Shakespeare's *Timon*); *KSA* 10:1[30]; *KSA* 10:2[22] bitch (cf. *KSA* 10:3[1].192); *KSA* 10:3[1].184; *KSA* 10:4[38]; *KSA* 10:4[91]; *KSA* 10:4[187]; *KSA* 10:5[1].75, *KSA* 10:5[1].190; *KSA* 10:7[22] dog-type (*Hunde-Art*); *KSA* 10:7[42]; *KSA* 10:8[1] dog liver; *KSA* 10:8[8] bitches; *KSA* 10:10[4] hell hound ("conversation with the hell hound (Vulcan)") and 10[28] now fire-hound; *KSA* 10:10[40], 11[13], 13[25], 13[27], and 13[28] fire hound (plans for section on fire hound); *KSA* 10:11[11] fire hound (saying of the fire hound; not in *Z*: " 'When the house burns, one forgets even lunch' "); *KSA* 10:13[1], p. 436 (ref. to dog and child looking over his shoulder into a picture book); *KSA* 10:13[3], p. 449 hell hound; *KSA* 10:18[55] chained watchdog (*Kettenhund*); *KSA* 10:21[3]; *KSA* 11:25[37] hunting dog (titled "misunderstanding of the beast of prey," refers to the health of Cesare Borgia and the hunting dog's qualities); *KSA* 11:25[126] (quoting Taine); *KSA* 11:25[194] (regarding Andrea Doria and loneliness); *KSA* 11:25[354]; *KSA* 11:25[516] dog-egoism; *KSA* 11:26[242]; *KSA* 11:28[9], 28[23], and 29[1] (devotion); *KSA* 11:29[11], 31[33], and 31[61] (mawkish dogs); *KSA* 11:29[62] and 31[45] (yelping hell hound); *KSA* 11:31[32]; *KSA* 11:34[141]; *KSA* 11:34[147] tracking dogs (*Spürhunde*); *KSA* 11:35[22] canine; *KSA* 11:38[20] (wild dogs in oneself, will to truth as wildest dog); *KSA* 11:40[65] (draft of new preface to *HH*); *KSA* 12:1[158] (Parisian *Windhund*, reiterated in *KSA* 12:5[109] only as "dog" but with attribution to Parisian poets instead of spirit); *KSA* 12:5[38] dog kennel-existence (*Hundesstahl-Existenze*) (refers to N's life, cf. letters cited at *KSA* 15, pp. 12 and 155); *KSA* 12:10[107]; *KSA* 13:11[9]; *KSA* 13:11[41], and 20[67]; *KSA* 13:14[155] (bite of conscience like the bite of a dog); *KSA* 13:15[23]; *KSA* 13:15[71] dog-manner (*Hunde-Art*; i.e., of attacking from behind and beneath).

Lion

Typical lion attributes such as courage, strength, and ferocity apply to almost all of the lions in Nietzsche's texts, and at least complicate the passages that do not seem leonine (such as the discussion of *mürbe* below or the presence of doves). As a symbol of courage, for example, the lion appears in *Z*:3 "Involuntary Bliss," in *GM* II:23 referring to the Greeks having made gods the source of evil, and at *KSA* 9:11[111]. There are two passages in the drafts for *Zarathustra* explicitly relating the lion to the child, *KSA* 10:4[177] and *KSA* 10:4[218], and these may shed some light on the role of *Zarathustra's* lion and the children that surround it, though nowhere else is it so clearly thematized. The mentioned fragments indicate a tension between one's child and one's lion that one must keep in proper relation, whereby the lion does not overcome the child. For a plausible explanation for the quizzical lines of Z:4 "On the Higher Men" 20—"what milks lionesses"—see Walter Otto's comments on lions and maenads, in *Dionysus: Myth and Cult.*

Nietzsche often likes to use his animals to characterize a relationship to knowledge or wisdom, both in acquisition and expression—and the lion is no exception. Alongside fox and wolf paths, there are "lion paths of epistemology" (*KSA* 8:34[14] and cf. AOM 27). Zarathustra asks, in Z:P 3, "Does reason desire after knowledge as the lion after its nourishment?" Some truths require being leonine in courage (*KSA* 9:11[111], where we are told a lamb's innocence is needed too). Z:2 "On the Famous Wise Men" mocks the wise men as false images of a leonine voracity for wisdom and demands that one be lion-willed, "hungry, violent, lonely and godless"; also in this vein is Z:3 "Old and New Tablets" 16. In Z:2 "The Child with the Mirror," Zarathustra's wild wisdom is a lioness. A fascinating passage describing his own aphoristic style, *KSA* 11:37[5] gives one the difficult to translate: "und eine Einsiedler-Philosophie, wenn sie selbst mit einer Löwenklaue geschrieben wäre, würde doch immer wie eine Philosophie der 'Gänsefüßchen' aussehen."

In the notes to *Zarathustra* (*KSA* 10:16[51]), Nietzsche writes of a third animal companion, the lion, which is to be a "symbol of his *ripeness* [*Reife*] and *tenderness* [*Mürbe*]." *Mürb* is an adjective denoting that which is no longer resistant, but pliant (often indicating a being past the prime, e.g., brittle); in this sense, Grimm's dictionary gives as its second definition "that which is easily bitten," that is, tender, just right. In this way, it makes sense alongside ripeness (*Reife*). Zarathustra being *mürb* ("mellow" in Kaufmann's Z) is required, in Z:2 "The Stillest Hour," for his readiness to have followers, to command great things with a lion's voice; thus the laughter says to him. In Z:3 "On the Three Evils" 2, the lion-willed—opposed to the wilted for whom sex (*Wollust*) is a poison—find sex an invigorator; they are ripe and mature enough for it. The king to the right, in Z:4 "The Welcome," speaks of loneliness growing *mürb* and breaking open, letting forth those destined for Zarathustra. Notes at *KSA* 10:21[2] narrate that "the 4 animals (pride with cleverness—power with mildness [*Milde*]) come closer to one another"—here perhaps ripeness is power, readiness to use power, as when the laughing lion roars at the higher men—but the lion definitely nears the dove swarm, connoting a certain passivity in the mixture. However, one year later, Nietzsche ties the coming of the laughing lion with a hardening (e.g., KSA 11:31[11] and KSA 11:31[16]).

The final scene of Z involves both the laughing lion and the accompanying flock of doves. The first mention of these two animals together in Nietzsche's corpus is in GS Appendix "My Happiness." Predating him in combining these two, however, is Schiller, in his *Piccolomini* act 3, scene 8, line 1872: "Mit Löwenmuth den Taubensinn bewaffnen." Laughter surrounds Zarathustra in both Z:2 "The Child with the Mirror" in connection to his lioness "wild wisdom" and Z:2 "The Stillest Hour" while Zarathustra is encouraged to command like the lion. Z:3 "Old and New Tablets" 1 is the first pairing of the laughing lion and the dove in Z; and in Z:4 "The Welcome" we are told that these lions are Zarathustra's children, for whom he is waiting. Though referring to eagles and panthers, the lines in Z:4 "The Song of the Melancholy" 3 seem relevant to the preying, laughing lion: "*tearing to pieces* the god in man / no less than the sheep in him, / and *laughing* while tearing" (so too perhaps, the lamb and eagle of GM II:13). Finally, in "The Sign," the prophesy is fulfilled and the laughing lion and the swarm of doves appear. For more on the meaning of this lion see Paul S. Loeb and Babette E. Babbich's essays in this collection.

Several commentators have understood the "blonde beast" in GM to resemble a lion, and it certainly has strong similarities to those in Z, especially the "grim, blonde, curly / lion monster" in "Among the Daughters of the Wilderness" and the "yellow, powerful animal" of KSA 11:32[15]. Moreover, there are strong similarities between the discussion in GM and Callicles' use of lions in Plato's *Gorgias* (483e–484a), where lions are natural rulers taken from their natural habitats, but who might one day unfetter themselves and return to conquer and rule. In addition, the similarities between the "blonde beast" and Callicles' lions seem to share the ideology put forth by the Athenians to the Melians as reported by Thucydides. (For more on these connections see Brennecke, Calder, Dodds [esp. pp. 387–391], Ginzburg [esp. pp. 1–25], Müller and, in this collection, articles by Schank and Loeb.) Further utilizing a politicized lion, KSA 7:5[98] and KSA 11:36[42] both employ the lion to represent a ruling caste or individual and its influence on the people or caste not in power.

FEI 5, p. 137 (Schiller's "Robbers" frontispiece); GS 99; GS 314; GS "My Happiness" (*Lowendrange*); Z:P 3; Z:1 "Three Metamorphoses"; Z:2 "Child with the Mir-ror" lioness wisdom (cf. KSA 10:11[4]); Z:2 "Famous Wise Men" lion's skin and lion-will (cf. Aesop fables 267 and 279, see also the index entry for the ass); Z:2 "The Stillest Hour" lion's voice; Z:3 "Involuntary Bliss" "overbearing, prankish bearing" (*Löwen-Übermuthe und-Muthwillen*) and lion's voice; Z:3 "Three Evils" 2 lion-willed; Z:3 "Old and New Tablets" 1; Z:3 "Old and New Tablets" 16 lion-willed; Z:4 "Welcome" laughing lion; Z:4 "Higher Men" 20 lioness (cf. KSA 11:29[11], 31[50] and 31[64]); Z:4 "Daughters of the Wilderness" 2 (wanderer sings of moral lions); Z:4 "The Sign" (cf. KSA 11:31[21], 32[14] (draft called "The Last Sin"), and 32[15]); BGE 204 (sarcastically referring to Dühring and von Hartmann); GM II:23 lion-hearted; GM III:26 (quoting Anacreon); A 45; DD "Among Daughters of the Wilderness" 3; KSA 7:5[98]; KSA 7:7[122]; KSA 8:3[53]; KSA 8:34[14] lion's ways (*Löwengänge*); KSA 9:9[13]; KSA 9:11[111]; KSA 10:4[77] (cf. KSA 10:5[1].136); KSA 10:4[177]; KSA 10:4[218]; KSA 10:4[222]

lion tamer dies by the lion (lion tamer may be the god of love, following the ancient Greek representation of love as a lion); KSA 10:15[7], 16[83], 20[3], and 18[45] lion-dove pairing in Z:3 drafts; KSA 10:16[45], 16[51], and 21[2] lion as Zarathustra's animal; KSA 10:16[64] draft of Z:3 ending; KSA 10:17[75] lion of mania and caprice; KSA 10:18[37] lion-willed; KSA 10:19[7] lion's laugh; KSA 11:29[14], 29[26], 31[9], and 31[56] lion-dove pairing in Z:4 drafts; KSA 11:31[11], 31[14], 31[16], and 31[22] laughing lion drafts; KSA 11:31[23]; KSA 11:32[16] prospective chapter title "The Laughing Lion"; KSA 11:36[42]; KSA 11:37[5] lion claws; KSA 13:20[104] lion foot (*Löwenfuß*); KSA 13:24[10] lion-novella (Goethe wrote the first of its kind—it lets-ripen, is autumnal, "something golden, sweetened, mild, *not* marble").

Mole

As it is a subterranean creature that does little but works hard with poor eyesight, the mole appears in Nietzsche's writings with these primary characteristics. For *SE* 6 (and its draft) the working, scholarly mole is not only short sighted but 'sees' in (or reads into) history human motives that are much like his own. This is because his inclinations are shared with most of society; the mole's isolated activity makes it see itself in his work object. Similarly, in *HH* 18, the logician's maxim that a substance is always mostly self-same and unchanging is due to a mole-like predisposition for the same, limited in scope. In both *D* 41 and *D* 435, the mole's work is contrasted with the active life (and in the latter with the life of great sensations), which leaves behind noble ruins (not mere mole tunnels) when it dies. *GS* 86 finds a mole worker forced into the wings and conceits of a culture and sentiment he does not truly understand, but which he thinks he can evaluate anyway. This mole is also called a mule, so its receiving wings may prefigure the ass given wings in Z:4 "Higher Men" 20.

The mole also takes on two distinct political meanings in Nietzsche separated by more than twenty years. The first appears in "The Greek State," referring to "the slave, the blind mole of culture." What Nietzsche seems to mean by slaves is a working class (be it ancient, feudal, or modern), a necessary element for culture. These workers (the defeated, in his story of the state's origin) are blinded beneficently by dust from the victor's chariot's wheels (i.e., his culture) (p. 8), such that they can proclaim the dignity of labor and of man. They are also blind because they unconsciously let the "state-instinct" act through them for its "state-purpose." Some years later the mole's digging returns (KSA 11:37[11]), as the agitating work of the socialist and communist. Presumably for reasons similar to those in "The Greek State," a socialist society, one lacking a slavish working class, would be antithetical to life. However, Nietzsche finds the burrowing undermining work of the socialist agitator a positive force, making the herd element retain its cunning and warlike qualities just that much longer. (For more on the mole see David Farrell Krell's chapter on the mole in *Infectious Nietzsche* and Debra B. Bergoffen's essay in this collection.)

SE 6, p. 227 incl. mole tunnel (*Maulwurfsloch*) (cf. KSA 7:29[13]); "The Greek State" p. 9 ("the slave, the blind mole of culture," cf. KSA 7:10[1], p. 342 fragment for *BT*); HH 18 mole's eyes; D P 1; D 41 mole tunnel; D 435 mole hills; KSA 9:4[36] ("The blind mole is descended from those who see well—the effect of the darkness on the optical nerve."); GS 86; Z:3 "Vision and the Riddle" 1 (mole and dwarf); Z:3 "Spirit of Gravity" 2 (mole and dwarf); KSA 11:37[11].

Snake

The biblical snake, a major source for Nietzsche's snakes, appears in Gen. 3:1 as the more cunning (*listiger*) animal who convinces Eve to eat from the tree granting knowledge of good and evil The snake is also described as wary (*klug*) (Matt. 10:16). It is referenced explicitly at BGE 44, BGE 152, EH "Books" BGE:2, and A 48. In contrast to the chthonic powers of snakes in antiquity, one should compare the lowly, dust-eating position the Bible allocates its snakes (Gen. 3:14–15 and Isaiah 65:25) and how this influences Zarathustra's snake and those of GS "Rhymes" 8. Among the ancient Greeks, snakes were believed, among other things, to be carriers of the deads' souls, thus continuing life in its mental and spiritual capacities in a new body, partially because they were considered chthonic beings, who passed, like worms, through graves. Perhaps this added to the use of the widespread image of a snake eating itself as a symbol for eternity.

In an early fragment to *Zarathustra*, Nietzsche imagines that the "snake of eternity lies coiled" in the light of the "sun of knowledge" (*KSA* 9:11[196]). However, in the published work the roles have changed; the snakes of knowledge (*Z*:1 "Gift-Giving Virtue" 1) lies around the sun, whose cycles, at noon and midnight, often indicate the eternal (return); yet at the end of the chapter "On the Gift-giving Virtue" the sun returns as the *knowledge* of one who has gone under and beyond. For other indications of this back and forth see *KSA* 10:2[9] and *KSA* 10:4[261].

The dangerous snake being an impediment to progress (e.g., *KSA* 7:5[65], *KSA* 7:34[14], and *KSA* 8:28[39]) naturally causes one to approach it as an opponent. There are many precursors to this in Greek mythology (e.g., infant Hercules against the snakes, and when grown up against the serpentine hydra, and Apollo defeating the python guarding the Delphic oracle) and in the Bible (e.g., Bel & Snake 23–27 and Isaiah 27:1). *HH* 498, *D* 494, *Z*:1 "Adder's Bite," *Z*:2 "Human Prudence," and *KSA* 10:12[1].4 all discuss the need to have a proper enemy (be it snake or dragon) in order to achieve the desired end or to be a "hero." A more specific struggle is found in *KSA* 7:5[65] and *KSA* 7:11[1] (see additional notes below).

Nietzsche sometimes uses unwieldy and desirous snakes to represent one's desires or drives (as with the war-mongering kings of *Z*:4 "Conversation with Kings" 2 and in *DD* "Das Feuerzeichen"). Guilt-ridden and misunderstanding his drives and true intentions, the pale criminal is "a heap of diseases" and "a ball of snakes" that, not finding repose among themselves, seek their prey in the world (*Z*:1 "Pale Criminal"). A draft to this passage attests to this reading: "What is the human? A heap of passions . . ." (*KSA* 10:5[1].185). This heap of struggling passions may recall the "fight among your virtues" (*Z*:1 "Enjoying and Suffering the Passions") and the idea that it is better to have one virtue, rather than many, to overcome. Moreover, *KSA* 9:6[83] describes the struggle between opposing moral drives, so highly valued by some moralists, as like the attack on Laocoön by snakes. This would follow with Nietzsche's reframing of virtues as aspects of drives and passions. In contrast, compare the constricting snakes of metaphysical conceptions of *HH* 236.

HL 4, p. 110; *HL* 10, *Schlangentödtern*; "Dionysian Worldview" 1, p. 559 (cf. "Birth of Tragic Thought," p.587, both paraphrasing *The Bacchae* 677ff and also the chorus' parodos earlier on); *TL* 1, p. 82; *HH* 13; *HH* 236; *HH* 498 (snake into dragon, cf. *Z*:1 "Adder's Bite"); *HH* II P:2, snake's cunning (*Schlangenklugheit*); *AOM* 36, snake tooth; *AOM* 49, snake's skin; *AOM* 62; *AOM* 172; *WS* 74 snake's cunning; *D* 77; *D* 84 (see John 3:14, Num. 21:6–9, and 2 Kings 18:4); *D* 193 rattle snake; *D* 455 incl. shedding; *D* 494; *D* 573 incl. shedding; *GS* P2:4 shedding; *GS* "Rhymes" 8 incl. snake's diet; *GS* "Rhymes" 11; *GS* 165 (on the need to shed often); *GS* 259 (cf. *KSA* 9:18[6], *KSA* 10:4[38], 5[1].74, and 12[1].157); *GS* 342; *GS* 371 shedding; *Z* P 1; *Z* P 10 (cf. *KSA* 10:2[7] snake's cunning knows what strengthens a heart, eagle is to take and carry the heart where ever it wants); *Z*:1 "Pale Criminal"; *Z*:1 "Adder's Bite" incl. adder, snake poison; *Z*:1 "Gift-Giving Virtue" 1; *Z*:2 "Child with the Mirror"; *Z*:2 "Immaculate Perception" incl. snake's filth and snake rings (*Schlangengeringel*) (cf. the drafts at *KSA* 10:2[19], 3[1].197, 9[16], and 13[1], p. 422); *Z*:2 "Human Prudence" rattle snake; *Z*:3 "Vision and the Riddle"; *Z*:3 "Three Evils" 2; *Z*:3 "Convalescent" 2; *Z*:3 "Other Dancing Song" 1 (life becomes snake-haired and full of desire); *Z*:4 "Conversation with Kings" 2 (swords like red flecked snakes, cf. *KSA* 11:29[64] and 31[35]); *Z*:4 "Magician" 2; *Z*:4 "Ugliest Man" ("snake death" valley); *Z*:4 "Voluntary Beggar"; *Z*:4 "Shadow" shedding; *Z*:4 "Welcome"; *Z*:4 "Song of Melancholy" 1; *Z*:4 "Science" snake cunning; *Z*:4 "Drunken Song" 2; *BGE* 44 snake like; *BGE* 152; *BGE* 202; *CW* 3 rattlesnake (Wagner); *CW* 5 rattlesnake's happiness (Wagner); *A* 48 (utilizing the etymological connection between Eve and snake, *heva* in Hebrew, cf. *KSA* 13 11[289] and 2 Cor. 11:3); *A* Epilogue 1 (cf. Milton's *On Reformation*, p. 590 "The soure levin of humane Traditions mixt in one putrifi'd Masse wth the poisonous dregs of hypocrisie in the hearts of *Prelates* that lye basking in the Sunny warmth of Wealth, and Promotion, is the Serptents Egge that will hatch an *Antichrist* wheresoever, and ingender the

same Monster big, or little as the Lump is which breeds him."); *EH* "Books" *BGE*:2; *DD* "Zwischen Raubvögeln" incl. snake poison; *DD* "Das Feuerzeichen"; *NCW* Epilogue 2 shedding; *KSA* 7:5[65] incl. vipers (unidentified quote of the northern European myth of Geenar and Atli, cf. *KSA* 7:7[20], relating this to Prometheus, so that snakes are the punishment for the promethean type); *KSA* 7:11[1] (draft of "Foreword to R. Wagner," snakes are impediments to culture's progress and Greek rebirth, cf. *KSA* 7:5[65] and its notes above); *KSA* 7:13[1] python; *KSA* 7:34[14] snake writhing (*Schlangengewimel*) (one isolated returns to life as to a writhing mass of snakes); *KSA* 8:23[30]; *KSA* 8:28[39] (image of Mithras killing the bull on which a snake hangs); *KSA* 9:6[83] (Laocoön's struggle, see Vergil's *Aen.* Book 2); *KSA* 9:6[154] shedding; *KSA* 9:16[22]; *KSA* 10:2[9]; *KSA* 10:4[95]; *KSA* 10:4[260]; *KSA* 10:4[280] adder's bite; *KSA* 10:5[1].184 ("So long as your moral hangs over me, I breath as one suffocating. And thus I strangled this snake. I wanted to live, therefore it had to die."); *KSA* 10:5[1].185; *KSA* 10:9[17] snake haired (cf. *KSA* 10:12[43] and 13[1], p. 435); *KSA* 10:12[1].4; *KSA* 10:12[1].51 snake's teeth; *KSA* 10:13[1], p. 443; *KSA* 10:13[2] (sketch of things to happen in Z, cf. *KSA* 10:13[3], p. 446); *KSA* 10:13[3], p.450 adder; *KSA* 10:16[45] (alternate ending where his snake poisons Zarathustra, then all the animals kill each other fighting); *KSA* 10:16[83] (outline of *Z*:3 "snake in high, precipitous mountains"); *KSA* 10:18[21] (snake at end of path through seven solitudes); *KSA* 10:18[38]; *KSA* 10:18[39] ("This is *my* word that wants to strangle me! This is *my* snake that slithers into my throat!" cf. *KSA* 10:5[1].184); *KSA* 10:18[53]; *KSA* 10:20[2] ("snake and herdsman" rings and greatness an eternal goalless *game*); *KSA* 10:20[3] (within outline of *Z*:3, "he tears apart his snake; the herdsman dies; he struggles with his eagle"); *KSA* 10:20[8] (plan for *Z*:3 "death of the boy with the snake"); *KSA* 10:21[6] (sketch involving the biting off of snake's head); *KSA* 10:22[2] (plan for *Z*:3 incl. "the boy and the snake"); *KSA* 11:29[26] (plans for *Z*:4); *KSA* 11:31[52]; *KSA* 11:31[62]; *KSA* 11:32[13]; *KSA* 12:9[26]; *KSA* 12:9[72] (cf. *A* 48 daemon snake); *KSA* 13:16[25] ("the snake vanity"); *KSA* 13:16[42] rattlesnake's happiness.

Spider

Nietzsche's spiders follow closely from their natural attributes, emphasizing their spinning of threads into webs and nets. However, there are several passages that trade on spinning out stories or conversation (e.g., *HH* 625, *WS* P 1, *KSA* 8:11[39], and *KSA* 8:23[133]). This common literary use readily admits of application to theoretical speech and explanation. Indeed, Nietzsche sometimes writes as if spinning mental webs are necessary to all human life, something endemic to sensation and thought (e.g., *TL* 1, pp. 85 and 87, and *D* 117). Though, occasionally applied to historians (e.g., "Relation of Schopenhauer's Philosophy," *HL* 6, p. 126, and *HL* 8, p. 145), he far more often calls the philosopher, especially the metaphysician, a spider. Socrates (*BT* 15), Parmenides (*PTA* 10), Plato (in his style, *WS* P 1), Kant (*A* 11), Schopenhauer (*KSA* 12:2[197]), and Spinoza (*A* 17 and *TI* "Skirmishes" 23) are all implicated in this manner of spinning.

And while Nietzsche overwhelmingly refers negatively to this kind of conceptual web spinning (as in the many passages discussed in Alan D. Schrift's paper herein), it is also the drive and pleasure of the theoretical human to *uncover* the illusory spider webs of life (*KSA* 7:5[33]). Perhaps they search for those webs in the complex of mental states that compose the human character (*D* 115; cf. *D* 539), in the spirit's previous, symbol- and form-constructing mode of thought (*HH* 3), or beneath the different layers of valuations humans have spun around the same activities over the years (*KSA* 9:1[111]). It could be for Nietzsche that one should recognize knowledge as one kind of artifice and illusion among several: for human experience, beauty itself is a tightly-woven web, tighter than the more transparent web of knowledge ("Birth of Tragic Thought," p. 596). Artistic drives, too, can also be expressions of the arachnoid in humans (e.g., *HL* 6, p. 126 and *KSA* 7:19[221]).

Another interesting thread along which Nietzsche sets his spiders stretches between causality, chance, and purpose. The "spider's web of purposes" stands in common opinion as delicate against the brute force of disruptive chance (D 130), however Nietzsche emphasizes that we ourselves can often break this web by our own doing. In Z:3 "Before Sunrise," Zarathustra praises chance and change over purposes, the eternal spider, and the web of reason. Claiming it to be hubris to posit God as the purposive and moral underpinning of the causal world (GM III:9), Nietzsche implies that the causal web lacks purposes in itself and therefore that we can disrupt it, as previously described, with our own doings. As Alan Schrift notes, the spiders in GS 341, Z:3 "Vision and the Riddle" 2, and Z:3 "Virtue that Makes Small" 3 are all connected by the theme of the eternal return of the small. The small things too, even when abstained from, "weave the web of the future" and figure in the causal web; but as God is not necessitating them (with some intent or purpose), they need to be "cooked in the pot" (Z:3 "Virtue that Makes Small" 3) and made into proper food. It may be that there is a manner in which the insignificant little spider will not return exactly as before, because there is some way in which one can break the web of purposes.

BT 15 spinning (cf. same at "Socrates and Greek Tragedy," p. 639, KSA 7:6[12], and as its opposite in KSA 7:5[33]); BT 21 web (Gespinnst), (the stage as a delicate web); "Dionysian Worldview" 1 web (Gespinnst) (and the same in "Birth of Tragic Thought," p. 584); HH P 5 spinning; "Birth of Tragic Thought," p. 596 web (Gespinnst); "Relation of Schopenhauer's Philosophy" spider webs; PTA 10 incl. cobwebs; TL 1, pp. 85, 87 incl. spider webs and spinning; HL 6, p. 126 überspinnt (cf. KSA 7:2[96]); HL 8, p. 145 net and spinning; HL 9, pp. 147–48 spider webs, unraveling (Zerspinnen), cross spider, and net; RWB 5, p. 282 enmeshing (einspinnen) (education enmeshes one in the net of "clear concepts" regardless of one's feelings); HH 2 spinning out (some philosophers think the whole world is spun out of one's ability to think); HH 3 spinning out (cf. KSA 8:24[1]); HH 9 spider webs; HH 427 incl. net and webs; HH 625 spinning out (fort-

spinnen); HH 637 web (Gespinnst); AOM 32 spinning out (Ausspinnen), world-net, and world-spider (artists self-deceive to think they know the creation of the world); AOM 153 incl. net; AOM 171 cobwebs; AOM 172; AOM 194 incl. thread, spinning, and net ("Three Thinkers equal one Spider"); WS P 1 long-spun-out and spinning (Plato's literary works as well); WS 9 (silkworm's spinning, finding freedom in own necessities, because feeling of life is greatest, cf. KSA 8:41[66] and KSA 9:3[161]); WS 168 spinning out (weiterspinnen) (an extending); D 33 spinning (spinning the higher world out of our higher feelings); D 71 (great spider to suck up the blood out of hopes for Rome's demise); D 115 web (Gespinnst); D 117 incl. net; D 130 incl. spider web (Spinnennetze); D 539 web (Gespinnst); GS 306 threads and spinning (Epicureans can draw a long delicate thread and enjoy much on its light strength); GS 341 (cf. KSA

9:11[206]); GS 358; GS 366 spinning (scholarly specialists spinning in a nook); Z:2 "Tarantula" incl. tarantula and poison spider (cf. KSA 10:12[43] and 4[71]); Z:2 "Scholars" incl. weaving (thinkers as malicious); Z:3 "Vision and the Riddle" 2; Z:3 "Before Sunrise" incl. spider webs; Z:3 "Virtue that Makes Small" 3 incl. spider net and web; Z:3 "Apostates" 2 incl. cross-spider and spinning; Z:3 "Three Evils" 2 cross spider; Z:3 "Great Longing"; Z:3 "Seven Seals" 2 cross spider; Z:4 "At Noon" incl. thread and spinning (cf. GS 306 and the draft KSA 11:31[33]); Z:4 "Drunken Song" 4 incl. spinning (scene of Z:3 "Vision and the Riddle" 2 returns); BGE 25 cobweb spinners (*Spinneweber*); BGE 209 ("the spider skepsis" [*Skepsis*] a female vampire [*Blutaussaugerin*]); GM III:9 spider of purpose and of morality, captious web (*Fangnetz-Gewebe*), and *araignée*; GM III:14 spinning and net (malicious, vengeful web being spun by the sickly); GM III:17 web-spinners (cf. BGE 25); TI "Reason" 4 web spinners; TI "Skirmishes" 23 conceptual web spinning (*Begriffs-Spinneweberei*); A 11 (Kant as the spider of catastrophe); A 17 incl. spinning (cf. KSA 13:17[4] below); A 18 ("god as spider" cf. GM III:9, A 17, and AOM 32, where God is in some way considered a spider, and the draft KSA 13:17[4] below); A 38 poison-spider (i.e., priests); KSA 7:1[94]; KSA 7:5[33] spider webs; KSA 7:19[221] spidery (*spinnenartig*) (limbs of the painters); KSA

7:29[215] spider webs; KSA 8:11[39] spinning (*weiterspinnen*); KSA 8:12[33] spinning out (artist to remove the veil of cold and artificial concepts); KSA 8:17[9] self-spinning out (a lengthening); KSA 8:22[80] spinning; KSA 8:23[133] enmesh (*umspinnen*); KSA 8:40[25] incl. web; KSA 9:1[111] enmesh (*umspinnen*); KSA 9:6[439] incl. net (cf. KSA 9:15[9]); KSA 9:9[15] spider's existence and spider's happiness; KSA 9:15[9] incl. net and spinning out; KSA 10:4[71] spinning and thread ("The scientific human shares his lot with the rope spinner: he spins his thread longer, but in so doing goes—backwards."); KSA 10:4[255] ("they spin at the edge of the earthly and their fine eyes grow blind in the twilight"); KSA 10:7[197] enmesh (*umspinnen*) (quoting Roux's *Der Kampf der Teile im Organismus*); KSA 10:22[1], p. 606 web, web-master, and net-spider (*Netzespinnerin*); KSA 11:28[9] gold-spider nets; KSA 11:38[7] spiders of concepts; KSA 12:2[6] conceptual-spider webs; KSA 12:2[197] spinning and spider's thread (the last connections between world and God); KSA 13:11[83] spin out (*fortspinnen*) and thread ("the task to spin out the entire chain of life so that the thread becomes ever stronger"); KSA 13:11[55] conceptual-spider's weaving; KSA 13:16[58] incl. spinning (cf. A 17); KSA 13:17[4] incl. spinning (sections entitled "On the History of the Concept of God").

Worm

Trading upon common associations with the worm, Nietzsche often uses it to represent what is small, rotten, or corrosive—sometimes describing life generally as in SE 3 and KSA 8:23[50]; the insignificant or weak individual as in D 298, KSA 10:9[17], and DD "Ruhm und Ewigkeit" Z; an individual work or interpretation as in *AOM* 147 and *GM* III:6 (Kant's conception of the beautiful); or groups of people as in his neologism "Reich-worm" in *CW*. In this last regard, there are several passages connecting the behavior or results of academics and scholars to wormy corrosiveness or triviality: *PTA* 2, *DS* 6, *HL* 7, *TI* "Ancients" 4, and *EH* "Books" HH:4.

More psychologically, the worm is also an image of self-contempt (*Selbst-Verachtung*). From the Summer of 1883, Nietzsche writes at *KSA* 10:8[15] of how the ancient Greek nobles, for whom gnawing at and subverting oneself is ignoble, act and judge instinctively—qualities of "the *good* type"; "the evil human enjoys partly veneration, partly commiseration (*Mitleid*); he is not even himself devoured by worms—all destroying, stirring self-contempt is missing." In *Z*:3 "Great Longing," Zarathustra teaches his soul the contempt that "does not come like the worm's gnawing, the great, the loving contempt. . . ." Science, in *GM* III:23, is a hiding place for discontent, gnawing worms, *despectio sui*, bad conscience, "it is the unrest of the lack of ideals, the suffering from the *lack* of any great love. . . ." (Cf. *Z*:4 "Higher Men" 8 and *KSA* 11:40[60] for other descriptions of what it might mean to poorly create or produce in a worm-eaten state.) Yet, if all human life requires disguise and deceit (that is to say, is worm-eaten), its origin might be sought in the "artist-creator" (*KSA* 8:30[68]), one who does not despise himself or herself, is self-transparent about this creative disguising, and has goals, ideals, and love. Seemingly less ravenous gnawing worms of bad conscience prefigure a good conscience in the creator (*AOM* 90, see also the worms of self-doubt at *AOM* 169 and *KSA* 12:1[174]) and "the worm of conscience is a matter for the masses, and a real inheritance of the noble attitude" (*KSA* 11 25[259]). These worms can grow and be amplified by either moralization (via the sting or bite of conscience) of the difference between human and the Judeo-Christian God (see *KSA* 11:22[442], *A* 25, and *A* 62) or by *ressentiment* in opposition to the greater person (see *Z*:2 "On the Pitying" and *GM* III:14, this later one is a combination of these possibilities). (The worm of conscience seems to stem from both Bible passages referenced at *A* 45 (see below) and was the title of a play by Anzengruber in 1874. There is a connection, in this regard, between the worm of conscience and undermining. In this respect, the worm has characteristics that resemble the mole's. (See Bergoffen's essay in this volume and David B. Allison's "A Diet of Worms.") In either case, inward self-contempt devises means to turn outward while not admitting the cause. Except in cases of outward-turned, malicious intent and self-negation, Nietzsche does say that it "does not speak against the ripeness of a spirit that he has several worms" (AOM 353); as we have seen, such worms often accompany creativity. Another way in which human life is worm-eaten for Nietzsche is through instincts. KSA 8:19[110]: "Instinct is like a worm from which one has cut off its head and yet moves on in the same direction." KSA 8:23[10] is very similar while linking this with Platonic anamnesis. D 477 speaks of struggling with moral skepticism as either making one worm-eaten or yielding a repossession of instincts, where one must often work like a worm (cf. D 449 on working in worm paths [Wurmgänge] in the soul). Z:P 3 finds Zarathustra proclaiming that "You have made your way from worm to man, and much in you is still worm," while its draft at KSA 10:4[139] amends: "much in us is still worm and a memory of our way" (emphasis added).

Lastly, four passages (TI, "Maxims" 31, "Skirmishes" 3, KSA 13:11[9], and 12 7[4], p. 269) relate to a German proverb: "wenn man den Wurm tritt, so krümmt er sich," or "tread on a worm and it will turn." However, the last of these sections is on "the metaphysicians," specifically Kant and Schopenhauer, where a twist on the phrase is quoted from Kant's Metaphysics of Morals (KSA 12:7[4]: "Wer sich aber zum Wurm macht, kann nachher nicht klagen, daßer mit Füßen getreten wird"; cf. Kants Gesammelte Schriften, vol. 6 [Berlin, Walter de Gruyter], p. 437) and may help explain why Nietzsche indicates "that famous worm [jener beruhmte Wurm]."

KSA 8:11[29] Höhlenwurm (cf. KSA 8:40[12]), 27[28] Riesenwurm; KSA 8:40[12] Lindwürmern; and KSA 9:12[96] Lindwurm, though related by the root word, refer to dragons of a sort (see Paul S. Loeb's "The Dwarf, The Dragon, and the Ring of Eternal Recurrence: A Wagnerian Key to the Riddle of Nietzsche's Zarathustra"). However, some such relations (Holzwurm, Ohrwurm, Ringelwurm, Flügelwurm, Leucht- and Lichtwurm) have been provided for inclusiveness and because sometimes Nietzsche is thinking of their similarities to worms.

PTA 2 Kerbwürmern; PTA 3; DS 6, p. 32; HL 7, p. 136; SE 3, p. 193; SE 4, p. 200 ("selfish worm and canine fear"); TL 1, p. 82; TL 1, p. 87; KSA 7:15[2] ("Nach einem nächtlichen Gewitter"); KSA 8:22[53] and 23[50] worm rot (Wurmfrass); HH 243 ("timidity (the worm rot of all sick people)"); AOM 90 (cf. AOM 353); AOM 147; AOM 169; AOM 353 (cf. KSA 10:12[1].34); WS 9 silkworm (cf. KSA 8:41[66] and KSA 9:3[161]); WS 57; WS 211 (illogical worm); KSA 8:30[68]; D 49 earwig (Ohrwurm) (we, as the earwig, cannot move up in the order of things—similar to Z [connnecting ape, worm and overcoming] but with the opposite teaching); D 298; D 449 worm paths (Wurmgänge); D 477 (cf. KSA 8:19[110] and 23[10]); GS 122 (cf. D 477); KSA 9:6[279]; KSA 9:12[205] (bites into my heart); Z:P 3 (cf. *KSA* 10:4[139]); *Z*:1 "Pale Criminal"; *Z*:1 "Flies of the Market Place" poison worm (parasitic); *Z*:1 "Free Death" poison worm, worm eaten; *Z*:2 "On the Pitying" nagging worm (*Nage-Wurm*); *Z*:2 "Night Song" *Leuchtwürmer* (cf. EH "Books" *Z*:7 and *KSA* 10:13[9]); *Z*:2 "Land of Education" and *KSA* 10:13[3], p. 450 *Flügelwürmer*; *Z*:2 "Immaculate Perception" ringworm (a pun on the German "in eines Gottes Larve," or "in the mask of God." Cf. *KSA* 10:9[16] and 13[1], p. 422); *Z*:3 "Three Evils" 2; *Z*:3 "Convalescent" 1 (abysmal thought . . . sleepy worm); *Z*:3 "Great Longing" worm rot; *Z*:4 "Higher Men" 8 worm rot; *Z*:4 "Drunken Song" 5 incl. termite (*Holzwurm*), worm of the heart (*Herzenswurm*); BGE 44 (free spirits are "grateful to god, devil, sheep and worm in us"); BGE 46; GM II:14 gnawing worm; GM III:6; GM III:8 (gnawing worms of ambition); GM III:14 incl. *Kranken-Wurmfrasses*, worm-eaten (*Wurmstichigen*); GM III:23 gnawing; *CW* "Postscript" 2 *Reich-worm* (*Rhinoxera*); *TI*, "Maxims" 31, and *TI* "Skirmishes" 3 (cf. *KSA* 12 7[4], p. 269

and *KSA* 13:11[9]); *TI* "Skirmishes" 24; *TI* "Ancients" 4 (cf. *KSA* 13:24[1], p. 627); A 25 "worm of conscience [*Gewissens-Wurm*]"; A 45 and *KSA* 12:10[200] quoting Mk. 9:47–48 (cf. Isaiah 66:24); A 62 (Worm of sin); *EH* "Books" HH:4 book-wormishness (*Bücherwürmerei*) (i.e., philology); *DD* "Ruhm und Ewigkeit" 2; *KSA* 10:4[273]; *KSA* 10:8[1]; *KSA* 10:8[15] (part of draft called "The Greeks as Experts on Humans"); *KSA* 10:9[17] and 13[1], p. 435 *Regenwürmen* (combatant for the small, cf. *Z*:II "Human Prudence" and similar passages involving the snake); *KSA* 10:15[13] and *KSA* 13:20[108] ("grave, worm!"); *KSA* 10:17[84] ("foolish worm and abyss of thought"); *KSA* 11:25[24] and *KSA* 12:2[22] (asceticism to prevent worms in productive spirits); *KSA* 11:25[259]; *KSA* 11:26[382]; *KSA* 11:26[442]; *KSA* 11:40[60]; *KSA* 12:1[174]; *KSA* 13:11[259]; *KSA* 13:11[297](it is a worm-eaten person who eternally wages war for peace; for more on this passage see the cow's index entry).

Bibliography

Aesop, the Complete Fables. Trans. Olivia Temple and Robert Temple. New York: Penguin, 1998.

Allison, David B. "A Diet of Worms: Aposiopetic Rhetoric in *Beyond Good and Evil.*" *Nietzsche-Studien* 19 (1990): 43–58.

Brennecke, Detlef. "Die blonde Bestie. Vom Missverständnis eines Schlagworts." *Nietzsche-Studien* 5 (1976): 113–145.

Calder, William M. III. "The Lion Laughed." *Nietzsche-Studien* 14 (1985): 357–359.

Chaucer, Geoffrey. *The Riverside Chaucer.* 3d ed. Ed. Larry D. Benson. Boston: Houghton Mifflin Company, 1987.

Euripides. *The Bacchae of Euripides.* Trans. G. S. Kirk. Cambridge: Cambridge University Press, 1979.

Freeman, Kathleen, ed. *Ancilla to the Pre-Socratic Philosophers.* Cambridge, Mass.: Harvard University Press, 1948.

Ginzburg, Carlo. *History, Rhetoric, and Proof*. Lebanon, N.H.: University Press of New England, 1999.

Gooding-Williams, Robert. *Zarathustra's Dionysian Modernism*. Stanford, Calif.: Stanford University Press, 2001.

Higgins, Kathleen Marie. *Nietzsche's Zarathustra*. Philadelphia: Temple University Press, 1987.

———. *Comic Relief: Nietzsche's Gay Science*. New York: Oxford University Press, 2000.

Köhler, Joachim. *Zarathustra's Secret: The Interior Life of Friedrich Nietzsche*. Trans. Ronald Taylor. New Haven, Conn.: Yale University Press, 2002.

Krell, David Farrell. *Infectious Nietzsche*. Bloomington: Indiana University Press, 1996.

Loeb, Paul S. "The Dwarf, the Dragon, and the Ring of Eternal Recurrence: A Wagnerian Key to the Riddle of Nietzsche's Zarathustra." *Nietzsche-Studien* 31 (2002): 91–113.

Milton, John. *Complete Prose Works of John Milton*. Vol. 1. Ed. Don M. Wolfe. New Haven, Conn.: Yale University Press, 1953.

Müller, F. "Die blonde Bestie und Thukydides." *Harvard Studies in Classical Philology* 63 (1958).

Otto, Walter F. *Dionysus: Myth and Cult*. Trans. Robert B. Palmer. Dallas: Spring Publications, 1993.

Parkes, Graham. *Composing the Soul: Reaches of Nietzsche's Psychology*. Chicago: University of Chicago Press, 1994.

Plato. *Complete Works*. Ed. John M. Cooper. Assoc. ed. D. S. Hutchinson. Indianapolis: Hackett Publishing Company, 1997.

———. *Gorgias*. Ed. E. Dodds. Oxford: Oxford University Press, 1959.

Schiller, Friedrich. *Sämtliche Werke*. Eds. Gerhard Fricke and Herbert G. Göpfert. Munich: Carl Hanser Verlag, 1985.

Shakespeare, William. *The Works of William Shakespeare*. London: Studio Editions, 1993.

Index

Note: As references to Zarathustra and Thus Spoke Zarathustra occur in nearly every essay, relevant index entries proved impractical. Those interested in Nietzshe's Zarathustra should find the entire collection useful.

Aesop, 327, 332
Agamben, Giorgio, 60n6
aggression, 223–24. *See also* violence
alchemy, 266, 270, 277
Allen, Barry, 269
Allison, David, 82n7, 268, 281n2
ambition, 37
animality (general), 1f, 7, 223, 302, 309f, 312, 315
animals: ant, 62; ape, 17–29, 319f; ass, 101–18, 296, 320, 325; beast (general), 5, 121, 134, 140–53, 326; beast of prey, 56, 68, 142, 146, 150, 156–74, 252; bee, 62, 177n27; bird (general), 83–87, 95–97, 181, 190n7, 254, 280; blond beast, 5, 121–22, 133–34, 140–55, 156–58, 159; butterfly, 96, 135n6, 173, 177n27; camel, 5, 27–28, 32–41, 121, 124, 252, 257, 267, 321, 324f; cat, 56, 97, 133, 182–83, 186, 190n6, 190n7, 203f, 251–61; caterpillar, 173; centaur, 6; child and children, 27–28, 33, 37, 87, 123, 135n6, 257f, 281, 321, 325f; cow, 89–98, 183, 190n7, 254; dog, 53–59,

66, 96, 252–53, 320, 325; dove, 87, 122, 135n3, 135n6, 136n11, 138n33; dragon, 94, 131, 135n5, 289; eagle, 53, 76, 247, 250, 296, 298; fox, 171, 296, 298; goat, 211–13; halcyon, 83–87, 279. (*See also* bird); hedgehog, 300n18; herd animal, 9, 57, 159, 182, 189–90n1, 228, 252; horse, 214, 265, 296; human (general), xv–xxvi, 18, 88, 152–3, 157–59, 285–300; hydra, 48; hyena, 181; lamb, 138n33, 296; leech, 30n4, 87; lion, 5, 27, 28, 32–33, 87, 121–34, 146, 148, 149–50, 204, 252, 257–58, 265, 267ff, 297, 321, 325; lizard, 264–81; "maggot-man," 172; mole, 65, 242–50, 300n17; nymph, 214; octopus, 48n2; ostrich, 296; overhuman, 6, 12n20, 19, 23f, 92–93, 149–50, 196, 220–37, 298, 325f; oyster, 297; panther, 122, 133, 139n37, 252; polar bear, 171, 298; polyp, 42–49; rabbit, 296; satyr, 124, 211–17; sea animal or sea-beast, 183, 278, 313. (*See also* halcyon); sea monster, 48; silkworm, 70n12;

snake, 45, 53, 59, 71–81, 94, 183, 237, 268; sphinx, 202–4; spider, 53, 61–70, 297; squid, 296; swine, 207, 296; tarantula, 30n3, 67f; tiger, 122, 171, 183, 186, 190n6, 252, 258, 298; wolf, 55, 252, 287; woman as animal, 97, 181–92, 193–208, 254ff; worm, 81n3

Ansell-Pearson, Keith, 30n5, 152, 174n7, 175n16, 299n3

anthropocentrism, 4, 19, 86, 310

anthropomorphism, 17

Apollo and the Apollinian, 141, 143f, 213, 255, 270, 277f

Apuleius (The Golden Ass), 112–15

Arendt, Hannah, 239n13

Aristotle, 80, 190n4, 194

artistry and artists, 36–38, 63, 84, 88n5, 90, 143, 166–69, 173, 254ff, 261

Aryan myth, 145–47, 148–49, 151–52

ascetic ideal, 172, 267

Ass Festival, 104–111

bad conscience, 160, 163–64, 172, 174n5, 175n13, 175n15

Bataille, G., 238n16

Bayreuth, 129–30

beauty, 35ff, 38f, 171

becoming, 13n35, 29, 59, 85–87, 220–37, 280, 298–99, 302–315. See also overcoming

Behler, E., 262n10

being, 32, 309–11

Bennholdt-Thomson, Anke, 127

Biblical references, 54, 71–74, 77ff, 81, 84, 129, 136n20

Bizet, 188ff

blondness, 145–49, 283n19

Borgia, Cesare, 150

breeding, 152–53, 220f

Brennecke, D., 149–50, 152, 153n1

Burckhardt, J., 150

Cadmus, 92–94

Caspari, Otto, 182, 189n1

Christ, Jesus, 72, 135n5, 138n30, 223, 268

Christianity and the Church, 6, 20f, 63, 65, 67, 69n8, 70n11, 71–73, 76, 105–12, 116, 144, 167f, 182, 224–25

Circe, 206–7

civilization and civilizing, 9, 149, 168, 182, 221f, 226, 228–30, 236–37

Colder III, William M., 133

comedy, 105–11, 111f, 215f, 218n19

contest (including agon), 37, 146, 150, 212f, 222, 225, 228

convalescence, 265, 268, 278. See also illness; health

Conway, Daniel W., 31n20

counter-memory, 226

Cox, Christoph, 300n11

creativity, 5f, 27, 33, 37, 68, 94, 168, 256ff, 288, 321, 357

cruelty, 134, 144–45, 163, 258, 263n21, 268, 269, 288, 297. See also violence

cultivation, 7, 165–69, 227, 288

culture, 164ff, 221f, 226, 290

dance, 39f, 98, 198, 214

Darwin, Charles, 3, 19, 144f, 194–95

Darwinism, 3, 149, 181

deception, 251–60, 354

Deleuze, Gilles, 84, 88n5, 237n1, 301–315

democracy, 176n20

Derrida, Jacques, 85, 87, 204–7, 238n10, 260–61, 262n16

desire, 86f

destruction, 94, 168

Diethe, Carol, 111

Diogenes, 56, 344

Dionysus/Dionysian, 79, 91–93, 139n37, 141, 143f, 152, 211–16, 236, 255, 270, 314, 324

discipline and disciplining, 57f, 165f, 170f

disease, 8, 92, 223

domestication, 8f, 54, 59, 164–65, 167,
172–73, 176n21, 176n22, 176n23,
182f, 200f, 251, 288, 337, 344. *See also*
training; discipline
domination, 41, 227f
dreams, 221–37
drives, 43–48, 75, 159f, 169, 189n1, 212f
dualism, 91, 92, 97
dwarf, 53ff, 58, 93, 247, 281, 300n17

education, 7, 57
ego, 55–59
envy, 37
Epictetus, 268
eternal return, 21, 53f, 59, 61, 76f, 79, 80f,
86, 91, 94, 136n10, 267
evolution, 4, 20ff, 182–86, 294f, 303, 319.
See also Darwinism

Falcón, Jaime Juan, 320, 322f
fear, 33f
feminine, 261
feminism, 185f, 256
ferity, 7ff
fertility, 77f, 80f, 97
folly, 115–16. *See also* comedy; laughter
forgetting and forgetfulness, 95, 220–37,
246f, 253, 290
Förster-Nietzsche, Elisabeth, 187
Foucault, M., 57, 60n6, 238n15, 311f
freedom, 57, 84–85, 229–36, 306
Freud, 86, 160, 204, 206, 237n4
friendship, 97, 238n12

Gadamer, H., 258–59
Gast, Peter, 184
Gavarni, 190n9
Gebhart, É., 192n17
genealogy, 159, 163, 175n12, 243–50
Gerber, G., 282n14
Gobineau, 147–49, 150–52
Goethe, 125

Gooding-Williams, R., 123, 125, 135n7,
135n9
Greek culture, 141, 143f, 212ff, 258, 275f
Guattari, F., 84, 88n5, 237n1, 301–15

Hagenbeck, Carl, 200ff
Harries, Karsten, 260, 261n5
Hartmann, Eduard von, 63
Hatab, Lawrence J., 176n20
health, 9, 20, 44–46, 108, 150, 171, 226–
27, 235, 255
Heidegger, Martin, 32, 35, 85, 244, 265,
274, 283n22, 293, 308–11
Heracles, 26ff
Heraclitus, 29, 31n17, 33, 226, 258,
263n20
Higgins, Kathleen Marie, 59n3, 73,
191n14
Homer, 262n8, 269
honor, 33f, 37
Hume, 46
Husserl, 249

ideas, 276–80
illness, 157f. *See also* convalescence; health
illusions, 220–37, 257, 353
imagination, 36f
imitation (*mimêsis*), 23–26
individuality, 45–47, 57–59, 213f, 227,
249, 345. *See also* individuation
instincts, 160, 357. *See also* drives
interpretation, 11n13, 258ff, 275, 285–
300, 355f. *See also* Gadamer
Irigaray, Luce, 85–86, 212, 312ff

joy, 33f, 40f, 87, 134, 214, 268
judgment, 37, 49n9
Jung, C., 135n3

Kant, Immanuel, 44–45, 49n9, 61, 62f,
67–68, 261n3, 353, 357
Kierkegaard, S., 24

Kleist, 279f
knowledge, 73–75
Kofman, Sarah, 3, 238n5, 259, 263n26, 291f
Kogi Indians, 247–49
Krell, D., 260–61, 283n22

lactation, 97f, 341
LaMettrie, 43
Lampert, L., 30n11, 127, 136n15, 136n18, 174n3, 269
Lange, 42f
language, 206, 270f, 291ff, 309, 315, 326n9, 333, 338
last man, 9, 22, 91
laughter, 59, 94, 96f, 111ff, 116, 123, 125, 133–34, 136n9, 138n34, 138n35, 139n36, 139n37, 139n38, 217, 258–77, 268f, 281, 282n10, 332, 347f
Lingis, A., 310, 317n25
Lippitt, J., 138n34
Loeb, Paul S., 77, 94, 219n20
love, 24, 97, 135n6, 186–88, 253
Lukàs, G., 151
Luther, M., 116n3

man (male), 183, 191n11
Mann, T., 151
memory, 220–37, 248f. See also forgetfulness
metamorphosis, 27, 86, 95, 115f, 122, 173–74, 208f, 257–58, 267f, 290f, 296ff, 298, 319–27, 328n7, 337. See also transfiguration
metaphor, 96, 259, 263n26, 272, 285–99
metaphysics, 34, 41, 60n5, 67, 70n11, 244, 246f
mimêsis, 23ff, 215. See also imitation
misogyny, 183, 185–86, 193, 256
Montaigne, 258
morality, 72, 74, 77, 78, 142, 144f, 154n12,

163f, 172–74, 224–25, 330, 356. See also Christianity; value creation
Moses, 100, 102, 125, 129, 131, 137n20
Motley Cow, the town of, 92–96
Müller-Lauter, Wolfgang, 294–95
music, 272–76, 280–81
myth, 98, 218n2, 218n4, 218n6, 218n17

naturalism, 5, 29, 212
Naumann, G., 103ff
nausea, 24, 94, 132, 172, 176n23
Nazism (including Hitler), 140, 149, 151, 155n42, 283n19
necessity, 68
Nehamas, A., 260
Newton, I., 266
Norris, Margot, 2, 196
nourishment, 43–44

obedience, 40. See also training; discipline
ontology, 293–99, 302, 304, 307, 316n5
opposition, 37ff. See also contest
Orpheus, 84, 87
Ottmann, H., 144, 150
over-animal (Überthier), 181, 183, 190n3, 224. See also overman
overcoming, 31n23, 220–37. See also becoming; transfiguration
overman, 92, 196, 320
Ovid, 27, 86
Owen, David, 175n15

pain, 47, 55, 87
Pangle, Thomas, 127
Parkes, Graham, 47, 174n4, 191n13, 261n6, 269, 299n2
Parmenides, 62
Paul, Saint, 72
perspectivism, 64, 260, 294–95, 297
Pharisees, 138n30
philosophy, 34
pity, 30n15, 44, 54, 176n23

Plato, Platonism, 31n17, 35, 57, 63, 66, 68, 194, 245, 247, 256, 261n6, 335, 353
play, 25, 198, 214, 239n20, 251–61, 323
pleasure, 47, 259
poets and poetry, 63, 280
predation, 68f, 133, 157f, 164, 165–69, 182–85, 188–89
pregnancy, 92, 97, 174n5, 253, 256, 262n13
priest, 65, 67, 169–73, 176n24
promising, 220–37
propagation, 130. See also sexuality; fertility

race, 149–52
rationality, 292–93
reading, 89, 95–96, 271f, 287
Rée, Paul, 144f
Reed, T. J., 2
resentment, 24, 60n5
responsibility, 229–34
reverence, 33f, 37f
Ridley, Aaron, 137n25, 175n13, 175n17
Rilke, R., 87, 206
Rousseau, 68, 145, 152

Salaquarda, Jörg, 118n1, 118n4, 120n33
Salomé, Lou, 184–88, 198, 202, 281n2
Schacht, Richard, 174n6
Schiller, 153n5, 335
Schlegel, F., 143
Schopenhauer, Arthur, 59n3, 153n7, 194, 196, 252, 261n3, 353, 357
Schutte, O., 138n28
science, 62f, 266
self, 45–47, 306f. See also ego; individuality
self-improvement, 43, 47
self-overcoming, 121, 134, 171, 173, 267. See also overcoming; transfiguration
sensuality, 251–60
Seung, T., 108, 111, 118n30
sexuality, 79–81, 86f, 260n3

Shepard, Paul, 175n12, 176n22
shepherd (in Z), 56, 58f, 79, 135n4, 267f
sickness, 157, 167, 223–24, 226–27. See also health; convalescence
Socrates, 63, 64, 287, 334, 353. See also Plato
solitude, 90f, 124, 127, 265
song, 84f, 87, 88n5, 92, 95, 334. See also music
speciation, 58f, 290, 294, 298
Spinoza, Baruch, 61, 62, 66–67, 69, 303, 353
spirit, 30n13, 32–41, 116, 121, 173–74
state, the emergence of, 161–64
Staten, Henry, 175n14, 177n24
strength, 33, 201–2
style, 205f, 259–60, 266–68, 270f
sublimation, 6, 34f, 38f, 184, 186, 188, 190n4, 212, 217

taming, 142, 149f, 191n13, 199–202, 226, 252, 288, 345. See also domestication
Tongeren, Paul van, 152, 175n11, 176n19
tragedy, 94–95, 214–15, 272ff, 333
training, 55, 57, 149, 199–202, 288, 345. See also domestication
transfiguration, 208, 266–69, 277–81, 290–91, 298–99
Trembley, Abraham, 42
truth, 62f, 66, 97, 205ff, 217, 221–22, 246, 248f, 255, 274, 291, 297

Umgekehrten, 235–36

value creation (including revaluation), 100, 108, 121, 123ff, 122, 130, 135n7, 137n25, 235–36, 253, 280, 289f, 295–96. See also morality
virtue and virtù, 95, 150

Wagner, Richard, 30n14, 84, 93, 129, 149, 151, 154n24, 155n42, 273

war, 130f, 161, 171, 283n20
White, R., 176n19
wildness, 165–66, 168, 175n12, 215, 251f
will to nothingness, the, 164, 172
will to power, 59, 211, 280

women, 80f, 85f, 97, 193–208, 214, 312ff, 316n19. *See also* animal, woman as animal
Wood, D., 315

About the Contributors

Christa Davis Acampora is Assistant Professor of Philosophy at Hunter College of the City University of New York. She is the North American Review editor for the *Journal of Nietzsche Studies*, and author of numerous articles on Nietzsche. Her current research focuses on completing a book on Nietzsche's conception of competition and struggle.

Ralph R. Acampora is Assistant Professor of Philosophy at Hofstra University. He has published journal articles and book chapters on topics in environmental philosophy and animal studies as well as on Nietzsche. Fond of ferine fauna, his recent research has focused on the interspecies ethics of captivity and of domesticity.

Babette E. Babich is Professor of Philosophy at Fordham University in New York City and Adjunct Research Professor of Philosophy at Georgetown University. She is author of *Nietzsche's Philosophy of Science: Reflecting Science on the Ground of Art and Life* (1994), *Words in Blood, Like Flowers: Philosophical Essays on Poetry, Language, and Music* (forthcoming), and essays on the philosophy of science and technology, as well as aesthetics and the museum. She is also founding and executive editor of *New Nietzsche Studies*.

Debra B. Bergoffen is Professor of Philosophy, Women's Studies and Cultural Studies at George Mason University. Her publications bring an existential, phenomenological, psychoanalytic, gendered perspective to questions of truth, value, and justice. Her recent book is titled *The Philosophy of Simone De Beauvoir: Gendered Phenomenologies, Erotic Generosities* (SUNY).

Thomas H. Brobjer is Professor in the Department of History of Science and Ideas at Uppsala University. He is the recipient of numerous prestigious grants supporting his research on Nietzsche's intellectual heritage. Brobjer has published articles on Nietzsche in several well-known journals, among them *Nietzsche-Studien, Journal of the History of Ideas, Journal of Nietzsche Studies*, and *International Studies in Philosophy*.

Daniel W. Conway, Professor of Philosophy at the Pennsylvania State University, is the author of many important books and articles on Nietzsche and political philosophy. His most recent books include *Nietzsche's Dangerous Game: Philosophy in the Twilight of the Idols* (Cambridge) and *Nietzsche & The Political* (Routledge). He is also the chief editor of the multi-volume *Nietzsche: Critical Assessments* (Routledge).

Brian Crowley is a graduate of Hunter College/CUNY, who intends to continue studying philosophy as a graduate student, developing his interests in axiology, modern German philosophy, and the history of philosophy.

Brian Domino is Associate Professor of Philosophy at Miami University, Middletown Campus. He is the editor of the *Journal of Nietzsche Studies*. His current research interests concern the pre-modern conception of ethics, particularly as Nietzsche retrieves them.

Peter S. Groff is Assistant Professor of Philosophy at Bucknell University. He is coeditor of the four-volume anthology, *Nietzsche: Critical Assessments* (Routledge), and has published and given papers on Nietzsche's philosophical naturalism. His most recent research focuses on comparative philosophy, particularly on establishing a dialogue between Nietzsche and the Islamic philosophical tradition.

Jennifer Ham is Associate Professor of German and Humanistic Studies at the University of Wisconsin-Green Bay. She is the author of numerous articles on German culture and the co-editor of the recent book *Animal Acts: Configuring the Human in Western History* (Routledge).

Lawrence J. Hatab, Professor of Philosophy at Old Dominion University, has written extensively on Nietzsche, Heidegger, political philosophy, and the role of myth in philosophy. He is the author of the highly acclaimed *A Nietzschean Defense of Democracy* (Open Court). His most recent book, *Ethics and*

Finitude (Rowman & Littlefield), explores the relationship between Heidegger's ontology and ethics, and his next book, *Nietzsche's Life Sentence: The Literal Meaning of Eternal Recurrence* (Routledge) will appear soon.

Kathleen Marie Higgins is Professor of Philosophy at the University of Texas at Austin. She is the author of several books, including *Nietzsche's Zarathustra, Comic Relief: Nietzsche's Gay Science,* and (with Robert C. Solomon) *What Nietzsche Really Said.* She is also editor (with Bernd Magnus) of *The Cambridge Companion to Nietzsche* and (with Robert C. Solomon) *Reading Nietzsche,* as well as books on world philosophy, erotic love, aesthetics, and ethics.

Vanessa Lemm is affiliated with the departments of Philosophy and of Political Science at Northwestern University, Evanston, Illinois. She is currently completing a book on animality, freedom, and culture in the philosophy of Friedrich Nietzsche.

Paul S. Loeb is Professor of Philosophy at the University of Puget Sound. He is currently completing a book on Nietzsche's *Thus Spoke Zarathustra.*

Nickolas Pappas is Associate Professor of Philosophy at the City College and the Graduate Center of the City University of New York. He is the author of the Routledge *Guidebook to Plato and the Republic* and of articles on Plato, aesthetics, film, and other topics. He is now at work on a book, *The Nietzsche Disappointment.*

Richard Perkins is an independent scholar and Adjunct Professor of Philosophy at Canisius College in Buffalo, N.Y. He has published numerous articles on Nietzsche in periodicals such as *International Studies in Philosophy* and *Nietzsche-Studien.*

Gerd Schank is a member of the workgroup of the Nietzsche Dictionary Project at Nijmegen University. His publications include: *Dionysos gegen den Gekreuzigten: Eine philologische und philosophische Studie zu Nietzsches' "Ecce homo"* (Verlag Peter Lang, 1993); *"Rasse" und "Züchtung" in Nietzsches Philosophie* (De Gruyter, 2000) and "Dionysos und Ariadne im Gespräch: Subjektauflösung und Mehrstimmigkeit in Nietzsches Philosophie" in: *Tijdschrift voor Filosofie.*

Alan D. Schrift, Professor of Philosophy and Director of the Center for the Humanities at Grinnell College, has published numerous books and articles on Nietzsche and French philosophy. His most recent books include *Why Nietzsche Still? Reflections on Drama, Culture, and Politics* (California), *The Logic of the Gift: Toward an Ethic of Generosity* (Routledge), and *Nietzsche's French Legacy : A Genealogy of Poststructuralism* (Routledge). He is currently editing a collection of essays on *Modernity and the Problem of Evil* (Indiana) and is finishing a book that chronicles the history of twentieth-century French philosophy.

Gary Shapiro is Tucker-Boatwright Professor in the Humanities and Professor of Philosophy at the University of Richmond. He is the author of dozens of articles in Continental philosophy. His books include *Archaeologies of Vision: Foucault and Nietzsche on Seeing and Saying* (Chicago), *Earthwards: Robert Smithson and Art After Babel* (California), *Alcyone: Nietzsche on Gifts, Noise, and Women* (SUNY), and *Nietzschean Narratives* (Indiana).

Tracey Stark is Assistant Professor of Philosophy in the Department of Organizational and Political Communication at Emerson College. Her interests include: Continental Philosophy, Ethics, Political Theory, and DIY radio and theatre.

Charles Senn Taylor, Professor and Chair, Department of Philosophy at Wright State University, is the author of numerous articles on topics ranging from Schopenhauer to the aesthetics of wine. He has also edited a trilingual on-line edition of Descartes's *Meditations* and developed a multi-media version of Nietzsche's *The Birth of Tragedy*.

Jami Weinstein is visiting at Vassar College where she teaches gender studies, philosophy, and technoscience studies. She is concurrently completing her PhD in philosophy at the City University of New York Graduate Center and her Doctorate *l'histoire des techniques* at L'École des Hautes Études en Sciences Sociales in Paris, France.

Martha Kendal Woodruff is Assistant Professor of Philosophy at Middlebury College. She received a B.A. from Haverford College and a Ph.D. from Yale University; she also studied for two years at Universität-Freiburg with a research grant from DAAD (German Academic Exchange Service). Her main areas of interest include ancient Greek and modern Continental philosophy. She has published articles on Plato, Aristotle, Nietzsche, and Heidegger and she is currently working on a book entitled *The Pathos of Thought: Aristotle and Heidegger on Mood, Poetry, and Philosophy.*